Days of the Lord

THE LITURGICAL YEAR

Days of the Lord

THE LITURGICAL YEAR

Preface by ✝ Godfried Cardinal Danneels

Volume 1.

Season of Advent

Season of Christmas / Epiphany

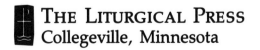

THE LITURGICAL PRESS
Collegeville, Minnesota

The English translation of Volume 1 of this series is by Gregory LaNave and Donald Molloy. The original French text of *Days of the Lord* (*Jours du Seigneur,* Brepols: Publications de Saint-André, 1988) was written by the authors of the *Missel dominical de l'assemblée* and *Missel de l'assemblée pour la semaine* under the direction of Robert Gantoy and Romain Swaeles, Benedictines of Saint-André de Clerlande.

ACKNOWLEDGMENTS
Excerpts from the English translation of *Lectionary for Mass* © 1969, International Committee on English in the Liturgy, Inc. (ICEL); excerpts from the English translation of *The Liturgy of the Hours* © 1974, ICEL; excerpts from the English translation of *Documents on the Liturgy, 1963–1979: Conciliar, Papal, and Curial Texts* © 1982, ICEL. All rights reserved.

Scripture selections taken from the *New American Bible,* copyright © 1970 by the Confraternity of Christian Doctrine, Washington, D.C., are used by license of said copyright owner. All Rights Reserved. No part of the *New American Bible* may be reproduced in any form without permission in writing from the copyright owner.

Cover design by Monica Bokinskie.

Library of Congress Cataloging-in-Publication Data
Jours du Seigneur. English.
    Days of the Lord : the liturgical year.
        p. cm.
    Translation of: Jours du Seigneur.
    Includes bibliographical references.
    Contents: v. 1. Advent, Christmas, Epiphany.
    ISBN 0-8146-1899-5 (v. 1)
    1. Church year. 2. Catholic Church—Liturgy. I. Title.
BX1970.J67313   90-22253
263'.9—dc20   CIP

Contents

Preface

The Second Vatican Council accomplished the most important reform of the Church's liturgy ever undertaken, while at the same time profoundly respecting its great tradition. This is exactly what the Fathers of the Council wanted: to restore in all its height, length, and depth, the great flow of the Church's liturgical tradition. Only thus can we contemplate, in all its splendor, the architecture of the liturgical year. The edifice is there, the architects have done their work, the masons and engineers theirs.

Yet there is a need to understand the great laws of the liturgy; guides are still required for examining and understanding this structure.

Days of the Lord, as a contribution to the long tradition of liturgical commentaries, is an excellent guide for understanding the riches of the Church's liturgy. I am delighted by its publication. The commentaries, written by several different authors, who for some years have contemplated the mystery—the "sacrament"—of the liturgical year, have this particular quality in common, which is indispensable for the nourishment of the people of God: they do not get bogged down in anecdotal annotations or purely moral discourse when looking at the liturgical texts. They have the contemplative eye that can see beyond the obvious and ecclesial meaning of the texts. They allow the texts themselves to speak. For this is the secret of all genuine liturgical commentaries: they awaken the slumbering heart of the texts, that it may beat more strongly in the body of the Church. No one can explain the liturgy better than it does itself. It is the liturgy itself that enlivens Christian existence and transforms it. The liturgy is the "stream whose runlets gladden the city of God" (Ps 46:5).

I am confident that *Days of the Lord* will be a tool that will enable many Christians and their pastors to enter into the mystery of the liturgical year, to pray with understanding, to proclaim the beauty of the liturgy and its riches to their brothers and sisters who long to know the Christian message with mind and heart.

✝ Godfried Cardinal Danneels
Archbishop of Malines-Brussels
Malines, July 20, 1988

Foreword

During several years of working together to prepare the *Missel dominical de l'assemblée* and the *Missel de l'assemblée pour la semaine,* we studied, one after another, the formularies for each Mass of the whole liturgical cycle, from Sunday to Sunday (Years A, B, C), from week to week (odd and even years), and from day to day. While doing so, and especially after having finished the project, we found ourselves faced with the question of the liturgical year—its meaning, its unity, its dynamic in the continuity and diversity of the days of the Lord.

The liturgical year sets forth "the whole mystery of Christ from the incarnation and nativity to the ascension, to Pentecost and the expectation of the blessed hope of the coming of the Lord," says the council's Constitution on the Sacred Liturgy (n. 102).

But how is this concretely realized? How do we progress from Sunday to Sunday, from stage to stage? Do the long weeks of Ordinary Time have an internal dynamism comparable to that of the other seasons of the year? How is the liturgical year different from a calendar of Sundays and feasts? What sort of full, conscious, and active participation does it require? What is the grace proper to this "mystery," this "sacrament"?

These questions and others, which present themselves in a rather challenging way, have led us to attempt a complete presentation of the days of the Lord.

We hope to furnish, therefore, so far as we are able, an aid to our brothers and sisters in faith, that they may enter, with some competency, into the mystery of Christ and its unfolding in our time, which is the time of God among us.

THE AUTHORS

The Sacrament of the Liturgical Year

Typically, ''the liturgical year'' calls to mind only the Christian calendar of Sundays and feasts that, instead of beginning on January 1 and ending December 31, goes from the first Sunday of Advent to the Saturday at the end of the thirty-fourth week of Ordinary Time.[1] This deviation from the common secular calendar does not create a real problem. One reason is that we are used to other, similar deviations, particularly those of the school year. Another is that Christmas is the only date one needs to know in order to determine the date of the first of the four Sundays of Advent. However, this first, superficial picture of a simple, annual schedule of Christian celebrations is not enough to fully appreciate the profound reality of the liturgical year and all its values. We must begin, therefore, with a certain understanding of time.

Time: Measure of Duration

According to one idea, time is a uniform and indefinitely extended line upon which certain events are placed with precision and objectivity. This line is divided into segments: years, months, weeks, days, and even hours, as in our schedules. These place marks allow us to measure the distance between what has happened, what is happening now, and what will happen. This distance is expressed in terms of duration. According to this conception, time is a neutral mathematical value, a succession of units and, ultimately, an abstraction. It is, in fact, dissociated from those things it measures.

Time: Dimension of What Lasts

Time is not an abstraction, but a dimension of that which is born, lives, and dies. We can perceive it if, abandoning the realm of abstraction, we come to reflect upon ourselves. We can be conscious of our identity throughout the vicissitudes of life that affect our being, on all levels: physical, psychical, intellectual, moral. Blessed with reflective memory, we perceive the continuity—though it be marked with sudden jumps, highs

1

and lows, longer and shorter periods—between yesterday and today; most important, we can project ourselves into the future and prepare for it. Finally, we can reflect on our own experience and that of others, putting them into relation with each other, communicating them and, from this collection of data, drawing profit. In short, we are not a point on the line of time, which carries us away like a straw in a hurricane until one day we founder. Ronsard understood it: "Time is fleeing, time is fleeing, madame. Alas! not time, but we ourselves are fading, and soon we will sleep under its waves."[2]

Concrete Time: Object of Experience

We cannot ignore the great "clocks" of the sun and the moon. They determine and measure night and day, the seasons, and, among other cycles, the year.[3] It is possible to be content with this and take into account only their regular movement. In this perspective, time is a neutral value. In spite of variations (mostly minor or accidental) that can change the seasons from one year to the next, time is characterized by the cyclical regularity that brings about monotony, or even the jaded boredom of which Ecclesiastes speaks:

> One generation passes and another comes,
> but the world forever stays.
> The sun rises and the sun goes down;
> then it presses on to the place where it rises.
> Blowing now toward the south, then toward the north,
> the wind turns again and again, resuming its
> rounds.
>
> All rivers go to the sea,
> yet never does the sea become full.
> To the place where they go,
> the rivers keep on going.
>
> What has been, that will be; what has been done, that
> will be done. Nothing is new under the sun. Even the
> thing of which we say, "See, this is new!" has already
> existed in the ages that preceded us.
> (Eccl 1:4-7,9-10)

It is true that we are not free simply to do anything at any moment. "Each thing in its time." Nature sets its rhythms: times of sowing, of reaping and harvests, etc.; time to rest in the field and time to bring in the cattle, etc. This regularity can, in itself, be perceived as constraining and monotonous. But this way of looking at time is concrete. It takes its historical content into consideration and is not concerned with the philosophical question of its nature. Thus is it dealt with in the Bible. It calls *kairos* "favorable time" or "opportune moment," what the Greeks would simply call *chronos*, i.e., abstract duration, mathematically measurable.

Favorable Time, Time of Humankind

Like everything else in the universe, especially living beings, each of us, from birth to death, is under the influence of the rhythms of nature and its inexorable laws.[4] However, we are not totally or blindly submissive to this determinative and cyclical regularity.

According to the conception in the Bible, our time—the time of our life— is qualified and determined not by chance or the caprices of nature or the stars, but by our own personal responsibility.[5] This life—whether short or long—has its value, for better or worse, in the conduct of the person who has the wisdom to perceive it as "favorable time" (*kairos*), for which he or she is accountable. People in the Bible know that both their time and that of the universe are oriented toward "a day" that God alone knows, when there will no longer be a cycle of day and night, nor of the seasons: "on that day" God will reign over all the earth (Zech 14:6-8).

It is a fact that people, because of their experience, cannot help asking, "On whom, on what depends the time of beings who are born, live, and die? On what forces or superior gods?"[6]

Cosmic Time and God

Faced with these fundamental questions, the people of the Bible, living amidst surrounding civilizations and often enticed by their seductions, have maintained firm and original affirmations. God is the unique creator of the universe and of all humankind. He created everything "from the beginning" without being constrained by anyone or anything. The "day when God made heaven and earth" is the absolute beginning, the absolute starting point of our time. This time is good, as is the rest of creation. God has created and ordered everything with an eye toward men and women, and he guides his destiny toward a mysterious end. He does not exercise his power as Creator in a tyrannical or capricious manner, but with goodness and love: he is, actually, Providence.

Time not only involves perpetual new beginnings; it also involves the dynamic orientation of the lives of individuals and nations—the entire universe—toward God.

The sun and the moon, the stars and the constellations, and the seasons have all been created by God, who has determined and governed their movement; in no way are they gods or demiurges.

The man or woman of the Bible is progressively more conscious of all this, more through experience than reflection. These convictions are sometimes expressed in terms of wisdom, but always in a language that is concrete, not philosophical.

Cosmic Time Sanctified

Religious beings are naturally compelled to sanctify, by rites and feasts, the rhythms of cosmic time: the changing of the seasons, the months, the days. They do this not only because the secret of these rhythms eludes them, but also because they suspect that divine forces rule them and are manifested through them. It is essential to win over these forces, calming or preventing their ill humor, often with the hope of channeling or diverting their power. Myths about them have flourished in polytheistic religions.[7] The people of God were tempted to join with these pagan cults, and sometimes they even adopted some of their practices. Accordingly, the prophets never ceased denouncing laxity, syncretism, and the subtle or overt paganization of feasts and celebrations that were linked to the cycles of nature and of time:

> I will bring an end to all her joy,
> her feasts, her new moons,[8] her sabbaths,
> and all her solemnities (Hos 2:13).

In fact, the Old Testament integrated into its calendar the celebration of cosmic cycles. While it eliminated all their references to polytheistic myths, it did portray such celebrations as acts of worship rendered to the Lord—the one God, Creator and Provider. Thus in the spring, the beginning of the barley harvest, the feast of Unleavened Bread (Exod 23:15); the offering of the first-fruits (Deut 26:2) and of the first sheaves (Lev 23:10-11); the feast of the harvest, called the feast of Weeks or Pentecost (Exod 23:16; 34:22; Lev 23:16); and those of the autumn harvests (Exod 23:16; Deut 16:13; Lev 23:34-43).

> Never mention the name of any other god; it shall not be heard from your lips. Three times a year you shall celebrate a pilgrim feast to me (Exod 23:13-14).

On the other hand, the content and object of these feasts changed: the feasts of Passover and of the Unleavened Bread commemorated the flight from Egypt and the entry into Canaan (Exod 12:17, 26-27; Josh 5:10-12); Pentecost, the covenant at Sinai; the autumn feast, the journey in the desert (Lev 23:43). The new celebrations were instituted in memory of other events in sacred history: thus the Dedication in 1 Maccabees (4:36-59).

So we pass from cosmic into historical time.

Cosmic Time and History

Cosmic time, essentially characterized by its cyclical regularity, involves a perpetual new beginning. History does not obey this law of perpetual new beginning. It contains unique events that the human race retains in its memory, but which are not repeated.

In pagan religions, historical time is sacred only insofar as particular events reproduce the primordial time of the gods. In the Bible, there is no history that predates the creation by God of the universe and of humankind.[9] History is sacred because in it is unfolded the plan of God that, after the sin of Adam and Eve, became the sacred history of redemption.

This sacred history is marked by interventions of God: he reveals himself; he appeals to the responsibility of men and women that they might choose to enter freely into his plan and turn back to him when they have sinned; he guides events toward the fulfillment of his plan of redemption. This history moves toward an end: the full realization of the desire of God for the salvation of each and every person by the coming of the Messiah, the Savior.

God Among Us

The Old Testament is the revelation of God through his acts, the "wonders" he accomplishes for all people in their history.

When Jesus appears—Son of God born of the Virgin Mary, a man among men—"This is the time of fulfillment. The reign of God is at hand!" (Mark 1:15).

The history of people and salvation takes a decisive turn. Jesus is born "during the reign of King Herod" (Matt 2:1). The preaching of John the Baptist began: "In the fifteenth year of the rule of Tiberius Caesar, when Pontius Pilate was procurator of Judea, Herod tetrarch of Galilee, Philip his brother tetrarch of the region of Ituraea and Trachonitis, and Lysanias tetrarch of Abilene, during the high-priesthood of Annas and Caiaphas" (Luke 3:1-2). "Crucified under Pontius Pilate, he suffered, died and was buried. On the third day he rose again from the dead" (Nicene Creed).

The event of Jesus Christ—God among us—ushers in the "last days," leading history to its end. "Today" the Scriptures are fulfilled. Jesus, who ascended to the right hand of the Father, will come again in glory. Between these two moments is the "intermediate time," the time of passage from the present world to the world to come, the "favorable time"—the "today"—of God and of the salvation that comes and is unfolded; the time of the Church guided by the Spirit; the time of the liturgy that celebrates and announces, indeed that sacramentally crosses the distance between what is "already" acquired, once and for all; and the "to come," given in hope, that will be manifested in full.

A Road Begun

The "intermediate time" is that of the Church, of the proclamation of the gospel to all nations, of the disciples baptizing and preaching the faith (Matt 28:19-20; Acts 1:6-8).

The gospel cannot be reduced to a body of doctrines to which one adheres, nor to a moral code that one submits his or her life to. Being a disciple does not just mean placing one's faith in Christ; rather, this faith is *communion* with the Lord, following in the wake of his Passover. This is what is expressed and realized when we participate in the liturgy within the framework of the liturgical year.

The Church calendar is not simply a list of feasts and commemorations celebrated on specific dates. It is more like an itinerary, in the sense that it is vitally, effectively integrated into a journey toward salvation, a dynamic that we experience today, because the events we celebrate sacramentally have taken place once and for all. Having happened historically, they are not really reenacted. Rather they have an importance and presence that transcends time. We have a share through the sacrament that unfolds them and at the same time grants us grace, here and now. Today is the time of the coming (Advent) of the Lord for whom we must prepare the way. Today Christ is born for us. Today the Church strives for its conversion (Lent). Today believers pass with Christ from death to life (Easter) and are continuously formed in paschal community (Easter season). Today the Spirit is given to the Church that it might proclaim the wonders of God in every tongue (Pentecost). Today the Church marches on in the rhythm of Ordinary Time, to the encounter with the Lord who came, who comes, and who will come again.

The mystery of the kingdom cannot be divided up. The liturgical year never ceases to unfold its totality, but it does so according to a focus that is proper to each season. Believers must become part of history, not only in its celebrations but in the return to daily life within the perspective of the liturgy, the "source and summit" of the life of the Church.[10]

The liturgical year is therefore not a neutral framework—and ultimately an abstraction—but the mystery of salvation itself, and the means of sharing in it in time. That is why it is the time of God and the time of all people who are brought together, just as the sacraments are acts of God and acts of the Church that sanctifies. It speaks without ceasing—but always in a new way—of the coming of the Lord throughout the Old Testament until his return, which is always coming nearer, not because time elapses but because *we* are progressing. So the sacraments guide our lives from their birth in Christ till the encounter with him face to face, of which the sacrament of anointing is the sign and promise. Thus the dismissal of the assembly—"Go in the peace of Christ"—becomes the parting word to a brother or sister at the threshold of eternity: "May the Lord Jesus Christ protect you and bring you to life everlasting."[11] "Father . . . may he [she] enjoy happiness and peace for ever in the life to come."[12]

The liturgical year is not merely a succession of weeks out of which come a certain number of Sundays and feasts. It is not a kind of time-line dotted with celebrations to be observed and lived, so to speak, from one point to another. On the contrary, it constitutes a unity where everything participates, without meaningless (weak) times—even if there are strong times[13]—in the mystery of salvation. For God acts—and saves—always. Each moment is a "favorable time," an "opportune moment" (*kairos*) given for salvation. This true nature of the liturgical year arises from the way it grows out of the Easter celebration, the event that is its center, heart, core, and seed.

Origin and Formation of the Liturgical Year

The history of the formation of our present liturgical year is quite complex. It involves the relationship between the liturgy and cosmic time and its cycles (solar and lunar); computations and references to historical time, different cultures, etc.; also by decisions of the several that throughout the course of history have determined the liturgical calendar. Some of these decisions were not always the best in terms of options and liturgical or pastoral considerations. Moreover, whatever one might say, some changes took place that, objectively, were deviations. For instance, at one time the overflow of saints' celebrations supplanted the normal Sunday celebration far too often. This brought about reforms, the last of which, for the Latin Church, dates from Vatican II, with the publication of the new Roman Calendar (March 21, 1969). We should understand that all the elements contributing to a construction of a liturgical year, some of them poorly made compromises, always remain open to the possibility of correction and, above all, to adaptation to diverse times and places.[14] In short, the liturgical year as we know it is the result of numerous factors mingled with numerous cultures and traditions. This is not the place to describe its history, even in summary, for a history cannot be reduced or simplified without more or less distorting it.[15] However, we can point out some significant highlights of its formation.

From the beginning, the one great Christian celebration has been the observance of the Lord's Passover on the first day of the week, that is, the day after the Sabbath (Acts 20:7; 1 Cor 16:2; Rev 1:10; Matt 28:1; Mark 16:9; Luke 24:1; John 20:1). This was the day of the assembly and of the Eucharist. This "Day of the Lord"—later called "Sunday"—this weekly Passover, is the core of what will be the liturgical year and what gives it its fundamental meaning. It truly is paschal. The "first day of the week" makes one think of the first day of the first week and thereby suggests that the resurrection of the Lord inaugurates a new creation. On the other hand, this day comes after the seventh: it has thus been called the "eighth day." This term evokes what will come at the end of all weeks. Is it perhaps a witticism that certain Fathers of the Church took pleasure in? No. It is, rather, an expression of a symbolic perception of things. In all the names for this day a fundamental reality is expressed. The resurrection of the Lord marks the beginning of a new world. Its weekly celebration moves forward to the fullness of time beyond time. Yesterday, today, tomorrow: here is found the internal dynamic of the liturgical year.

The first Christians were children of Judaism who each year, on the fourteenth day of Nisan,[16] celebrated the Passover. Their faith in Christ enabled them to see this annual celebration in a new light. However, it was not until the first years of the second century—the second half of the century at Rome—that there was an institution of a Christian feast of Easter.[17] This celebration rapidly developed into a feast that lasted fifty days, "a week of weeks" according to St. Hilary (315-367).

A fast of forty days appeared in Egypt at the beginning of the fourth century. It became "Lent" at the end of the fourth century, and continued to evolve until the sixth.

In the fourth century we see testimony to the feast of the Nativity of the Lord, as well as to the feast of Epiphany, which perhaps had an earlier origin in the East.

The history of the Roman Advent begins in the sixth century, but there was some form of an Advent known previously at the end of the fourth and in the fifth centuries in Gaul and Spain.

This quick recital of the genesis of the liturgical year brings out the fact that it is—and remains—fundamentally a paschal celebration. The cycle of Advent and Christmas-Epiphany is the last to appear. The longest series of Sundays during this time, which we now call "Ordinary," still testifies to one basic practice: weekly celebration of the Passover of the Lord. The later developments, the evolving structures, the reforms, the development of worship, and the memorial of the saints—primarily the martyrs—changed nothing. The most recent reforms of Vatican II are explicitly concerned with the reevaluation of Sunday.

> Holy Mother Church believes that it is for her to celebrate the saving work of her divine Spouse in a sacred commemoration on certain days throughout the course of the year. Once each week, on the day which she has called the Lord's Day, she keeps the memory of the Lord's resurrection. She also celebrates it once every year, together with his blessed passion, at Easter, that most solemn of all feasts.

> In the course of the year, moreover, she unfolds the whole mystery of Christ from the incarnation and nativity to the ascension, to Pentecost and the expectation of the blessed hope of the coming of the Lord.[18]

> The liturgical year is to be revised so that the traditional customs and discipline of the sacred seasons shall be preserved or restored to suit the conditions of modern times. Their specific character is to be retained so that they duly nourish the piety of the faithful who celebrate the mysteries of the Christian redemption and, above all, the paschal mystery.[19]

The Liturgical Year: Present Calendar

The liturgical seasons of Advent, Christmas-Epiphany, Lent, Easter, and Ordinary Time constitute the seasons of the liturgical year, whose framework is determined by the feasts inserted into it. These different seasons begin and end on certain dates that vary from year to year because of the movability of the great feasts (or solemnities) to which they are wed.[20]

Many are always celebrated on a Sunday: Epiphany,[21] Easter, Trinity, Body and Blood of Christ.[22]

Since December 25—Christmas—can fall on any day of the week, the date of the first Sunday of Advent depends on it.

Ascension is always the Thursday following the sixth Sunday of Easter.[23]

During Ordinary Time, the feasts of the Lord and the solemnities can be observed on a Sunday if they fall on that day: Presentation of the Lord (February 2), Birth of St. John the Baptist (June 24), Sts. Peter and Paul (June 29), Transfiguration (August 6), Assumption (August 15), the Triumph of the Cross (September 14), All Saint's Day (November 1), Commemoration of All Souls (November 2), Dedication of the Lateran basilica or of the Holy Savior (November 9). In certain years, there are several Sundays in Ordinary Time that are put in parentheses, so to speak.[24]

Finally, when there is no Sunday between Christmas and Epiphany, the feast of the Holy Family is celebrated during the week, on December 30. In the same way, if Epiphany is celebrated on January 7 or 8, the Baptism of the Lord is moved to the following Monday, that is to say January 8 or 9.

Several series of variables must be calculated in order to establish the calendar for the liturgical year. One need not make his or her own computations to know in advance which Mass is celebrated on which Sunday and on what date, each year, the movable feasts are found. One can simply refer to a liturgical calendar.[25] Nevertheless, the movability of too many feasts—especially Easter—poses some problems.[26]

One simple reform would be to assign an annual date for the feast of Easter, fixed on a determined Sunday once and for all. The Church does not oppose this idea. However, it would be necessary to gain the assent of the entire body of Churches and Christian communities for the date to become fixed.[27] Here is where the difficulty lies, even in the West.[28]

Some people wish that we might go further: to introduce, in civil society, a perpetual calendar. The Church is not opposed to this either, but it does have some even stricter conditions: "Among the various systems that are being devised with a view to establishing a perpetual calendar and introducing it into civil life, the only stipulation of the Church is that the calendar retain and safeguard a seven-day week, with Sunday, and without the introduction of any days outside the week, so that the succession of weeks may be left intact, unless in the judgment of the Apostolic See there are extremely serious reasons to the contrary."[29]

Such a calendar, however, would be even more difficult to adopt, because beyond the agreement of the Churches, it would be necessary for all countries to decide together which system among all those in present use would become the new, perpetual calendar.

At any rate, the liturgical year will always preserve its originality. It is qualitatively different; not a simple division of time but a mystery—sacrament—of the coming of salvation in time.

It is not enough to abandon oneself to appointed "holy times," to celebrate faithfully and piously every Sunday and feast day on the calendar. The liturgical year demands that one enter into its mystical, sacramental perspective. This requires a "full, active, and conscious" participation which, in turn, depends on our progress, and that of the whole Church, toward the Day of the Lord and the full realization of the plan of salvation that God accomplishes in time.

The Liturgical Year and Salvation History

History is made up of single events that often never recur. Historical time is therefore qualitatively different from cosmic time, which is characterized by the cyclical regularity of the unceasing and foreseeable return of the seasons and days. We do not obtain history by observing the revolution of the sun or the phases of the moon, but by seeing on earth the lives and deeds of men and women. History is written, certainly, in chronological form, but it is not like an impassive clock, whose movements all take place in an invariable and arbitrary manner. History has a meaning that we can decipher, because it records a memory of events.[30] History involves meaning and memory.

The revelation of this meaning by God, the experience and memory of his interventions in the lives of those who are born and die, make this history holy, that is, defined by the orientation that God gives to it, by the setting forth of his plan and by the free involvement of humanity in its unfolding.

Sacred history is not superimposed on us. But it is a history that is perceived as the unfolding plan of salvation. Nothing is neutral or completely worldly. History is touched and made holy, for each man and woman and for the whole world, by the intercession of God, by his grace. This history involves the responsibility of nations, of the Church, and of all who walk in the paths of God, or who deviate from them, fall into sin, and are converted. But in spite of all these vicissitudes, indeed through them, sacred history moves inexorably toward its end—the coming of the kingdom—because God is faithful, and no one can do anything to hinder the ultimate accomplishment of his will.

The liturgical year is situated in this context and perspective. It is the great trajectory of salvation history, from beginning to end, traveled symbolically, but efficaciously. Its stages and rhythms are those of the advancement of the kingdom from its preparation in the Old Testament to the return of the Lord and its end in the heavenly Jerusalem.

The liturgical year recalls the events of salvation, but not in the way in which a commemorative ceremony recalls past events. "Today" is the key word that one must understand first of all in a concrete, nonmetaphorical sense.

Today God reveals his Law to us and allows us to choose between good and evil, between life and death (Deut 30:19). Today resounds the call to prepare the ways of the Lord. "Today, in our world, the Word is born."[31] Today Christ is baptized in the Jordan, water is changed into wine.[32] Today the kingdom is at hand. Repent and believe the good news (Mark 1:15). Today, if you hear his voice, harden not your hearts (Ps 95). Today Christ dies on Calvary and is raised from the dead; he ascends to heaven and is seated at the right hand of the Father. Today the Spirit is given to us. Today is the favorable time *(kairos)*. For God transcends time, submitting not to its limits: what he does once for all remains always. The living Christ is present and active in the world where he became incarnate. The Spirit, sent by the Father, continues to act.

For all its divine nature from beginning to end, this sacred history is, nonetheless, human. The day of God is proclaimed and lived in the day of men and women. The activity of God in the world determines the true nature of our time, of our history—and consequently the destiny of humanity. Biblical and Christian religion ignores any primordial time, the primordial history that human beings have produced throughout time by way of myths.

The time and history of humankind contribute their own worthy contributions to the successive stages of God's unfolding plan. New insights are generated by and through the sacrament of the liturgical year. Each liturgical season, each feast of the year in progress, is different from its counterpart of the preceding year; the celebrations of the next year will be new again, and so on. This does not result only, or even primarily, from the fact that we ourselves change from year to year, that we celebrate with different dispositions, etc. It comes from the nature of an act, an event that is always unique, in which we find that God is involved to the highest degree.

One might say that *everything* is involved in each celebration of every new liturgical year: the weight of eternity and the importance of the divine; the unique character of the present and the aspect of the human

dimension; the halfhearted passivity and unfocused participation of today that may certainly be atoned for tomorrow. In any case we move—or
we ought to move—from conversion to conversion. There is lull in the
history of salvation; there is no break in the liturgical year.

Spirituality of Wakefulness and Vigilance
If one wished to characterize the spirituality of the liturgical year, one
would have to speak of wakefulness and vigilance. We have been ad-
monished to practice these virtues from the time of the announcement
of the first manifestation of the Lord until his anticipated return as King
of the universe.[33]

In the gospels for the First Sunday of Advent, we hear Jesus say to us:
"Stay awake, therefore"; "Be on guard"; "Be on the watch. Pray constantly."[34]

This call to vigilance is sometimes more intense, more explicit. But in
one way or another, it is always in our celebrations. Moreover, we see
it there, since, in the acclamation that follows the consecration of bread
and wine we say: "Christ will come again"; "Lord Jesus, come in glory";
"We proclaim your death, Lord Jesus, until you come in glory."

In the same way, throughout the liturgical year we are urged without
ceasing and in a variety of ways to be attentive to the signs of the times.
Far from encouraging us to escape from this world into another more or
less mythical one, the liturgical year calls us insistently to take daily realities seriously, repeatedly reminding us that "God is working in this age,
these times are the last."[35]

The liturgical year develops, therefore, a spirituality of responsibility,
of acting to bring about the reign of God, its peace, justice, and joy in
a world that is never without meaning, into our own historical time. It
opens the pathways of our creative imagination, enlightened and stimulated by the word of God.

The Liturgical Year and the Word of God
Without the word of God there would be no sacred history; nor would
there be a liturgical year. "In the beginning was the Word" (John. 1:1).
The word of God created heaven and earth and all they contain. His word
called us to life and entrusted the universe to us. This was God's first
revelation of himself and of his plan: sacred history had begun. After
Adam and Eve sinned, God revealed that he would henceforth pursue

a plan of salvation. This promise is called in the Christian tradition the "proto-gospel," the "first announcement of the good news" of salvation (Gen 3:14-15).

God called Abraham, whose vocation was to begin gathering a nation of believers (Gen 12:1); then he called Moses, that he might lead the people out of Egypt and receive the Law (Deut 4:10; 9:10; 18:16). The history of salvation, though, begins with the Exodus, the fundamental event. It is always this event that is referred to in order to evoke the past, reform the present, and prepare the future.

Afterward came the prophets, by whom God spoke to his people and led them. They confirmed and revealed God's plan to the people. By denouncing the people's sins and calling for their conversion, the prophets forced them to return to the ways of the Lord, to remain faithful to the covenant. The prophets made them aware of the signs of the times and revealed to them the meaning of happy or unhappy events in their lively history, which was always under God's guidance. They taught the people "to hope for salvation" patiently.[36]

The inspired writings, the living memory of Israel, recount many striking and significant deeds, and they reveal the unity and continuity of the sacred history that sages continue to read and reread in order to interpret their meaning for the present, as well as their meaning for the future. This reading of the events of salvation history finds its warrant—indeed its reason for being—in studying God's actions: happening once in the past, they transcend time, and they involve both the present and the future. In Scripture we discover the expression of the liturgy, which always associates yesterday, today, and tomorrow.

At the juncture of the Old and New Testaments, John the Baptist is presented as the voice that urges sinners to be converted and prepare themselves for imminent salvation (Luke 3:1-18). Finally, Jesus is the Word—the voice of God— made flesh (John 1).

We have already seen that the great Jewish feasts celebrate major events of salvation history that stood out from others by the decisive word of God. As the word has held a primary place in the synagogal liturgy since the beginning, so it does in the liturgy of the Christian assembly. Now, however, new writings are added to the ancient Scriptures—the Gospels, apostolic letters, the Book of Revelation—a collection that we call the New Testament.[37] As early as St. Justin (c. 100/110–165), the readings of the prophets and the memoirs of the apostles already appear to be a tradition and essential part of the Sunday assembly.[38]

One of the most notable reforms of Vatican II has been the immense enrichment of the liturgical Lectionary. Since the First Sunday of Advent in 1969 (November 30), three readings have become part of the Sunday Mass: the first taken from the Old Testament, the second from an apostolic writing (Acts, Letters, or Revelation), the third from the Gospels. There has been an admirable response to the request of the council: "The treasures of the Bible are to be opened up more lavishly so that . . . a more representative part of the sacred scriptures will be read to the people in the course of a prescribed number of years."[39]

The first and truly important innovation is the introduction of a reading from the Old Testament into the course of the Sunday Mass. It is true that portions of the Old Testament had been included in liturgies long before Vatican II, but they were read only on weekdays: on the Ember days, during Lent, and on various feasts.[40] Read in the course of the Sunday assembly, the Old Testament takes its rightful place in the economy of salvation and in the celebration of the liturgy. It is undoubtedly an integral part of salvation history. Apostolic readings (Letters, Acts, Revelation) have a particular significance and importance. The apostles constitute an indispensable link in the transmission of the good news, and they retain a unique authority for its interpretation. It is essential that their voice reverberate in Christian communities in all ages, especially in liturgical assemblies where the faithful gather.

The second innovation is the three-year cycle that allows for a much wider reading of the texts, beginning with the Gospels, since in each of the years (reading cycles A, B, C) emphasis is given to one of the three Synoptic Gospels.[41]

The council's wishes have been truly honored, not only because the scriptural texts have been considerably augmented but because the Lectionary for Sundays and Feasts has been composed in an extraordinary manner, as anyone who uses it can testify.[42]

In sum, the liturgical year is presented as an itinerary marked by the word of God proper to each Sunday. During Ordinary Time, those appropriate words set the tone for each celebration. The other elements—the antiphons and songs at the opening of Mass and at communion, the prayers—are invariable and therefore not characteristic of the celebration of each separate year. So there is reason to be particularly interested in the biblical readings of the day.

During the other times of the liturgical year and on the feasts, the texts and songs are proper to the Sunday of the week. One must be attentive to the whole formulary and each of its parts, which together determine the meaning and significance of the celebration.

The Calendar of Saints (Sanctoral)

The Second Vatican Council prescribed that the liturgical reform must restore the Sunday celebration to its original dignity and primacy. "Other celebrations, unless they be truly of the greatest importance, shall not have precedence over Sunday, which is the foundation and kernel of the whole liturgical year.[43] For this reason, the Proper of the Time shall be given due preference over the feasts of the saints so that the entire cycle of the mysteries of salvation may be suitably recalled."[44]

In the course of time, the Sanctoral has been considerably amplified.[45] In the Code of Rubrics (1960) there were no less than 338 separate feasts and commemorations. With such a proliferation, the formularies of the Sunday Masses were rarely taken up again during the week, and they were never used during Lenten weekdays. Many popes, among others Benedict XIV (1740-1758), Pius X (1903-1914), and Pius XII (1939-1958), envisioned a reform of the calendar that would reduce the number of feasts, but they were not able to bring such a project to fruition.

Certainly, "the saints have been traditionally honored in the Church, and their authentic relics and images held in veneration. For the feasts of the saints proclaim the wonderful works of Christ in his servants and offer to the faithful fitting examples for their imitation."[46] It is not a question of contesting what may be the legitimacy or value of a cult of the saints, nor of yielding to any sort of iconoclastic enterprise. For all that, the multiplication of feasts and memorials of the saints was surely at odds with the normal celebration of the mystery of the time. The council launched a reform whose time had certainly come.

It also enunciated a principle: "Lest the feasts of the saints should take precedence over the feasts which commemorate the very mysteries of salvation, many of them should be left to be celebrated by a particular Church, or nation, or family of religious. Only those should be extended to the universal Church which commemorate saints who are truly of universal importance."[47]

As for the others, it divided them into four categories: solemnities, feasts, obligatory memorials, and optional memorials. The weekly Lectionary was not to be used for those feasts and obligatory memorials that have their own readings.[48]

This reform was received warmly because from this point on, there are specific scriptural texts for each day of every week of the liturgical year. Moreover, during Ordinary Time, the books of the Bible are read sequentially according to the style of reading known as "semi-continuous."[49] During the rest of the year, the choice is made according to the current liturgical time. It was regrettable that until the reform, one frequently had to abandon the weekly Lectionary in order to read other texts.

The reform of the Calendar of Saints has been successful. It has, moreover, greatly facilitated the practice of venerating the saints. In fact, these "feasts and memorials" are now fully integrated into the celebration of the mystery of salvation and no longer smack of the occult. God is "glorified in the assembly of saints." Their lives are models for us. Their witness of faith revives the strength of the Church. "Their example inspires us." "Their fraternal prayer strengthens us to work for the coming of the kingdom."[50] Far from turning us from the Lord, they lead us resolutely toward him.[51] The fact that local saints are now fully approved and inscribed into particular calendars again makes the celebration of the liturgical year even more concrete today—here and now—in each ecclesial community.

Our Purpose

Our purpose in this book is to help our brothers and sisters in faith to fully participate in the mystery of the liturgical year in the most active and conscious way possible.

We will read attentively the scriptural texts designated by the Church for each Sunday and feast so that we may understand them in the framework and context of the liturgical celebration that unites believers today.[52]

These readings are situated within the context of the universal Church. Hence the appeal to tradition: the tradition of yesterday, represented above all by the Fathers, but also that of today, expressed in various forms; especially hymns and songs, poetic prayers, and spiritual reading.

But the liturgy is not just composed of readings. It is also punctuated with prayers, antiphons, etc. None of these elements should be neglected.

We will apply ourselves principally to the Sunday Eucharistic celebration. But there is also the Divine Office—the Liturgy of the Hours—that is prayed by a good number of people who wish to be in touch with more than just the Sunday celebration. We will appeal to them, above all in the seasons of Advent and Easter, drawing especially from the hymnal.

Must we speak of this as a work of "spirituality"? The term runs the risk of being misunderstood or of being vague. We prefer to speak, in a more concrete manner, of a book for the spiritual life whose source and summit are in the celebration of the liturgical year. From this perspective, we can see endless interplay between the announcement of the good news, the daily life of believers and of the Church, and the celebration of the holy mysteries.

The sacred liturgy does not exhaust the entire activity of the Church. Before people can come to the liturgy they must be called to faith and to conversion. "But how can they call on him in whom they have not believed? And how can they believe in him of whom they have not heard? And how can hear without someone to preach? And how can people preach unless they are sent?" (Rom 10:14-15).

> Therefore the Church announces the good tidings of salvation to those who do not believe, so that [all] may know the one true God and Jesus Christ whom he has sent and may be converted from their ways, doing penance. To believers also the Church must ever preach faith and penance; she must prepare them for the sacraments, teach them to observe all that Christ has commanded, and encourage them to engage in all the works of charity, piety, and the apostolate, thus making it clear that Christ's faithful, though not of this world, are to be the lights of the world and are to glorify the Father before [all peoples].
>
> Nevertheless the liturgy is the summit toward which the activity of the Church is directed; it is also the font from which all her power flows. For the goal of apostolic endeavor is that all who are made [children] of God by faith and baptism should come together to praise God in the midst of his Church, to take part in the Sacrifice and to eat the Lord's Supper.
>
> The liturgy, in its turn, moves the faithful filled with "the paschal sacraments" to be "one in holiness"; it prays that "they hold fast in their lives to what they have grasped by their faith." The renewal in the Eucharist of the covenant between the Lord and man draws the faithful and sets them aflame with Christ's insistent love. From the liturgy, therefore, and especially from the Eucharist, grace is poured forth upon us as from a fountain, and the sanctification of [all] in Christ and the glorification of God to which all other activities of the Church are directed, as toward their end, are achieved with maximum effectiveness.[53]

Finally, at the heart of Scripture we find the lives of believers, the liturgy and the liturgical year, and we find the Lord Jesus himself, "the Alpha and Omega, the beginning and the end" of all things (Rev 21:6).

It is of him that the Scriptures speak: even more than that, he is the good news. It is at his side that believers march, conformed to his likeness. It is both him and the mystery of salvation that the liturgy celebrates.

He is, truly, the decisive event of sacred history from which dynamics the liturgical year draws.

Through his words and deeds, it is Jesus who is revealed and who reveals the Father. Through the lives of believers and the Church, animated by the Spirit, it is his reign that comes. It is he who is given as nourishment at the table of the Word and the Eucharist. It is through him, with him, and in him that the liturgical assembly gives to God, the Father almighty, all honor and glory. It is he who, by the mystery of the liturgical year and the celebration of the Days of the Lord, draws us toward the day when God will be all in all.

The Season of Advent

The season that opens the liturgical year was initiated and given a framework by the end of the fourth century, at about the same time as the celebrations of Christmas-Epiphany were being organized and encouraged.[1]

In Gaul and Spain there was a desire, at first, to undergo ascetic preparation before these feasts, a time for fasting and intensive prayer. The length of this kind of preparation differed from place to place. In some places, it continued until Christmas or Epiphany, those solemnities not being distinct at the time. There were three weeks of preparation—sometimes forty days—from St. Martin (November 11) to January 6.[2] The Council of Saragossa (380) prescribed an intense period of preparation for the feast of Epiphany, from December 17 onward,[3] significantly different, however, from Lent. From the very first, the community's preparation for the baptism of new members had little influence on it.[4] This primitive Advent did not have its roots in liturgical piety but rather in piety itself. Historically, there had been a long wait for the birth of the Savior. Mustn't this figure somehow among the sentiments that would inspire the Fathers? The feast of Christmas, consequently, took on great psychological importance. An even greater degree of piety must be in order when preparing for Christmas, for is it not "the long-awaited time"?[5] A response in the Office expresses this orientation well: "Watching from afar, I see the power of God advancing, and the whole earth enveloped in a cloud. Go out to meet him crying: 'Tell us if you are the One who is to reign over the people of Israel.' "[6] Since Lent at this time seemed already perfectly structured, everything was naturally compared to it.

The practice of fasting suggests a comparison. Although it does not seem to have been a definitive and essential practice during the early development of Advent, there was already the custom of fasting twice a week. *The Rule of St. Benedict* (c. 480–547) testifies to a daily fast from mid-September to Easter and twice per week the whole summer, after Pentecost, except when field work and summer heat made fasting hazardous to health.[7] We cannot hope, with our present-day mentality, to fathom the customs of ancient times, however, nor should we try. Suffice to say that St. Benedict explicitly associates the observances of Lent with the joy of preparation for the paschal feasts.[8]

At Rome, however, things came about differently. First of all, Advent came into being much later, toward the middle of the sixth century. More importantly, its orientation was entirely different. No trace of ascetic preparation for Christmas; still less for Epiphany.[9] At first, Advent was a liturgically determined time. Six Sundays were calculated before Christmas. Pope St. Gregory the Great (591–604) reduced them to four, probably hoping to simplify and perhaps more clearly mark the difference between Advent and Lent.

Until that time, Christmas was a secondary feast, especially at Rome. From the seventh century on, it took on more and more importance. Advent evolved in the same way. It was more solemn, but its orientation had also changed. From being a time to prepare for Christmas, it became a time to attend to the glorious *return* of the Lord. It received a clearly eschatological orientation, that is, it was directed toward the end of the world, to "last things." Christmas and Epiphany—two feasts, each complete in themselves yet forming together one great solemnity—thus became the celebrations of the birth of Christ the King.

The Eastern Churches did not develop a cycle of Advent comparable to that of the Roman liturgy.[10] Scarred by the Christological controversies of the fourth to sixth centuries, they were anxious to strongly affirm the orthodox faith regarding the mystery of the incarnation and the person of Christ.[11] The liturgies that preceded Christmas were, therefore, preparation for celebrating the mystery of the incarnation in all the purity of the faith.

Accordingly, on the Sunday that precedes the feast, the Byzantine Rite celebrates all those who, in the course of the ages, were heralds of Christ.

> Lift up your voice, Zion, holy city of God; proclaim the blessed memory of the Fathers. With Abraham, Isaac, and Jacob we praise them with our songs. Behold how, with Judah and Levi, we glorify Moses, and Aaron, inspired of God. We celebrate with David, Joshua, Samuel. Let our songs preview the divine birth of Christ, and let us beg that his kindness will grant great mercy to our world.
>
> Come, Elisha, you who one day saw Elijah drawn off in a heavenly chariot of fire, together with Hezekiah and Josiah, rejoice! You inspired prophets, lead the dance for the Nativity of the Lord; sing, you just ones; blessed

children, who by the dew of the Spirit were able to withstand the fiery fur-
nace, pray for us in holy awe: that Christ might grant our souls abundant
mercy.

Behold, the Virgin proclaimed through the ages by the prophets comes
in our world; she who gladdened the hearts of the wise and all upright
people. With them dances Sarah, most honored among women, Rebekah
and Rachel, Anna and Moses' glorious sister Miriam. The ends of the earth
rejoice with them; all of creation celebrates, for God will come to be born
in the flesh and fill the world with his mercy.[12]

From December 20 on, eyes are turned toward Bethlehem, where the
mystery of the birth of the one who is true God and true man is accomplished:

> Listen, O heavens, and earth take heed, for the Son, the Word of God the
> Father, will be born of a virgin, known by no man, through the power of
> one who without changing it communicates his nature, and the coopera-
> tion of the Holy Spirit. Bethlehem, be ready; Eden opens its doors, for the
> One who is becomes what he was not; the One who fashioned all creation
> is fashioned in his turn, he who will fill the earth with his mercy.[13]

The Virgin Mary, Mother of God (Theotokos: Council of Ephesus, 431),
is in the foreground:

> The Virgin, on this day, comes to the cave to give birth in an unspeakable
> manner to the eternal Word. May the universe leap for joy when it learns
> of it; may all creation together with the angels and the shepherds glorify
> him, the newborn child, the eternal God. The sacred words of the prophets
> are fulfilled: Behold, the Virgin bears God in the flesh, in the town of Beth-
> lehem, within a cave. All creatures glorify the One who has filled them with
> good things; let them dance! The Master of all things partakes of our ser-
> vile state in order to ransom us from the power of the Unknown One, we
> who sink under corruption; he comes as an infant lying in the crèche, a
> newborn child, the eternal God.[14]

This preparation takes place in an atmosphere of joy and festivity: it
is purely a matter of dancing and merrymaking.

In the Syrian liturgies, this preparation is stretched out over many weeks
called "annunciations." Successively evoked are the annunciations to
Zechariah and Mary, the visitation of Mary to Elizabeth, the birth of John
the Baptist, and the annunciation to Joseph. Finally, on the Sunday before Christmas, the liturgy evokes the prophets, that they might bear their
witness to the Savior and sing his praises.

Throughout all these evocations, the Eastern liturgy prepares to celebrate the day of the mystery, the coming of the Lord. But for which event,
exactly, does one prepare? That which has taken place already in the in-

carnation or that which we look for at the end of time? Clearly, not every liturgy has the same perspective or puts the accent on the same dimension of the mystery that we are preparing to celebrate. This is particularly evident in the evolution of Advent in the Latin liturgy.

The Double Meaning of the Season of Advent

The Roman Calendar says most explicitly: "Advent has a twofold character: as a season to prepare for Christmas when Christ's first coming to us is remembered; as a season when that remembrance directs the mind and heart to await Christ's Second Coming at the end of time."[15]

In its liturgical sense, the Christian word "advent"— *adventus*—is of pagan origin. The shift in the meaning of the word came about when the feasts of Christmas-Epiphany were instituted to celebrate the manifestation of the Lord in the flesh.

Pagans observed a manifestation of the divinity that came to dwell in its temple at a certain time each year. The feast honoring this divinity was called *adventus*. On these days the temple, customarily closed, would be opened. Sometimes a statue of the divinity would be moved into a space much larger than the small sanctuary where it was usually placed. The *adventus* thus was in the nature of a return, an anniversary.

In its imperial context, the *adventus* celebrated the anniversary of the coming of the emperor.

So the word was available to describe the coming of the Son of God in the temple of his flesh—his return, his visit. Moreover, the word's usage gradually became limited to describe what was considered the only real coming—*adventus*—the coming of the Lord. In the same way this *adventus*, this anniversary of the birth (*dies natalis*) of Christ, replaced the *adventus* and *dies natalis* of the unvanquished sun of the winter solstice. This usage gained prominence at about the time when the emperor Constantine (306–337), in an effort to tolerate all religions, issued the Edict of Milan (313), allowing the open and free practice of Christianity. With the ensuing adoption of Christian feasts—Christmas among them—pagan festivals were soon supplanted and forgotten.

This ancient idea of the *adventus* is found underlying the prayers of Advent that evoke "the coming" of the Lord,[16] the presence in our midst of the one who must "come."[17] This same vestige of meaning is discernible in the prayer of December 20, with the same image of the temple.

> At the message of an angel
> [Mary] welcomed your eternal Son

and, filled with the light of your Spirit,
she became the temple of your Word.

For most Christians, Advent remains a time to prepare for Christmas, which celebrates the first coming of the Lord. Nevertheless, the texts give evidence of further enrichment resulting from a later perspective.

The readings of the Fourth Sunday of Advent are centered on the birth of the Lord at Bethlehem. The prophecies announce him in the first readings. "The virgin shall be with child" (Isa 7:10-14: Year A). "Your house and your kingdom shall endure forever before me" (2 Sam 7:1-16: Year B). "From Bethlehem shall come forth one who is to be ruler in Israel" (Mic 5:1-4: Year C).

The Gospels report the announcements to Joseph (Matt 1:18-24: Year A) and to Mary (Luke 1:26-38: Year B), and the visitation of the mother of the Savior to her cousin Elizabeth (Luke 1:39-45: Year C).

The second readings reveal the same perspective. The Son of God is born of David's lineage (Rom 1:1-7: Year A). The mystery hidden from the beginning is now made manifest (Rom 16:25-27: Year B). In coming into the world, Jesus said to the Father: "I have come to do your will" (Heb 10:5-10: Year C).

This is also the case on the Third Sunday, with, however, a call to prepare the way of the Lord for his coming, a call not limited to the idea of his birth.

The strong voice of John the Baptist is heard, who calls us to recognize the one who is among us. The liturgy of this Sunday begins each year with this urgent invitation: "Rejoice in the Lord always; again I say, rejoice! The Lord is near." Joy of Christmas, certainly, but also of the last days that will see the glorious return of Christ (Isa 35:1-6, 10; 61:1-2, 10-11; Zeph 3:14-18).

The second readings speak, moreover, of a coming of the Lord for which Christians still wait and for which they must prepare in patience, prayer, and peace (James 5:7-10; 1 Thess 5:16-24; Phil 4:4-7).

By contrast, the First and Second Sundays place Advent within a much larger context. The prophetic oracles glimpse the day when the Lord will call together all nations in the eternal peace of the kingdom of God (Isa 2:1-5: First Sunday, Year A), when God will judge the poor with justice (Isa 11:1-10: Second Sunday, Year A), when he will manifest his glory (Bar 5:1-9: Second Sunday, Year C). They shout out the hope of believers in God, our justice (Jer 33:14-16: First Sunday Year C): "Oh, that you would rend the heavens and come down!" (Isa 63:16-19; 64:2-7: First Sunday, Year B). They call for the preparation of the way of the Lord (Isa 40:1-5, 9-11: Second Sunday, Year B).

This is the call of John the Baptist: "Reform your lives! The reign of God is at hand" (Matt 3:1-12; Mark 1:1-8: Second Sunday, Years A and B). Jesus uses it in speaking of the coming of the Son of Man who will be shown to "all flesh" (Luke 21:25-36; 3:1-6: First and Second Sundays, Year C). Hence the exhortation to be watchful, for we do not know when the Lord will come (Matt 24:37-44; Mark 13:33-37: First Sunday, Years A and B). The opening antiphons set the tone:[18]

> To you, my God, I lift my soul, I trust in you; let me never come to shame. Do not let my enemies laugh at me. No one who waits for you is ever put to shame. (First Sunday)

> People of Zion, the Lord will come to save all nations, and your hearts will exult to hear his majestic voice. (Second Sunday)

At the beginning of the celebration, we pray that God may increase in us the "strength of will for doing good," "removing the things that hinder us from receiving Christ with joy." The perspective is one of judgment and the eternal life to come:

> All-powerful God, increase our strength of will for doing good that Christ may find an eager welcome at his coming and call us to his side in the kingdom of heaven. (First Sunday)

> God of power and mercy, open our hearts in welcome. Remove the things that hinder us from receiving Christ with joy, so that we may share his wisdom and become one with him when he comes in glory. (Second Sunday)

This same orientation is present in the prayers after Communion:

> Father, may our communion teach us to love heaven. May its promise and hope guide our way on earth. (First Sunday)

> Father, you give us food from heaven. By our sharing in this mystery, teach us to judge wisely the things of earth and to love the things of heaven. (Second Sunday)

In this way the Sunday liturgy celebrates Advent in its double perspective of waiting for the second coming of the Lord (First and Second Sundays) and the immediate preparation for the feast of Christmas (Third and Fourth Sundays). The same orientation is in the present repertoire of hymns, particularly those that the Liturgy of the Hours presents.[19]

The Invitatory of each day's Office has the refrain "Come, let us worship the Lord, the King who is to come" (first and second weeks), or "The Lord is close at hand; come, let us worship him" (third and fourth weeks). The first is a traditional prayer to remain wakeful while awaiting the return of the Lord.[20] On December 24 we sing: "Today you will know the Lord is coming, and in the morning your will see his glory." This last invitatory antiphon makes the synthesis.

There are three distinct accents to the liturgy of the Advent season, which are defined by the three comings of the Lord: yesterday, at Bethlehem, when the Son of God was born of the Virgin Mary; today, in our world, where he is always incarnate; tomorrow, when he returns in glory.

Such is the rich meaning of Advent. From this beginning of the liturgical year, we celebrate the whole panorama of the mystery: from the beginning, when God created heaven and earth, until its fulfillment at the end of time, passing through the times of preparation—through the Scriptures— nearer and nearer to the approaching realization of "today in our world." This is a far cry from the simple, ascetic, and pious Christmas preparation of earlier days.

Heeding the Fathers

In their preaching, the Fathers knew how to present the rich mystery of Advent to the faithful. At this point we should review what the Liturgy of the Hours has selected for the Advent Office of Readings. To begin, we cite two readings, from the First Sunday and the following Monday. The first is an excerpt about the twofold coming of Christ, taken from the prebaptismal catechesis of St. Cyril of Jerusalem (c. 315–386):

> We do not preach only one coming of Christ, but a second as well, much more glorious than the first. The first coming was marked by patience; the second will bring the crown of a divine kingdom.
>
> In general, what relates to our Lord Jesus Christ has two aspects. There is a birth from God before the ages, and a birth from a virgin at the fullness of time. There is a hidden coming, like that of rain on fleece, and a coming before all eyes, still in the future.
>
> At the first coming he was wrapped in swaddling clothes in a manger. At his second coming he will be clothed in light as in a garment. In the first coming he endured the cross, despising the shame; in the second coming he will be in glory, escorted by an army of angels.
>
> We look then beyond the first coming and await the second. At the first coming we said: "Blessed is he who comes in the name of the Lord." At the second we shall say it again; we shall go out with the angels to meet the Lord and cry out in adoration: "Blessed is he who comes in the name of the Lord."[21]

The second excerpt is from a pastoral letter of St. Charles Borromeo, archbishop of Milan (1538–1584), on the meaning of Advent:

Beloved, now is the acceptable time spoken of by the Spirit, the day of salvation, peace and reconciliation: the great season of Advent. This is the time eagerly awaited by the patriarchs and prophets, the time that holy Simeon rejoiced at last to see. This is the season that the Church has always celebrated with special solemnity. We too should always observe it with faith and love, offering praise and thanksgiving to the Father for the mercy and love he has shown us in this mystery. In his infinite love for us, though we were sinners, he sent his only Son to free us from the tyranny of Satan, to summon us to heaven, to welcome us into its innermost recesses, to show us truth itself, to train us in right conduct, to plant within us the seeds of virtue, to enrich us with the treasures of his grace, and to make us children of God and heirs of eternal life.

Each year, as the Church recalls this mystery, she urges us to renew the memory of the great love God has shown us. This holy season teaches us that Christ's coming was not only for the benefit of his contemporaries; his power has still to be communicated to us all. We shall share his power, if, through holy faith and the sacraments, we willingly accept the grace Christ earned for us, and live by that grace and in obedience to Christ.

The Church asks us to understand that Christ, who came once in the flesh, is prepared to come again. When we remove all obstacles to his presence he will come, at any hour and moment, to dwell spiritually in our hearts, bringing with him the riches of his grace.

In her concern for our salvation, our loving mother the Church uses this holy season to teach us through hymns, canticles and other forms of expression, of voice or ritual, used by the Holy Spirit. She shows us how grateful we should be for so great a blessing, and how to gain its benefit: our hearts should be as much prepared for the coming of Christ as if he were still to come into this world. The same lesson is given us for our imitation by the words and example of the holy men of the Old Testament.[22]

Two texts from the Second Vatican Council are read on Tuesday of the second week and on Thursday of the third. They are a timely reminder that the last days have come for us, and that Christ, whose coming we celebrate, is the fullness of revelation:

The Church, to which we are all called in Christ Jesus and in which we acquire holiness through the grace of God, will reach its perfection only in the glory of heaven, when the time comes for the renewal of all things, and the whole world, which is intimately bound up with man and reaches its perfection through him, will, along with the human race, be perfectly restored in Christ.

Lifted above the earth, Christ drew all things to himself. Rising from the dead, he sent his life-giving Spirit upon his disciples, and through the Spirit established his Body, which is the Church, as the universal sacrament of salvation. Seated at the right hand of the Father, he works unceasingly in the world, to draw men into the Church, and through it, to join them more closely to himself, nourishing them with his own body and blood, and so making them share in his life of glory.

The promised renewal that we look for has already begun in Christ. It is continued in the mission of the Holy Spirit. Through the Spirit it goes on developing in the Church: there we are taught by faith about the meaning also of our life on earth as we bring to fulfillment—with hope in the blessings that are to come—the work that has been entrusted to us in the world by the Father, and so work out our salvation.

The end of the ages is already with us. The renewal of the world has been established, and cannot be revoked. In our era it is in a true sense anticipated: the Church on earth is already sealed by genuine, if imperfect, holiness. Yet, until a new heaven and a new earth are built as the dwelling place of justice, the pilgrim Church, in its sacraments and institutions belonging to this world of time, bears the likeness of this passing world. It lives in the midst of a creation still groaning and in travail as it waits for the sons of God to be revealed in glory.[23]

***

God, who through the Word creates all things and keeps them in being, provides men with unfailing testimony to himself in creation. With the intention of opening up the way of salvation from above, he also revealed himself to our first parents from the very beginning.

After their fall, he lifted them up to hope for salvation by the promise of redemption, and watched over mankind with unceasing care, in order that he might give eternal life to all who in persevering in good works seek out salvation.

In his own good time God called Abraham, to make of him a mighty nation. After the patriarchs, he taught this nation through Moses and the prophets to acknowledge himself alone as the living and true God, a provident father and just judge, and to look forward to the promised Savior. So, through the ages, he prepared a way for the gospel. After speaking "at various times and in different ways through the prophets, God has finally spoken to us in these days through the Son."

He sent his son, the eternal Word who enlightens all men, to dwell among men and make known to them the innermost things of God. Jesus Christ, the Word made flesh, sent as "a man to men, speaks the words of God," and brings to perfection, the saving work that the Father gave him to do.[24]

The Day of Salvation: Already Here, Yet Not Quite

It might be possible to convey the meaning of Advent with a simple definition, but it would be a limited one. The meaning and significance of the season do not lend themselves to simple definitions because Advent is not confined to any one focus. The various songs appropriate to this time and that recur most often are witness to this.[25] Such hymns as "Come, Divine Messiah," "God Comes to Save Us from Death," "New

Dawn,'' ''The Old World Has Fled,'' ''The People That Walked in Darkness,'' ''The Times Are Renewed,'' and ''Yet a Little While, and the Lord
Will Be Here.''

Variety is not only desirable, it is most appropriate, because the season of Advent is at one and the same time oriented toward the one *who
has come once and for all* (''God Among Men, God on Our Paths''), *who
is coming* (''The Times Are Renewed''), and *who will come* (''When the
Lord Will Show His Face''). This threefold aspect of Advent is implicit
in any liturgical definition of it.

> The day of God is not one day,
> an historical moment, never to return.
> The day of God is God forever,
> forever living, without night, without sleep.[26]

The beginning of the liturgical year plunges us immediately into the
dynamic of the mystery—the sacrament—of time, set forth season by season throughout the uninterrupted Days of the Lord.

First Week of Advent

> To you, my God, I lift my soul, I trust in you;
> Let me never come to shame.
> Do not let my enemies laugh at me.
> No one who waits for you is ever put to shame.
> (Entrance Antiphon)

This antiphon, taken from Psalm 25,[1] immediately places Advent within the context of the coming of God and the salvation whose full realization we await with confidence. Following this proclamation of faith and hope, the assembly turns to God to ask for his grace:

> All-powerful God,
> increase our strength of will for doing good
> that Christ may find an eager welcome at his coming
> and call us to his side in the kingdom of heaven.
> (Opening Prayer)

So from the beginning of the liturgical year we clearly express what is at the heart of the life of believers, the Church, and the liturgy: the ardent desire for God and his reign, the hope for the return of the Lord who is already present among his own, what waiting for the Lord's coming means for each believer, and the absolute need for the Spirit to fulfill our hope lest it be in vain.

Psalm 25 ends with a pathetic cry: "Redeem Israel, O God, from all its distress" (Ps 25:22). Waiting may in fact be intolerable if there is no certainty of God's faithfulness, and if we do not know that the one who must come has already come. But we must not give up hoping. The most assured hope—that which draws on our past experience that waiting for the future is best served by patiently enduring the present[2]—carries with it a dramatic connotation. We are sure of God, of course, but we are also conscious of all the perils, interior and exterior, that beset us!

In evoking the centuries that preceded Christ, that is, by recalling in the liturgy the ancient oracles of a bygone era, the Church is not inviting us to return to the past or to act as if Christ has not yet come. But it does remind us that at the end of Advent we celebrate what is not merely the birthday of the Lord, but rather an event that happened once, and for all time, so that we might enjoy today the grace it generated.

The experience of Israel still has meaning for today. The desire for God is never fulfilled, because "God is greater than our hearts" (1 John 3:20). The fullness of salvation overwhelms our capacity to receive it: we never cease being open to the immensity of the gift that has been given to us. Known and recognized as it is, however, God's love yet dwells in a hidden place. Furthermore, as we perceive God's wonders, we realize that we have seen scarcely anything, that we still have everything to discover. The temptations that assail our abiding hope do not alter its genuine nature or diminish its strength.

The Eucharist is the sacrament of the presence of the Lord in the midst of his people. But we are no less open to a gift that is yet to come.

> Father, may our communion teach us to love heaven. May its promise and hope guide our way on earth. (Prayer after Communion)

Such is the Advent we are introduced to by the liturgy of this First Sunday. There are, however, three cycles of readings from Scripture prescribed by the Church in the Lectionary: Years A, B, and C.

First Sunday of Advent—Year A

Light Pierces the Night

"He Will Come . . . in the Future"

The Liturgy of the Word opens with a solemn proclamation from Isaiah, whose voice is often heard during the course of Advent.[3] It is an oracle of revelation concerning the one who is to come. The prophet has had a vision. He was at prayer. He heard and saw the crowds who were ascending the hill to the Temple. In his ecstasy, he heard and clearly saw what lay "in the future," the great spectacle of what "will come to pass": the gathering of the nations to the place where the Lord will show himself at his coming.

The Lord is in the ideal temple on high, on a mountain that no one can climb, and which is clearly not of this world.[4] This "future" that Isaiah contemplates is not marked on a calendar, but neither is it illusory. This coming is not conditioned by the vagaries of history: it is the fulfillment of the plan of God, who dwells in high places.

This coming concerns "all the nations," "the multitude of peoples" who will ascend to the Lord in order to submit themselves to his will, to receive his teaching and his light. The one who "will come in the future," is thus the manifestation—the epiphany—of the universal rule of the Lord, an era of utterly pure peace. "They shall beat their swords into plowshares and their spears into pruning hooks." It is difficult to imagine how one could speak of these things in a stronger or more suggestive manner.

In our own day we spend money that should be used to feed starving people on ever more deadly weapons of war. Yet, it is from where we find ourselves "now" that we must march toward the future. The time of waiting for the manifestation of the Lord, the time of Advent, is that of taking the road toward what must come.

> *I rejoiced when I heard them say: let us go*
> *to the house of the Lord*
>
> I rejoiced because they said to me,
>   "We will go up to the house of the LORD."
> And now we have set foot
>   within your gates, O Jerusalem—

Jerusalem, built as a city
  with compact unity.
To it the tribes go up,
  the tribes of the LORD,

According to the decree for Israel,
  to give thanks to the name of the LORD.
In it are set up judgment seats,
  seats for the house of David.

Pray for the peace of Jerusalem!
  May those who love you prosper!
May peace be within your walls,
  prosperity in your buildings.

Because of my relatives and friends
  I will say, ''Peace be within you!''
Because of the house of the LORD, our God,
  I will pray for your good. (Ps 122:1-9)

At an hour when you least expect . . .

We are going toward an encounter with the Lord who will manifest himself. But when will he come? At certain times and in certain places—even today—some say ''Very soon!'' They seem unable to resist the temptation to point to a certain date. There is an apocalyptic fervor attached to it that resurfaces time and again. New dates are successively put forward, and no matter how many false prophecies there are, another date is scheduled.

Others, opposed to this, are content with the certitude of immediate experience. Time passes, and nothing comes. Then why be uneasy? It is not apocalyptic fervor that afflicts these people. On the contrary, they are asleep, they are really not concerned, and they lack true vigilance.

Jesus speaks to both these groups in this Sunday's gospel (Matt 24:37-44).

The coming of the Son of Man (the parousia) will be sudden and unexpected. Jesus, in order to make this comprehensible, recalls what happened before the Flood. All were busy with their own pursuits—''people were eating and drinking, marrying and being—oblivious to anything else: ''the flood came and destroyed them.''

Does this mean that the Lord's coming is itself a catastrophe? Certainly not: it is, rather, a question of attitude, the personal attitude of each of us. If we are negligent, we will end in disaster, as the example of the two women grinding meal clearly describes. They are working together, each doing the same task. But ''one is taken, the other left.''

Jesus teaches, first of all, that his coming cannot be doubted. And he insists, moreover, that it will be a completely unexpected event and therefore unpredictable. This unambiguous teaching lays to rest any idea of determining the date of his coming, but at the same time, it also tells us that it would be folly to lose sight of it. This Gospel is at the heart of the season of Advent. It reminds us that we must continue to live with renewed watchfulness.

Jesus affirmed that the kingdom is already present, in his person, while proclaiming forcefully that it is still to come. Everything has been fulfilled in the person of Jesus. His life, death, and resurrection—decisive historical events—fulfill the Scriptures and their promises, and satisfy the longing of all the prophets since Moses (Luke 24:27). But not everything is yet fully manifested. Faith in the victorious redemption wrought by Christ also means that we look forward with a renewed hope to that glorious epiphany of the Lord's kingship upon his return. In the face of these certainties, questions of "when and how" are meaningless, and it matters nothing if there have been errors in approximating the date.

The first Christians, for example, earnestly believed that Jesus' return was imminent—a brief wait. But they never forgot—and this is the important thing—the words of Jesus himself: "As for the exact day or hour, no one knows it, neither the angels in heaven nor the Son, but the Father only" (Matt 24:36). What counts is the manner in which we live our lives today, for it is how we live that determines how we hope.

"Stay awake, therefore"
Sure of the coming of the Lord, of which we know neither the day nor the hour, knowing only that it will be sudden, we must live in a state of watchfulness. This command is delivered as a simple imperative: "Stay awake, therefore!" The reason? Always the same: "You cannot know the day your Lord is coming"; "The Son of Man is coming at the time you least expect."

The miniparable, in one phrase—"like a thief in the night"—is enough to illustrate this command. Not that it means that the Lord is a thief: rather, that he will come like one. It insists again on the unpredictable character of his arrival, which demands that we remain prepared. The thief image seems to have struck the imaginations of the first Christians (1 Thess 5:2; 2 Pet 3:10; Rev 3:3).

The Gospel of Matthew for this Sunday speaks of different kinds of vigilance: the parables of the faithful servant (24:45-51), the ten virgins

(25:1-13), and the talents (25:14-30). The apostolic writings are also strongly centered on the return of the Lord: the resurrection of the dead, the awaiting of the day (1 Thess 4:13; 5:2; 2 Pet 3), the letters to the seven Churches (Rev 2–3), and the final chapter of the Book of Revelation (Rev 22:12-21).

This vigilance is not a vague disposition of the spirit or soul. It is, rather, an active force, a dynamic prompting that makes one act, always and everywhere, with full reason. It is a question, really, of faithfully doing one's work, of assuming our daily responsibilities with the conviction that we will not be surprised by the unforeseen arrival of the Lord. The Christian believer is one whose life is active and serious but without anxiety, because each day may be the one when Christ will knock at the door. Whatever the hour, that visit will not surprise the faithful and vigilant servant. He will open the door, and the Lord will enter his house and seat himself at the table, which is always ready.

> Like a friend whom one has invited,
> Jesus will come when he wishes.
> The table will be quickly set for him
> if he has a place at our supper.
> The night of his sudden arrival
> will fulfill those who wait.[5]

"The Night Is Over, the Day Begins"
In this context, the exhortation of Paul is put into sharp relief (Rom 13:11-14).

It is a declaration of urgency that is reflected in the style of the verses. Quick phrases follow each other breathlessly. Images are strewn together hurriedly. The image of awakening gives way to the image of day and night, then darkness and light. There is a certain rhythm to it all that helps us to understand, but the words themselves are enough, and they are all the richer if we take time to linger over them, a swift succession of images, each in relation to the other.

Salvation is the goal we approach, step by step, from the moment of our conversion and baptism. We find ourselves already beginning to wake from the dark night, as little by little the dawn presents itself to light our glorious morning. Morally, we remain in the theological context of "the present time." We are moving toward a day so bright that the obscurity of night is already dispelled. Present time is thus characterized by an illumination that gets gradually brighter as life goes on. Entering into this dynamic of time, the Christian must already live according to the rising light. In other words, the definitive salvation yet to come already acts within us by the hope it creates and the vigilance it provokes. For we have been given faith, grace, and the gift of the Spirit.

Act as if You Were in Broad Daylight

Those of us who are already conscious of receiving the grace of salvation, and who wait for final salvation, do not consider this dawn-pierced night as darkness. Nevertheless, we remain caught in the unceasing battle between light and darkness, a battle that everyone must fight by putting on the appropriate armor that Paul describes:

> Put on the armor of God so that you may be able to stand firm against the tactics of the devil. Our battle is not against human forces but against the principalities and powers, the rulers of this world of darkness, the evil spirits in regions above. You must put on the armor of God if you are to resist on the evil day; do all that your duty requires, and hold your ground. Stand fast, with the truth as the belt around your waist, justice as your breast-plate, and zeal to propagate the gospel of peace your footgear. In all circumstances hold faith up before you as your shield; it will help you extinguish the fiery darts of the evil one. Take the helmet of salvation and the sword of the spirit, the word of God (Eph 6:11-17).

The contest will be difficult, especially if one lives in a pagan environment. In any case, as sincere as our conversion and faith, this does not mean that we are exempt from any temptation, for the evil spirit is not destroyed in the first defeat. Driven from its dwelling, it is forced to return to it (Matt 12:43-45). It is a question, rather, of remaining on guard, so that we can unceasingly resist these repeated temptations and not fall asleep. One would have to be very naive not to feel worried by Paul's warning. All this is explicit. But this battle exists on a level beyond simple morality.

Put On the Lord, Jesus Christ

Paul sums up all that he says by giving us a way to deal with this combat between darkness and light. Our struggle should not be merely the struggle to become a morally perfect person, but rather a struggle to let the light of Christ shine through our being, keeping in mind the day when God will be "all in all" (1 Cor 15:28). It is behaving in a manner "dead to sin but alive for God in Christ Jesus" (Rom 6:11). It is to become "Christian"—or "Christ-like"—in order to contribute to the coming of the "whole Christ" and to have a part in him. For this coming is the end toward which we move throughout our time: the First Sunday of Advent opens our eyes to it, and we celebrate in hope.

Looking Forward to the Day

Hope is at the heart of Christian faith. It is at the heart of the life and activity of the Church, of the individual communities within it, and of each believer.

It is not only prayer, the sacraments, and liturgical celebrations that express this hope with words unceasing; hope is also expressed in human activity—in deeds.

The confession of faith in God, as expressed in the Creed, culminates in a cry of hope: "We look for the resurrection of the dead, and the life of the world to come." From baptism to the anointing of the sick, each of the sacraments is celebrated and administered within the context of this never-ending hope.

In receiving the grace of God here and now, and in giving thanks to the Father for this outpouring of the sanctifying Spirit, the Christian takes another step toward the threshold of the future in joy and confidence. And remembering the gifts already received by the Church from Jesus Christ our Lord, each step reveals a little more of what our future has in store for us.

From the assembling of the ecclesial community to its return to daily life and being sent forth on a mission, from hearing the word proclaimed to the prayer and profession of faith, the Eucharist is the sacrament par excellence, the "holy liturgy"—as the Eastern Christians say—because it defines the Church as a community of hope progressing toward the showing forth of the Lord and the coming of the kingdom. It is both the "source and summit" of the sacramental order, of the life of the Church and all believers, because it is the efficacious celebration of the mystery that is continuously unfolded until its full realization: yesterday, today, and tomorrow.

Hope Is Better Than Expectation

More importance seems to be given to expectation than to hope. Whatever hope's strength may be, it is always more or less marked with an anxious uncertainty or a certain passivity. Everything depends on so many uncontrollable, unforeseeable, and fragile factors! Those who wait with great hope are subject to so many vicissitudes and interruptions that their hope seems limited. Expectation has its foundation in God, the all-powerful and faithful one, whose plans know neither the slightest failure nor limitation. Expectation relies upon the experience, past and present, of the "already," which guarantees, sustains, and begets the "not yet."

Punctuated and reactivated without end by liturgical celebration, the life of the Church and of Christians is, at all times, given life and breath by the tension that exists between the "already" and the "not yet."

The One Who Has Come Is Coming Again

Each year, the season of Advent allows us, through various liturgies, to truly experience the coming of the mystery of salvation that we share in the Church.

In the incarnation of the Son of God, the Lord has surely come: Christmas, each year, is a celebration of this first, decisive coming. But the kingdom of justice and peace that Jesus inaugurated—"Glory to God and peace to those whom he loves!"—will not be fully realized until some future time.

We have to build peace now, and we must labor to make justice prevail. But it is the Lord himself who will establish them definitively and forever. The prophecy of Isaiah solemnly assures us, the good news raising our hope and inviting us to proceed again with a more confident step: "Come, let us walk in the light of the LORD" (Isa 2:5). "I rejoiced because they said to me, 'We will go up to the house of the LORD'" (Ps 122). Let us join the solemn procession of all peoples, marching toward the assembly on the mountain of Zion where the Lord will show himself (First Reading).

Ready to Receive the Welcome Surprise

Nowadays, we do not like having to wait for something without knowing the day, even the hour, of its arrival, because few of us know how to wait calmly, to continue our daily activities without the paralyzing nervousness that often accompanies the waiting process. It is natural for us to ask about the date of the Lord's return. "No warning," says the Gospel firmly, recalling the suddenness of the Flood that "the people" were not waiting for, or the coming of a thief who does not announce exactly when he will be breaking into the house.

On reflection, this uncertainty about the day and hour of the Lord's coming must engender feelings that are opposite to those of excitement and anxiety. It's like when true friends have promised to visit us "as a surprise one of these days." We're always ready to receive them, knowing that they won't be offended at finding us occupied with our daily tasks. This is how it should be waiting for Jesus, as if he were saying: "Stay awake and wait for me. I promise you the welcome surprise of my return."

It is not a question of our becoming numb and tired of waiting in vain, but of being active, knowing that each passing day draws us closer to the coming of the Lord. It will be a triumph of light over darkness, an end to the daily battle we all wage today. Orgies and sinful pleasures that now bedazzle our minds will no longer be the order of the day. How sorry we will be if we are occupied with such matters or are fighting one another when Christ appears!

Let us not be mistaken, however: it is not a particular "moral" conduct that the apostle is extolling when he tells us to "put on the Lord Jesus Christ" (Rom 13:14), that is, conform ourselves to him, allowing ourselves to be increasingly penetrated by his light (Epistle).

Our expectation appears to be an attitude of faith—even mystical—and the expression of an immense confidence: " 'Yes, I am coming soon!' Amen! Come, Lord Jesus!" (Rev 22:20).

> God is at work in this age;
> these times are the last.
> God is at work in this age;
> his Day will arise!
> Fear not, the Day will come,
> the night is at its end,
> And the glory of the Lord will fill the universe
> more than water covers the sea!
>
> What is the task of those people
> that God comes to assemble,
> other than to build the kingdom
> of the Prince of Peace?
> How can we hasten
> this long-awaited day,
> when the glory of the Lord will fill the universe,
> more than water covers the sea?
>
> That we may not be lost on this Day,
> which comes like a thief;
> let us not sleep in the darkness;
> let us keep watch in the Lord.
> As the light of the rising Sun
> even till its setting,
> he will come in glory on the clouds,
> the Lord, the God of love.
>
> May our pathway be lit
> with the sign of Jesus!
> He alone can save our earth,
> where love is no longer among us.

We must defend the downtrodden,
free the prisoner,
and the glory of the Lord will fill the universe
more than water covers the sea.

God is love for his people,
he loves to forgive.
God is love for his people,
he desires their liberty.
Fear not, the Day will come,
the night is at its end.
Let us rend our hearts and return to the Lord,
For he is the God who will return![6]

First Sunday of Advent—Year B

The Long Wait Fulfilled

Throughout salvation history, we have always been, and always will be, between two comings of the Lord. The time of Advent will only end with the last manifestation (called the "eschaton") of the one who has already come but for whom we nevertheless still wait. However, time is neither perpetually uniform nor indefinitely cyclical; one doesn't travel in circles, but advances. Each day is unique, as is each era. Some things happen that create or modify rhythms, or start them up again, things that have a decisive character. In all these matters is the event of Jesus Christ, an event that brings about a new advent—the final one—that cannot be modified in any way and which fulfills the hope of those that precede it. Because of this, earlier cries of appeal take on a new ring, and are enriched with unforeseen harmonies.

"Oh, That You Would Rend the Heavens and Come Down!"

The Liturgy of the Word this Sunday opens with a prayer in the form of a psalm (Isa 63:16-17, 19; 64:2-7). A prayer that is easy for the Christian assembly today to make its own, because this psalm text is effectively situated between two comings of the Lord.[7]

"You, Lord, are our father, our redeemer you are named forever." We are used to naming God in this way, and we understand these titles in their truest sense. But do we know all the connotations of the term "redeemer"? This term translates a Hebrew word—*go'el*—that denotes one who defends the interests of a person or group, especially the poorest members of a family. This person provides posterity for one who has died without having children, by marrying the widow and fathering a child (Ruth 3:12–4:14), pays the debts of a relative fallen into poverty, redeems one who has been sold as a slave (Lev 25:23-28, 47-49), and avenges blood unjustly spilled (Num 35:19-27).

Applied to God, this title suggests that he is our kinsman, that he has taken upon himself, so to speak, the fulfillment of responsibilities to his people.[8] Consequently, it is not improper to call on him. On the contrary, so that we might appeal with confidence to these "covenants," he has voluntarily assumed them to his "name forever," to what he is in himself and for others.

The "whys" that we address to him are signs of humility, respect, and confidence. If our Redeemer does not intervene, we will continue to stray from his path, and our hearts will remain indifferent to his power, which is the source of justice.

One even dares to demand that he "return," a term habitually applied to persons that they may "turn away from sin" and "return to God" (Jer 3:22; 4:1). We do not even have the capacity of converting ourselves; divine grace must open us to the salutary movement of returning to our God. The refrain of Psalm 80 plays on this double conversion of the Lord and the sinner:

> O Lord of hosts, restore us;
> if your face shine upon us,
> then we shall be safe.
> O Lord of hosts, restore us!

The audacity of this prayer is founded on the love of God for "his servants" and for "the tribes that belong to him." These are terms and expressions that arise from the language of the covenant, the use of which expresses, with new force, the bond between God and his people. "Servant of the Lord" is, in the second part of the Book of Isaiah, the title of Israel, as it will be of the Messiah. In other texts it is said: "For your name's sake" (Jer 14:7, 21; Ezek 20:9, 14; Isa 48:9; 66:5), Israel "your heritage" (Deut 9:26, 29; etc.). In the final analysis, it is a theophany that one is asking for: "Oh, that you would rend the heavens and come down!"

Such a divine manifestation can only be evoked with the help of images that despite their ancient traditions and out-of-date cosmology, nonetheless retain their evocative power. God inhabits "the heavens," which is to say, he is beyond our reach. In order to come near to us, he must take the initiative of "rending" the veil that conceals him from our eyes, for we are not able to elevate ourselves to his dwelling place.

To render an account of the glory that accompanies this manifestation, and to signify the presence of this God whom we do not know how to see, we speak of lightning, thunder, and earthquakes.

> The earth swayed and quaked;
> the foundations of the mountains trembled. . . .
> From the brightness of his presence

coals were kindled to flame.
(Ps 18:8, 13)

In the Bible, and in the religious memory of Israel, the theophany par excellence is that of Sinai: "Oh, that you would rend the heavens and come down!"

This strong call still echoes in the assembly of believers. But as in all prayers of this kind, the fixation on future hope does not cause one to lose sight of the recent past, a sign of a new grace of which we know ourselves to be unworthy.

"You Have Descended"

Confidence in God is such that any prayer asking him to intervene becomes a prayer of thanksgiving. Actually, being assured of the response of the Redeemer—the *go'el*—who will never slip away or deceive those who wait for him, we see him as the Lord who comes to meet with those who joyfully practice justice and remember him by following his way. What has happened a short while ago, what happens today, and what will happen shortly—these three levels are merged together; rather, they are but a single "today" to God, who encompasses and joins together as "one" what remains for us the past, present, and future. It is always thus, especially in the liturgy, where the eternity of God and his action touches the world and all the people in it, who live according to the sequential measuring of time.

This is why God, at every moment, can save sinners who are wasting their lives away from him. If they invoke God with faith and trust, he will again turn his face toward them. He is always their Father: he cannot forget the work of his hands.

> *Lord, make us turn to you,*
> *let us see your face and we shall be saved.*

> O shepherd of Israel, hearken,
>   O guide of the flock of Joseph!
> From your throne upon the cherubim, shine forth.
> Rouse your power,
>   and come to save us.

> Once again, O LORD of hosts,
>   look down from heaven, and see;
> Take care of this vine,
>   and protect what your right hand has planted.

> May your help be with the man of your right hand,
>   with the son of man whom you yourself made strong.

Then we will no more withdraw from you;
  give us new life, and we will call upon your name.
(Ps 80:2-3, 15-16, 18-19)

In the Heart of the Night

With this dialogue between God and his people, the Gospel brings us back to our particular place in this world and to the manner in which we wait for the coming of the Lord (Mark 13:33-37).

Mark repeats Matthew's urgent warning (First Sunday, Year A): "Stay awake!" And always for the same reason: "You do not know when the appointed time will come." But there is one difference between the two. Mark places the return of the Lord at night.

This may not seem like a significant variation. The return of the Master will take place unexpectedly; that is what is essential. Whether it takes place during the day or the night matters nothing: a simple detail of the presentation. Is this in fact the case?

These days, most people can enter their homes at any time, whether daytime, evening, midnight, or dawn (cockcrow), in spite of the danger that exists in certain cities. Such was not the case when Jesus recounted the parable of the watchful gatekeeper (Mark 13:33-37). To place the moment of the Master's return at night is unusual, and must have a meaning.

A great deal of symbolism is attached to night in the Bible. While no one can work during nighttime hours (John 9:4), nevertheless, that is the time when the powers of evil display their activity: it is then that the enemy sows weeds in the wheat field (Matt 13:24-30). Night is the time of suffering and the threat of surprise attacks (Job 7:3; Isa 15:1; Jer 6:5), the sorrowful time of waiting for the coming of the Son of Man (Rom 13:12; 1 Thess 5:4-6). The term "night," therefore, often—and quite naturally[9]—has a negative connotation.[10]

In the parable of the gatekeeper, night signifies the present time with all its ambiguity and tension: in itself it is dark, but those who are "sons of light," "sons of day," do not belong to it. One should read the passage from the First Letter to the Thessalonians, which concerns the explication of this Gospel:

> As regards specific times and moments, brothers, we do not need to write you; you know very well that the day of the Lord is coming like a thief in the night. Just when people are saying, "Peace and security," ruin will fall on them with the suddenness of pains overtaking a woman in labor, and there will be no escape. You are not in the dark, brothers, that the day should catch you off guard, like a thief. No, all of you are children of light

and of the day. We belong neither to darkness nor to night; therefore let us not be asleep like the rest, but awake and sober! (1 Thess 5:1-6)

Like everyone, Christians live in the night of this world, but they do not belong to it. They will not be surprised by the day that will come during this night: the light is within them and keeps them in a state of watchfulness.

Nevertheless, the vigil between the departure of Jesus and his return is an ordeal in which Jesus, in praying for them, supported his disciples before leaving them (John 13:31–17:26). Hiding from them none of the difficulties and temptations they would have to face, he said to them: "I will not leave you orphaned" (John 14:18). He promised them peace (John 14:27) and the gift of the Spirit (John 16:7-15): " . . . he will bear witness on my behalf. You must bear witness as well . . ." (John 15:26-27).

Patience, Peace, Joy, Thanksgiving

These themes are at the heart of apostolic preaching, as witnessed by an excerpt from the First Letter of Paul to the Corinthians, which the Lectionary has retained (1 Cor 1:3-9).[11]

This letter "to the church of God which is in Corinth" is explicitly addressed to "all those who, wherever they may be, call on the name of our Lord Jesus Christ" (1 Cor 1:1-2).

It begins with a thanksgiving by the apostle for the favor given in Christ Jesus, in whom the faithful "have been richly endowed with every gift of speech and knowledge. . . . The witness I bore to Christ has been confirmed among you," writes Paul. "You lack no spiritual gift as you wait for the revelation of our Lord Jesus Christ." It is true: we have "been consecrated in Christ Jesus"; we are "called to be a holy people" (1 Cor 1:1-2). How can we not give thanks? How can we not, at the same time, receive the "Eucharist" as a lesson of modesty and a call to order? We can only boast because of the abundance of the grace of God on our behalf. How can we receive so many riches? Surely, that question is asked, but St. Paul says, "Force yourselves to become what you are."

"Hold fast till the end!" Thus "you will be blameless on the day of our Lord Jesus Christ. God is faithful, and it was he who called you to fellowship with his Son, Jesus Christ our Lord."

The apostle's exhortation joins and prolongs that of the Gospel: "Keep on guard! Stay awake!"

The Vigorous Song of the Seasons of Faith

This Sunday sings and celebrates long-term faith, the long delay in the expectation of the "good news of Jesus Christ, the Son of God," about whom Mark will tell us throughout this year. The gospel of Jesus Christ, the gospel that is Jesus Christ, is always a beginning that must ring forth in our memories in order to be revived in all its capacity for renewal and enthusiasm. The gospel? . . . an event that "is coming": the opposite of a dead text or an ancient, dusty manuscript that one analyzes, dissects, and examines. Its written outline is there, in narrative form, but as a signature inspiring each of us to forge ahead toward the beginning, toward Advent; to retrace the footsteps of Jesus Christ who has come and is always coming; to walk in his steps, struck by the difference between his extraordinary life and ours. Nothing is yet lost, and we can seize the hope that is offered us. Nothing is yet played out. Each Advent is there to remind us of it.

The cry of the ages is still ours today: "Oh, that you would rend the heavens and come down . . ." (Isa 63:19). Let us accept the insistent call to stay awake: "You do not know when the appointed time will come" (Mark 13:33). Let us receive the assurance that nothing will go wrong for the one who waits for the Lord: "He will strengthen you to the end" (1 Cor 1:7-8). Living in expectation, our souls open to whatever comes, waiting patiently for it day to day, ministers of vigilance for the world. Christians are people of the dawn.

Live in Expectation: The Lord Comes

In the waning years of the twentieth century, many discern the faint glimmers of imminent apocaypse. Still, in nature and the cosmos, there are many depths and dimensions as yet unexplored, many forces to unlock, to discipline in order to heal, to cleanse, to bring life to its fullest potential! There are yet many unknown colors, shapes, smells, and sounds to bring to light! Is not creation-in-waiting an image of the real condition of humanity and of each individual?

This might not seem to be evident or may appear too optimistic. Are there not two sides of human nature? Human conflict throughout the centuries seems to have been part and parcel of all kinds of belief, of politics, of ideologies. "Two loves have built two cities: love of self to the point of contempt for God, and love of God to the point of contempt for oneself" (St. Augustine). On the one hand we have selfishness based on egoism and greed, impatience, and a refusal to be disciplined. On the other, we have self-sacrifice and an ardent desire to receive life from the hands of an Other, an openness to one greater than oneself, to gift-giving and to sharing. Once freed from our helplessness and our illusions, aren't we all more authentically ourselves as we confusedly await a better life, as we desire to put off the finality of death, the paralysis of anguish and psychosis, the sclerosis of obsessions of all kinds?

Is this possible? Is it true that one may still live today in the hope of salvation, when so many dreams turn out to be fantasies, when so many noble ambitions turn out to be pretentious to the point of being renounced? Isn't this a form of killing the soul? Yes, the Gospel affirms, it is more urgent than ever to hope. To live in the spirit of Advent is, in spite of all we have said, to bear in ourselves the hope of a harvest to come, fruits sown by an Other on whom our hopes fall back even when everything else contradicts them. Thus it is possible to badger this God with our "why," this God who is affirmed as our Father and our Redeemer, who apparently leaves his people in agony (Isa 63:17–64:7). Such questions are not the least bit blasphemous: they do not doubt the divine capacity to rend the heavens and to heighten in our world the burgeoning clarity of a new heaven and a new earth where justice will reign. Night is the time when it is best to believe in the light.

Unconditionally Open to the Light

Asked about his coming, Jesus recommends only one thing to his followers: "Stay awake" (Mark 13:33-36). He is quite insistent on this. Besides, how could it be otherwise when no one—not even the Son of Man (Mark 13:32)—knows anything about the "when" of this coming? One should call this to the attention of those self-deluded Christians who seek the false security of certain sects that live in a world of heightened readiness, a world somewhat removed from the real one. But each person must be constantly convinced of his or her condition as *homo viator*, as a "voyager" called to constant pilgrimage under the motivating force of the Spirit who sighs deep within nature and the cosmos. One must learn the asceticism of the watchman, an active vigilance that is not headlong flight, but the honest, courageous, creative attitude of one who aspires to open his or her life to the infinitude of God.

Keeping watch is one of the most important activities of the human heart, a focusing of energy that endeavors to rid the night of the evil spirits that hold back the dawn in the world. Watching in prayer gives our full attention to God and to others. But one must watch "with me," recommends Jesus at Gethsemani: with the one who is already come but who will come again "at dusk, at midnight, when the cock crows, or at early dawn" (Mark 13:35), the four times in the night when the temptation to give ourselves over to sleep is strongest. "Stay here" with the Lord who is praying (Mark 14:32) because "Jesus will be in agony till the end of the world: we must not sleep during that time."[12] Watch with him amidst universal helplessness or fall prey to the peril we face if we do not live vigilantly. Watch because of him, the first-born of the dead. The great vigil of Advent prefigures the vigil of Easter, and the splendid dawn of the new time.

Wait to the End with Patience

It is difficult to be patient, a virtue that many people reject today. We no longer know how to be content with what comes to us in our world. We want everything now. We wish to bear fruit, but we resent the time it takes to ripen. As a result, the world is now host to generations of selfish, immature, and greedy people, who want everything for themselves.

The infinite patience of God is just the opposite. For millions of years God surveyed the appearance of life on the earth; for millions of years, the development of humanity. For seven or eight millennia, the growth of moral conscience. Finally, in the last four thousand years, God forged the chain of the living, culminating in the body of Christ. God is not an impatient magician, but a gardener: he does not tug at the flowers in order to make them grow. He knows that nothing matures by some miraculous single stroke. He grows the roots deep in the ground of grace that they might "hold fast till the end."

It becomes possible to give thanks for all that the Father has already given in Christ Jesus, because hope, as well as patience, takes us out of ourselves and out of what we consider our worth. Far from weakening us, God's grace helps us to give thanks for all that God has given us in his Son Jesus and for all that he does, through the power of the Holy Spirit, that affects us. This happens without any great to-do or smugness on our part. It is simply good to say "thank you" to the one who has planted in us the seed of the harvest to come. Already present, though hibernating under the ice and snow, is all that we hope and wait for: the kingdom of God, peace, and joy.

> Our nightwatch is long, Lord,
> and the cold wind of sloth threatens to put out the
> fire of our hearts;

will it still burn to light up your face,
when you knock at our door?

"When the Son of Man comes,
will he find faith on the earth?"

Watch in prayer, I come like a thief,
to surprise you.

Watch in prayer, that you fall not into temptation:
he who holds fast to the end will be saved.

Watch in prayer: the one who is ready,
I myself will wait on in my kingdom.[13]

First Sunday of Advent—Year C

To Appear Before the Son of Man

Each year, the First Sunday of Advent focuses on the coming of the Lord, of which no one knows the day nor the hour. The certainty of this manifestation is at the heart of Christian faith, of the liturgy, of the assembly, and of the Sunday Eucharist especially. It gives to the life of believers and the Church its dynamism and proper goal. The liturgy not only celebrates the end of human life and of all things: it allows us, here and now, to participate sacramentally in the salvation that has already come, that comes now, and will come again. Everything proceeds on its way from this time toward the end of time. This is the meaning and importance of Advent, this season that opens the liturgical year and also defines it from beginning to end.

Jesus himself spoke to his disciples about his coming. He said: "No one knows the day nor the hour. Stay awake, therefore!" Sts. Matthew, Mark, and Luke each makes mention of this teaching, which they received from tradition.[14] However, each treats it in his own way; in light of the sources each used, each aimed at a certain audience.

On the First Sunday of Advent (Year C), we hear the witness of Luke. He stresses, on the one hand, the attitude that the disciples must assume when they see the signs pointing to the Lord's return; on the other hand, he emphasizes the role of prayer in their vigilance (Luke 21:25-28, 34-36).

With this Gospel, we read a passage from the Book of Jeremiah (Jer 33:14-15) and an extract from Paul's First Letter to the Thessalonians (1 Thess 3:12–4:2).

The Promise to David Has Not Been Forgotten
"Again and again [God] offered a covenant to man, and through the prophets taught him to hope for salvation."[15] Sacred history is punctuated with God's solemn promises reiterated from the past and proclaimed again at specific moments to reawaken the hope of his people.

Among the words of the Lord that emerge are those the prophet Nathan transmitted to David: "And when your time comes and you rest with your ancestors, I will raise up your heir after you, sprung from your loins, and I will make his kingdom firm. It is he who shall build a house for my name. And I will make his royal throne firm forever. I will be a father to him, and he shall be a son to me. Your house and your kingdom shall endure forever before me; your throne shall stand firm forever'' (2 Sam 7:12-14, 16).

This promise is engraved in the memory of Israel and the Church. It is particularly contemplated in the psalms:

> You who gave great victories to your king
>   and showed kindness to your anointed,
>   to David and his posterity forever. (Ps 18:51)
>
> ''I have made a covenant with my chosen one,
>   I have sworn to David my servant:
> Forever will I confirm your posterity
>   and establish your throne for all generations.''
> (Ps 89:4-5)
>
> ''Once, by my holiness, have I sworn;
>   I will not be false to David.'' (Ps 89:36)
>
> The LORD swore to David
>   a firm promise from which he will not withdraw:
> ''Your own offspring
>   I will set upon your throne;
> If your sons keep my covenant
>   and the decrees which I shall teach them,
> Their sons, too, forever
>   shall sit upon your throne.'' (Ps 132:11-12)

Nothing can turn God away from keeping his promise, not even the sin of David's descendants. What he has sworn, once for all, the Lord will accomplish, but under a new form, raising up a shoot from the stump of David: the tree fallen to the ground will blossom again, because God cannot forget ''his first love,'' that which he swore to David (Ps 89:50).

The Promise of Happiness

As sincere and assured as it may be, this expectation, over time, has been subjected to doubt and indifference. At certain moments, one even wonders whether the word of God has any real substance. Thus is raised the voice of the prophets, who repeat the promise, reawaken hope, and widen our perspectives.[16]

Yes, proclaims Jeremiah, ''the days are coming'' when God ''will fulfill the promise.'' This ''gospel'' is no longer concerned only with the royal line, but with "the house of Israel" and the "house of Judah," i.e., the northern and the southern kingdoms. It has ecumenical scope.

The symbolic name "The Lord our justice" is no longer given to the new David, but to the city itself.[17] Ezekiel said that its name will be "The Lord is here" (Ezek 48:35). It is the place where, "in those days, in that time," salvation will come. In the last book of the Bible, Revelation, one reads that when "the former heavens and the former earth had passed away," "a new Jerusalem, the holy city" will descend "from God" (Rev 21:1-3). The seer of Patmos hears a voice cry out: "This is God's dwelling among men. He shall dwell with them and they shall be his people and he shall be their God who is always with them."[18]

This Jerusalem is not an earthly city. It symbolizes the flowing of a new world into the present one, inaugurated by the coming among us of "The Lord our justice."

On the First Sunday of Advent, Jeremiah's prophecy reawakens our hope, confronted with the defiance of history. This world of injustice, suffering, war, division, even in the Church: Isn't this proof that the words of the promise are dead?

"No!" responds Jeremiah vehemently. God acts in a more subtle and complex way than we are inclined to imagine. The Word is there, at work among visible realities through the Spirit, whose coming and going we do not perceive. Nothing can hold it in check. The time will come when the great day of salvation will finally appear, a process that is being accomplished now, in secret.

The earthly Jerusalem is not the City on High, nor is the Church the Heavenly Kingdom. Nevertheless, the kingdom is already among us, in gestation. This assurance grants us hope "against hope" (Rom 4:18), with all who have believed, who believe now, and who will believe in the promise.

As if they already see the invisible, the faithful march toward "those days," their eyes lifted to the Lord who teaches them his paths.

> To you I lift up my soul,
> O LORD, my God.

> Your ways, O LORD, make known to me;
>   teach me your paths,
> Guide me in your truth and teach me,
>   for you are God my savior,
>   and for you I wait all the day.

> Good and upright is the LORD;
>   thus he shows sinners the way.

He guides the humble to justice,
  he teaches the humble his way.

All the paths of the LORD are kindness and constancy
  toward those who keep his covenant and his decrees.
The friendship of the LORD is with those who fear him,
  and his covenant, for their instruction.
(Ps 25:1-2; 4-5; 8-10; 14)

Lift Up Your Heads: Your Redemption Is at Hand
Jesus also spoke of those things that would happen "in those days," in the day of his coming. To do this, he made natural use of a literary genre that was familiar to his contemporaries,[19] but he gave it a perspective and style closer to the prophets than to apocalyptic writing.[20] Jesus actually spoke with his own authority, and preached first of all about how his disciples were to behave while waiting for his coming. This is particularly clear in Luke.

Cosmic disorder—"signs in the sun, the moon and the stars . . . the roaring of the sea and the waves"—is a traditional style of apocalyptic literature and is therefore obligatory. Is the coming of the Son of Man "with great power and glory" thinkable without the movement of "the powers in the heavens"?

Having said this, the evangelist focuses on the attitude of believers "when these things begin to happen." People will be fearful, "dying of fright in anticipation of what is coming upon the earth." That is when, therefore, they must "stand up straight . . . raise [their] heads." Not because they will be animated with an extraordinary courage or, even less, unaware of the presence of danger, but because they will see in these manifestations signs that foretell that their redemption is at hand. Are not "those days" the object of their hope? The disciples have nothing to fear in the events that will declare the victory and lordship of their Master. Like wanderers leaving the mist and finally seeing the splendor of the sun, they will straighten up, they will lift their heads, radiant with joy: their final liberation is in sight.

It is nonetheless important not to forget the unforeseeable suddenness of the coming of the Lord. Jesus insists on that.[21] Constant vigilance is required. We must neither revel in debauchery and drunkenness[22] nor be engrossed by earthly cares that distract our attention.[23]

The net will be cast upon everyone on earth, but it will not be a snare for the disciples, because they will be found "standing ready," i.e., like good and faithful servants fulfilling the task conferred on them by their Master (Luke 12:35-48).

"Stay Awake and Pray"

Luke, not surprisingly,[24] clearly states that prayer "at all times" is part of the attitude of being alert. This instruction is one that tradition has retained and put in practice. It is ritually expressed in monasteries in nocturnal prayer, rightly called "vigil prayer," particularly on Saturday night, celebrated and experienced as a vigil, waiting for the coming of the Lord who will manifest himself at dawn. In fact, according to *The Rule of St. Benedict,* at the end of this night office the abbot solemnly proclaims the gospel, which all listen to, standing. This is a rite filled with significance: Christ comes amid the assembly under the double sign of the Book and the Word. Then all sing the hymn *Te decet laus:* "Praise and glory to you! God the Father, Son, and Holy Spirit, forever and ever. Amen."[25] The dawn of the Day of the Lord can then resound with earthly praises (lauds) and unite them to those of heaven:

> The Lord God has come,
> let us sing his glory.[26]

> The LORD is king, in splendor robed;
>   robed is the Lord and girt about with strength
> (Ps 93:1).

> I will extol you, O LORD, for you drew me clear
>   and did not let my enemies rejoice over me
> (Ps 30:2).

> Bless the Lord, all you works of the Lord (Dan 3:57).

> Blessed be the Lord the God of Israel
>   because he has visited and ransomed his people
> (Luke 1:68).

The wonder of liturgical prayer! By it, the Church, taking into consideration the present condition of "not yet," celebrates that which it possesses "already" in hope, i.e., the redemption that is coming. In the communion of saints, this prayer exalts the glory of the Day of the Lord that rises up from the darkness. There is nothing artificial in the poetry of this prayerful vigil. On the contrary, the Lord is here, among his people. He is shown through the efficacious signs of the liturgy. Each celebration unveils his presence a little more. To keep watch in prayer while remaining upright before him is to keep oneself ready to receive him, without fear, when he will come "on a cloud with great power and glory."

To Live in Holiness

"The sacred liturgy does not exhaust the entire activity of the Church."[27] Not just prayer "at all times," the liturgy is more. It is a source of grace because of its sanctification in Christ,[28] which "increases you and makes you overflow with love" with regard to all, as Paul says (1 Thess 3:12–4:2).

The apostle has witnessed to this love by devoting himself to it in addition to announcing the good news, itself true spiritual worship (Rom 1:9; 15:16), of the Christian life (Rom 12:1). To live "blameless and holy before our God and Father" is the other side of watching for "the coming of our Lord Jesus Christ with all his holy ones." On this day will the true nature of each be shown.

God Is Present in Our Waiting

The grace of the season of Advent is a reawakening of our hope in the salvation that has already come, that comes now, and will come in the fullness of the "Day of the Lord." Nevertheless, it is true that insistence on this grace somewhat hides the primordial role of God. Would we do anything but wait if God were not the Master of the Game? The liturgy of this Sunday reminds us that God is not inactive.

Once again, he solemnly swears to us that the days are coming when he will fulfill the promise he made to the house of Israel and Judah: "I will raise up a righteous shoot for David . . . he shall do what is just and right in the land" (First Reading).

When the prophet Jeremiah proclaimed this word of God, David's dynasty had ended. Today, we hear this promise at a time far removed from the time when Jesus lived in our world and left it to rejoin the Father. But humanity continues to aspire to a happiness that always seems to escape it, as if the promise were empty.

God, then, calls us to him to reestablish our confidence now and always, that we may not be discouraged by delays, tribulations, and troubles of every kind, for he is present in our world.

None Who Wait Are Deceived

Today, the Church, each Christian community assembled for the liturgy, hearing this divine protestation, this cry from the heart of God, responds with all the faith it can muster: "To you, my God, I lift my soul, I trust in you; let me never come to shame . . . for you are God my savior" (Ps 25: Entrance Antiphon and Responsorial Psalm). Far from being presumptuous about what comes from God, the Church recognizes the gift he has given.

Certainly we ask God to "increase our strength of will for doing good" (Opening Prayer). But the Father gives to his faithful ones not only the means, but also the knowledge of it: "Your ways, O Lord, make known to me; teach me your paths" (Ps 25:4).

It is the God who can make us "increase and overflow with love" that Christians must show to their brothers and sisters in faith, and to everyone. It is he who by the gift of charity establishes believers, "making them blameless and holy . . . at the coming of our Lord Jesus with all his holy ones" (Second Reading). Through the Eucharist he forms us, "teaching us to love heaven and guiding our way on earth" (Prayer after Communion).

We are assured of seeing the Son of man "coming on a cloud with great power and glory." God, though, retains the initiative in this decisive encounter (Gospel). The future belongs to God; it is for this that we wait and must wait with confidence.

Not a Promise Without Responsibilities

Knowing that God is working toward the time of fulfillment does not free us from responsibility. On the contrary, after Jeremiah's prophecy that announces the days of deliverance, a kind of security prepared by "the Lord our justice," we feel compelled to praise God for all his wonders. Now, the liturgy gives us a song that recalls the terms of the covenant, the necessity of observing the commandments.

The Letter of Paul to the Thessalonians follows the same line of thought. The disciples are reminded of their duty: to please God by their conduct, to dwell firmly in a life of holiness, to progress continuously in this way "until the coming of our Lord Jesus with all his holy ones."

This warm and encouraging speech echoes the grave warning of the Lord: "Be on guard. . . . Pray constantly."

"Your redemption is at hand!" From the perspective of looking toward the end of things, we are able to look critically at our present time, to discern what really matters today, to engage in our daily work with courage and assurance. Then, when the foreshadowing signs appear, we will not have to be afraid.

A thrill of joy runs through the liturgy for this First Sunday of Year C. It is a joy that allows one to hear the divine promises, to accept the responsibility fighting against the inner and outer darkness, to proceed without fear, head held high, to meet the One who has come and is coming.

Behold, the time is coming
when the Lord of justice
will fulfill his promise of peace
for those he loves!

Read the signs of God
in the moon and the sun:
He is coming,
coming on the clouds!

See the nations shake
before the storms of the sea:
He is coming,
He is coming, victorious!

Reform yourselves, for look:
Our salvation is at hand!
He is coming
coming for our joy!

Let us stay awake,
and escape the snare.
And we will stand
before the Son of man
on the day of judgment!

Happy the one who believed
that one day would be fulfilled
the words of his God
for all whom he loves![29]

Monday Through Saturday—First Week

The Missal, the Lectionary, and the Liturgy of the Hours offer particular formularies for each day of the four weeks of Advent: texts from the Scriptures and the Fathers, antiphons and psalms, responses and prayers.[30]

It would be useless to try to place these diverse elements within the rigid framework of a logical presentation, thematically arranged, for example. This is a rather different thing than the liturgy, which serves as a buffet, abundantly stocked with various foods that everyone can sample.[31]

People can find in these readings a variety of collateral material that will satisfy their desire to continue the mood of the Sunday celebration or deepen their appreciation of it during the course of the week.[32]

The Missal and the Lectionary
These two books are accessible to everyone, since the Missal for the faithful, as opposed to the Missal of the altar, contains the texts of the Lectionary.[33]

The Opening Prayers are all about the final coming of the Lord, which is this Sunday's perspective. Each prayer approaches the idea in its own way, but the inspiration for all of them is biblical.

> Lord our God,
> help us to prepare
> for the coming of Christ your Son.
> May he find us waiting,
> eager in joyful prayer (Monday).

> Lord our God,
> grant that we may be ready
> to receive Christ when he comes in glory
> and to share in the banquet of heaven (Wednesday).

These are the prayers of believers that are filled with the teaching of Jesus and the apostles. "Here I stand, knocking at the door. If anyone hears me calling and opens the door, I will enter his house and have supper with him, and he with me" (Rev 3:20). "Stay awake and pray" (the gospels of the First Sunday). "Let us live honorably as in daylight" (Rom 13:13). God "will strengthen you till the end" (1 Cor 1:8).

Accordingly, we do not find ourselves unaware of the long wait for the coming of the Lord, nor of the constant struggle that accompanies it.

God of mercy and consolation,
help us in our weakness and free us from sin.
Hear our prayers
that we may rejoice at the coming of your Son (Tuesday).

Father,
we need your help.
Free us from sin and bring us to life.
Support us by your power (Thursday).

Jesus, our Lord,
save us from our sins.
Come, protect us from all dangers
and lead us to salvation (Friday).

God our Father,
you loved the world so much
you gave your only Son to free us
from the ancient power of sin and death.
Help us who wait for his coming,
and lead us to true liberty (Saturday).

The Readings from the Old Testament are all taken from the Book of Isaiah. These prophecies dwell on the one who will come "in the future," on the "day" when God will institute his reign.[34] But they always attach a reminder to this announcement about the conditions necessary for participating in the glory that will manifest itself.

The good news is addressed at first to the remnant of Israel (Isa 2 and 4: Monday; Isa 25: Wednesday; Isa 26: Thursday). It will gather together the multitudes coming from every nation (Isa 2: Monday). All righteous and humble people will benefit from the mercy of God (Isa 30: Saturday). Even more, all of nature will participate in the renewal that the Lord will accomplish (Isa 29: Friday). Then, peace will reign among the peoples (Isa 2: Monday). Joy will be given to the whole world (Isa 25: Wednesday). All of this will come from the Messiah who will issue from the line of David, and on whom the Spirit will rest (Isa 11: Tuesday).

The Psalms that follow the readings from the prophet (Pss 122; 72; 23; 118; 27; 147) are songs of the joy and hope of a people who are marching toward the coming of the Lord.

I rejoiced when I heard them say:
let us go to the house of the LORD (Ps 122).

Justice shall flower in his days,
    and profound peace, till the moon be no more (Ps 72).

The LORD is my shepherd. . . .
And I shall dwell in the house of the LORD
for years to come (Ps 23).

Give thanks to the LORD, for he is good,
    for his mercy endures forever (Ps 118).

The LORD is my light and my salvation;
    whom should I fear? (Ps 27).

The LORD sustains the lowly;
    the wicked he casts to the ground (Ps 147).

The Gospels proclaim that Jesus has inaugurated the era of when these wondrous promises will be accomplished.[35] During his earthly ministry, he addressed himself directly to the people of his country, and it was in the midst of them that he went about doing good, exercising his mercy on their behalf. His pity for the crowds without a shepherd (Matt 9:35: Saturday), his miracles (Matt 9:27-31: Friday) show that the reign of God has come.

Make no mistake: "None of those who cry out, 'Lord, Lord,' will enter the kingdom of God but only the one who does the will of my Father in heaven" (Matt 7:21: Thursday). Jesus reserved the revelation of his Father's secrets for the humble and the childlike (Luke 10:21-24: Tuesday), for those who put their faith in him. There will be a great number who "will come from the east and the west and will find a place at the banquet in the kingdom of God with Abraham, Isaac, and Jacob" (Matt 8:11: Monday).

Such is the message that the Church announces to the world: "Nations, hear the message of the Lord, and make it known to the ends of the earth: Our Savior is coming. Have no more fear" (Entrance Antiphon: Monday).

During the first week of Advent, the Mass liturgy insists on "the true meaning of the things of this world," completely refocusing our attention on the good things to come (Prayer after Communion: Friday).

The Liturgy of the Hours
The Liturgy of the Hours has always been characterized by an abundance of biblical readings, both short and long. At vigils (or matins), the reading from a patristic text is traditional.[36]

The Biblical Readings for Advent are all taken from the Book of Isaiah.[37] God is not content with being distanced from his people who have abandoned him, nor with the blows of every kind that bruise them because of their sinfulness. But to change all this, great numbers of sacrifices and prayers are not enough. How could God be moved by such demonstrations? "Your hands are full of blood! Wash yourselves clean! Put away your misdeeds from before my eyes; cease doing evil; learn to do good. Make justice your aim: redress the wronged, hear the orphan's plea, defend the widow." Then, "though your sins be like scarlet, they may become white as snow; though they be crimson red, they may become white as wool" (Isa 1:1-18: Sunday).

God's constant fidelity to his people will triumph. "Zion shall be redeemed by judgment, and her repentant ones by justice" (Isa 1:21-27: Monday).

Yes, God will intervene. "On that day, the branch of the Lord will be luster and glory, and the fruit of the earth will be honor and splendor for the survivors of Israel. He who remains in Zion and he that is left in Jerusalem will be called holy: every one marked down for life in Jerusalem" (Isa 4:2-6: Tuesday).

This is the magnificent song of the friend and his vineyard. "My friend had a vineyard on a fertile hillside; he spaded it, cleared it of stones, and planted the choicest vines; within it he built a watchtower, and hewed out a wine press. Then he looked for the crop of grapes, but what it yielded was wild grapes" (Isa 5:1-7: Wednesday).

This lamentation is not a depressing song evoking despair, but an urgent call to conversion, as attested by the response that follows this reading:

> Never let us be far from you,
> let us live and call your name.
>
> A boar from the forest has torn down the vine you planted; the beasts of the field have devoured it. See, Lord, and arise in your mighty power; let not the work of your hands be destroyed.

Indeed, the following text evokes the day when "man shall look to his maker, his eyes turned toward the Holy One of Israel. He shall not look to the altars, his handiwork, nor shall he regard what his fingers have made: the sacred poles or the incense stands" (Isa 17:7-8: Thursday):

> And this is the name they will give him: the Lord is our righteousness.
>
> I shall raise up an heir for David,
> one who is just;
> he will make fair judgment prevail on earth.

A throne of mercy will be set up;
there a true judge will set,
one who seeks justice and is swift to do right (Response).

The opposite of the situation will be such that hereditary enemies will be reconciled as fellow beneficiaries of salvation. Behold ''a blessing in the midst of the land, when the Lord of hosts blesses it: 'Blessed be my people Egypt, and the work of my hands Assyria, and my inheritance, Israel' '' (Isa 19:24-25; Friday).

This series of oracles ends with the proclamation of the watchman: ''Here he comes now'' (Isa 21:6-12: Saturday), to which the Church responds in prayer:

Stay awake,
for you know neither the day nor the hour!
Reform yourselves to the Lord! (Response)

The Patristic Readings speak about the meaning of Advent and what one could call the ''spirituality'' of this liturgical season.

At first—on Sunday—there is a passage (which we have already cited)[38] from Cyril of Jerusalem (c. 315–386). It is from a prebaptismal catechesis concerning the second coming of Christ.[39]

We do not preach only one coming of Christ, but a second as well, much more glorious than the first. The first coming was marked by patience; the second will bring the crown of a divine kingdom.

In general, what relates to our Lord Jesus Christ has two aspects. There is a birth from God before the ages, and a birth from a virgin at the fullness of time. There is a hidden coming, like that of rain on fleece, and a coming before all eyes, still in the future.

At the first coming he was wrapped in swaddling clothes in a manger. At his second coming he will be clothed in light as in a garment. In the first coming he endured the cross, despising the shame; in the second coming he will be in glory, escorted by an army of angels. We look then beyond the first coming and await the second.

St. Bernard (1090–1153) speaks of a triple coming of the Lord.

We know that there are three comings of the Lord. The third lies between the other two. It is invisible, while the other two are visible. In the first coming he was seen on earth, dwelling among men; he himself testifies that they saw him and hated him. In the final coming ''all flesh will see the salvation of our God,'' and ''they will look on him whom they pierced.'' The intermediate coming is a hidden one; in it only the elect see the Lord within their own selves, and they are saved. In his first coming our Lord came in our flesh and in our weakness; in this middle coming he comes in spirit and in power; in the final coming he will be seen in glory and majesty.

Because this coming lies between the other two, it is like a road on which we travel from the first coming to the last. In the first, Christ was our redemption; in the last, he will appear as our life; in this middle coming, he is our rest and consolation.[40]

These two texts are truly remarkable. It is impossible to find any better ones about the meaning of Advent. Notice, moreover, that St. Cyril is addressing candidates for baptism. What excellence and depth there is in this catechesis of a bishop of the fourth century!

The other patristic readings focus on some fundamental attitudes appropriate to Advent. It is the time of a great yearning for God, the theme of St. Anselm of Canterbury (1033–1109). The archbishop of Canterbury addresses God in a heart-rending prayer that is full of confidence: "Where and how to seek you, where and how to find you . . . you dwell in 'light inaccessible.' " Where is it and how does one reach it? "Who will lead me and bring me into it that I may see you there? And then, by what signs and under what forms shall I seek you?" Questions, always questions. But at the end, this confidence is placed in the hands of God:

Teach me to seek you, and when I seek you show yourself to me, for I cannot seek you unless you teach me, nor can I find you unless you show yourself to me. Let me seek you in desiring you and desire you in seeking you, find you in loving you and love you in finding you.[41]

It is the time of vigil, which St. Ephrem (c. 306–373) extols.

To prevent his disciples from asking the time of his coming, Christ said: "About that hour no one knows, neither the angels nor the Son. It is not for you to know times or moments." He has kept those things hidden so that we may keep watch, each of us thinking that he will come in our own day. If he had revealed the time of his coming, his coming would have lost its savor: it would no longer be an object of yearning for the nations and the age in which it will be revealed. He promised that he would come, but he did not say when he would come, and so all generations and ages await him eagerly.

Keep watch; when the body is asleep nature takes control of us, and what is done is not done by our will but by force, by the impulse of nature. When deep listlessness takes possession of the soul, for example, faintheartedness or melancholy, the enemy overpowers it and makes it do what it does not will. The force of nature, the enemy of the soul, is in control.

When the Lord commanded us to be vigilant, he meant vigilance in both parts of man: in the body, against the tendency to sleep; in the soul, against lethargy and timidity.[42]

It is the time of patience in hope, a theme developed by St. Cyprian, bishop of Carthage (end of second century–258).

> Patience is a precept for salvation given us by our Lord, our teacher: "Whoever endures to the end will be saved." And again: "If you persevere in my word, you will truly be my disciples; you will know the truth, and the truth will set you free."
>
> Dear brethren, we must endure and persevere if we are to attain the truth and freedom we have been allowed to hope for; faith and hope are the very meaning of our being Christians, but if faith and hope are to bear their fruit, patience is necessary.
>
> We do not seek glory now, in the present, but we look for future glory. . . . Patient waiting is necessary if we are to be perfected in what we have begun to be, and if we are to receive from God what we hope for and believe.[43]

From St. Charles Borromeo (1538–1584), we read an extract from a pastoral letter. The archbishop of Milan exhorts the faithful of his diocese to celebrate Advent with fervor, "the day of salvation, peace and reconciliation." He puts it in the perspective of the first coming of Christ and his uninterrupted presence among us.

> Each year, as the Church recalls this mystery, she urges us to renew the memory of the great love God has shown us. This holy season teaches us that Christ's coming was not only for the benefit of his contemporaries; his power has still to be communicated to us all. We shall share his power, if, through holy faith and the sacraments, we willingly accept the grace Christ earned for us, and live by that grace and in obedience to Christ.
>
> The Church asks us to understand that Christ, who came once in the flesh, is prepared to come again. When we remove all obstacles to his presence he will come, at any hour and moment, to dwell spiritually in our hearts, bringing with him the riches of his grace.[44]

Finally, the Liturgy of the Hours gives us the words of St. Gregory Nazianzus in Cappodocia (329–389). Out of many select passages, this one is, curiously enough, taken from a pastoral homily. These passages are consecrated to the incarnation of the Word of God. We must retain, most of all, what it says in accordance with Advent:

> Christ, the light of all lights, follows John, the lamp that goes before him. The Word of God follows the voice in the wilderness; the bridegroom follows the bridegroom's friend, who prepares a worthy people for the Lord by cleansing them by water in preparation for the Spirit.[45]

This text takes us to the Second Sunday of Advent, consecrated each year to the preparation, by the preaching and ministry of John the Baptist, for the manifestation of Jesus.

Second Week of Advent

People of Zion,
the Lord will come to save all nations,
and your hearts will exult
to hear his majestic voice.

This antiphon, repeated each year at the beginning of the Second Sunday of Advent, quietly foreshadows its atmosphere and perspective.

The liturgy of last Sunday was clearly oriented toward the coming of the Son of Man at the end of time that, though sudden and unpredictable, is centered around the uninterrupted coming of salvation in the day of each generation. From this comes the necessity of keeping watch and not allowing oneself to be discouraged or to let down one's guard.

Nothing changes at the beginning of the Second Sunday. In sketching the acts of the Messiah to come, the prophet Isaiah describes a new world that is clearly not of this earth (Isa 2:1-10: Year A). Yet, another prophecy from the same book speaks as if the prophet foresaw a kind of acceleration of history.[1] "Give comfort to my people. . . . In the desert prepare the way of the Lord. . . . Here is your God! Here comes with power the Lord God" (Isa 40:1-5, 9-11: Year B). The prophet Baruch, finally, urges Jerusalem to make preparations for a feast. "Take off your robe of mourning and misery. . . . Up, . . . and see your children gathered . . ." (Bar 5:1-9: Year C).

It is true that on this Sunday the voice of the Precursor is raised. "Reform your lives! The reign of God is at hand" (Matt 3:1-12: Year A). "One more powerful than I is to come after me" (Mark 1:1-8: Year B). "Make ready the way of the Lord" (Luke 3:1-6: Year C).

There is, then, a sense of nearness to the time of the Lord's coming, but there is also a sense of the universality of salvation. "The Gentiles glorify God" (Rom 15:4-9: Year A).

Finally, as so often during this part of the liturgical year, there is a call to personal responsibility. The Lord does not delay, "since he wants none to perish but all to come to repentance" (2 Pet 3:8-14: Year B). The work that God has so well begun "he will carry . . . through to completion, right up to the day of Christ Jesus.'' This is the way of walking without stumbling toward that day (Phil 1:4-6, 8-11: Year C).

Indeed, aware of their frailty and the absolute necessity for rescue by divine grace (prayer over the gifts), the faithful who gather for the celebration this Sunday plead urgently with God:

> God of power and mercy,
> open our hearts in welcome.
> Remove the things that hinder us from receiving Christ with joy,
> so that we may share his wisdom
> and become one with him
> when he comes in glory (Opening Prayer).

> Father,
> you give us food from heaven.
> By our sharing in this mystery,
> teach us to judge wisely the things of earth
> and to love the things of heaven (Prayer after Communion).

Second Sunday of Advent—Year A

We Must Be Converted

In Those Days, John the Baptist . . .

The liturgy always celebrates the unique mystery of the salvation of God: this mystery enters into its most important phase with the incarnation of the Son. It is set forth throughout the ages under the power of the Spirit, and will attain its complete and decisive fulfillment with the Lord's return. That is why we are always celebrating in the presence of the Trinity. However, it can happen that something else appears to occupy center stage. This is the case, each year, on the Second and Third Sundays of Advent, with the figure of John the Baptist, whose voice resounds in the Christian assembly. But let us not be deceived about this.

He who "arose" (appeared) "in those days" "in the desert of Judea," was not simply a key figure in salvation history who belongs irrevocably to the past, to that point in time when the Old Testament bordered on the New.[1] He is the prophet whose preaching retains all its power in the time when the Lord comes, when we strive toward his ultimate coming; this preaching is given to us that we might prepare.

John the Baptist says that we must focus our attention on another. "I baptize you in water for the sake of reform, but the one who will follow me is more powerful than I. I am not even fit to carry his sandals. He it is who will baptize you in the Holy Spirit and fire" (Matt 3:11). "No one can lay hold on anything unless it is given him from on high. You yourselves are witnesses to the fact that I said: 'I am not the Messiah; I am sent before him.' It is the groom who has the bride. The groom's best man waits there listening for him and is overjoyed to hear his voice. That is my joy, and it is complete. He must increase, while I must decrease" (John 3:27-30).

Who Is the One Who Will Come?

John characterizes the one who is to come after him as truly exceptionable. In contrast, the Precursor presents himself as not so exceptionable, but like Elijah, wearing "a garment of camel's hair, and a leather belt around his waist," and eating "grasshoppers and wild honey." All the same,

69

Christians today aren't all that impressed by the description of the one "greater" than John.

The baptism "in the Holy Spirit," as opposed to the "baptism in water" given by the Precursor, is, we are assured, merely a matter of two distinctive rites, one that Jesus will institute, and the other (John's) that prefigures him. But "baptism in fire"(!) and with such a graphic description! "His winnowing-fan is in his hand. He will clear the threshing floor and gather his grain into the barn, but the chaff he will burn in unquenchable fire" (Matt 3:12).

The general picture here is that of judgment, undeniably attributed to the Messiah. One ought not to forget that this is also found in Jesus' preaching. He also has spoken of the day when, separated from the wheat the chaff will be bundled together to be burned, while the wheat will be placed in the barn (Matt 13:24-30). But this reminder of judgment is not brandished like a sword of Damocles over our heads, and it is clearly not meant to be feared. It is, really, an event that is meant to impress us. We are not to forget it, but to have it always in our minds as a stimulus.[2] At least, it allows one to avoid self-delusion and false security.

Do Not Say Among Yourselves . . .

The gospel of this Sunday allows us to hear John the Baptist's strong reproach that, in Matthew, is addressed to the Pharisees and Sadducees.[3]

We would be wrong to think that this condemnation no longer concerns us, that the Evangelist reports it only to inform us of the behavior of certain of John's listeners, whom he castigates. In fact, in the Gospel According to Matthew, it is a passage, characteristic of Matthew's writing, that is notable for the way it expresses and illustrates the faith of the Church in his time. It is to nourish the faith of Christians that it has been written.[4] It is not only proclamation of the faith but also "catechesis," that is, instruction on the demands of faith. This Gospel retains, consequently, all of its power.

The Church for which Matthew wrote was already threatened by grave dangers. Among the Christians there were "bad as well as good" (Matt 22:10), some pretentious leaders who, rather than serving their people, took advantage of the authority conferred upon them for their personal vanity.[5]

The Evangelist wrote for these Christians. In repeating the warnings of John the Baptist, he reminds them that they also will be judged on their conduct. But they wouldn't have been heard saying to themselves:

"We bear the name of Christians, we have been marked with the sign of redemption, we come together for the Sunday liturgy." "God can raise up children to Abraham from these very stones."

Jesus himself, clearly addressing the disciples gathered around him, declared: "When that day comes, many will plead with me, 'Lord, Lord, have we not prophesied in your name? Have we not exorcised the demons by its power? Did we not do many miracles in your name as well?' Then I will declare to them solemnly, 'I never knew you. Out of my sight, you evildoers!' " (Matt 7:22-23). For it is a question of producing a fruit that expresses one's conversion, acceding to the will of the Father. "Every tree that does not bear good fruit is cut down and thrown into the fire."

John the Baptist is revealed as a true Precursor of the Lord who, with his sovereign authority, will issue the same call: "Reform your lives! The kingdom of heaven is at hand" (Matt 4:17). And he will proclaim the same demands of a faith put into practice. John is also the model of all precursors because of the manner in which he shows himself receptive to all who, with a sincere heart, acknowledge their sins, that they may receive the mercy and grace of God, of which every sacramental step is a sign and a gift.

Knowledge of the Lord Will Fill the Universe

The gravity of this teaching, which reverberates today in Christian assemblies, is in sharp contrast to the words read at the beginning of the liturgy, which evoke messianic times (Isa 11:1-10).

Isn't this a marvelous dream of a universal paradise? It's the kind of dream that gives our sleep a translucent, radiant feeling; but, upon waking, we are suddenly shocked into remembering the real world, where we experience the age-old absence of justice, peace, and gentleness.

This state of affairs smacks of scandal; it is a test for faith. For, "a shoot" has come from the "stump of Jesse, father of David," "a bud" has blossomed "from his roots": "Jesus Christ, son of David, son of Abraham" (Matt 1:1: Nativity of the Lord, Evening Vigil). Yes, it is certainly Jesus— meek and humble of heart, filled with the Holy Spirit and the fear of the Lord—whom the prophet describes. How, then, is it possible that this kingdom, which it is his mission to institute, has not yet come, that he does not yet appear (far from it!) "as a signal for the nations," and that he is largely misunderstood, forsaken, ignored? It would be wrong to interpret Isaiah's text today in this fashion. The psalm that follows calls us to see ourselves as we truly are and, once again, provides a key to the correct understanding of this Old Testament text.

The refrain reaffirms the unshakable certainty of the Christian assembly: "Justice shall flourish in his time, and fullness of peace for ever." Then, after an appeal to God for the one to come who will govern his people with justice and give the unfortunate their due, the verbs of three other couplets are in the future tense and turn us toward that for which we wait. This attitude and this prayer are familiar to us: ". . . hallowed by the name; thy kingdom come, thy will be done on earth as it is in heaven. . . . Deliver us from evil in this life where we hope for the happiness that you have promised and the coming of Jesus Christ, our Savior." We are now firmly rooted in the dialectic of "already" and "not yet" that characterizes the mystery of Advent and its celebration, indeed the whole of Christian life.

> *Justice shall flourish in his time,*
> *and fullness of peace for ever.*
>
> O God, with your judgment endow the king,
>   and with your justice, the king's son;
> He shall govern your people with justice
>   and your afflicted ones with judgment.
>
> Justice shall flower in his days,
>   and profound peace, till the moon be no more.
> May he rule from sea to sea,
>   and from the River to the ends of the earth.
>
> For he shall rescue the poor man when he cries out,
>   and the afflicted when he has no one to help him.
> He shall have pity for the lowly and the poor;
>   the lives of the poor he shall save.
>
> May his name be blessed forever;
>   as long as the sun his name shall remain.
> In him shall all the tribes of the earth be blessed;
>   all the nations shall proclaim his happiness.
> (Ps 72:1-2, 7-8, 12-13, 17)

All That Scripture Foretold Is Fulfilled in Your Sight

Without ignoring crisis situations and the discouragement they can produce, we look for light in the holy books. All that they say "was written for our instruction, that we might derive hope from the lessons of patience and the words of encouragement in the Scriptures" (Rom 15:4-9).

The ultimate basis for this assurance, the supreme guarantee of this hope, the inexhaustible source of this courage is found in "the faithfulness of God" manifested clearly by Christ who "became the servant of the Jews because of God's faithfulness in fulfilling the promises to the patriarchs," and because of his "mercy," thanks to which "the Gentiles glorify God."

When we become discouraged over our everyday problems, we must lift up our eyes. What were only recently pagan areas of the world are today Christian lands with extraordinarily vibrant and dynamic Churches that have received, in Christ Jesus, "every gift of speech and knowledge" (1 Cor 1:5; First Sunday of Advent, Year B). They have become examples to believers who tell one another how the pagans welcomed the apostles, how others like themselves have been "turning to God from idols, serving him who is the living and true God and awaiting from heaven the Son he raised from the dead—Jesus, who delivers us from the wrath to come" (1 Thess 1:7, 9-10).

Give Thanks to the Lord

We ourselves, children of pagans—haven't we been received by Christ for the glory of God, and made by him to be, in some sense, ministers for the reception of Christ, precursors of the Lord for one another? Not so much in words but in deeds, by living in the unity that is given by the Spirit of Jesus Christ and by practicing mutual acceptance.

How can we not give thanks and "glory to God, the Father of our Lord Jesus Christ" for the things he has done for us and for all people?

Perhaps we feel that we are but a handful of the faithful assembled for the Sunday liturgy, but we must not become discouraged or lose hope. We must continue to do our part and, in our own desert, we must prepare the way of the Lord and make straight his path, so that all may come (or return) to embrace him. We have much to be thankful for.

Throughout the whole world, many communities, large and small, celebrate the same liturgy of the coming of the Lord, and we are in communion with them. The same word of God is proclaimed to everyone, each hearing it in his or her own tongue. Their voices unite with ours to form an immense choir, and therefore everyone can truthfully say, "I sing your praise among the nations."

> Stand up! The Lord comes!
> A prophet's voice
> has risen from the desert . . .
> Desire and waiting
> have ripened our hearts . . .
> Let us prepare!

Stand up! The Lord comes!
The word creeps in
and shakes our hearts . . .
And behold the Kingdom,
it draws near, it is here . . .
Let us awake!

Stand up, the Lord comes!
Our new hope
between the currents of our lives . . .
Its fertile mystery,
a silent faith . . .
Let us be purified!

Stand up, the Lord comes!
Happy those called
to his table of love . . .
God himself invites us
and we shout for joy!
Let us assemble!

The Lord comes![6]

Second Sunday of Advent—Year B

The Lord Is Come:
He Is Here!

"Here begins the gospel of Jesus Christ, the Son of God." Thus begins the Gospel According to Mark, the first page of which we read today (Mark 1:1-8).

To speak of a "beginning" normally implies an end that is more or less near, more or less certain. This is not the case in the Gospel According to Mark. This short book stops abruptly and unexpectedly with the discovery of the empty tomb "on the first day of the week" by Mary Magdalene, Mary the mother of James, and Salome (Mark 16:1-8).[7] "They made their way out and fled from the tomb bewildered and trembling; and because of their great fear, they said nothing to anyone" (Mark 16:8; Easter Vigil, Year B).

We know that this is not the end. By ending this way, Mark doubtlessly wants to make us understand that each of us must continue the story thereafter with the personal response that we make to the "mystery" of the empty tomb. The evangelist's story stops abruptly, as if suspended, which invites others to "begin the gospel of Jesus Christ, the Son of God" in light of which they must now live until the Lord comes again.

The gospel is not a closed, private matter. Always proclaimed in a new manner, it must be read in the present, in following the one who has already come, and in expectation of the one who will come. The liturgy in which the gospel is proclaimed turns out to be, actually, the celebration of the mystery of salvation that comes in our time and in which we have a share.

The Lord Your God Comes with Strength
The Liturgy of the Word this Sunday begins with an oracle from the Book of Isaiah (40:1-5, 9-11).

> "Comfort, give comfort to my people, says your God. . . . In the desert prepare the way of the Lord! Make straight in the wasteland a highway for our God! . . . Cry out at the top of your voice, Jerusalem, herald of good news! . . . Here is your God! . . . Like a shepherd he feeds his flock. . . . "

If "faith is confident assurance concerning what we hope for and conviction about things we do not see" (Heb 11:1), what assurance is in this prophecy! It was pronounced when the people of the promise no longer had a country, or temple, or political power. Nevertheless, the prophet sees the return of the exiles and their gathering before the Lord in glory. He sees the great return as a new and marvelous Exodus. No more wearisome wandering in a hostile desert; rather, there is a triumphal procession. No longer is it the cloud that guides the people, but the Lord himself, like a shepherd leading his flock. "In his arms he gathers the lambs, carrying them in his bosom, and leading the ewes with care."

How marvelous! What dazzling proof of God's care for his own! It is they who constitute the glorious spoils of his victory. He has never abandoned or forgotten them. He is here, he is coming even today. If you feel inclined to doubt it, "Go up onto a high mountain." Then you will see; you will shout the good news to all.

Psalm 85 expresses this same assurance:

> Lord, let us see your kindness,
> and grant us your salvation.
>
> I will hear what God proclaims;
> the Lord—for he proclaims peace to his people. . . .
> Near indeed is his salvtion to those who fear him,
> glory dwelling in our land.
>
> Kindness and truth shall meet;
> justice and peace shall kiss.
> Truth shall spring out of the earth,
> and justice shall look down from heaven.
>
> The Lord himself will give his benefits;
> our land shall yield its increase.
> Justice shall walk before him,
> and salvation, along the way of his steps.
> (Ps 85:9-14)

"The word of the Lord is peace for his people." Peace, a summary of all the benefits of the messianic age, is associated with salvation in the New Testament. Because the Father of our Lord Jesus Christ is the God of peace, Christ himself is our peace, and his gospel is the good news of peace.[8]

At Bethlehem the angels sang: "Glory to God in high heaven, peace on earth to those on whom his favor rests" (Luke 2:14), to those whom he has shown "kindness and love" (Titus 3:4; Christmas, Mass at Dawn). But we also partake of it in the season of Advent, asking God to show us his love and give us his salvation, which have yet to be manifested in their fullness.

A New Heaven, a New Earth: We Are Still Waiting Today

The wait for the last coming of the Lord remains at the heart of faith, even after Christ's coming. One must realize that this does not preoccupy the minds of many Christians today; whereas in the early Church, the faithful were somewhat frantically inclined toward the imminence of the final days. Certainly, there is always the possibility of a planetary catastrophe: "The heavens will vanish with a roar; the elements will be destroyed by fire." But this fear, which we try to exorcise anyway, has nothing to do with waiting for the coming of the Lord. The exhortation of the Second Letter of Peter, which is read this Sunday, seems not to concern us at first. But this impression does not last long. The six verses prove themselves to be a source of great riches for faith and for life. Moreover, it seems to be of great importance precisely at this time when the prospect of the final days hardly seems to matter to us (2 Pet 3:8-14).

God remains faithful to his promise, the day of the Lord will come, and it will come like a thief, that is to say, suddenly. This is the whole mystery of Advent that is once again affirmed.

Does time, then, stretch on without any end in sight? This is an instance of the patience and mercy of God. "He wants none to perish but all to come to repentance." Because of this, we are able to return to the serious concern of our present life and our responsibility. "So, beloved, while waiting for this, make every effort to be found without stain or defilement, and at peace in his sight."

The mention of a possible cataclysm in which the heavens disappear, the elements are destroyed by fire, and "the earth and all its deeds will be made manifest," is not a prophecy of evil. These violent cosmic upheavals are those that will accompany the birth of a new heaven and earth where justice will dwell. This world, though it is "to be destroyed," will not be annihilated; on the contrary, it is promised a marvelous future. The Second Letter of Peter takes up and extends the prophecy of the Book of Isaiah. In fact, it makes clear that there will be a continuity in the change between the heaven and earth that we know and the new heaven and earth that "we await according to his promise." It also says that the "adventure" of this world and of all peoples has a meaning, that it moves toward an end that we must not fear, but prepare and hope for. Each person knows, in a sense, what is to be his or her fate at that moment, because it is the responsibility of each to do what is necessary for that day to be a personal day of salvation.

Believers are told to witness to this hope. Not by what they say, but above all by what they do and are, the holiness of their life, their respect for God and the works of the Creator entrusted to them. Under their eyes, by the work of their hands, by their personal involvement in all areas of life—political, social, etc.—a new world is coming into being. Such is the mystery of Advent that we participate in.

The Indispensable Ministry of Precursors

The good news is not imposed by force: it requires the free acceptance of those who hear it. We will find that the ground in which the seed falls is not prepared for all time by the prophets and the precursors of old, by the traditions to which one belongs, by whatever is the soil's natural disposition: the good earth can become a wasteland if it is not constantly cultivated.

John the Baptist came, and the multitudes crowded together on the banks of the Jordan where he preached and baptized. But not all turned quickly toward Jesus—far from it!—when he in his turn proclaimed: "This is the time of fulfillment. The reign of God is at hand! Reform your lives and believe in the gospel" (Mark 1:15).

Despite the enthusiasm of the crowds that crushed in upon him from all over—from Galilee, Judea, Jerusalem, Idumea, from across the Jordan, Tyre, and Sidon (Mark 3:7-9)—Jesus was left with only a handful of disciples at his death. Yet he never gave up teaching and performing miracles.

Since the day of Pentecost, the newborn Church has known an extraordinary kind of mission. The gospel has been preached to all the nations by the original apostles and their successors. But some Churches that once flourished are now only a memory. Others, as a result of sometimes dramatic crises, have become so indifferent that one might ask, "Have you forgotten your baptism?"[9] On the other hand, in some countries and even on entire continents, we see some young Churches becoming models for longtime Christians who seem to be running out of steam. Contemporary life and ancient history both bear witness to this: the reception of the good news, the vitality of the Churches, their internal and missionary dynamism will require precursors, leaders who will prepare the way of the Lord and make straight his path, prophets and saints to nourish and quicken the faith of believers, whether new or longstanding.

Without them—we see it only too well—the old idols reappear and impose their dominion anew: hate, injustice, egoism, and indifference regain the upper hand; people become progressively more inhuman, oblivious to the impact of the good news and incapable of receiving the Spirit who frees and sanctifies.

Servants of a Greater One

John the Baptist is the model of the prophet-precursor who is at all times conscious of his mission, but who also possesses an exemplary humility. He never does or says anything that would focus attention on him rather than on the one he wishes to focus upon. On the contrary: ''One more powerful than I is to come after me. I am not fit to stoop and untie his sandal straps. I have baptized you in water; he will baptize you in the Holy Spirit'' (Mark 1:1-8).

We find in this serene humility a certain quality that allows one to recognize a true prophet. John does everything in his power to prepare the way of the one who is coming, but he puts himself in the background. John the Baptist speaks and acts as if he had already heard and meditated on the parable of the master and his useless servants (Luke 17:7-10). He accomplishes his mission: that is enough for him.

The world and the Church always need such prophet-precursors who call for conversion. Wherever they appear, *there* is the ''beginning of the gospel'' for those who do not yet know Christ. In the Church, in the Christian communities, at the heart of all renewal, of all new beginnings, we find prophets, sometimes invested with a ministry, often without any official title, but in every case animated by the Spirit of the Father, who reveals his secrets to the meek and the humble.

> New dawn in our night;
> to save his people, God will come.
> Joy and feasting today for the poor:
> We must prepare the way of the Lord.
>
> Good news, cries and songs:
> to save his people, God will come.
> A voice rises up in our deserts:
> We must prepare the way of the Lord.
>
> New earth, new world:
> to save his people, God will come.
> Peace on earth, heaven among us:
> We must prepare the way of the Lord.[10]

Second Sunday of Advent—Year C

God Speaks Anew

The Second Sunday of Advent in Year C is also dominated by the figure of John the Baptist. Each Synoptic Gospel recalls his preaching and his role as the immediate precursor of the Lord. If read quickly, these three accounts appear to be identical, except for some details that one may be tempted to neglect. And we shouldn't give in to the temptation of trying to synthesize them so as to come up with one story. This would be regrettable, because we would erase the particular styles of these three witnesses, however comfortably Matthew, Mark, and Luke[11] may otherwise fit into the context—the collection—of the three different Liturgies of the Word, accompanied on the Second Sunday of Year C by texts from Baruch and the Letter of Paul to the Philippians.

Throw Off Your Robe of Sadness and Misery
In the first reading we hear the end of the poem by Baruch. The prophet sends, on behalf of God, a message of consolation and hope to a personified Jerusalem.[12]

The city to which they always hoped to return bore the sorrow of its departed children (Bar 4:9, 11, 23). It is told to throw off its "robe of mourning and misery," to put on "the splendor of glory from God forever," to wrap itself "in the cloak of justice from God," to place on its head "the miter that displays the glory of the eternal name."[13] The return of the exiles is at hand: the city must prepare to receive them.

In the Bible, a change in a given situation or in the character of a person is often indicated by the imposition of a new name that signifies God's taking possession.[14] Thus it is that the City will henceforth be called "the peace of justice, the glory of God's worship."[15] What a magnificent conclusion to an already long litany!

> City of justice, faithful city (Isa 1:26)
> The Lord's throne (Jer 3:17)
> The Lord our justice (Jer 33:16)
> Center of the nations (Ezek 5:5)
> The Lord is here (Ezek 48:35)
> Salvation (Isa 46:13)

The holy city (Isa 48:2; 52:1;ff.)
City of the Lord (Isa 60:14)
Espoused (Isa 62:4)
Frequented (Isa 62:12)
Joyful city (Isa 65:18)
Mother Zion (Ps 87:5)
Peace of justice, the glory of God's worship (Bar 5:4)

Rise Up, Jerusalem, and See Your Children Coming Toward You

As always, salvation, as the work of God—"because he is mindful"—is a gathering of those who were dispersed and isolated. And as always, this gathering takes place around the word of God, by his intervention.[16] It takes the form of a triumphal return, in contrast to the confused rout of the dispersion. Driven out in forced marches, the people return walking cheerfully along easy paths, sometimes even carried in triumph. The difficulties of the terrain are smoothed out, whether the highest mountains, the hills, or the valleys. The sun does not overwhelm them: they walk in the shade of forests and fragrant trees! The mercy of God and his justice escort them.

The last book of the Bible—the Revelation of John—ends with a vision of the heavenly Jerusalem, which the seer contemplates from the top of a mountain.

> Then I saw new heavens and a new earth. The former heavens and the former earth had passed away, and the sea was no longer. I also saw a new Jerusalem, the holy city, coming down out of heaven from God, beautiful as a bride prepared to meet her husband. I heard a loud voice from the throne cry out: "This is God's dwelling among men. He shall dwell with them and they shall be his people and he shall be their God who is always with them. He shall wipe every tear from their eyes, and there shall be no more death or mourning, crying out or pain, for the former world has passed away." The One who sat on the throne said to me, "See, I make all things new!" (Rev 21:2-5).

Christians can profit by studying the poetry portions of the Book of Baruch. This is even more the case when the architect of this reunification of all nations, coming from the four corners of the earth is henceforth the Word made flesh: Jesus the Word of God, whose nativity at Bethelehem we celebrate and whose coming at the end of time we await. So the Church, gathered around the Word, makes its own, on this Sunday of Advent, the old psalm of ascent:

> *The Lord has done great things for us;*
> *we are filled with joy.*

When the LORD brought back the captives of Zion,
  we were like men dreaming.
Then our mouth was filled with laughter,
  and our tongue with rejoicing.

Then they said among the nations,
  "The LORD has done great things for them."
The LORD has done great things for us;
  we are glad indeed.

Restore our fortunes, O LORD,
  like the torrents in the southern desert.
Those that sow in tears
  shall reap rejoicing.

Although they go forth weeping,
  carrying the seed to be sown,
They shall come back rejoicing,
  carrying their sheaves.
(Ps 126)

The Fifteenth Year of the Reign of Tiberius

Now comes the presentation of John the Baptist and his ministry in the Gospel According to Luke (Luke 3:1-6).

What strikes one at the beginning of this text is the solemnity of the first phrase, which sounds like an official proclamation:

> In the fifteenth year of the rule of Tiberius Caesar, when Pontius Pilate was procurator of Judea, Herod tetrarch of Galilee, Philip his brother tetrarch of the region of Ituraea and Trachonitis, and Lysanias tetrarch of Abilene, during the high-priesthood of Annas and Caiaphas, the word of God was spoken to John son of Zechariah in the desert.

Especially in the first two chapters of his Gospel, Luke, the historian, takes care to give chronological benchmarks that situate the events of which he speaks: the announcement to Zechariah of the birth of John "in the days of Herod, king of Judea" (Luke 1:5); the birth of Jesus at Bethlehem "while Quirinius was governor of Syria" (Luke 2:2). The accumulation of this sort of thing here is unique.

This is not surprising if one remembers that from the beginning of his Gospel, Luke treats jointly of John the Baptist and Jesus. It is not only the beginning of the ministry of the Precursor that Luke places here. He is doubtlessly thinking more of Jesus than the Baptist.

This reference to secular history is followed by a traditional citation of the prophecy of Isaiah (40:3-5).[17] The important thing to realize is that by joining them, Luke suggests that the history of salvation is integrated into the course of the history of all people.

Everyone Will See the Salvation of God

Note also that Luke cites the prophetic text of Isaiah 40 at greater length than the other evangelists, going as far as verse 5: "Then the glory of the Lord shall be revealed, and all mankind shall see it together." The universal importance of the event is thus affirmed. This is already suggested by the mention of the emperor Tiberius, the princes of Iturea, and the region of Trachonitis, pagan territories.

Readers of this Gospel who are aware of the full revelation of Easter can see in this prophetic announcement the true fullness of the salvation that Jesus brings.

Simeon, having taken the infant Jesus in his arms, said: "My eyes have witnessed your saving deed" (Luke 2:30). At the end of the Book of Acts, Paul, after having cited another prophecy of Isaiah (Isa 6:9-10), declared: "Now you must realize that this salvation of God has been transmitted to the Gentiles" (Acts 28:28). Luke is the only one of the Synoptics to give the title of Savior to Jesus (Luke 2:11) as well as to God (Luke 1:47). He is the only one to speak of salvation in Jesus (Luke 1:69, 71, 77; 19:9; cf. Luke 23:35-43; Acts 4:12). The way Luke presents the mission of John the Baptist is oriented not only to the immediate manifestation of Jesus after his baptism in the Jordan but also to the foreshadowing of all his work of salvation, of which Easter is the summit in this world, and the moment of its full realization when "all mankind shall see the salvation of God."

This announcement is quite unobtrusive, characteristic of Luke. In Luke's writings, revelation is always approached gradually, almost pedagogically.

The gospel for this Sunday puts us in the context and dynamic of the Advent season: immediate preparation for the celebration of Christmas; the beginning of a new liturgical year that sets forth, at this time, the mystery of salvation in Jesus Christ—from nativity to Easter—its continuity in the mission of the Church,[18] and its final fulfillment in the triumphal return of the Son of Man.

God Will Accomplish What He Has Begun

"May God bring to a good end what he has begun in you." This is a traditional formula by which the celebrant responds to those who are making a life commitment, for example, in religious profession. Paul wrote the same thing in his Letter to the Philippians, as seen in the excerpt that is read this Sunday. However, he did not imagine this perseverance lasting only for the duration of this life, but even until the coming of the Lord. "I am sure of this much: that he who has begun the good work in you will carry it through to completion, right up to the day of Christ Jesus" (Phil 1:4-6, 8-11).

"I am sure . . . ." At all times, Paul expresses his unalterable confidence in the grace of God, which gives rise to all his thanksgiving and joy. In the same way, when he writes a letter, he cannot hide the sentiments he feels for the recipients, whether rejoicing in their conduct or reproaching them.

"With the affection of Christ Jesus." The Greek terms are so expressive that one hesitates to translate them literally: "with the bowels" of Christ. There is, perhaps, a transposition here of one of the Hebrew words that denotes love, the root of which signifies "bowel," "maternal womb." In one of its prophecies, the Book of Isaiah does not hesitate to say of God: "Can a mother forget her infant, be without tenderness for the child of her womb?" (Isa 49:15). Paul wrote to the Corinthians: "Granted you have ten thousand guardians in Christ, you have only one father. It was I who begot you in Christ Jesus through my preaching of the gospel" (1 Cor 4:15). And to the Galatians: "You are my children, and you put me back in labor pains until Christ is formed in you" (Gal 4:19). We are not surprised, then, by his visceral tenderness with regard to the Philippians.

In his prayer, he asks for them what is essential in order to walk without stumbling toward the day of Christ: growth in charity, this gift of the Spirit (Gal 5:22) "which binds the rest together" (Col 3:14). From it springs "the true knowledge," that of the heart, of God and his mystery, so that they might perceive directly and intuitively "what is most important" in view of the return of the Lord.

So much for Paul. His teaching is not in the least moralistic but, on the contrary, the theological dimension of Christian conduct that has for its object "the glory and praise of God."

Celebration of the Mystery of Salvation by Christ

In the gospel for this Sunday, John the Baptist occupies center stage: "Make ready the way of the Lord." The one for whom we must make the path straight is not named. Nevertheless, it is he, and not the Precursor, who is found at the heart of the gospel as well as at the heart of the celebration. Not only his person, though, but also the "salvation of God" that he accomplishes in fulfillment of the Scriptures. He who was born at a specific time in human history, who, with a unique authority accompanied by miracles, announced the good news, who died and was resurrected, was raised to the right hand of God, from whence he shall come to judge the living and the dead. All this can be read in the passage from the gospel this Sunday. The proclamation in the Creed makes it explicit. The Eucharist makes a memorial of it in the offering of the bread of life and the cup of salvation, while we sing the praises of the Father through Jesus Christ, his beloved Son,[19] and where we receive the Body and Blood of Christ for eternal life.

John the Baptist, the faithful Precursor, turns us toward the celebration of the mystery of salvation by Christ. Luke recalls, in citing a prophecy from the Book of Isaiah, that all men and women will see the salvation of God.

The Twofold Coming of the Lord

The preaching of John the Baptist is oriented toward the first manifestation of the Lord who comes after him to announce the good news of the kingdom that is at hand and to call for conversion.

Before this announcement, there are others to which Luke rightly witnesses: to Mary and Joseph by an angel; at the Temple by Simeon and the prophetess Anna; to the shepherds at Bethlehem.

In each of these announcements the same dimensions of the mystery are proclaimed. For instance, they speak of the coming of a Savior. "The angel said to Mary, 'You shall conceive and bear a son and give him the name Jesus,' " which means God saves (Luke 1:31); "This day in David's city a savior has been born to you," the angels announce to the shepherds (Luke 2:11); God "has raised a horn of saving strength for us," chants Zechariah (Luke 1:69), to which the Canticle of Simeon echoes: "My eyes have witnessed your saving deed" (Luke 2:30), while Anna "talked about the child to all who looked forward to the deliverance of Jerusalem" (Luke 2:38). This salvation concerns all "those on whom God's favor rests" (Luke 2:14), because it is a revelation of light "to the Gentiles," "displayed for all the peoples to see" (Luke 2:31-32).

At the same time, it is said that this coming of the Lord manifests the glory of God. "Glory to God in high heaven" (Luke 2:14). The shepherds understood this well: after having seen the child at Bethlehem, "they glorified and praised God'' (Luke 2:20), as did Simeon and Anna (Luke 2:28, 38).

Last, but not least, the angel said to Mary that his "reign will be without end" (Luke 1:33), which suggests another coming of the Son of the Most High upon this earth. This is completely in line with what the prophets had announced (First Reading). This is why Paul can say that we march toward the day when we will be "found rich in the harvest of justice which Jesus Christ has ripened in you, to the glory and praise of God" (Second Reading).

To Prepare the Way of the Lord

Like the first coming of the Lord, the second must be prepared personally in the community of believers, by fidelity to the will of God and the active reception of his grace. God who has begun in us his "work" asks only that it be followed to its end: "up to the day of Christ Jesus" (Second Reading). Actually, there are still many mountains and hills, many valleys that are obstacles on the road to peace and justice, "glory and piety to God," and divisions between men and women and the scattered faithful! (First Reading). There are also many who have not seen the salvation of God! (Gospel). For all that, Advent is a time of hope and joy, of confidence as expressed in the prayer: "Our Father . . . your kingdom come!" It moves us toward the approaching celebration of the Nativity of the Lord, which is not a simple commemoration of his first coming long ago, but an actualization of this first manifestation that announces and guarantees what is already on the horizon.

> Leave your sorrows and tears,
> put on your garments of joy:
> The one who is coming
> comes on the clouds!
>
> The love of God guides us;
> his glory is our light:
> The one who is coming
> comes victorious!
>
> Why do you not hasten
> toward the day of your God?
> The one who is coming
> comes for our joy!
>
> Prepare his way,
> accept his pardon;
> each of us will see

the grace of our God
on the day of judgment!

Happy the one who believed
that one day would be fulfilled
the words of our God
for all men whom he loves!

Behold, the times are come
when the Lord of justice
will fulfill his promise of Peace
for all men whom he loves![20]

Monday Through Saturday—Second Week

The liturgical books for the week are filled with readings for each day: prayers and psalms, biblical and patristic readings for the Mass and the Office. Those who have the chance to integrate the celebration of these liturgies into the rhythm of their lives can profit most from this abundant, varied, and well-chosen spiritual nourishment. But what about other people—the greater number—who cannot do this? It is a regrettable fact that most people regard this abundance and multiplicity of spiritual foods as reserved to those who have the leisure to partake in them regularly: priests who celebrate the Eucharist and the Office every day, religious, monks whose lives are organized around the liturgy. But perhaps there is an alternative to this "all or nothing" situation.

In fact, the various liturgies of the week are not formed as a homogeneous ensemble, but rather with several means of access. Even without participating in the celebrations of the Eucharist and the Office, one can read and meditate on a certain text from the Missal or the Liturgy of the Hours, or pray, be it only for a few moments, a psalm or a prayer of the day. This kind of reading and prayer refreshes the spirit and the heart in the course of the day, forming them and allowing one to live in the spirit of the liturgy of the season.

The Missal and the Lectionary

Some of the prayers of this week seem to have been composed for the intention, rightly enough, of working persons.

> Lord,
> free us from our sins and make us whole.
> Hear our prayer,
> and prepare us to celebrate the incarnation of your Son (Monday).

> We await the healing power of Christ your Son.
> Let us not be discouraged by our weaknesses
> as we prepare for his coming.
> Keep us steadfast in your love (Wednesday).

> Give us the joy of your love
> to prepare the way for Christ our Lord.
> Help us to serve you and one another (Thursday).

> Help us to look forward in hope
> to the coming of our Savior.
> May we live as he has taught,
> ready to welcome him with burning love and faith (Friday).

Help us to look forward
to the glory of the birth of Christ our Savior:
his coming is proclaimed joyfully
to the ends of the earth (Tuesday).

Let your glory dawn to take away our darkness.
May we be revealed as the children of light
at the coming of your Son (Saturday).

The Readings from the Old Testament, still taken almost exclusively from the Book of Isaiah, speak of the wonders that will announce and accompany the return of the Lord, as if vying with each other.[21] The earth will be changed, and no longer will there be the slightest weakness. "Be strong, fear not!" (Isa 35:1-10: Monday). "I will open up rivers on the bare heights, and foundations in the broad valleys; I will turn the desert into a marshland, and the dry ground into springs of water. I will plant in the desert the cedar, acacia, myrtle, and olive; I will set in the wasteland the cypress, together with the plane tree and the pine" (Isa 41:13-20: Thursday). Like a concerned shepherd, God himself will lead his flock in order to gather and console them (Isa 40:1-11: Tuesday). His coming will give strength and vigor to the weak and disheartened (Isa 40:25-31: Wednesday). One must hear the voice of the Lord and walk on the path traced by his teaching (Isa 48:17-19: Friday). For the coming of the Lord is like a refiner's fire (Sir 48:1-4, 9-11: Saturday).

The Psalms that follow these readings extend their meaning in prayer and meditation, they praise the Lord, and beg for his coming.[22] After having said them, one will want to inwardly sing parts of them in one's heart.

I will hear what God proclaims;
   the LORD—for he proclaims peace to his people. . . .
Near indeed is his salvation to those who fear him,
   glory dwelling in our land.
Kindness and truth shall meet;
   justice and peace shall kiss . . .
The LORD himself will give his benefits;
   our land shall yield its increase. (Ps 85: Monday)

O shepherd of Israel, hearken.
From your throne upon the cherubim, shine forth.
Rouse your power,
   and come to save us. (Ps 80: Saturday)

I will extol you, O my God and King,
   and I will bless your name forever and ever.
The LORD is good to all
   and compassionate toward all his works. (Ps 145: Thursday)

> Bless the LORD, O my soul;
>   and all my being, bless his holy name. . . .
> Merciful and gracious is the Lord,
>   slow to anger and abounding in kindness.
> Not according to our sins does he deal with us,
>   nor does he requite us according to our crimes. (Ps 103: Wednesday)

> Let the heavens be glad and the earth rejoice;
>   let the sea and what fills it resound;
>   let the plains be joyful and all that is in them!
> Then shall all the trees of the forest exult,
>   before the LORD, for he comes;
>   for he comes to rule the earth. (Ps 96: Tuesday)

> Happy the man who follows not
>   the counsel of the wicked
> Nor walks in the way of sinners,
>   nor sits in the company of the insolent,
> But delights in the law of the LORD
>   and meditates on his law day and night. (Ps 1: Friday)

The Gospels are divided into two groups of three.[23] Jesus, under the eyes of his contemporaries, has accomplished "wondrous deeds" in healing the paralytic who was lowered to him from the roof of the house, and in forgiving his sins (Luke 5:17-26: Monday).

He has called and received unto himself all those who labor under heavy burdens (Matt 11:28-30: Wednesday).

By his behavior, he has revealed the Father, who desires that not even a single one be lost, who acts like the shepherd who leaves the ninety-nine sheep in the hills in order to look for the one who is lost (Matt 18:12-14: Tuesday).

After this come three readings from the Gospel of Matthew, who recalls the words of Jesus regarding John the Baptist. He is certainly the greatest among men, but the greatest of all is the one who possesses the king-dom of heaven by way of listening to the voice of the prophets and the one whom they announce (Matt 11:11-15: Thursday).

We cannot, then, behave like capricious children, never content with what is offered them. How sad it is to see the Word denied, however it presents itself: the messengers of God rejected one after another, what-ever their style; the initiatives, the calls, the reforms of the Church—always greeted with disdain! (Matt 11:16-19: Friday).

It seems as if we were always waiting for another prophet, because they were one after another persecuted like Jesus himself, put to death by those who did not wish to recognize him (Matt 17:10-13: Saturday).

Each of these Gospels returns to the responsibility of the present time, when we must prepare the way of the Lord who comes.

The Liturgy of the Hours

The Liturgy of the Hours includes a certain number of variable elements that are designed to create a special tone or color for each liturgical season. From week to week, however, it varies less than the Liturgy of the Word in the Mass. The Office is organized around the psalmody, which acts as a framework, i.e., a prescribed course of readings for a given year.[24] The brief biblical texts for Lauds, Midday, and Compline are chosen according to the liturgical season, but they are not rigorously imposed. The same is true of the Office of Readings, where the patristic texts (readings from the Fathers) may or may not be directly related to the biblical texts: it is sufficient for them to have a theme that is appropriate to the season. One can find in the Office whatever will provide nourishment for reflection, meditation, and prayer.

The Biblical Readings

From Monday to Friday of the Second Week of Advent, the Office includes the entire text of what is called the "Apocalypse of Isaiah" (Isa 24:1–27:13).[25] These four chapters "see beyond the immediate events to the final judgment of God; of this they give a poetic description interspersed with supplicatory and thanksgiving psalms" (JB).[26]

Here is the beginning of a terrifying passage on the judgment to come (Isa 24:1-8):

> Lo, the Lord empties the land and lays it waste; he turns it upside down, scattering its inhabitants: layman and priest alike, servant and master, the maid as her mistress, the buyer as the seller, the lender as the borrower, the creditor as the debtor.

> The earth mourns and fades, the world languishes and fades; both heaven and earth languish. The earth is polluted because of its inhabitants, who have transgressed laws, violated statutes, broken the ancient covenant. Therefore a curse devours the earth, and its inhabitants pay for their guilt; therefore they who dwell on earth turn pale, and few men are left.

But there is also the small remnant of the just, for whom this judgment will bring glory:

> These lift up their voice in acclaim; from the sea they proclaim the majesty of the Lord: "For this, in the coastlands, give glory to the Lord! In the coastlands of the sea, to the name of the Lord, the God of Israel!" From the end of the earth we hear songs: "Splendor to the Just One!"

On this day, sin will be wiped out by God, "[for he is] a refuge to the poor, a refuge to the needy in distress; shelter from the rain, shade from the heat, as with the cold rain, as with the desert heat" (Isa 24:19—25:5: Tuesday).

Immediately thereafter comes a poem that sings with confidence of God the Savior (Isa 25:6–26:6: Wednesday), and an ardent prayer of hope (Isa 26:7-21: Thursday), of which one part (Isa 26:1-4, 7-9, 12) has been retained to constitute a canticle of the Old Testament.

> On this mountain the Lord of hosts will provide for all peoples a feast of rich food and choice wines, juicy, rich food and pure, choice wines. On this mountain he will destroy the veil that veils all peoples, the web that is woven over all nations; he will destroy death forever. The Lord God will wipe away the tears from all faces; the reproach of his people he will remove from the whole earth; for the Lord has spoken. On that day it will be said: "Behold our God, to whom we looked to save us! This is the Lord for whom we looked; let us rejoice and be glad that he has saved us!" For the hand of the Lord will rest on this mountain, but Moab will be trodden down as a straw is trodden down in the mire. He will stretch forth his hands in Moab as a swimmer extends his hands to swim; he will bring low their pride as his hands sweep over them. The high-walled fortress he will raze, and strike it down level with the earth, with the very dust.

> On that day they will sing this song in the land of Judah: "A strong city have we; he sets up walls and ramparts to protect us. Open up the gates to let in a nation that is just, one that keeps faith. A nation of firm purpose you keep in peace; in peace for its trust in you."

> Trust in the Lord forever! For the Lord is an eternal Rock. He humbles those in high places, and the lofty city he brings down; he tumbles it to the ground, levels it with the dust. It is trampled underfoot by the needy, by the footsteps of the poor. The way of the just is smooth; the path of the just you make level. Yes, for your way and your judgments, O Lord, we look to you; your name and your title are the desire of our souls. My soul yearns for you in the night, yes my spirit within me keeps vigil for you; when your judgment dawns upon the earth, the world's inhabitants learn justice. The wicked man, spared, does not learn justice; in an upright land he acts perversely, and sees not the majesty of the Lord.

> O Lord, your hand is uplifted, but they behold it not; let them be shamed when they see your zeal for your people: let the fire prepared for your enemies consume them. O Lord, you mete out peace to us, for it is you who have accomplished all we have done. O Lord, our God, other lords than you have ruled us; it is from you only that we can call upon your name.

> Dead they are, they have no life, shades that cannot rise; for you have punished and destroyed them, and wiped out all memory of them. You

have increased the nation, O Lord, increased the nation to your own glory, and extended far all the borders of the land.

O Lord, oppressed by your punishment, we cried out in anguish under your chastising. As a woman about to give birth writhes and cries out in her pains, so were we in your presence, O Lord. We conceived and writhed in pain, giving birth to wind; salvation we have not achieved for the earth, the inhabitants of the world cannot bring it forth. But your dead shall live, their corpses shall rise; awake and sing, you who lie in the dust. For your dew is a dew of light, and the land of shades gives birth.

Go, my people, enter your chambers, and close your doors behind you; hide yourselves for a brief moment, until the wrath is past. See, the Lord goes forth from his place, to punish the wickedness of the earth's inhabitants; the earth will reveal the blood upon her, and no longer conceal her slain.

On this day, God will intervene on behalf of his people (Isa 27:1-13: Friday).

On that day—the pleasant vineyard, sing about it! I, the Lord, am its keeper, I water it every moment; lest anyone harm it, night and day I guard it.

I am not angry, but if I were to find briers and thorns, in battle I should march against them; I should burn them all. . . . Shall he cling to me for refuge? He must make peace with me; peace shall he make with me!

The exiles will be reassembled: "Prostrate you shall speak from the earth, and from the base dust your words shall come" that they may never forget that their redemption is conditional upon the fidelity of God (Isa 29:1-8: Saturday).

Throughout these texts, God urges his people to vigilance and confidence.

Jerusalem, fear not; you shall not be put to shame; for the Lord of hosts will come to visit you. The passing multitudes of all nations, which have struggled against you, will be like flying dust.[27]

The Patristic Readings are taken from the works of St. Irenaeus (c. 135–202: Friday), St. Augustine (354–430: Wednesday), St. Peter Chrysologus, archbishop of Ravenna (c. 380–450: Thursday), Isaac of Stella, English Cistercian abbot (1147: Saturday), St. John of the Cross (1542–1591: Monday), and the constitution *Lumen gentium* of Vatican II (November 21, 1964: Tuesday).

The texts, from authors of various times, is quite interesting and, surprisingly, seem to speak for all time. Some speak directly of Christ: who he is in himself and for us, what he has done since his first coming, his coming return and what it means about how we should behave in this world. In others, the authors evoke attitudes, essential approaches to the life of Christians, that are at the heart of the season of Advent.

St. John of the Cross, the great mystic, writes:

> God has spoken so completely through his own Word that he chooses to add nothing. Although he had spoken but partially through the prophets he has now said everything in Christ. He has given us everything—his own Son.
>
> Therefore, anyone who wished to question God or to seek some new vision or revelation from him would commit an offense, for instead of focusing his eyes entirely on Christ he would be desiring something other than Christ, or beyond him.
>
> God could then answer: "This is my beloved Son in whom I am well pleased; hear him." In my Word I have already said everything. Fix your eyes on him alone, for in him I have revealed all, and in him you will find more than you could ever ask for or desire.[28]

Commenting on Psalm 110, St. Augustine says that God is not content to give us his Son in order to show us the way: "He has made him the road by which you travel under his direction, the road that you follow."[29]

In a homily on the mystery of the incarnation, St. Peter Chrysologus recalls how "God, seeing the world falling to ruin because of fear, immediately acted to call it back to himself with love. He invited it by his grace, preserved it by his love, and embraced it with compassion." He evokes the purification of "the earth hardened in evil"; he calls Noah "to be the father of a new era" and Abraham whom he made "the father of all believers"; Jacob is comforted by visions; Moses is invited "to be the liberator of his people."

The archbishop of Ravenna adds: "In all the events we have recalled, the flame of divine love enkindled human hearts and exhilarated them. Wounded by love, they longed to look upon God with their bodily eyes."

Imagining objections that might be made regarding this desire to see God, he responds:

> Yet how could our narrow human vision apprehend God, whom the whole world cannot contain? But the law of love is not concerned with what will be, what ought to be, what can be. Love does not reflect; it is unreasonable and knows no moderation. Love refuses to be consoled when its goal proves impossible, despises all hindrances to the attainment of its object. Love destroys the lover if he cannot obtain what he loves; love follows its own promptings, and does not think of right and wrong. Love inflames desire, which impels it toward things that are forbidden. But why continue?

It is intolerable for love not to see the object of its longing. That is why whatever reward they merited was nothing to the saints if they could not see the Lord.

St. Irenaeus[30] and Isaac of Stella[31] speak of the Virgin Mary. She is the new Eve, but she is also the image of the Church.

Both are mothers, both are virgins. Each conceives of the same Spirit, without concupiscence. Each gives birth to a child of God the Father, without sin. Without any sin, Mary gave birth to Christ the head for the sake of his body. By the forgiveness of the every sin, the Church gave birth to the body, for the sake of its head. Each is Christ's mother, but neither gives birth to the whole Christ without the cooperation of the other.

In the inspired Scriptures, what is said in a universal sense of the virgin mother, the Church, is understood in an individual sense of the Virgin Mary, and what is said in a particular sense of the virgin mother Mary is rightly understood in a general sense of the virgin mother, the Church. When either is spoken of, the meaning can be understood of both, almost without qualification. . . .

The Lord's inheritance is, in a general sense, the Church; in a special sense, Mary; in an individual sense, the Christian. Christ dwelt for nine months in the tabernacle of Mary's womb. He dwells until the end of the ages in the tabernacle of the Church's faith. He will dwell for ever in the knowledge and love of each faithful soul.[32]

The promised renewal that we look for has already begun in Christ. It is continued in the mission of the Holy Spirit. Through the Spirit it goes on developing in the Church. . . .

The end of ages is already with us. The renewal of the world has been established, and cannot be revoked. In our era it is in a true sense anticipated: the Church on earth is already sealed by genuine, if imperfect, holiness. Yet, until a new heaven and a new earth are built as the dwelling place of justice, the pilgrim Church, in its sacraments and institutions belonging to this world of time, bears the likeness of this passing world. It lives in the midst of a creation still groaning and in travail as it waits for the sons of God to be revealed in glory.[33]

Third Week of Advent

"Rejoice in the Lord always;
again I say, rejoice!
The Lord is near."

This antiphon, which every year opens the liturgy of the Third Sunday of Advent, gives it a particular character. It is like a backdrop on which are superimposed different elements of the celebration, or a musical theme developed with variations from year to year. This day has been called Gaudete Sunday, after the Latin *gaudere,* to rejoice. And "rejoice" is a term that suits it well.

The mention of joy is found in the opening prayer and in the communion antiphon:

Lord God,
may we your people,
who look forward to the birthday of Christ
experience the joy of salvation
and celebrate that feast with love and thanksgiving.

God of mercy,
may this eucharist bring us your divine help,
free us from our sins,
and prepare us for the birthday of our Savior.

Third Sunday of Advent—Year A

Courage! Do Not Fear!

The Desert Resounds with Exultation and Cries of Joy

Again, at the beginning of the Liturgy of the Word for the Third Sunday, it is a text from the Book of Isaiah that is proclaimed (Isa 35:1-6, 10).

The prophecy read last Sunday announced a marvelous future of justice and peace: on the day when "a shoot shall sprout from the stump of Jesse, and from his roots a bud shall blossom." "On that day, the root of Jesse, set up as a signal for the nations, the Gentiles shall seek out, for his dwelling shall be glorious" (Isa 11:1-10).

That "day" has already dawned, declares a disciple of Isaiah.[1] Sadness gives way to joy, even in nature, which is one with the fate of humanity.[2]

The bold image of a desert that again flourishes and is covered with great trees—the fabled cedars of Lebanon—is easily envisioned by everyone, perhaps more easily by those who live in cultivated areas.[3] But the Bible always has particular connotations linked to religious memories and faith. It is through the experience of the desert that the people came to a covenant with God (Exod 24:3-8), where they were given the Law that made them the people of God (Exod 19:5). Consequently, in the collective memory of the people of the Bible, the desert evokes not so much the sufferings borne during the Exodus but, rather, intimacy with God: "This word of the Lord came to me: 'I remember the devotion of your youth, how you loved me as a bride, following me in the desert, in a land unsown" (Jer 2:2).

In addition, the verbs "rejoice," "exult," "cry for joy" derive from a liturgical vocabulary.[4] Consequently, to say that "the desert and the parched land will exult; the steppe will rejoice and bloom," is not simply a poetic way of speaking. The prophet sees the scene as a liturgical celebration in which the desert plays a part; along the way, the roads are lined with freed captives, and voices are united in songs of praise. For in biblical poems, the mountains, heaven, and the sea take an active part in the events of salvation—particularly in the Exodus[5]:

98

When Israel came forth from Egypt . . .
Judah became his sanctuary . . .
The mountains skipped like rams,
   the hills like the lambs of the flock. . . .
Before the face of the LORD, tremble, O earth,
   before the face of the God of Jacob (Ps 114:1-7).

Behold, It Is Your God; Do Not Fear!

The reveling of nature is a reflection and echo of the joy of the ransomed who are addressed after the prophecy. The "feeble hands," "the knees that are weak," are images that evoke the abasement of a people who are profoundly disturbed, trembling with fear—"panicking."[6] After these images come the clear and explicit words "Be strong, fear not! Here is your God . . . he comes to save you."

The blind see, the deaf hear, the lame leap like deer, the mute cry out with joy. Miraculous cures, yes; but, more importantly, they are acts that signify salvation, according to the biblical tradition and the gospel.[7]

This is why the evangelists, when they report the miraculous healings of Jesus, take care to use the verb "save" and not "heal."

God himself comes to save. The captives ransomed by the Lord "will return and enter Zion singing, crowned with everlasting joy; they will meet with joy and gladness, sorrow and mourning will flee" (Isa 35:10). This description calls to mind the vision of St. John in Revelation: "I heard a loud voice from the throne cry out: 'He shall be their God who is always with them. He shall wipe every tear from their eyes, and there shall be no more death or mourning, crying out or pain'" (Rev 21:3-4).

Let us pause a bit on the verb "return." It does not refer to a purely exterior act, a kind of journeying; rather, it is the return to intimacy with God. This verb has, in the Old Testament, a vast spectrum of meanings, which the prophetic literature and the psalms did not fail to exploit. Hebrew, in fact, allows a play on the various nuances of the root of a word, which is impossible in English. At the most, we can sometimes point up a play of significant words: "If you return (to me), I will allow you to return (to your country), and you will stand before me (you will turn yourself toward me)" says God (Jer 15:19); "If you allow me, I will return," pleads Ephraim (Jer 31:18).[8]

This is truly a question of salvation, a salvation whose initiative belongs to God, but which implies conversion, the return of a person sustained by grace.

Lord, come and save us.

The Lord GOD keeps faith forever,
  secures justice for the oppressed,
  gives food to the hungry.
The LORD sets captives free;
  the LORD gives sight to the blind.
The LORD raises up those that were bowed down;
  the LORD loves the just;
The LORD protects strangers;
  the fatherless and the widow he sustains,
  but the way of the wicked he thwarts.
The LORD shall reign forever;
  your God, O Zion, through all generations.
(Ps 146:7-10)

Have Patience; Be Firm

The desert flourishes, the arid earth becomes a verdant forest. This change is brought about right before our eyes. But we must determine its meaning and allow time for it to develop. Christian faith, assured of the return of the Lord—"His coming is at hand" and "The judge stands at the gate"—is essentially related to patience. The word occurs four times in the four verses of the Letter of James read this Sunday (James 5:7-10).

The image of the farmer is eloquent. Farmers know that wheat puts forth a shoot under snow. They do nothing to hasten its growth. "See how [the farmer] awaits the precious yield of the soil." Everything comes in its season. But make no mistake: if patience is a human virtue, a healthy attitude, in regard to the coming of the Lord, it becomes an authentically Christian virtue, a component of faith that is characterized by steadfastness.[9]

Similarly, the peace that flows from it is not just peace of mind, or a matter of temperament. It is, rather, based on faith, which shuns all spitefulness, grumbling, and turmoil in time of distress. It is an imitation of God himself, patient and slow to anger.[10] It is the fruit of the Holy Spirit, of grace, and a mark of the true Christian. "The fruit of the spirit is love, joy, peace, patient endurance, kindness, generosity, faith, mildness, and chastity" (Gal 5:22). "Because you are God's chosen ones, holy and beloved, clothe yourselves with heartfelt mercy, with kindness, humility, meekness, and patience" (Col 3:12; see Eph 4:2).

The prophets are examples. Mistreated, sorely tried, they never wavered, never doubted God, and despite all pitfalls, pursued their mission. And what about Jesus' example!

The disciples hold fast: they wait in patience, like fruit ripening for the final harvest at the coming of the Lord.

Happy Are Those Who Persevere Because of Me

Waiting for harvest time puts patience to the test. What is worse, however, is the temptation to reject whatever comes because it doesn't correspond to one's idea of what was anticipated. It seems that John the Baptist knew this, but he at least had the wisdom to doubt his own judgment and not get caught up in the problem (Matt 11:2-11).

Preaching conversion, "for the kingdom of heaven is near," he exhorted the people to "flee the wrath that comes." He already saw the axe "at the base of the trees" that do not produce good fruit, and which will soon be "cut down and thrown into the fire." He described the one "greater" than he as holding "the winnowing-fan in his hand," preparing to "clear the threshing floor," and burn the straw "in unquenchable fire" (Matt 3:1-12: Second Sunday).

For reproaching Herod because he was living with his brother's wife, John the Baptist was arrested and imprisoned in the fortress of Machaerus, near the Dead Sea. Here, news came to John of the preaching and works of Jesus. Was he perhaps confused by the attitude of the one whom he had baptized? Did he doubt his own judgment? Whatever the case, he sent his disciples to ask Jesus: "Are you the one who is to come or do we look for another?"

The reply forces John again to judge for himself. He knows enough Scripture to recognize the references to the prophecies of Isaiah: "The blind recover their sight, cripples walk, lepers are cured, the deaf hear, dead men are raised to life" and, above all, "the poor have the good news preached to them."[11]

Can we suppose that John sang his *Nunc dimittis* when his emissary came back with Jesus' reply? Jesus' praise of the Precursor allows us to understand that, in fact, the Baptist knew well the meaning of the message, and that he died believing in the one whom he had announced. In any case, the response is perfectly understandable to the Christian familiar with the initial preaching of Jesus of Nazareth (Luke 4:16-22), and the Sermon on the Mount (Matt 5:1–6:34), which in a sense summarizes the Gospel.

But this saying of Jesus is also applicable to the Church. It is through these same works that we recognize the one whom the Lord has sent. The Church is truly present when it announces the good news to the poor, not only in words but also in actions. "Happy are those who find no stumbling block"—who are not scandalized—because of the Church and Christ, in whom it finds its very being!

We must remember this, because bishops, priests, and Christian communities often appear unconcerned about the poor, not merciful enough to the weak, etc., and such a scandalous situation does not correspond to our idea of the Church and its mission. Instead of invoking God's vengeful anger against sinners, we see the Church presenting itself as the manifestation of the merciful tenderness of the Lord! We become disappointed, even resentful, much like Jonah felt when he saw that God had decided not to punish Nineveh (Jonah 4:1). "Happy are those who find no stumbling block in me."

John the Baptist and Jesus

While John's envoys return, Jesus speaks to the multitudes about John the Precursor. His words must be understood—in the Christian context—of John the Baptist's relation to Jesus.

The characteristic traits of John the Baptist are emphasized from the beginning. In the first place, there is his unshakable firmness. He showed nothing, in fact, of the appearance of a reed bending in the wind, he who bent before no one. He was just like Jeremiah, of whom the Lord said: "Be not crushed on their account. . . . For it is I this day who have made you a fortified city, a pillar of iron, a wall of brass, against the whole land: Against Judah's kings and princes, against its priests and people" (Jer 1:17-18).

At the same time, this prophet of the desert, clad in camel's hair, with a leather belt around his waist (Matt 3:4), was extremely austere in his living habits. Even in his manner of dress he recalls Elijah, who wore "a hairy garment, with a leather girdle about his loins" (2 Kgs 1:8).

Without a doubt, he was a prophet "and more than a prophet." No wonder the multitudes wondered if he was the Messiah (Luke 3:15)!

To take a further look at John and his mission, one must consider "what is written." We read in the Book of Malachi (3:1): "Lo, I am sending my messenger to prepare the way before me." When this prophecy comes from Jesus' lips, "before me" becomes "before you" (Matt 11:10). The change, in itself, is minimal, but it is loaded with meaning. The word "you," for us Christians, points to Jesus himself. Consequently, what Malachi announced about the coming of the "Lord God" is taken by Christians as referring to the earthly coming of Jesus. To recognize John the Baptist as the precursor of whom Malachi spoke is to recognize Jesus as the Lord in whom dwells the glory and power of God himself.

On close examination, we find another teaching. The mission of John, and of saints in general—of all precursors—of the Church, of each Christian, is not to focus attention on themselves, but to direct it to the Lord whose witnesses they are—each according to his or her own vocation—in the midst of humanity.

The Greatest and the Least

"I solemnly assure you, history has not known a man born of woman greater than John the Baptizer. Yet the least born into the kingdom of God is greater than he."[12]

The first part of this formal declaration—"I solemnly assure you"—is easily understood in light of the previous affirmation: John is a prophet, and "more than a prophet." But what is meant by the following, which truly is a paradox?

John is great, the greatest among all in their earthly existence. One must admit to this and not have the slightest doubt about the part played by the Precursor in the glory of the kingdom to come. The Roman canon places him highly among those who belong to the community of the blessed, to which we ask that we may be joined one day. He is also among the saints invoked in each of the three other Eucharistic Prayers.[13]

But what significance does this man's greatness have, a man blessed with charisma and other spiritual gifts, in view of the kingdom of heaven? When the the seventy-two who were returning from their mission told Jesus that "even the demons are subject to us in your name," Jesus shares in their joy, saying: "I watched Satan fall from the sky like lightning." But he adds: "Nevertheless, do not rejoice so much in the fact that the devils are subject to you as that your names are inscribed in heaven" (Luke 10:17-20). Admire John, yes, but above all see to it that we belong to the kingdom of heaven.[14]

We Proceed in Joy

Isaiah's prophecy assures us that we are on the right path, close to the end. He shows us "the parched land" that is progressively covered with wildflowers. Our cries of joy resound in the vastness of the desert to the point where it seems to cry out with us. In our enthusiasm, we say: "You too exult, cry for joy!"

Is this an illusion, a collective delirium? No, because all peoples, all the assemblies gathered throughout time and space, raise the same cries. The wind carries them to us, and these chants are so blended as to form virtually a great "symphony of a new world" that is endlessly amplified and enriched by new voices, new harmonies, and a wondrous variety of new sounds.

Certainly the road remains something of an ordeal; we still get tired. But, reechoing the encouragement of the prophet, which far exceeds our complaints and our shortness of breath, we say among ourselves: "Stand fast! Courage! Fear not! See the ears of the deaf opened, the lame and crippled dancing, the dumb singing for joy."

We are like prisoners who know that their liberator is at hand. They no longer fear the jailers who torture them. They remain prisoners, but "already" it is no longer an infamous thing. How many of our contemporaries have known such a liberation (First Reading)!

It is thus with a new tone of voice that they cry: "Come, Lord, save us!" Justice for the oppressed, bread for the hungry, liberty for captives, sight for the blind, strength for the weary—this is to be "already" today. "The Lord shall reign forever" (Ps 146).

The tension between "already" and "not yet" is, and will remain, a part of the daily experience of the Church and of believers. It is a trial of faith and hope, but a vivifying trial that must reawaken the sustaining power of those who wait for the coming of the Lord. The example of the farmer helps us to understand: we live in a state of patience.

The seed of the kingdom has been sown. It grows even under snow and storm; it must yield its precious fruit. At the harvest—a traditional biblical image of the last day (Matt 13:24-43)—our astonished eyes will see that our patience has not been tried in vain, that the splendor of the fields, which but lately seemed to be arid land, infinitely surpasses what we imagined.

This has been said; now it must be believed. It is in God, in his word and his promises that we must believe.

It would be dangerous to wait for nothing; in the end, it would lead to neither sowing nor to growth. We would stand back, arms folded, waiting for the wheat to grow by chance. Perhaps we would just hope that while doing something else there would be some unknown "miracle" of a spontaneous harvest. That is not what Jesus said when he spoke of the wheat that grows by itself (Mark 4:26-29) or of the lilies of the field (Matt 6:28). Neither panic, which makes one helpless, nor impatience, which is a vicious circle, is called for. Neither can it be animosity among ourselves; that can only result in fruitless confrontations. What we must do is to collaborate, to practice trust and enthusiasm for working together, while we await the not-far-off coming of the Judge of the harvest whom we will find at our doorstep. Patience! Endurance! (Epistle).

John the Baptist is a living testament to this endurance and patience. He has ceaselessly followed his mission as precursor "in the desert of Judea," and it is he who pointed out to two of his disciples "the Lamb of God," who immediately attached themselves to Jesus (John 1:35-38). He was then able to retire, to leave the stage and give the entire scene to the One whose way he prepared (John 1:30). Thrown in prison for offending King Herod, he sent his own disciples to investigate the "first fruit of the harvest" that he waited for patiently.

Was he disturbed by the behavior of Jesus, who did not really fit the figure of the Messiah-Judge that he had imagined? And this in spite of his assured witness to the one who stood before him and whom the Spirit pointed out to him (John 1:29-34)?

These questions do not matter much, and they are always somewhat useless to ask, because the Gospel is not really concerned about a person's psychological makeup or the state of one's soul. One thing remains: Jesus' response to John's emissaries reveals to us the signs that point to the coming of the kingdom and the presence of the one whom the prophets announced.

From the beginning of his ministry in the synagogue at Nazareth, Jesus will call our attention to these same signs (Luke 4:16-21). They are signs that solicit everyone's involvement: "Happy are those who find no stumbling block in me" (Gospel).

Such is the case with all the signs and particularly with the greatest one of all, the sign par excellence, that of the Body and Blood of Christ, the sacrament of "already" and "not yet," memorial of the Lord and of his work of salvation, the pledge and anticipation of the realities to come.

But this sign suggests a decisive choice. Either one rejects it as scandalous ("This sort of talk is hard to endure") or else one receives it in faith ("We have come to believe; we are convinced that you are God's holy one" [John 6:60-69]). We hear this beatitude at each Eucharist: "Happy are those who are called to his supper."

> A voice cries out around the earth,
> God is approaching in the night;
> the seed of light
> is finally bearing fruit.

Behold the hour of the kingdom,
the dead tree flowers again;
but before the Son of man
who can stand?

In the East his day arises,
no one can escape his coming;
his word, like a sword,
lays hearts bare.

Only the poor find grace,
only the poor know love:
God invites them to take their places
near his eldest Son.

And the Lamb of new life,
God made flesh in our time,
each day under humble signs
comes before us.

Offer him your open hands,
take his body which is given for you;
his love will be your feast,
give him your faith.

March toward the City
where your eyes will see the Lamb.
Look to him for the road to follow,
leading to the new day![15]

Third Sunday of Advent—Year B

Joy, Prayer, Thanksgiving

Anointed by the Lord God for the Good News

The first reading for this Sunday consists of two passages from the Book of Isaiah: the announcement of a prophet sent by God to bring the good news to the poor and to proclaim a year of favor and a cause for rejoicing among the people (Isa 61:1-2, 10-11).

> The spirit of the Lord GOD is upon me,
>   because the LORD has anointed me;
> He has sent me to bring glad tidings to the lowly . . .
> To announce a year of favor from the LORD.

When hearing this reading, one immediately thinks of the first time Jesus preached, in the synagogue at Nazareth. On that day, having read this passage, he closed the book and said: "Today this Scripture passage is fulfilled in your hearing" (Luke 4:14-21). There is justification for the Christian interpretation of this scriptural passage. We cannot determine with certainty who the prophet was that pronounced it,[16] but gospel and Christian traditions have seen in it the figure of the Messiah to come, the announcement of Jesus—the Anointed One, i.e., the Christ of the Lord God. This interpretation is not only sound: Scripture itself—the Gospel According to Luke—and the Church, under the power of the Spirit, give it the ring of authority.[17]

But the earthly coming of the Messiah cannot be dissociated from the coming of the Lord at the end of time. The prophecy of the Book of Isaiah must be read according to this dual perspective, above all in the context of the liturgy of Advent. The "year of favor from the Lord" was inaugurated when Jesus appeared. "Today this Scripture passage is fulfilled," but it will be truly consummated when the Lord returns.

The Good News for the Poor

The recipients of the good news that the Anointed One of the Lord God is to announce are "the poor," the broken-hearted, "prisoners," and "captives." The first term inspires the others and explains them.

The theme of the "poor of Yahweh"—'anāwîm—is basic in the Old Testament and is found in all its richness in the New Testament. Etymologically, the Hebrew word for "poor" means "bowed down," an attitude of humble submission. The "poor of Yahweh" stand before God, whose benevolent kindness they recognize, whose mystery they adore, and for whom they wait with utter confidence. It is the cry of these poor—the persecuted, afflicted, and unfortunate—their form of prayer and protestation that we often hear in the psalms.[18] As friends and servants of God, they can count on him. It is to them that the kingdom of heaven belongs, as Jesus proclaims in calling them "blessed." These "poor" are, by definition, those who constitute the people of God.[19]

I Leap for Joy in God My Savior

This people of the "poor," when given the good news, "leap for joy" in the Lord; they "exult" in God their Savior.

In order to express this joy accurately, the Greek translators of the Old Testament used a word unknown in classical language. They wanted to express an outburst of joy that breaks forth in song, music, and dancing— an exultation, a trembling under the intoxicating breath of the Spirit. It is a complete celebration because God breaks in to make it so, to transform it. "He has clothed me with a robe of salvation, and wrapped me in a mantle of justice, like a bridegroom adorned with a diadem, like a bride bedecked with her jewels." It is difficult to express in words this enthusiasm that, slowly but surely, wins over all the nations who are called to the same praise, insofar as they benefit from the year of favor granted by the Lord.

No chant is more appropriate here than the *Magnificat*. It is the canticle not only of Mary but of all the "poor" that God calls together.

Every word of the *Magnificat*, woven with biblical memories,[20] can be sung by the Church, the pilgrim people that works to bring about a new evangelical order. For it to become our song of thanksgiving, we must be moved by the same sentiments that moved the heart of the Virgin. "May the soul of Mary dwell in you to glorify the Lord; may the spirit of Mary dwell in you to exult in God!"[21] By singing it, our soul is filled with these sentiments. In this way we prepare ourselves to receive anew the One who has come and continues to come, so that our joy may be perfect.

> My soul rejoices in my God.
>
> My being proclaims the greatness of the Lord,
>   my spirit finds joy in God my savior.
> For he has looked upon his servant in her lowliness;
>   all ages to come shall call me blessed.

God who is might has done great things for me,
    holy is his name;
His mercy is from age to age
    on those who fear him.

The hungry he has given every good thing,
    while the rich he has sent empty away.
He has upheld Israel his servant,
    ever mindful of his mercy (Luke 1:46-54).

Rejoice Always

After the *Magnificat*, the liturgy for this Sunday contains an extract from the First Letter of Paul to the Thessalonians (1 Thess 5:16-24).

It begins with an exhortation to rejoice "always." To understand this properly, one must realize that so many of the poor really do live in sorrow and anguish. It is not a question of trying or appearing to be happy in order to get rid of or hide a profound sadness, something that is impossible to do. That way, a person would be ignoring the fact that the Christian joy Paul speaks about is a fruit of the Spirit: "The fruit of the spirit is love, joy, peace, patient endurance, kindness, generosity, faith, mildness and chastity" (Gal 5:22); "The kingdom of God is . . . justice, peace, and the joy that is given by the Holy Spirit" (Rom 14:17). Furthermore, this joy, as a fruit of the Spirit, is not and cannot be separated from the other gifts of the same Spirit. It is ultimately on the certitude of faith that Christ grants the grace of God, opens the "day of salvation" (2 Cor 6:1-2) by inaugurating the reign of God, and that God will take us into glory, because "the Lord is near" (Phil 4:5).

Christian joy is therefore rooted in hope, and is invulnerable. Paul testifies to this: "I find my joy in the suffering I endure for you" (Col 1:24). "We are called imposters, yet we are truthful; nobodies who in fact are well known; . . . sorrowful, though we are always rejoicing" (2 Cor 6:9-10). The apostle was able to say that he was himself inspired by the example of the Churches of Macedonia: "In the midst of severe trial their overflowing joy and deep poverty have produced an abundant generosity" (2 Cor 8:1).

Pray and Give Thanks Without End

It is an easy step to go from constant joy to constant prayer, and vice versa, because the one is based in the confidence and hope that the other expresses.

God has made us "worthy to share the lot of the saints in light" (Col 1:12). He has "bestowed on us in Christ every spiritual blessing in the heavens! God chose us in him before the world began, to be holy and blameless in his sight, to be full of love; he likewise predestined us through Christ Jesus to be his adopted sons'' (Eph 1:3-5). Our march toward the fullness of salvation is the work of his benevolence (Rom 8:29-30; Eph 1:3-14). We ask him, in prayer, to bring to a good end what he has begun in us, and for the coming of his reign.[22]

Asking and giving thanks go together. One goes constantly from one to the other, as does the Eucharistic Prayer. This happens naturally, but also because ''God wills this in Christ Jesus,'' according to Paul.

Being Open to the Spirit and Recognizing Its Gifts

In certain places and communities, people are very much interested in extraordinary manifestations of the Spirit. In others, they are not held in high esteem. This was true even in Paul's time. Early on he had to remind the faithful of the primacy of love among the gifts of the Spirit (1 Cor 13:13), so that they would not misunderstand them. In each particular case, it is important to know what is actually present. Without hedging, the apostle here gives the general principle to which one can always refer: receive the ''charismatic gifts'' with sympathy but without naïveté; hold on to the ones through whom the Spirit truly speaks, that they may guide you, and discard the others.

Surely, we cannot suspect Paul of being unfairly prejudiced, given the extraordinary manifestations of the Spirit with which he was favored (2 Cor 12:1-10). He knew that these are precious gifts, that they can serve to edify, exhort, and comfort, indeed even to convert nonbelievers (1 Cor 14:1, 3-5, 12, 25). He wrote to the Corinthians: ''Thank God, I speak in tongues more than any of you.'' But he immediately adds: ''. . . in the church I would rather say five intelligible words to instruct others than ten thousand words in a tongue'' (1 Cor 14:18-19). He concludes: ''If anyone thinks he is a prophet or a man of the Spirit, he should know that what I have written you is the Lord's commandment. If anyone ignores it, he in turn should be ignored'' (1 Cor 14:37-38).[23]

He also sorrowfully acknowledged that there are ''false apostles,'' people who ''practice deceit in their disguise as apostles of Christ.'' He adds: ''And little wonder! For even Satan disguises himself as an angel of light. It comes as no surprise that his ministers disguise themselves as ministers of the justice of God'' (2 Cor 11:13-15). Therefore, ''Seek out the value of each thing. What is good, keep hold of; flee everything that bears the slightest mark of evil.''

Love is the supreme criterion. All that hinders the moral improvement of the Christian community or sows disorder "bears the mark of evil" (1 Cor 14:4-5, 19, 33, 40). A false charism that contradicts a certain truth contained in the gospel is to be rejected, for the Spirit and Christ do not oppose each other (Gal 1:7-8). It is Scripture that judges charisms, not vice versa.

Perfect and Without Reproach, for the Coming of the Lord

Paul recognizes the holiness of Christians in the works of charity, in joy, and in the life of prayer and thanksgiving. This sanctification, though it requires active cooperation, is fundamentally the work of "God who, in his good will toward you, begets in you any measure of desire or achievement" (Phil 2:13). The call to faith is a sure sign of it, since God is faithful: he has not called us in vain; he does not lose interest in us.

Sanctification is aimed at the whole person, body and soul. It remakes us in the image of the Creator (Col 3:10).

It does not focus on ourselves, rather it prepares us to receive "the coming of our Lord Jesus Christ."

John the Baptist, Precursor and Witness to the Light

Beyond his historical role, John the Baptist is the one whose person and preaching continues to prepare us for the coming of the Lord. It is significant that, in the great and densely packed prologue to the Fourth Gospel, we read a phrase about the Precursor and, immediately following, his firm witness to Jesus (John 1:6-8, 19-28).

We notice immediately the solemnity of this introduction to the Precursor: "There was a man named John sent by God" (v. 6), parallel to that of the first verse, "In the beginning was the Word." The evangelist John, like the Synoptics, especially Luke, shows the Precursor's relation to the Son of God made flesh. He does this in the prologue, thus underscoring the importance of the Baptist's mission in the mystery of salvation that the Son has accomplished, he "who is in the bosom of the Father" and "has brought us to know him," he through whom "we have received grace upon grace."

The hierarchy is well defined between Christ and the Baptist, whose dignity is nonetheless affirmed. "He himself was not the light," but he came "as a witness to testify to the light, so that through him all men might believe." Truly, "history has not known a man born of woman greater than John the Baptizer" (Matt 11:11: Third Sunday, Year A). He is, moreover, unequaled as a model for believers who, in their own vocations, have given witness to the Light "that all might believe" in the Lord.

What Do You Say About Me?

What John the Evangelist wants to say, in presenting the man sent by God whose name was John, does not only correspond to the manner in which Christians have understood the mission of the Baptist; he has, in fact, without the slightest ambiguity, declared who he was. And he has testified to John the Baptist in a manner that almost seems like an official inquest.

We should not be surprised that the priests and Levites sent messengers from Jerusalem to interrogate John. It was incumbent on them to pass judgment on the man and his mission and on the meaning and authenticity of what he was doing. They were careful, however, not to pronounce judgment based on their first impressions. Authority in the Church works similarly. It intervenes in situations when people give themselves permission to follow certain opinions uncritically, and thus risk being led astray.[24]

In John the Baptist's testimony, he cuts short any false notions: "I am not the Messiah." The response is decisive: "I am not Elijah," who some thought would come again to anoint and manifest the Messiah,[25] although John may indeed have come, as Luke says, "in the spirit and power of Elijah" (Luke 1:17).[26] Finally, one last denial: " 'Are you the prophet?' 'No.' " But what does this mean?

The title "prophet" occurs twice in the Fourth Gospel. After the multiplication of the loaves, "When the people saw the sign he had performed they began to say, 'This is undoubtedly the Prophet who is to come into the world' " (John 6:14). Again, some of those who heard his teaching in the Temple said: "This must be the Prophet" (John 7:40). He is easily mistaken for the Messiah. We can then understand that John responds: "I am not he."

There must have been a certain irritation in these responses, but John endured these cases of mistaken identity. Far from being naïve or sullen, or keeping others in doubt, he almost angrily, at least sharply, responds with a vigorous "No" to those who take him for someone else. To those who press him to give a positive response, he offers a text from Isaiah: "I am a voice in the desert, crying out: Make straight the way of the Lord"

(Isa 40:3).[27] Thus he is placed in relation to an Other, whose servant-precursor he is, an Other whose name we know: Jesus.

John's Baptism of Jesus

Knowing the one of whom John speaks, what "happened in Bethany, across the Jordan" has more meaning for us today than merely historical interest.[28]

First there is the matter of baptism. It is not surprising that it was of interest to John the Evangelist. In fact, his Gospel, more than the others, is "sacramental." It pays particular attention to signs and their meaning. What he calls "signs" are more commonly known as the "miracles" of Jesus. He sees them as actions full of meaning, and this is apparent to Christians familiar with the sacraments. Note that he often speaks of them in the context of a celebration. This is especially true in chapter 6 on the bread of life, which involves a Eucharistic reading of Jesus' discourse in the synagogue at Capernaum. He does not report the institution of the Eucharist, but he has retained from the Last Supper Jesus' teaching on charity and caring for one another, which are the graces proper to the Eucharist. This interest in signs and symbols is so apparent that one often has the impression that the evangelist left blank areas in his writing, perhaps suggesting that we take time to reflect on the sacramental nature of these things.

"I baptize with water." This detail—"with water"—which is a restriction, is followed by a dramatic pause. Christian readers find themselves thinking of another baptism: the one *they* received. Often, we see that the evangelist's teaching sustains this memory by dwelling on this sacrament instituted by Jesus, which remits sins and gives us the gift of the Holy Spirit (Acts 2:38-41). And so the Fourth Gospel cannot be read quickly, but demands a time for meditation.

From John's ministry and baptizing to Jesus's ministry, there is continuity and forward motion. The relation is that of witness to the Light and Light itself. John was explicit: "There is one to come after me, the strap of whose sandal I am not worthy to unfasten."

There Is One Among You

Of this one he designates, John the Baptist says: "There is one among you whom you do not recognize." Not even John knew him until the day when he saw "the Spirit descend like a dove from the sky, and it came to rest on him." This Spirit revealed to the Precursor the one "who is to baptize with the Holy Spirit" (John 1:21-33).

On the day after his testimony to the envoys from Jerusalem, John the Baptist, seeing Jesus come to him, declared: "Look! There is the Lamb of God who takes away the sin of the world! It is he of whom I said: 'After me is to come a man who ranks ahead of me, because he was before me'" (John 1:29-30). The following day, the Precursor sent two of his own disciples to follow Jesus. One of them was Andrew, who eagerly told his brother Simon: "We have found the Messiah" (John 1:35-42). According to the Fourth Gospel, the mystery surrounding Jesus did not last long, and it was John the Baptist who dispelled it. One might say that John the Evangelist speaks of the Precursor only because of the part he plays at this moment: he does not recall his birth, he merely alludes to his imprisonment—"John, of course, had not yet been thrown into prison" (John 3:24)—and his death can be inferred only through the Gospel's use of the imperfect tense: "John was the lamp, set aflame and burning bright" (John 5:35).

Nevertheless, the evangelist could not ignore the fact that several years later, missionaries of the first Christian community found, in Ephesus, some disciples of John the Baptist who received the gospel eagerly (Acts 19:1-6). It may be that Jesus, and later the apostles, addressed themselves at first to the disciples of John, who were prepared to receive the good news, and who would be living witnesses to the saying "One man sows; another reaps. I sent you to reap what you had not worked for. Others have done the labor, and you have come into their gain" (John 4:37-38). Whatever the case, the fact remains that by announcing, "There is one among you whom you do not recognize," John the Baptist acted as an authentic precursor: he prepared himself to recognize and receive the Lord, while allowing the Lord to reveal himself.

Humility and abnegation, yes. But also the joy of the sower who, in faith, participates beforehand in the merrymaking of the harvest, to which the Precursor witnesses: "You yourselves are witnesses to the fact that I said: 'I am not the Messiah; I am sent before him.' It is the groom who has the bride. The groom's best man waits there listening for him and is overjoyed to hear his voice. That is my joy, and it is complete. He must increase, while I must decrease" (John 3:28-30).

The Time of Expectation: Humble and Joyous

The season of Advent is a parable of the life of the Church and of each believer, hoping in joy and humility for the hour of the great rendezvous. It is the time when eyes are uplifted to the One who dispenses all gifts in unpredictable ways; the time of spiritual joy for those who do not obstruct the Spirit and misunderstand the prophets; the time when one looks ahead to the coming of God.

It is also the time for praying that God himself, by the coming of his Son, may inaugurate his reign and help us to reduce the distance that always exists between the little that we are and all that God has in store and prepares for us.

It is the time when we awaken to God by opening our hearts and awakening the very center of ourselves that listens and, already secure in his mercy like a child in the love of his parents, gives thanks at all times.

You are the Other for whom we wait,
Jesus, Word and response,
you are our only song,
Emmanuel in our silences.

Are you the one who is to come
to make our deserts bloom,
to free our hearts,
to bring our seeds to life
by the waters of the Jordan?

You are the Other for whom we wait,
Jesus, Source of living water,
you are the springtime for the grain,
Emmanuel in our deserts.

Are you the one who is to come
and who comes each day
to free our lives,
to stir up our breath
by the movement of your own?

You are the Other for whom we wait,
Jesus, the world's strength,
you are the Living One who returns,
Emmanuel, God-with-us.[29]

Good News, Rejoicing, and Song!

Joy, Cries of Joy, Songs of Feasting

The first reading for this Sunday, taken from the Book of Zephaniah, is like a psalm, which appears clearly when we view the text in stanzas (Zeph 3:14-18).[30]

In the first verse, four imperative verbs call for rejoicing: "Shout for joy! Sing joyfully! Be glad and exult with all your heart!" Far from being an isolated instance in prophetic literature, this invitation is characteristic of all evocations of the messianic age. Salvation and joy are synonymous. The Lord brings liberation to his people, freeing them from having to serve the sentence that sin had placed on them.

"Do not fear," said the angel to Mary when he came to announce to her that she would conceive and bear the Savior (Luke 1:30). "Do not be afraid!" says the risen Jesus to the women who came to the tomb on Easter morning (Matt 28:10). "Fear not," announces the prophet to Zion. For "the Lord, your God, is in your midst, a mighty savior."

These events enliven the joy and good spirits of God himself. Zion, "forsaken" and "desolate," becomes again the one the Lord calls "my delight" and "espoused" (Isa 62:4). He goes so far as to "sing joyfully because of her." This prophecy becomes abundantly clear in the framework of the liturgy of Advent. We are truly "at a festival."

> *Cry out with joy and gladness:*
> *for among you is the great and Holy One of Israel.*
>
> God indeed is my savior;
>   I am confident and unafraid.
> My strength and my courage is the LORD,
>   and he has been my savior.
> With joy you will draw water
>   at the fountain of salvation.
>
> Give thanks to the LORD, acclaim his name;
>   among the nations make known his deeds,
>   proclaim how exalted is his name.

Sing praise to the LORD for his glorious achievement;
   let this be known throughout all the earth.
Shout with exaltation, O city of Zion,
   for great in your midst
   is the Holy One of Israel! (Isa 12:2-6)[31]

Joy, Serenity, and Peace in the Lord

"Rejoice in the Lord always! I say it again. Rejoice!" (Phil 4:4-7).[32]

It is common to say that one rejoices because of a person—for what he or she brings or for what happens to him or her—or that one shares in another's joy. But "in the Lord" is a common turn of phrase in St. Paul. Of great theological importance, it implies union with Christ, source of all that is evoked—in this instance, joy.[33] It means, moreover, that joy cannot be held in check by anything, by any exterior tribulation (2 Cor 7:4; Rom 12:12). Paul writes: "For I am certain that neither death nor life, neither angels nor principalities, neither the present nor the future, nor powers, neither height nor depth nor any other creature, will be able to separate us from the love of God that comes to us in Christ Jesus, our Lord" (Rom 8:38-39).

This joy is not demonstrated in untimely and noisy manifestations, often more or less forced, or in paradoxical expressions of sadness and deep anxiety. It is, rather, marked by "serenity," as can be seen, for example, in certain invalids or the elderly. It is a joy, also, that guards against anxiety, this formidable evil from which so many of our contemporaries suffer, and that frequently goes hand in hand with the unshakable feeling of being abandoned by God.[34] Above all, it is an interior peace "in the Lord," a surrendering to his providence and love, which Jesus, in the Sermon on the Mount, makes a fundamental requirement for the kingdom (Matt 6:24-34).

This placing of oneself in the hands of God does not signify resignation or fatalism. The Christian confides his or her cares to God in prayers of supplication and thanksgiving. For how can one petition for today and tomorrow without remembering what one received yesterday and the day before?

Among all the gifts of the kingdom, peace, "the peace of God," is the supreme gift: it is "beyond all understanding." We ask for it at Communion, the moment when, with the Body and Blood of Christ, we receive the pledge of eternal life. For this peace is almost equivalent to blessedness. Nothing can ruin it, neither wars, nor persecutions, nor trials. It is the last word pronounced at the moment of death and at Christian funerals, as at the end of all liturgical celebrations, the Eucharist in particular: "Go forth in the peace of Christ"; "Rest in peace."

What Ought We to Do?

Luke presents the ministry of John the Baptist in a manner equal to that of the Fourth Gospel. Moreover, his account includes a distinct portion, which is found in the reading for this Sunday, that portrays the typical concerns and aspects of Luke's Gospel (Luke 3:10-18).

The evangelist first sets the scene among "the crowds who came to be baptized by John." Throughout the Gospel of Luke, "the crowds" press around Jesus, witnessing with their good will, their eagerness to listen to him. So it is here.

They ask John: "What ought we to do?" One could say that, by instinct, "the crowds" perceive that it is not enough to listen to a teaching: it must be put into practice. The Baptist preaches conversion. Good enough, but how are we to do that? John's response is simple. On the whole, he requires nothing extraordinary: "Let the man who has two coats give to him who has none. The man who has food should do the same!" This sharing exemplifies "simple" charity on behalf of those who lack the basic necessities of clothing and food. Jesus will make greater demands: "When someone takes your coat, let him have your shirt as well. . . . When a man takes what is yours, do not demand it back" (Luke 6:29-30). Nonetheless, "simple" charity is truly a sure sign of conversion. The poor know better than to be fooled by its absence: "If a brother or sister has nothing to wear and no food for the day, and you say to them, 'Good-bye and good luck! Keep warm and well fed,' but do not meet their bodily needs, what good is that?" (James 2:15-16).

The tax collectors are the second group to question John the Baptist. They are typical examples, in Luke, of those to whom Jesus was sent as a friend and merciful Savior. They address the Baptist with the respectful title "Master." He does not tell them to abandon their profession: "Exact nothing over and above your fixed amount"; do not use your position to enrich yourselves unjustly. Zacchaeus will go further, and spontaneously, when he encounters Jesus (Luke 19:1-10).

The third group, strangely enough, is composed of soldiers, undoubtedly mercenaries of Herod Antipas. They leave the ranks of "the crowd" in order to pose the question "What about us?" The response comes without hesitation: "Do not bully anyone. Denounce no one falsely. Be content with your pay"; leave the populace in peace; do not abuse your power through pillage and plunder.

This kind of writing is typical of Luke's style and thought. He often stresses the importance of action, above all in the social realm, and, in a word, effective charity. He does not give us a set of precepts or detailed rules, but he suggests concrete principles of action that each person must employ in his or her particular situation.

Luke's Gospel places clear demands on those who believe in the Lord. The text here deals with the constant state of conversion that must always be present, even for those who already believe. The concrete character of the text and Luke's ability to adapt to circumstances make it a model Gospel for all preaching and exhortation that strives to reflect the realities of life.

A Sermon for Today

John the Baptist—as the four evangelists witness—clearly perceived that his mission was to prepare the way for an Other who was greater than he. He said that his "baptism with water" was only a rite of penance and conversion. The one to come would baptize in the Holy Spirit. But he would also be the farmer who gathers the grain in his storehouse and burns the chaff "in unquenchable fire." In order to drive home this point, John the Baptist, playing on words, speaks of a "baptism" of fire.[35]

Jesus, the Messiah, is the Judge at the end of time. The faith of the Church and its prayer must not neglect this aspect of his role. Today—more than ever before—the imperative remains: to live "baptized in the Holy Spirit."

Good News: God Is Coming!

Luke summarizes John the Baptist's mission by saying that "He preached the good news." Moreover, the urgent calls of the Precursor are nothing, compared to the trials and tribulations that will precede the coming of the Power immediately after him. In the manner of the ancient prophecies, he proclaims in startling words that the Day of Judgment will be one that none can escape. Believers know this and never cease preparing for the day of reckoning. They follow their path of conversion, and their hearts overflow with joy and gladness. Why should they fear when the Lord is in their midst? What can trouble their serenity when they have assurance that God hears their petitions and will give them his peace?

During the season of Advent, which is not limited to just the four preparatory weeks before the celebration of the Lord's nativity, there is room only for rejoicing and song.

> Sound the trumpets in Zion, summon the nations;
> call the people together and tell them the good news:
> Our God and our Savior is coming.
>
> Proclaim the good news, let it be heard;
> tell it to everyone, shout it aloud.
> Our God and our Savior is coming.[36]

Monday Through Saturday—Third Week

The Missal and the Lectionary

The Prayers—both at the Liturgy of the Eucharist and in the Office—return insistently to our sinful condition, to the obstacles within us that may hinder the coming of the Savior. They never cease to appeal to the mercy of God.

> Hear our voices raised in prayer.
> Let the light of the coming of your Son
> free us from the darkness of sin. (Monday)

> Our sins bring us unhappiness.
> Hear our prayer for courage and strength.
> May the coming of your Son
> bring us the joy of salvation. (Thursday)

> You made a new creation
> through Jesus Christ your Son.
> May his coming free us from sin
> and renew his life within us. (Tuesday)

> Guide us with your love
> as we await the coming of your Son.
> Keep us faithful
> that we may be helped through life
> and brought to salvation. (Friday)

Full of realism, they are nonetheless cries of confidence. We address God, recalling that he has "made a new creation through Jesus Christ your Son" (Tuesday). We ask him that "the coming celebration of the birth of your Son bring us your saving help and prepare us for eternal life" (Wednesday); we hope to obtain his "long-desired coming." A keen awareness of our unworthiness does not keep us from saying: "May we find the joy of salvation in the coming of your Son."

At first, the atmosphere of these prayers seems strangely different from that of the Third Sunday of the year, the Sunday of joy (*gaudete*). But this gladness can make one forget that the coming of the Lord sets in motion a gigantic and dramatic battle between darkness and light: a combat that is harsh and uncertain for each of us, however assured one may be that the final victory will belong to the light.

The Lord has certainly already come: we can neither forget this nor act ignorant of it. As risen Lord, he has vanquished sin and death. But the battle between Good and Evil continues, much more virulent now that the last times are fast upon us. Each of us, whether we want to or not, finds that we are indeed involved and must take part. God will never cease coming until the day of the glorious appearance of the Son of Man. The time of Advent is today.

The Readings from the Old Testament continue to call to mind the various stages, preparations, and consequences of the Lord's coming.[37]

The oldest texts of the Bible have no difficulty in showing that pagans may prophesy whenever the Spirit of God seizes them. This is indicated, rather humorously, in the story of Balaam in the Book of Numbers, a portion of which is read (Num 24:2-7, 15-17: Monday).

This Balaam was a celebrated soothsayer whom the king of Moab had ordered to curse the Israelites, who were preparing to enter into the Promised Land. But "the spirit of the Lord came upon him." Thus in place of the desired malediction, he pronounced, instead, a benediction and a prophecy: "I see him, though not now; I behold him, though not near: a star shall advance from Jacob, and a staff shall rise from Israel."

This vision and prophecy have made their mark on the biblical and Christian tradition. They make one think, surely, of the star the magi saw that led them to Jerusalem, where they asked, "Where is the newborn king of the Jews?" (Matt 2:2). But there is also the fresco in the cemetery of Sts. Peter and Marcellus at Rome—dating from the first half of the fourth century—where one sees Balaam, standing, pointing with his right hand to an eight-sided rising star.[38]

Here, then—whatever his personality or influence on others for good or bad[39]—is a stranger to whom the Spirit gave "a true eye" to foresee the dawn of a new era. How can we fail to recognize Balaam as a figure for those who, more or less on the fringes of the faith and the Church, discern the "signs" of the coming, or the presence, of the Lord?; or of those believers and communities recently evangelized, whose eyes are more open than Christians of an older persuasion?; and Churches lately animated with vibrant missionary energy? This reminder is not intended to accuse or discourage us, but, on the contrary, to stimulate us and bring us to thanksgiving.

The texts from the Book of Isaiah read during this week are so many reiterated proclamations of the promise of the salvation that God prepares and that he alone can realize. But the universality of salvation is affirmed more and more. "I am the Lord, and there is no other. . . . There is no just and saving God but me. Turn to me and be safe, all you ends of the earth'' (Isa 45:6-8, 18, 21-25: Wednesday). ''Let not the foreigner say, when he would join himself to the Lord, 'The Lord will surely exclude me from his people'. . . . For my house shall be called a house of prayer for all peoples'' (Isa 56:1-3, 6-8): Friday).

The love of the Lord for his people is unfailing. ''The Lord calls you back, like a wife forsaken and grieved in spirit, a wife married in youth and then cast off, says your God. For a brief moment I abandoned you, but with great tenderness I will take you back. In an outburst of wrath, for a moment I hid my face from you; but with enduring love I take pity on you, says the Lord, your redeemer. . . . Though the mountains leave their place and the hills be shaken, my love shall never leave you nor my covenant of peace be shaken, says the Lord, who has mercy on you'' (Isa 54:1-10: Thursday).

This salvation will certainly not pass by a ''lowly remnant'': humble and modest people will put their trust in God after having been purified by the test (Zeph 3:1-2, 9-13: Tuesday). Because for all, ''those already gathered'' and others, participation in salvation is contingent upon faithfulness to God. ''Observe what is right, do what is just; for my salvation is about to come, my justice, about to be revealed'' (Isa 56:1: Friday).[40]

The Psalms that follow these readings prolong their meaning in prayer. In the course of the liturgy one must read or sing the verses without stopping, even if the repetition of the refrain after each stanza allows them to be interiorized quickly. In private—''go to your room, close your door'' (Matt 6:6). In a small group, one should return to the psalms at one's leisure for a more fulfilling prayer, prolonged in meditation in the freedom of the Spirit. This is what the ancients meant when they spoke of ''ruminating'' on the psalms, the selection of which is especially apt for this week in the Lectionary. To be convinced of this, it will suffice to read quickly, in the Missal, Psalms 25 (Monday), 34 (Tuesday), 85 (Wednesday), 30 (Thursday), and 67 (Friday). One moves easily from the world of prayer to recognizing how God makes his ways known to us; recalling his kindness, we give thanks; remembering his past gifts to us, we admire the ones he gives today with the knowledge that there will be still more marvelous gifts to come tomorrow.

> Your ways, O LORD, make known to me;
>   teach me your paths (Ps 25).

> Remember that your compassion, O LORD,
>   and your kindness are from of old (Ps 25).

I will bless the Lord at all times;
  his praise shall be ever in my mouth (Ps 34).

I will extol you, O Lord, for you drew me clear . . .
O Lord, you brought me from the nether world;
  you preserved me from among those going down into the pit (Ps 30).

Finally comes the beautiful Psalm 67, which expresses with admirable simplicity the universality of salvation.

O God, let all the nations praise you!

May God have pity on us and bless us;
  may he let his face shine upon us.
So may your way be known upon earth;
  among all nations, your salvation.

May the nations be glad and exult
  because you rule the peoples in equity;
the nations on the earth you guide.

The earth has yielded its fruits;
  God, our God, has blessed us.
May God bless us,
  and may all the ends of the earth fear him!

The Gospels[41] report the words of Jesus regarding the ministry and preaching of John the Baptist and the reception they received.

The parallel of two of these texts is read on the Third Sunday of Year A (Luke 7:19-23 and 24-30: Wednesday and Thursday = Mt 11:2-11). Luke adds only one detail to what Matthew wrote, but it is significant and very much in line with his Gospel: "The entire populace that had heard Jesus, even the tax collectors, gave praise to God, for they had received from John the baptismal bath he administered. The Pharisees and the lawyers, on the other hand, by failing to receive his baptism defeated God's plan in their regard" (Luke 7:29-30: Thursday). Much more than merely an account about various reactions to John, it is a warning addressed to Christians today.

Matthew makes the same point with the story of the two sons. One at first refused to obey his father "but afterward he regretted it and went" as he had been asked. The other immediately responded "Yes" to his father's order. But he did not do the work asked of him. Therefore, Jesus says: "Let me make it clear that tax collectors and prostitutes are entering the kingdom of God before you. When John came preaching a way of holiness, you put no faith in him; but the tax collectors and the prostitutes did believe in him. Yet even when you saw that, you did not repent and believe in him" (Matt 21:28-32: Tuesday).

The Gospels are eminently clear on this point, Matthew and Luke especially: in order to have a share in the kingdom, it is essential to show one's conversion through actions, not merely in words.[42]

Finally, we read, as at the beginning of the liturgical year, two Gospel texts that deal with the mystery of Jesus' person. One day when he was teaching in the Temple, "the chief priests and elders of the people came up to him and said: 'On what authority are you doing these things? Who has given you this power?'" They knew very well that he had not received such power from men, since they were the only ones who could have given it to him. Jesus did not answer them but, in his turn, posed them a question: "What was the origin of John's baptism? Was it divine or merely human?" They did not want to answer. If they said "divine," they would be reproached for not having listened to the words of the Baptist. But if they said "human," they would have reason to fear the crowd "who all regard[ed] John as a prophet." They therefore responded: "We do not know." Then, Jesus concluded: "Neither will I tell you on what authority I do the things I do" (Matt 21:23-27: Tuesday).

If it were just an occasion where Jesus very neatly avoided a trap for himself, our interest in this text would be purely anecdotal. But beyond opening up the question of the mysterious origin of Jesus—an origin that *we* know since we believe he is the Son of God—there is an important teaching contained here. Everything is held together in the revelation of God. One must understand the prophets in order to come to knowledge of the One whom they announce. More generally: Christian faith cannot ignore the Old Testament.[43]

The testimony of the prophets is essential for us. Jesus, of course, has no need of it. "I have testimony greater than John's, namely, the works the Father has given me to accomplish. These very works which I perform testify on my behalf that the Father has sent me" (John 5:33-36: Friday).

John the Baptist, like all prophets yesterday and today, is "the lamp, set aflame and burning bright" in order to lead us, in this night, to the Light "until the first streaks of dawn appear and the morning star rises in your hearts" (2 Pet 1:19). Then will our joy be perfect.

The Liturgy of the Hours

"The Lord is close at hand; come let us worship him." This invitatory refrain which opens the Office each day explicitly makes the daily prayer of the Third Week of Advent an extension of the Sunday liturgy, with the same atmosphere. At the same time we continue to read and meditate on the Book of Isaiah in the perspective of the coming of the Lord.

The Biblical Readings are taken from that part of the Book of Isaiah that is entitled, in the Jerusalem Bible: "Poems on Israel and Judah" (chs. 28–35).[44]

They begin with a stern warning to those who think they can rule their lives as if God did not exist or who, by their way of acting, grossly mock him, claiming to be able to take him to task.

> The Lord said: Since this people draws near with words only, and honors me with their lips alone, though their hearts are far from me, And their reverence for me has become routine observance of the precepts of men, therefore I will again deal with this people in surprising and wondrous fashion: the wisdom of its wise men shall perish and the understanding of its prudent men be hid.

> Woe to those who would hide their plans too deep for the Lord! Who work in the dark, saying, "Who sees us, or who knows us?"

> Your perversity is as though the potter were taken to be the clay: as though what is made should say of its maker, "He made me not!" Or the vessel should say of the potter, "He does not understand."

Then, without transition, a new oracle of consolation and hope.

> On that day the deaf shall hear the words of a book; and out of gloom and darkness, the eyes of the blind shall see. The lowly will find every joy in the Lord, and the poor rejoice in the Holy One of Israel. For the tyrant will be no more and the arrogant will have gone; all who are alert to do evil will be cut off . . . .

> Now Jacob shall have nothing to be ashamed of, nor shall his face grow pale. When his children see the work of my hands in his midst, they shall keep my name holy; they shall reverence the Holy One of Jacob, and be in awe of the God of Israel. Those who err in spirit shall acquire understanding and those who find fault shall receive instruction (Isa 29:13-24: Sunday).

In his love and mercy, the Lord cannot endure the oppression of his people. He is on the watch, waiting for the moment when he can bless them and raise them up to show his mercy (Isa 30:18-26: Monday). He will avenge the evil done to his own by those who confide in idols made by their own sinful hands (Isa 30:27-33; 31:4-9: Tuesday). It is toward him that one must turn in order to obtain salvation and not toward people who offer only illusory protection (Isa 31:1-3; 32:1-8: Wednesday). What a wonder that day will be!

> In those days the spirit from on high will be poured out on us. Then will the desert become an orchard and the orchard be regarded as a forest. Right will dwell in the desert and justice abide in the orchard. Justice will bring about peace; right will produce calm and security.
>
> My people will live in peaceful country, in secure dwellings and quiet resting places. Happy are you who sow beside every stream, and let the ox and the ass go freely! (Isa 32:15-33:6: Thursday).

But this day of restoration will also be a day of judgment: do not forget it.

> O Lord, have pity on us, for you we wait. Be our strength every morning, our salvation in time of trouble! (Isa 33:2).

"Who among us can do this?"

> He who practices virtue and speaks honestly, who spurns what is gained by oppression, brushing his hands free of contact with a bribe, stopping his ears lest he hear of bloodshed, closing his eyes lest he look on evil—he shall dwell on the heights, his stronghold shall be the rocky fastness, his food and drink in steady supply.
>
> Your eyes will see a king in his splendor, they will look upon a vast land. Your mind will dwell on the terror: "Where is he who counted, where is he who weighed? Where is he who counted the towers?" To the people of alien tongue you will look no more, the people of obscure speech, stammering in a language not understood.
>
> Look to Zion, the city of our festivals; let your eyes see Jerusalem as a quiet abode, a tent not to be struck, whose pegs will never be pulled up, nor any of its ropes severed.
>
> Indeed the Lord will be there with us, majestic; yes, the Lord our judge, the Lord our lawgiver, the Lord our king, he it is who will save us (Isa 33:7-24: Friday).

The Patristic Readings are taken successively from St. Augustine (Sunday and Friday), William of St. Thierry (Monday), The Imitation of Jesus Christ (Tuesday), St. Irenaeus (Wednesday), and Vatican II (Thursday).

In a sermon on the birth of John the Baptist, St. Augustine (354–430), with the analytical finesse and simplicity of expression for which he is famous, shows the place of the Precursor, who was "the voice," in his relation to Christ, who is the Word.

> John is the voice, but the Lord *is the Word who was in the beginning.* John is the voice that lasts for a time; from the beginning Christ is the Word who lives for ever.

Take away the word, the meaning, and what is the voice? Where there is no understanding, there is only a meaningless sound. The voice without the word strikes the ear but does not build up the heart.

However, let us observe what happens when we first seek to build up our hearts. When I think about what I am going to say, the word or message is already in my heart. When I want to speak to you, I look for a way to share with your heart what is already in mine.

In my search for a way to let this message reach you, so that the word already in my heart may find place also in yours, I use my voice to speak to you. the sound of my voice brings the meaning of the word to you and then passes away. The word which the sound has brought to you is now in your heart, and yet it is still also in mine.

When the word has been conveyed to you, does not the sound seem to say: "The word ought to grow, and I should diminish"? The sound of the voice has made itself heard in the service of the word, and has gone away, as though it were saying: "My joy is complete." Let us hold on to the word; we must not lose the word conceived inwardly in our hearts.

Because it is hard to distinguish word from voice, even John himself was thought to be the Christ. The voice was thought to be the word. But the voice acknowledged what it was, anxious not to give offense to the word. "I am not the Christ," he said, "nor Elijah, nor the prophet." And the question came: "Who are you, then?" He replied: "I am the voice of one crying in the wilderness: Prepare the way for the Lord."

"The voice of one crying in the wilderness" is the voice of one breaking the silence. "Prepare the way for the Lord," he says, as though he were saying: "I speak out in order to lead him into your hearts, but he does not choose to come where I lead him unless you prepare the way for him."[45]

On the subject of the prayer which prepares the way of the Lord, the bishop of Hippo said, in another sermon, that it is the desire of a heart filled with love.

For the desire of your heart is itself your prayer. And if the desire is constant, so is your prayer. The Apostle Paul had a purpose in saying: "Pray without ceasing." Are we then ceaselessly to bend our knees, to lie prostrate, or to lift up our hands? Is this what is meant in saying: "Pray without ceasing"? Even if we admit that we pray in this fashion, I do not believe that we can do so all the time.

Yet there is another, interior kind of prayer without ceasing, namely, the desire of the heart. Whatever else you may be doing, if you but fix your desire on God's Sabbath rest, your prayer will be ceaseless. Therefore, if you wish to pray without ceasing, do not cease to desire.

The constancy of your desire will itself be the ceaseless voice of your prayer. And that voice of your prayer will be silent only when your love ceases.[46]

This desire and this humble prayer will not be deceived, declares *The Imitation of Jesus Christ* (15th c.), in a series of sentences.

> If you know how to suffer in silence, you will surely receive God's help. Since he knows best the time and the way to set you free, resign yourself to him, for God helps you and frees you from all confusion.
>
> God protects and frees a humble man; he loves and consoles a humble man; he favors a humble man; he showers him with graces; then, after his suffering, God raises him up to glory.
>
> He reveals his secrets to a humble man and in his kindness invitingly draws that man to himself.[47]

God has first loved us that we may love him and that, by this, we may be saved.

> Truly you alone are the Lord. Your dominion is our salvation, for to serve you is nothing else but to be saved by you! O Lord, salvation is your gift and your blessing is upon your people; what else is your salvation but receiving from you the gift of loving you or being loved by you? That, Lord, is why you willed that the Son at your right hand, the man whom you made strong for yourself, should be called Jesus, that is to say, Savior, "for he will save his people from their sins, and there is no other in whom there is salvation." He taught us to love him by first loving us, "even to death on the cross." By loving us and holding us so dear, he stirred us to love him who had first loved us to the end.
>
> And this is clearly the reason: you first loved us so that we might love you.[48]

To those who love him, says St. Irenaeus (135–202), God grants the vision of what the prophets announced.

> By his own powers man cannot see God, yet God will be seen by men because he wills it. He will be seen by those he chooses, at the time he chooses, and in the way he chooses, for God can do all things. He was seen of old through the Spirit in prophecy; he is seen through the Son by our adoption as his children, and he will be seen in the kingdom of heaven in his own being as the Father. The Spirit prepares man to receive the Son of God, the Son leads him to the Father, and the Father, freeing him from change and decay, bestows the eternal life that comes to everyone from seeing God.[49]

To Philip who asked of him, "Lord, show us the Father," Jesus responded: "Whoever has seen me has seen the Father" (John 14:7-14). Christ is the personal fullness of revelation.

> To see him is to see the Father also. By his whole presence and self-revelation, by words and actions, by signs and miracles, especially by his death and glorious resurrection from the dead, and finally by sending the

Spirit of truth, he completes revelation and brings it to perfection, sealing by divine testimony its message that God is with us to free us from the darkness of sin and death, and to raise us up to eternal life.[50]

Behold, the times are coming when the Lord of justice
will fulfill his promise of Peace
for all men whom he loves!

"Happy the one who believed
that one day would be fulfilled
the words of his God
for all men whom he loves!"

He is coming to baptize
in the Spirit and in fire:
The One who is coming
comes on the clouds!

"Happy the one who believed
that one day would be fulfilled
the words of his God
for all men whom he loves!"

He is coming to harvest the good grain
on his beloved earth:
The One who is coming
comes victorious!

"Happy the one who believed
that one day would be fulfilled
the words of his God
for all men whom he loves!"

He is in your midst,
he dances in the midst of his own:
The One who is coming
comes for our joy!

"Happy the one who believed
that one day would be fulfilled
the words of his God
for all men whom he loves!"

Exult in faith,
give thanks to the Most High,
and may the peace of God
place us with Christ
on the day of judgment![51]

John the Baptist, Watchman and Awakener

At the center of the most theological passage of the Gospels, at the heart of that which evokes the mystery of the eternal generation of the Word and his coming into the world according to the Father's plan, we find this affirmation concerning John, the messenger of God, "who came as a witness to testify to the light, so that through him all men might believe" (John 1:7). A man, a name, a mission. It is difficult to define him, this witness to whom everyone yields pride of place, whom Jesus himself eulogized, but who knew well that he was not to detract from the brightness of the Sun whose coming it was his task to announce.

His place in the economy of salvation? Greater than all men born of a woman, greater than a prophet. Born at the end of the old covenant, already he no longer belonged to it. But he was also less than the least in the kingdom. Strange paradox. He hears the voice of the Bridegroom, and that is enough for him to rejoice. He is the Beloved, but he will not see the Bride because he is kept on the threshold, not entering into the festal hall. He called for austerity, for penitence, but the joy that surrounded his birth has something cosmic about it, since "many will rejoice at his birth" (Luke 1:14).

His special place in the Gospels is clear in the chapters Luke devotes to the infancy of Jesus. For Luke, the destinies of Jesus and John are intertwined: their annunciation, their circumcision, their growing up—everything indicates it and allows it to be foreseen. Their destinies will be parallel, even though Luke is careful to qualify the differences between them.[1] In spite of this parallelism, there is an enormous disproportion between their persons. Yet they are the only ones for whom the Christian liturgy has set aside days that celebrate both their births and deaths. To the summer solstice (c. June 24) responds the winter solstice (c. December 25), with its ever increasing light. In the memorial of the martyrdom of John, there is a prophetic announcement of the passion of Jesus.

The liturgy of Advent is well marked by the parallel between the Messiah and his Precursor. To better appreciate the distinctive features of this Advent figure John the Baptist, one must start with the proposed readings, without necessarily being limited to them.

John the Baptist, a Watchman Greater than a Prophet

One can speak of John and the spirituality of the desert.[2] The Baptist portrayed by the Advent readings appears appropriately "in the desert." To be precise, in the "biblical desert," that place of all spiritual resources, of all divine new beginnings. Was it not there that Yahweh "allured" Israel to speak to it heart to heart (Hos 2:16)? The desert invites a "return" to the origins of faith, to the ideal (now somewhat mythical) of a nomadic people in quest of a country, a kingdom, a Messiah. A solitary quest, in the face of the Alone. Ignoring idols, Israel follows its God presiding in the cloud, guiding the life of those who are called to great things: separation, renunciation, ascetic discipline, spiritual combat. All these are necessary for the instruction of the great pilgrims of faith.

This is the case with John, although the image he leaves us surpasses the stark nature of the desert. He does not live a detached life there, like the monks of Qumran. He does not flee the multitudes, as the monks of Egypt will do later on, unable to cope with annoyance. On the contrary, the Baptist cries in the desert in order to be heard: must he not prepare the way of the Lord? Thus he speaks, exhorts, and receives visitors. He recruits disciples without demanding that they leave their livelihoods or normal social environment, and for a long time, they will be a tightly knit group of one mind. Again, if John has the reputation of someone who "does penance," he does not necessarily appear as a role model for asceticism, in the manner of Macarius the Egyptian: locusts and wild honey are the normal fare of the nomad in the wilderness.

One gladly associates him with biblical prophets like Elijah and Elisha. He has their abrupt and colorful speech, their apocalyptic imagination, and even the classical garb of camel's hair (2 Kgs 1:8; Zech 13:4). For a long time, the lion-like roar of prophetic speech was not heard in Israel (1 Macc 9:27; Amos 3:8). With John, it seems suddenly taken up again. Could he be Elijah, whose return is expected at the end of time as the precursor of the Messiah, and who is to purify the sons of Levi and reestablish concord among men (Mal 3:1-3, 23-24)? In this fierce prophet, the son of the priest Zechariah and Elizabeth, who was of the line of Aaron, one can see the resurgence of the fiery Elijah the Tishbite (Sir 48:1).

Jesus sees in John "more than a prophet," and Elijah himself, faced with great men who were called prophets, rejected the title—he, the defender of monotheism. Amos attributes this to several people he holds in poor esteem (Amos 7:14). Later, Isaiah and Jeremiah will also avoid the title. These men, so greatly blessed by the Spirit, are too conscious of what distinguishes them from "institutional" prophets, those attached to the sanctuaries: they are, instead, the thunderous mouthpieces of God, they speak "for" God and take a back seat to their mission.

It is well known how the spiriting away of Elijah in a chariot of fire fed the imagination of Judaism after the Exile (2 Kgs 2:11; 1 Macc 2:58; Sir 48:1). They wait for his return: he will appear just before the day of Yahweh, and he will prepare the way for the messenger of the covenant (Isa 40:3; Mal 3:1). When the Baptist cried, "Make ready the way of the Lord," people believed that Elijah had returned.[3] Worried perhaps about antagonizing other baptists, to which some passages of the Book of Acts testify (Acts 18:25; 19:3-4), Luke rather tones down the personal traits of the Precursor. He would most willingly compare the Baptist to Jeremiah,[4] the first in a line of which John claimed to be the last: "The law and the prophets were in force until John" (Luke 16:16). John was not the great eschatological prophet that Judaism had expected. The Fourth Gospel confirms this interpretation, because the Baptist says explicitly that he is not Elijah (John 1:21-23).

In that case, "if you are neither the Christ, nor the Prophet, who are you, John?" (John 1:25). He is only a voice. John is only the voice of one of those watchmen that God promised to his people that never, "by day or by night, shall be silent" (Isa 62:6). Such a term, even if it is not attributed expressly to the Baptist, suits his role of sentinel well, persistently pushing sleep aside, waiting for the first rays of dawn, remaining always vigilant and on his guard. Exasperated by the long night of desire for salvation in the old covenant, it is proper for the Watchman to cry: "There he is, the one who is to come, and I am the Voice who calls everyone to turns towards him and repent" (Isa 21:8-11; Ezek 3:16-21; 33:1-9; Hos 9:8; Hab 2:1).

John the Baptist: The Awakener Who "Prepares the Way"
"Come" to bear witness to the light, John "came" to make known the Lamb of God to the people of Israel (John 1:7, 31). He is coming; he came: The verb suggests the divine mission that he made his own. Nevertheless, what humility there is in this witness! His role is crucial, but he ef-

faces himself before the Other. He points him out that he may advance, while John himself retreats. Voice for the Word, lamp for the Light, he represents the Old Testament, of which he is the highest summit, that must give way to the New Testament. But that voice! Meditating on the role claimed by John, St. Augustine notes that in the activity of the intellect, the word always precedes the voice, which expresses the word outwardly, and it follows:

> If John is the Voice, the Word is Christ. Christ is before John in the bosom of the Father, but he is after John with respect to us. . . . In this mystery, it is John who represents the voice. Otherwise, he is not the only one. . . . How many preachers has the Word, resting in the bosom of the Father, raised up! He sent the patriarchs, he sent the prophets. . . . The immutable Word sent voices, and after a great number of them, he descended in his own voice, his own flesh. All the voices that preceded the Word are, so to speak, attributed to the person of John. He is the symbol of all these voices.[5]

It is fitting for John the Baptist to be presented to us under this symbolic and mystical title as the Awakener par excellence. Having seen the heavens open and the Spirit descend and rest on Jesus, he can henceforth concentrate his whole task as sole witness: to point out, to designate the Messiah to the crowds, retreating gradually from their sight and detaching himself from them. The depiction of the crucifixion by Matthias Grunewald comes to mind, where the enormous finger of John leaps out from the dark base of the painting, pointing toward the crucified Christ: "Behold the Lamb of God!" John's prophetic role can be summarized as the announcement and identification of the One in whom there is salvation. After that, he will demonstrate one last time the attitude of all those who by following him become "servants of the Word": he will efface himself before the Word.

This title "Awakener" indicates that his role is not finished: he remains the Awakener till the end of time, he who prepares the way of one greater than he. His watchfulness that leads to the discovery of the hidden Messiah, his total openness to his mission, which involves self-effacement, establish his value beyond the old covenant as a sign for all those who contemplate a similar mission. We have seen that John possessed various qualities that are prerequisite to an evangelical mission: humility, joy, hope, and an authenticity of witness that is confirmed in his death. John is the herald of all the manifestations of the Lord because he prepares for all the Lord's comings by awakening hearts that slumber, by fascinat-

ing, with the zeal of his witness, "those from outside," enabling them
to foresee the coming of Christ:

> He preceded the Lord before his birth; he preceded him in his public
> life. . . . He preceded him to the realm of the dead, . . . that is to say
> before Christ descended to the realm of the dead to free them by his de-
> scent into hell. John the Baptist, before Christ, preceded him into the world
> of those souls who were imprisoned by death. He will precede him at the
> Last Day, the Fathers of the Church tell us; in other words, he will announce
> the final coming of the Lord who will judge the living and the dead.[6]

This role of Awakener, this way John has of preparing the comings of
the Lord throughout the historical unfolding of salvation, is fulfilled by
the Precursor for each nation, for all cultures that may yet stand in need
of evangelization. For the axe of his preaching will always be ready to
cut through the hypocrisies that lie in wait even for Jesus' disciples: must
we not always go beyond the "letter" of religion and prefer to choose
the "spirit" of it—the religion of the heart—which is the fervent wish of
all the prophets? Will not all human wisdom be surpassed by the Wisdom of the Absolute, to which John himself witnessed by his works (Luke
7:35)? Even today, his plowshare breaks open the soil to the seed of the
sower; John the Awakener calls religions, philosophies, and cultures to
be fulfilled by the imitation of Jesus. To walk behind the Messiah, to carry
his cross, to follow him to his death in order to be resurrected with him—is
this not the Wisdom of God that human wisdom has trouble understanding?

With John, the same meaning of the Absolute can and must be
awakened in all people, whatever race or religion they may be. For only
the gospel is "the" Way, the Truth and the Life, which belong to the
One who said, "Whoever has seen me has seen the Father. . . ." (John
14:9).

> There is a perpetual "Advent" of Christ, and this Advent contains John
> the Baptist. He is present for the final preparation that precedes every great
> spiritual manifestation or missionary activity, and he is present now.[7]

There is one last reflection on this portrait, which has some bearing on
certain aspects of the spirituality of Advent.

In Eastern Churches, above the "royal doors" before the altar where
the faithful communicate, Jesus' mother and John the Baptist are depicted,
each at the side of the glorified Christ. On one side the Watchman-
Awakener, on the other the perfect woman-at-prayer; the one who ends
the old covenant and the one who ushers in the new. To be fully human

is to integrate in our Christian souls these two aspects of this mystery. "Vigilance is masculine; kindness, feminine."[8] It is to the tenderness of Mary that the Baptist returns, to the one who is full of grace and thanksgiving.

Fourth Week of Advent

Let the clouds rain down the Just One,
and the earth bring forth a Savior.
(Entrance Antiphon)

The liturgy of the Fourth Sunday of Advent "fills us with joy."[1] It is like the vigil for a feast,[2] because the times are fulfilled: "The Virgin is with child and shall bear a son, and she will call him Emmanuel" (Communion Antiphon). This celebration unfolds with our eyes fixed on the manger, where Mary brings her child into the world. But one cannot lose sight of the fact that this birth is but the first step to Easter, and that its ultimate importance lies in the mystery of salvation in which we share.

Lord, fill our hearts with your love,
and as you revealed to us by an angel
the coming of your Son as man,
so lead us through his suffering and death
to the glory of his resurrection.
(Opening Prayer)

This is what happens each time we receive the Body and Blood of Christ in the Eucharist.

In this sacrament
we receive the promise of salvation;
as Christmas draws near
make us grow in faith and love
to celebrate the coming of Christ our Savior.
(Prayer after Communion)

Such is the liturgy. It always celebrates the whole of the indivisible mystery, even when it seems to be dealing with only one of its facets. Even when it focuses on one of the particular stages—like today—it is oriented toward the final stage, to the end of time.

In his love Christ has filled us with joy
as we prepare to celebrate his birth,
so that when he comes he may find us watching in
prayer, our hearts filled with wonder and praise.
(Preface for December 17-24)

137

The formulation has a double meaning; at least, one can understand it that way. Vigilance in prayer, and joy in preparing to celebrate the nativity of the Lord in our flesh, yes, but these are also fundamental attitudes of the Christian and the Church, waiting for his return in glory: he has come, he comes, he will come.

The prayers over the gifts merit some attention.

> Lord, may the power of the Spirit,
> which sanctified Mary the mother of your Son,
> make holy the gifts we place upon this altar.

Perhaps we don't think enough about the essential role of the Spirit and its invocation (epiclesis) in the heart of the Eucharistic Prayer. It is through the Spirit that the bread and wine become, sacramentally, the Body and Blood of Christ, as it was by the Spirit that the Virgin Mary gave flesh to the Son of God.

Fourth Sunday of Advent—Year A

Son of David, Son of God

It Is God Himself Who Gives the Sign

Each year, the Liturgy of the Word for the Fourth Sunday of Advent contains a prophecy that the Christian tradition has understood as an announcement of the birth of the Savior. The first (Year A) is the celebrated passage from Isaiah: "The young woman [virgin] shall be with child [shall conceive], and bear a son, and shall name him Immanuel" (Isa 7:10-14).[3]

In reading Isaiah, it is natural to want to know the circumstances in which the prophet was sent to King Ahaz. The king was actively preparing for the siege of Jerusalem by the kings of Damascus and Samaria. Isaiah said, "Take care you remain tranquil and do not fear; let not your courage fail before these two stumps of smoldering brands" (Isa 7:1-10). But Ahaz would not believe it. Rather, he was disposed to appeal to the king of Assyria, paying him tribute and acknowledging his lordship. Isaiah responded, "Ask for a sign from the Lord, your God; let it be deep as the nether world, or high as the sky!"

A "sign" is not necessarily a miracle, but an act that verifies the truth of a promise, that anticipates its realization and announces it.[4] Ahaz did not wish to accept the sign, because to do so would mean that he was declaring himself ready to accept faith.[5] So he tried to justify his refusal by professing a horror of putting God to the test, especially by demanding a miracle of him.[6] Isaiah was not fooled. "O house of David! Is it not enough for you to weary men, must you also weary my God?" But while leaving to Ahaz the responsibility for his attitude, God does not renounce Israel: he himself will give a sign.

Whatever may be the historical circumstances in which it was proffered—which are of no concern to the liturgy— it is the prophecy itself and its Christian interpretation that interests us.

Behold: A Young Woman Will Bear a Child

The sign that God gives is the birth of a child. It is a sign, because this birth is a promise of salvation. Moreover, he will bear the significant name Emmanuel, that is, "God-with-us."

139

A similar "sign" had been given in other circumstances and in similar terms.[7] But of all these prophecies, it is this one of Isaiah that is read today. Its messianic interpretation is the reason why *almah* is translated "virgin." One notes, too, that the son of Ahaz—Hezekiah—was not worthy of the name "God-with-us." He did not know for a long time how "to reject the bad and choose the good." His politics led to great calamities. He was definitely not the sign come from the Lord! It was necessary to reinterpret the prophecy.[8] Isaiah himself probably did so toward the end of his life, or perhaps one of his immediate disciples. The salvation announced to the people goes beyond the person of Hezekiah. The child, the "sign" of the salvation of God, will be no ordinary person, and he will come from David's lineage: the Messiah himself. When Jesus appeared, born of a woman—a virgin whose name was Mary—to whom the angel of God said: "You shall conceive and bear a son. . . . The Lord God will give him the throne of David his father . . . and his reign will be without end" (Luke 1:31-33), one could easily surmise that he must be the promised Emmanuel. Not merely one sign among many, but THE sign of God, in a way that none can imagine: "God-with-us." He is the one the Church prepares to receive anew in the sacrament—the sign—of the liturgy, whose coming the Church implores and whose salvation it fervently awaits.

> *Let the Lord enter; he is king of glory.*
>
> The LORD's are the earth and its fullness;
>   the world and those who dwell in it.
> For he founded it upon the seas
>   and established it upon the rivers.
>
> Who can ascend the mountain of the LORD?
>   or who may stand in his holy place?
> He whose hands are sinless, whose heart is clean,
>   who desires not what is vain . . .
>
> He shall receive a blessing from the LORD,
>   a reward from God his savior.
> Such is the race that seeks for him,
>   that seeks the face of the God of Jacob.
> (Ps 24:1-6)

Jesus, Son of God of the House of David

St. Paul's genius makes even a simple letter into a profound doctrinal and spiritual text that transcends time. What might have been a commonplace letter written on an old parchment remains a precious message for our faith and Christian existence today. Such is the case with the beginning of the Letter to the Romans, which we read today (Rom 1:1-7).

This text is most appropriate as we approach Christmas[9] because at its center is affirmation, a profession of faith in the form of a hymn to Christ.

> The gospel of God
> that he promised long ago through the prophets,
> as the holy Scriptures record . . .
> concerning his Son.
> Descended from David
> according to the flesh
> but was made Son of God in power,
> according to the spirit of holiness,
> by his resurrection from the dead:
> Jesus Christ our Lord.

What an admirable witness to the faith and tradition of the early Church!

Jesus Christ, our Lord, is the good news. Everything that concerns him, from his birth to his passion, is set forth in Holy Scripture, in the historical accounts and in the words of the prophets. This is a point that the New Testament insists upon,[10] one that Paul will condense into the famous formula: "Whatever promises God has made have been fulfilled in him . . . " (2 Cor 1:20). His double sonship is clearly affirmed: " . . . descended from David according to the flesh but was made Son of God in power, according to the spirit of holiness . . . " (Rom 1:3, 4). Note the Trinitarian character of this confession of faith that names the Father (God), the Son, and the Spirit. It would be difficult to find a better formulation for the solemn proclamation of the mystery of the incarnation.

This good news must be announced to "all the Gentiles" that they may know and honor the name of the Lord. Like us, they are called to "obedient faith."

The apostle who has been "set apart," that is, called by God to announce this gospel, is writing to Christians living in small communities in the great city of Rome, a world where paganism reigns supreme in its institutions, its world of thought, and its morality. But far from securing merely their own safety, these communities, filled with missionary zeal, reached outward to the often hostile exterior world. The apostles themselves could not remain to teach the little flocks they had assembled. But through letters, they were able to keep watch over the Churches they had founded. They stimulated them, established new communities, and rebuked them when necessary—all the while continuing to carry the good news to the pagans.

It is good to look at these examples. Even if a community is reduced to a handful of faithful to celebrate the holy mysteries, they are "by the call of God, the holy people," bearers of the good news who must "bring to obedient faith all the Gentiles." It is not our weakness and insignificance that we must consider, but rather our strength in him who has been made the Son of God "by his resurrection from the dead: Jesus Christ our Lord" who has called us and given us his message: who brings us the "grace and peace" that come from God our Father.[11]

Origin of Jesus Christ and the Mission of Joseph

The very ancient profession of faith read in the epistle this Sunday (Rom 1:3-4), and the apostolic preaching to which the Book of Acts[12] gives witness, proclaim that Jesus is the "son of David." Matthew highlights this title in the first verse of his Gospel,[13] in the genealogy that comes all the way to "Joseph the husband of Mary. It was of her that Jesus who is called the Messiah was born" (Matt 1:16).[14] Immediately following this, the evangelist tells us how the Davidic sonship fell to Joseph, while—as readers of the Gospel know—Mary, to whom he was engaged, "was found with child through the power of the Holy Spirit . . . before they lived together" (Matt 1:18-24).

Mary's virginal conception of Jesus is the fruit of an unprecedented initiative of God, an initiative that God alone enjoys, which he reveals to those whom he pleases. Joseph was "an upright man." How could he interfere and press his claim for Mary his fiancée to be his wife, she who was already "with child through the power of the Holy Spirit"? Facing such a mystery, must he not, rather, retreat quietly and in secret, leaving to God alone to pursue the plan for which he had chosen Mary? Such is the attitude of "the upright man" according to Matthew: he abandons himself to providence (Matt 6:25-34).

> Does something molded say to its molder, "Why did you make me like this?" Does not a potter have the right to make from the same lump of clay one vessel for a lofty purpose and another for a humble one? (Rom 9:20-21).[15]

Joseph, having thus unconditionally abandoned his prerogatives, and thinking only of retreating before the mystery in which he assumes he has no part, receives a revelation from God. "In a dream"—in a vision[16]—an angel appears and says to him: "Joseph, son of David, have no fear about taking Mary as your wife, for it is certainly by the Holy Spirit that she has conceived this child; but she is to have a son and you are to name him Jesus."[17]

We have spoken, appropriately, of the announcement to Joseph. This was not so much to explain to him about Mary's virginal conception but rather to reveal to Joseph what his mission was to be. As for the conception, it is absolutely extraordinary; it is a mystery, and Joseph understood this. He, the "son of David," far from retiring from the scene, must take Mary into his home. Joseph's acceptance of this situation and the role given him by God brings to an end the genealogy of "Jesus Christ, son of David, son of Abraham" (Matt 1:1).

Like Mary, Joseph believed in God, who sent his angel to him. He agreed to what was asked of him. He was completely submissive, as an "upright man," to the divine initiative. "When Joseph awoke he did as the angel of the Lord had directed him and received her into his home as his wife."

The Coming of Salvation in Our History

Advent celebrates the fidelity and constancy of God in the accomplishment of his eternal plan: the institution of the kingdom that the Lord's return will inaugurate and bring to its full and definitive manifestation. But this coming involves an earthly and historical phase—in the formal and modern sense of the term—which is not merely important but decisive for us and, in some way, for God himself.

It is decisive for us because it is within history that salvation comes to us, that we have the responsibility of freely accepting or refusing its grace, that we are called, personally and collectively, to take an active part in the coming of the reign of God.

For God, because—if one can speak in this way—he is personally and totally involved in this project he has begun and, without interruption, will guide toward its end. He has sent to our earth his only Son, "a man like us in all things but sin," whom he did not spare the supreme test of death, a death freely confronted in order to bring his mission to its end. It is he who, after the resurrection, gives us his Spirit in order to continue the work of universal redemption. Who would have imagined that God would go so far, that he would implicate himself in the history and destiny of humanity?

To wait for a "sign" from him: is this not "to put him to the test," while he dwells on high—we know not where—far off, unknown, inaccessible, and impassible? When such thoughts arise, let us listen to the words of the prophet Isaiah: "Is it not enough for you to weary men, must you also weary my God?" At all times, it is God who takes and keeps the initiative. "God-with-us" is his name. This is not a name without meaning or a way of saying that we have rights over him, that is, the power to call him to the rescue, that he is at the mercy of our interests be they most ambiguous or ignoble. The "sign" of his presence and initiative was given to us when he chose a young woman—a virgin—to give birth to the Savior. The very fragility of this sign—the birth of a child—is the most extraordinary, the most unexpected, and at the same time the most visible of the manifestations of the strength and love of the God who is faithful to his promises (First Reading).

Everything belongs to the Lord: "the earth and its fullness; the world and those who dwell in it." No one can "ascend the mountain of the Lord." "He whose hands are sinless, whose heart is clean" is the one who receives sanctity from on high. So "the race that seeks for him, that seeks the face of God" cries out in a shout of faith and hope: "Let the Lord enter; he is king of glory" (Ps 24).

Joseph, to whom "Mary, the mother of Jesus, was engaged" is the full model of the "upright man" who, not without an interior struggle when faced with the incomprehensible unexpectedness of the situation, remains open to what is revealed to him, that he may enter humbly and resolutely into the plans of God.

His first reaction to the mysterious conception is to distance himself from it. But God reveals to him that he has a mission to fulfill with regard to this child who will be called "Jesus, which means 'God saves' " and who will be the mysterious "Emmanuel" announced by an ancient prophecy. It is enough. He responds to this "annunciation" without hesitation, without posing any questions, and without the least delay. From astonishment to faith and submission of one's life by the reception of the word, extraordinary as it may be—this is the path for all believers and the Church itself to follow to respond to the call of God and his word (Gospel).

Today as always, this apostolic preaching of "obedient faith" is extended to "all the Gentiles." This is the good news promised by the prophets. It concerns the Son born of the house of David, established in the power of the Son of God by his resurrection from the dead—Jesus Christ, our Lord.

This is the beatitude of which we are "already" the beneficiaries, which nevertheless has "not yet" reached its full potential: "grace and peace from God our Father and the Lord Jesus Christ" (Epistle).

Good news, beatitude and grace for all times, but received with more

conscious ardor during the time of Advent. Memory (anamnesis) of
benefits of yesterday. Thanksgiving (eucharist) for the gifts of today.
Promise and pledge for tomorrow.

Rejoice, Joseph, son of David;
the Virgin will give to the world the Savior:
the word takes flesh.
The Word takes on a name.
Rejoice!
You will give the Son of God
the name he will bear among men:

"Jesus, God with us!
Jesus, Savior of the world!"

At this name,
the whole earth will rejoice!

Through this name,
all sin will be forgiven!

At this name,
every knee will bend!

Through this name,
everything will be given to us!

"Jesus, God with us!
Jesus, Savior of the world!"[18]

Fourth Sunday of Advent—Year B

Manifestation of the Announced Mystery

God Dwelling Among Us

Religious men and women have always dreamed of a close and accessible god, one whose presence can be placed "somewhere," eventually showing or imposing itself to the attention of all, where one can summon people for worship and prayer. Sacred enclosures, temples, sanctuaries, and churches express and concretize these most profound and admirable aspirations.

It is true that such "presence" can often be contested, especially where it borders on the profane and the ambiguous, and is transparently political. Some rulers or governments on various occasions have built, and continue to build, religious edifices for the purpose of consolidating or sacralizing their own power, of setting up a rivalry, of currying favor with parts of the population, or neutralizing them, etc.[19] The possibility of such deviations, however, does not warrant prohibiting a priori all construction of houses of God. Thus Nathan approved David's intention to build a temple without hesitation, and one must admit that the prophet was not lacking in discernment. We are surprised, then, by God's refusal and the message it sends to David. Let us try to understand its meaning and significance (2 Sam 7:1-5, 8-11, 16).

Nothing Can Limit the Freedom of God

This refusal by God does not mean that all sanctuaries are to be condemned. The prophet is not concerned solely with the construction of the Temple, whose undertaking and completion will fall to Solomon, the son of David. David's intention was excellent, but he undoubtedly gave his project an importance it did not deserve. This is what the prophet makes known to him on behalf of God, and the contents of this message have not lost their interest.

It is essential that we not lose sight of God's sovereignty, his complete and limitless independence. We cannot confine him to a place, not even to a magnificent temple (Acts 7:44-50). He remains free to manifest himself, to be present where he chooses, even outside any sacred precincts. The Bible has preserved this famous instance of God's freedom: One day, two men—Eldad and Medad—had not answered Moses' summons to the tent of reunion to which he had called seventy of the elders of the people. In spite of this, they received a share in the spirit that rested on Moses, and they found themselves able to prophesy like the others (Num 11:24-29).

The Gospels report that Jesus encountered men and women who lived outside the ranks of those people who assembled in or near the Temple: the Syro-Phoenician woman (Mark 7:24-30), the Samaritan woman (John 4:1-42), Zacchaeus (Luke 19:1-10), Levi (Matt 9:9-13), and many others—"tax collectors and sinners." From the Church's beginning, the Spirit itself intervened in startling ways so that the apostles might understand that the gospel and salvation were reserved not only for Jews: hence the baptism of Cornelius and his family (Acts 10:1-11:18) and the Council of Jerusalem (Acts 15:1-35).

It is God who chooses, who takes the initiative—not people. Nathan's prophecy should make us think carefully about those who are tempted to limit religion and the Church according to some sociological principle or current ideology.

Salvation rests on a covenant, on the presence of God at the heart of history. It does not fear the erosion that gnaws at the foundations of all temples and eventually transforms them into piles of ruins. For God, who is present everywhere, is not tied to any. It is to temples of flesh and blood that he addresses his promises.

Son of David, Dwelling Place of God

"The Lord also reveals to you that he will establish a house for you. Your house and your kingdom shall endure forever before me; your throne shall stand firm forever." It is not a temple made by human hands that David can rely on, but rather the stability that God will give to his house, from which will be born a son, the beneficiary of the promises.

This prophecy has long been a point of departure for discussing a characteristic theme of Revelation. This "temple theme" has undergone great development, first by the prophets and later by the Christian Church.[20] From the beginning, the Church has seen in it Jesus of Nazareth, cornerstone of the new temple of God that sustains all the other living stones (the believers) (1 Pet 2:4-10). God dwells among us in the

Body of Christ, son of David and son of God (John 1:14). His resurrected Body, living in the Church, is the true temple (John 2:20-22; 1 Cor 3:17). Vanquisher of all the powers of evil, he reigns forever in justice and peace (Matt 25:31-46). He has been enthroned next to the Father since the resurrection.

This marvelous fulfillment of the old prophecy does not prevent the Church from applying to Jesus the psalms that speak of a royal enthronement, that mix certitude, hope, and uneasiness (Pss 2, 72, 110, 132). In the person of the Word made flesh, conceived by Mary of Nazareth and born of David's lineage, the oracle pronounced by the prophet Nathan has seen its fulfillment. It is to the child born in Bethlehem, "the city of David," that the Father has sworn love and faithfulness, forever.

Hope and uneasiness. Not everything is firm. Acceptance and refusal are possible; the contest between light and darkness continues. The only thing certain is the unshakable faithfulness of God who has "the words of the eternal covenant."

> *Forever I will sing the goodness of the Lord.*
>
> The favors of the Lord I will sing forever;
> through all generations my mouth shall proclaim your faithfulness.
> For you have said, "My kindness is established forever";
> in heaven you have confirmed your faithfulness:
>
> "I have made a covenant with my chosen one,
> I have sworn to David my servant:
> Forever will I confirm your posterity
> and establish your throne for all generations."
>
> "He shall say of me, 'You are my father,
> my God, the Rock, my savior.'
> Forever I will maintain my kindness toward him,
> and my covenant with him stands firm."
> (Ps 89:2-5, 27, 29)

Rejoice, Mary, Privileged One of God

Nathan's prophecy sees its realization in Nazareth of Galilee. "The angel Gabriel was sent from God" into this obscure village (John 1:46) where lived "a virgin betrothed to a man named Joseph, of the house of David. The virgin's name was Mary."

When we read about the annunciation to Mary, we should do so carefully even though we are familiar with it. Nor should we be primarily concerned with a psychological or subjective commentary on the scene that it depicts. Luke does not report the exact words of the exchange between the angel and Mary. But with consummate artistry and extreme delicacy, he constructs a story that is the divinely authorized presentation of what Mary experienced, an experience that is itself incommunicable. In an admirably structured dialogue filled with references to the Old Testament, he relates the substance of the event to us. There is not the least concession to the picturesque or the anecdotal in this remarkable passage.[21] It was not written to satisfy our curiosity, but to reveal a mystery and nourish our faith (Luke 1:26-38).

In his brief presentation of Mary, each detail is calculated to prepare us for the revelation of the mystery: the angel is sent to a "virgin," betrothed to a man "of the house of David." The same is true about the first words of the angel. We usually speak of this as the "salutation" of the messenger of God, and the Lectionary conforms to this usage: "Hail!" Luke, it is true, uses the word *chaire*, which corresponds to the ordinary form of the Greek greeting. But he also knows the Jewish greeting *Shalom* (peace), which would be more natural in the Semitic context of the first two chapters of his Gospel. Thus there is every reason to believe that he chose *chaire* because of its primary meaning "Rejoice."[22]

"Full of grace" ("O highly favored daughter"—New American Bible). The Greek is *kecharitomene*, i.e., "who is the object of a singular favor." This is "grace" (*charis*), if one understands the term in the sense of a "gracious gift" granted by God. It can also be translated as "favored." Whatever the translation, it is not a matter of a word or phrase that calls attention to the merits of Mary, but a proclamation that she is the recipient of divine favor. This is what the *Magnificat* says: "God who is mighty has done great things for me."[23]

The first words of the angel are neither a banal beginning to the conversation nor a simple salutation. Combined with what precedes, "The Lord is with you" immediately evokes a whole ensemble of expectations and mysteries. How, really, could one not think of the promise of the child whom one prophecy called "God-with-us" (Isa 7:14)?

"She was deeply troubled"—not because of the praise that the angel bestows. Mary's trouble is not of the psychological order.[24] Luke says explicitly that she was troubled "by his [the angel's] words," wondering about their meaning. Mary wonders because she perceives that the angel's salutation has a hidden meaning: it is a mystery. The messenger confirms her intuition. He had said: "Rejoice"; he adds "Do not fear." He called Mary by her own name after having given her the title of "favored," justifying this by the fact that she has "found favor with God," that she is the object of a singular divine favor. Finally, the angel explains what he has announced by saying: "The Lord is with you."

You Will Conceive and Bear a Son—"Jesus"

The conception and birth of a son is at issue. The announcement is made at first according to a stereotypical formula that is found many times in the Bible.[25] His name? That name he will carry throughout history: Jesus, Jesus of Nazareth; the name under which we will invoke him because he is "God saves." Immediately afterward come the titles of the promised child, which are clearly messianic.

"Great" is fairly indefinite: this epithet was given to John (Luke 1:15). "Son of the Most High" says much more, and this title is reinforced by that of "Son of God," which follows it.[26] Then come quite clear evocations of the messianic dignity of the child to whom Mary will give birth: "The Lord God will give him the throne of David his father. He will rule over the house of Jacob forever and his reign will be without end." Thus, what is announced to Mary is in line with the messianic promises of the Old Testament. What was awaited in a more or less distant future is now realized. The framework of the promise is concrete: it concerns a child that Mary will conceive and bear who will carry a certain name: Jesus.

After this, the story leaps, with consummate artistry, over an obstacle that lies in the way of the mystery. Mary asks a question that prompts the angel to reveal the answer to all this.

A Virgin Conceives

"How can this be since I do not know man?" Since St. Augustine (354–430), the entire Catholic tradition has thought that Mary did not understand how to reconcile the motherhood announced by the angel with her vow of virginity. Friends and foes continue to debate this interpretation, an issue of limited interest. But Mary's holiness is by no means at stake. What the Gospel attests to can be stated clearly: that Mary, betrothed to Joseph, was a virgin.[27] The question that she asks the angel serves to introduce what follows concerning this virginal conception, that is, the unique intervention of the Holy Spirit.

This intervention is enunciated in two statements placed one after another: "The Holy Spirit will come upon you and the power of the Most High will overshadow you."[28] The first expression, or an equivalent one, is found often in the Old Testament. Luke says, with regard to the Pentecost that Jesus announces: "You will receive power when the Holy Spirit comes down on you" (Acts 1:8). It is familiar to us.

By contrast, the second statement is filled with meaning. It reminds us of the cloud whose shadow covered the tabernacle and symbolized the glory of God that filled the dwelling place (Exod 40:35; Num 9:18-22). It is used in the image of God as a bird who shelters those he protects in the shadow of his wings.[29] It also recalls the beginning of Genesis. "The breath of God—the Spirit—moved over the waters" that covered the empty and unformed earth, like a brooding bird that brings forth life.

The angel announces to Mary more than protective help; an intervention of both the Spirit and the creative power of the Most High will produce new life in her. What he has done in various ways from the beginning, the creator Spirit will do in Mary's womb, causing the virgin to conceive and bear a son. Whether or not she had previously vowed virginity, Mary will henceforth always be the virgin mother. This is the mystery that God has made known to us through the message of an angel.[30] The virtually inexpressible divine action and Mary's ineffable experience are presented with extreme delicacy in accordance with the biblical style of storytelling.

Jesus, Son of the Most High, Son of God

Because a virgin conceives, "the holy offspring to be born will be called Son of God." In the first part of the dialogue with Mary, the angel says that the child, to whom his mother must give the name Jesus, would have the messianic title "Son of the Most High." The progression from one title to another here is of primary importance.

We understand "Son of God" in its strongest sense when speaking of Jesus. But to express the mystery of the incarnation and the person of the Lord, we say "Son of God made flesh" or, to speak like John (John 1:14) and the Creed—"Word made flesh." Did "Son of God" have that meaning when Luke wrote his Gospel, usually dated around A.D. 80? Whether or not it did, this title, applied to Jesus, has a completely new and unique meaning. Actually, having been conceived by the power of the Holy Spirit, he has no other father than God.

Let us look at Jesus' genealogy according to Luke (Luke 3:23-38). From Joseph, who was supposedly Jesus' father, it goes back to "Adam, son of God."[31] Jesus, who himself has life directly from God, without the intervention of a human father, is also "son of God," although in a completely transcendent manner; "Son of God" is the title that reflects his relationship to the Father. The parallelism between Adam and Christ is singularly suggestive and full of extended theological and useful meanings. Jesus, the new Adam who has his life directly from God, is the founder of a new humanity. In him is found the origin of a new humanity. St. Paul—of whom St. Luke was a disciple—developed this typology.[32]

The Sign Given to Mary

The epilogue to the story is short and simple. Mary receives a sign: "Know that Elizabeth your kinswoman has conceived a son in her old age; she who was thought to be sterile is now in her sixth month." Mary hadn't asked for it, but such information—stylistically is required in heavenly announcements.[33] Furthermore, the annunciation is thus related to what has preceded it (Elizabeth's maternity: Luke 1:5-25) and what follows (the visitation: Luke 1:39-45). It ends with Mary's acceptance: "I am the maidservant of the Lord. Let it be done to me as you say."

The greatness of Mary's acquiescence to the will of God and the vocation to which she has been called needs no additional consideration. This unhesitating "yes" is sufficient basis for calling Mary blessed, the one who for her entire life listened to and kept the word, and always heeded the will of God. Yet it is an exaggeration to make the "fiat" of the annunciation the summit of the story. Why should one imagine that the Father and all heaven and earth waited anxiously to see whether Mary would agree to become the mother of the Savior? As if God, uncertain of Mary's response, wondered until that last moment whether his message would be received!

In a famous sermon, St. Bernard calls upon the Virgin, and begs her to give the angel the response the whole world waits for.[34] The abbot of Clairvaux brings into his sermon all those who have waited for the Savior since the time of Adam. They implore Mary not to be hindered by her humility, but to break her silence, and to pronounce the "yes" on which their salvation hangs. This superb passage is a fusion of Marian piety and oratorical style. The Gospel is content to say, with all the discretion and sobriety that comes with such a mystery, that Mary, the perfect servant of the Lord, has made the will of God her own.

Her "fiat" was nonetheless pronounced in complete freedom, a freedom so great that nothing could affect it. This is something we are not always able to understand, because our experience is so much the opposite. Not being able to quickly distinguish good from evil with certainty, and having to overcome various obstacles to move toward the good (while evil seduces us with ease), we hesitate, often unable to rid ourselves of the fear of not having made the right choice. On the other hand, the more one is enlightened by the light of God that dispels the shadow and fog of sin, the more one clearly sees the good and the true, and the more one possesses a freedom that nothing can hinder. This is what Mary was able to do because—"full of grace"—she was free from any trace of sin.

This does not mean that her choice was without merit. Jesus himself, in his agony at Gethsemani, had to overcome a final temptation in order to obey, without regret, the will of his Father. Nor does it mean that the Virgin of Nazareth at once perceived all that she was getting herself into by saying "yes" to God. She would be called to acquiesce throughout her life: when Jesus left her to be about the work of his Father; on Calvary, when she saw her child give up his spirit on the cross; at the upper room, where the Spirit was given to the apostles so that they might go, without her, to preach the good news to all the nations; and finally, at the moment when she left her earthly life to enter into glory as the mother of the resurrected Christ and of the Church.

For God, Nothing Is Impossible

These last words of the angel express a general principle.[35] His reminder, in the context of the annunciation, accentuates its importance for each of us. Certainly, Mary's vocation is without equal. God has done for her great wonders that no other person has experienced. She nonetheless owes everything to the divine initiative.

No one could have foreseen that this humble daughter of Zion would be chosen and prepared by God to be, one day, the virgin mother of the long-awaited Messiah. She herself knew only one thing: her ardent desire to serve the Lord. This disposition in faith always lets God display his almighty power in those who receive his word, though they be sinners. How many unexpected individual or group conversions witness that nothing is impossible for God! Typically, the grace of God works through the long winding paths of human free choice. Mary appears and gives birth to Jesus after many generations and centuries of convoluted history. Occasionally, obstacles disappear that were thought impossible to overcome, a planted seed of an idea is quickly brought to fruition, ancient prejudices are no longer invoked, the laws of nature itself yield to the fulfillment of God's plan.

Communities that were thought to be disappearing are suddenly revived and become active. The torches of believers from whom one had not expected anything great are suddenly ablaze, their dying flames revived. Dim light bursts into brightness. Earth previously uncultivated suddenly yields abundant harvests. Christ does not put off being born into this world: "Nothing is impossible for God."

Glory to God

The almighty power of the divine is such that it can be exercised even in gentle ways, seemingly feeble at times, but manifesting itself to the humble. The Almighty God does not rule as a sovereign, as a dominating conqueror. Nevertheless, he has "the power to command," "to call the Gentiles to obedient faith." This is the good news, "the mystery which now is revealed: it had been hidden for many ages, but today it has been made known." The beautiful hymn that ends the Letter to the Romans is a wondrous cry that is appropriate for the Church today (Rom 16:25-27).

Like Mary, we are, though in varying degree, full of grace, privileged, objects of divine favor. Receiving the mystery, our "yes" is thanksgiving: "Glory to God!"

"Lord," on this vigil of Christmas, "as the last step in creation . . . come as God made man."[36]

> Be not afraid,
> Daughter of Zion:
> the breath of God
> has filled your life.
> In you, the Most High
> takes on human form.
>
> "Virgin Mary,
> God makes you his dwelling-place."
>
> Blessed be the Lord, the Great King:
> his house will be rebuilt forever.
>
> "Virgin Mary,
> God makes you his dwelling-place."
>
> The Lord fills the heavens and the earth:
> What house can be built for him?
>
> "Virgin Mary,
> God makes you his dwelling-place."
>
> The Lord is our God
> and we, his people:
> He is coming to dwell among us.
>
> "Virgin Mary,
> God makes you his dwelling-place."[37]

Fourth Sunday of Advent—Year C

Fulfillment of the Promises

Reading and Correctly Rereading an Old Prophecy

The Liturgy of the Word opens with the proclamation of a well-known oracle of the prophet Micah, which calls to mind its first sentence: "You, Bethlehem-Ephrathah, too small to be among the clans of Judah, from you shall come forth for me one who is to be ruler in Israel" (Mic 5:1-4).

It is true that we often remember only this first sentence. To turn it into an "apologetic" reading requires only one step: "Eight centuries before Christ, a prophet clearly announced that the Messiah would be born in Bethlehem." We may also note that "all the chief priests and scribes of the people" clearly and without hesitation cited this oracle when King Herod asked them where the Messiah was to be born. Having received this information, the king sent the magi to Bethlehem. Afterward, deceived by the magi, who had not returned to tell him what they had found, he "ordered the massacre of all the boys two years old and under in Bethlehem and its environs" (Matt 2:1-18).

Such a reading of this prophecy cannot be fully satisfactory. On the one hand, it is limited to the first verse, as if the others were only more or less oratorical extensions of it. With this mind-set, one tends to go quickly to the end of the text, content with just the symbolic sense of the shepherd and peace.

On the other hand, when looking at Matthew's account (Matt 2:4-5), it is important to consider the literary genre of his infancy narrative (Matt 1–2), the story of the manifestation to the magi in particular, and the use of ancient prophecies in the first two chapters and in the rest of the Gospel.

Matthew insists that the prophecies have been fulfilled by Jesus. He interprets the major events of Jesus' life by appealing to "fulfillment of the prophecies."[38] This fact invites a closer, more exact, more fruitful reading of the prophecy of Micah. Only then will we discover the reason why it has been retained in the liturgy for this Sunday. It is an announcement of a coming, an advent. This announcement, which sustained the hopes

of believers in the Old Testament, still fires our hope and our expectation. The Lord has come, certainly. But he must come again. Between
these two advents is the time of hope, of vigilance, the quality of which
conditions us for our complete liberation.

Micah's prophecy is thus not a simple prophecy that we read in a self-
satisfied way because we know that Jesus was actually born in Bethlehem. It is not merely a "scriptural argument" in defense of the justification of our faith. Rather, these words of Scripture sustain our hope and
determine our expectation of the "not yet" of the Lord's full manifestation.[39] This ancient oracle still retains all its power. Even now, it affects
the Advent experienced by the community of believers, and strengthens
the fruitfulness of our vigil.

The True Shepherd

"You, Bethlehem-Ephrathah, too small to be among the clans of Judah,
from you shall come forth for me one who is to be ruler in Israel." This
sentence is rich with reminiscences and biblical themes. Bethlehem recalls
the anointing of David, when Samuel recognized in the youngest son
of Jesse the one whom the Lord had chosen (1 Sam 16:1-13).[40] God took
David away from his flock so that he might be the commander of his
people (2 Sam 7:8). And Micah's prophecy, influenced by the imagery
established in the Book of Ezekiel (Ezek 34), also announces a shepherd.
Jesus will make use of this image in proclaiming himself to be the true
shepherd (John 10:1-18).

"He shall stand firm," with the attitude of a judge. His authority comes
from "the strength of the Lord," and he will act "in the majestic name
of the Lord, his God." Moreover, "his origin is from of old, from ancient times." He has been chosen from all eternity to lead the flock.[41]
He will allow it to live in security, because he himself is peace. "Now
his greatness shall reach to the ends of the earth." All this expresses the
tension between the insignificance of Bethlehem and the universal grandeur of the shepherd that the master of the flock will raise up for it.

A Day Will Come

The importance and pertinence of Micah's prophecy comes from a phrase
that is found in the middle of the text, which it would be wrong to pass
over without meditation. "Therefore the Lord will give them up, until
the time when she who is to give birth has borne, and the rest of his breth-

ren shall return to the children of Israel.'' In just a few words, Micah announces the three themes that bear on the prophecy's gradual fulfillment. The times of abandonment are the beginnings of the pangs of childbirth, a birth that is the prelude to the final assembly.

If the rest of the brethren have yet to come, it is because they are still in exile. ''She who is to give birth'' recalls Isaiah's prophecy that is read on the Fourth Sunday of Year A: ''The virgin shall be with child, and bear a son'' (Isa 7:14), and what is proclaimed at midnight Mass on Christmas: ''For a child is born to us, a son is given us; upon his shoulder dominion rests'' (Isa 9:5-6).

If one remembers the angel's salutation to Mary (Luke 1:31-33), and even more the *Magnificat* (Luke 1:47-55) or the *Benedictus* (Luke 1:68-79), one can see that the Christian community has taken Micah's prophecy to be an oracle of today—for today. The liturgy of the vigil of Christmas understands this well. The Church, upon studying this prophecy,[42] understands it as words of both hope and warning. Who the prophet announced has been born. He has ''come out'' of Bethlehem, the shepherd who is ''peace on earth to those on whom his favor rests.'' And yet ''all creation groans and is in agony even until now'' (Rom 8:22), while the signs that precede the end are evoked as ''the early stages of birth pangs'' (Matt 24:8; Mark 13:8; Rev 12:5; Isa 66:7).

This is why, after proclaiming Micah's prophecy, the liturgy suddenly focuses on the one who has come—the ''now''—and the one who must yet come—the ''not yet''—and sings Psalm 80.

Lord, make us turn to you, let us see your face and we shall be saved.

O shepherd of Israel, hearken. . . .
From your throne upon the cherubim, shine forth.
Rouse your power,
    and come to save us.

Once again, O LORD of hosts,
    look down from heaven, and see;
Take care of this vine,
    and protect what your right hand has planted
[the son of man whom you yourself made strong].

May your help be with the man of your right hand,
    with the son of man whom you yourself made strong.
Then we will no more withdraw from you;
    give us new life, and we will call upon your name.
(Ps 80:1-3, 15-16, 18-19)

From the Annunciation to the Visitation

After a brief introduction, the first two chapters of Luke's Gospel (1:5–2:40) present themselves as a rigorously composed diptych. On the first panel is what concerns the birth of John the Baptist; on the second, the birth of Jesus. The parallelism is remarkable: announcements to Zechariah (Luke 1:5-25) and to Mary (Luke 1:26-38); the birth, circumcision, and growth of John (Luke 1:57-80), and of Jesus (2:1-40).

This symmetrical and progressive construction underscores the continuity of the two narratives (Old and New Testaments) as well as the subordination of John (and the Old Testament) to Jesus (and the New Testament). This continuity and subordination is concretely verified at the encounter of Mary and Elizabeth. As a sign to Mary, the angel told her of her cousin Elizabeth's pregnancy. From the moment Elizabeth heard Mary's greeting, the baby she carried leapt for joy in her womb, and she proclaimed the blessedness of Mary. Furthermore, in the story of the visitation, the relationship between John and Jesus is symbolized in the analogous relationship of their mothers. This holds our attention not because of any Judeo-Christian controversy, but because there is material here for reflection and meditation that may help support our faith.

The first sentence of the story merits a second look: "Thereupon Mary set out, proceeding in haste into the hill country to a town of Judah." "Thereupon," a vague word, seems to indicate Mary's hasty departure from the scene of the annunciation.[43] The angel gave a sign: it was an implicit invitation to go—not to verify, but to experience firsthand this astonishing event. Mary's haste does not necessarily refer to the swiftness of the journey[44] but, in biblical style, rather to an interior disposition[45] that makes one act with fervor and zeal.

What moves Mary is the intense emotion excited by the wondrous events (Luke 1:29-30), her joy (Luke 1:28, 44, 47-48), and above all the enthusiasm of faith (Luke 1:38, 45). All these sentiments will burst forth in the *Magnificat* (Luke 1:46-55).

The rest of the details are of little importance; Luke does not even bother to name the town that Mary went to or tell us anything about the journey. Rather, he dwells on what happens between the two women when they meet.

From the Angel's Salutation to Elizabeth's

Luke does not tell us whether Mary, upon entering Elizabeth's house, greeted her cousin with the customary "Shalom" or, perhaps having pondered during the journey about what the angel had told her, with something akin to "Rejoice" or "Let us rejoice". We do not know. We can assume, however, that Mary's voice must have betrayed something extraordinary, causing Elizabeth to be moved by the joy, peace, and grace that lit up her young cousin's face. In any case, at this first moment—Luke insists on this point (vv. 41–44)—Elizabeth perceived that she was in the presence of a great mystery, that Mary bore salvation in her, and that her own joyous greeting was announcing the divine presence: "Who am I that the mother of my Lord should come to me?"

"The baby stirred in my womb for joy." All pregnant women feel the child's movements in their womb and are aware of life within. But Luke uses a verb that implies a certain astonishing power or strength: "to bounce," "to leap," "to dance,"[46]—not merely "to stir" or "to move." Then Luke says that Elizabeth "cried out in a loud voice."[47] Such words do not seem appropriate—and Luke is a good writer—if they refer only to the natural joy or emotion conveyed by an old woman about to become a mother to her visiting young cousin, herself pregnant. This is a truly charismatic setting. The writing is comparable to those in the Old Testament and in the early years of the Church that described instances of the overflowing of the Holy Spirit. When she heard Mary's greeting, Elizabeth, "filled with the Holy Spirit, was moved to prophesy."[48]

This passage is essentially theological, and it must be understood in this perspective. It bears upon the relation between the Precursor and the one for whom he would prepare the way. John will speak one day of his joy at having heard "the voice of the bridegroom" (John 3:29). The story of the visitation anticipates this testimony. However, it is Mary who occupies center stage, and it is toward her that Luke turns our eyes.

Faith of Mary, Mother of the Lord, Blessed Among Women
It is a prophetic discourse that Luke puts in Elizabeth's mouth. Inspired by the Holy Spirit, these words, glowing with religious fervor and holy enthusiasm, are modeled along the lines of biblical lyricism: benediction and beatitude. They witness to an already active Christian reflection. Luke, in line with his theology, rightly bases them in the Holy Spirit.[49]

"Blessed are you among women and blessed is the fruit of your womb." Elizabeth's exclamation has become familiar to Christians, who continue to extol it from one generation to another. "Blessed are you," an exclusively religious turn of phrase, is frequently found in the Bible.[50] "Blessed" is Mary, in an incomparable manner,[51] she whom the angel greeted and called "privileged" and "highly favored," as no other creature.

It is because of her Son and by reason of her faith in the word that the Virgin is elevated to such joyous and wondrous blessedness. This Gospel establishes an authentic Marian piety by defining its Christological and theological orientation. This is also expressed in the Rosary: it begins with the recitation of the "Creed," and each decade of "Hail Marys" is bracketed by the "Our Father" and the Trinitarian doxology of the "Gloria."

Mother of the Lord, Mother of God

Elizabeth's outburst culminates in prophetically giving Mary the title "mother of my Lord." In the Old Testament, the term "Lord" designates the Messiah, as witnessed, among others, by Psalm 110: "The Lord said to my Lord." In the Gospel, this name has an overt meaning. Luke, who is writing nearly eighty years after the event, must know that this term will receive great respect. The Council of Ephesus (431) will define it and make its meaning forever sacred by solemnly proclaiming Mary the "Mother of God" (Theotokos), not as a completely new title but as the proper understanding of the given revelation, the meaning of which the Christian people had never hesitated to believe. Moreover, this definition by the third ecumenical council comes about as a corollary of faith in Christ as the Son of God. It is upon Christological faith that the veneration all Christians give to Mary is based.[52] They single her out as the supreme exemplar of the believer. Because she received the word of God in total, humble obedience, God's saving grace can display all of its strength in her. She is, therefore, the image—the icon—of the Church, ransomed by obedience to the Son of God made man and his perfect fulfillment of the Father's will.

"I Come, My God, to Do Your Will"

In God, the ideas of being, desiring, and acting are one and the same. Therefore, to conform our own will to his and to live in obedience to him is the only way of personally uniting ourselves to him, of becoming again what he willed and created: his image. Obedience to God is not simply a moral virtue; it is not merely servile behavior. Rather, it is the highest road—a mystical one—to the holiness that will transform us and divinize us.

This union with God is the vocation of all men and women who come into the world. But, as close to God as one can get—whether "highly favored," i.e., free from all sin like the Virgin Mary—there will always be a gulf—an abyss—beyond which is found the Holy One. Whatever the path traveled, no creature can be elevated to the transcendence of God.

Christ traveled a reverse path. He was near to God: he received the body of a man that moved according to the rhythms of the human heart. He handed over this body on the cross, consecrating his heart to the fulfillment of the Father's plan: "I have come to do your will, O God." This declaration must be taken in the strongest sense, says the second reading (Heb 10:5-10).

Divine and human will are indissolubly united in the person of Christ, man and God. In him, in his assumed humanity, all humanity is sanctified. In a single stroke he has obtained for all people, for all time, the remission of sins that traditional acts of worship had sought to obtain. There is always the dichotomy between the desire to make sacrifices and holocausts on the one hand, and adherence to the will of God on the other: thus, the hazardous and limited efficacy of cultic offerings. Like the Son of God who made to the Father an offering of his body, we are able to offer a sacrifice that is pleasing to God, being truly consecrated and united to the Father: "through him, with him, in him."

Nothing less than our freedom and responsibility are involved in this spiritual sacrifice. We must be more and more incorporated into Christ. "Obedience is better than sacrifice" (1 Sam 15:22). Real worship in spirit and in truth is that of a holy life, which the liturgy, the source and summit of all the activity of the Church,[53] brings together and transforms into the praise of his glory.

In Faith and Hope Toward the Coming of the Lord

Liturgical time intensifies one of the most dynamic components of believers and the Church: the reaching out in faith and hope to the coming of the Lord.

He has come, and Christmas celebrates that coming. He has proclaimed and instituted his kingdom. He has recalled his people from exile and reassembled them. Nevertheless, this is not yet the age of gold that one would have imagined. We live in faith and hope for the total fulfillment of the promises; this constitutes a test, and calls for a continual overreaching of ourselves.

Christ is the guarantor of our hope. In him we are sanctified; through him we can offer God new worship; with him we have access to the presence of the Father—all because of the obedience of the Son made man.

The Virgin Mary is the model of creaturely faith in the fulfillment of the promises. Everyone profits, in his or her own measure, from the blessedness of the one who, because of the fruit of her womb, is "blessed among women."

> At the fiery passage of the one who comes,
> The new song that Mary sings,
> The song of the poor whom God chooses,
> Echoes over the ancient world.
>
> A long defiance has held them captive,
> But God recognizes in them his Christ!
> The Son of man made flesh with them
> Drinks their cup and vanquishes their death.
>
> Open your hearts to God's holy battle,
> The Lamb will come to add his fire to it;
> Purge yourselves, for the time is short,
> Follow the road that love has traced.
>
> Your possessions tie your hands,
> Keep hold of nothing, you will be filled:
> You must lose everything and let rise up
> The new song that Mary sang.[54]

December 17
Through December 24

From December 17 to December 24, the Lectionary, the Missal, and the Liturgy of the Hours have prescribed formularies for each day. Usually, the preparatory week for Christmas begins with the Fourth Sunday of Advent.[55] It always involves at least one Sunday (which retains its own formulary) and in certain years, two.[56] That is to say, one never uses all eight available formularies. Nevertheless, it is worthwhile to examine all of them.

The Missal and the Lectionary

The entrance and communion antiphons express impatience for the day of the feast, and anticipate the joy of celebrating it.

> You heavens, sing for joy, and earth exult! Our Lord is coming; he will take pity on those in distress. The Desired of all nations is coming, and the house of the Lord will be filled with his glory. (December 17)

Under one form or another, this cry of hope and joy is taken up day after day. It is amplified more and more as the feast approaches. Arriving, so to speak, in sight of Bethlehem, where this long-awaited event will take place, we gather around the manger to receive the child and welcome him on this earth.

> Gates, lift up your heads! Stand erect, ancient doors, and let in the King of glory. (December 22)

> A little child is born for us, and he shall be called the mighty God; every race on earth shall be blessed in him. (December 23)

> The appointed time has come; God has sent his son into the world. (December 24)

> Blessed be the Lord God of Israel, for he has visited and redeemed his people. (December 24)

We turn also to the Virgin:

> Blessed are you for your firm believing, that the promises of the Lord would be fulfilled. (December 21)

And increasingly, we chant and meditate on certain phrases of the prophecies and apostolic writings that resound in our hearts.

> He who is to come will not delay; and then there will be no fear in our lands, because he is our Savior. (see Heb 10:37; December 19)

> The dawn from on high shall break upon us, to guide our feet on the road to peace. (Luke 1:78-79; December 19)

> A shoot will spring from Jesse's stock, and all mankind will see the saving power of God. (see Isa 11:1; 40:5; Luke 3:6; December 20)

> The angel said to Mary: you shall conceive and bear a son, and you shall call him Jesus. (Luke 1:31; December 20)

These Prayers place our own prayer in a much larger context: the mystery of the Lord's nativity. Some are centered on the approaching feast of Christmas and our spiritual preparation for it: the purity of an obedient heart and freedom from sin by the mercy of God (December 19 and 23); faith (December 18; joy (December 24).

Others ask God for faithfulness in serving him, the vigilance required to watch for the glorious coming of the Lord, the desire to shine like living lights when he comes (December 17, 21, 23, 24). The three comings of the Lord—in humility at Bethlehem and today, in glory tomorrow—cannot be separated. We are going to meet our Savior, the only Son who is made one with us, in order to partake in his divine life (December 17 and 22).

The preparation for a feast—especially a religious one—is always a time to become more aware of all that is involved, of the consequences of total participation. Moreover, it is a time for not sulking over any difficult tasks one may be given, but for laboring in joy. When all is ready, all that remains is to put on one's finest clothes, and forget all weariness.

The Liturgies of the Word speak of what might be called the immediate history of Jesus' birth: his origin, i.e., his genesis (Matt 1:1-17); the annunciation to Joseph (Matt 1:18-24); the announcement of the birth of John the Baptist (Luke 1:5-25); the annunciation to Mary (Luke 1:26-38); the visitation (Luke 1:39-45); the Canticle *(Magnificat)* of Mary (Luke 1:46-56); the circumcision of John (Luke 1:57-66); the Canticle *(Benedictus)* of Zechariah (Luke 1:67-79).

The reading from the Old Testament, chosen with the day's gospel in mind,[57] helps us realize that the event is in the context of the flow of sacred history, that it is one stage in the fulfillment of the plan of God, that it has to do with the mystery of salvation.

An ancient prophecy had said that authority would not depart from Judah "while tribute is brought to him, and he receives the people's homage" (Gen 49:2, 8-10: December 17). The genealogy given by Matthew mentions Judah among the ancestors of Jesus (Matt 1:1-17).

Today, we do not regard this kind of "proof-texting" as necessarily decisive.[58] But look at all the teachings that this list of Jesus' ancestors suggests! He is inserted into a truly human line that is not composed only of holy men and women. He did not fall from heaven. He is a man, in the most carnal sense of the word. Before this seed came to fruition, there were centuries of preparation throughout a long and circuitous history. It is impossible to dissociate the New Testament from the Old to understand Jesus—as person and event—without constant recourse to past history.

This "genesis" of Jesus is like a parable of the "genesis" of the Church and of our communities. Their origins also go way back in time. Coming out of a long line of generations where the good fruit barely avoided the bad, they will, in turn, give birth to future generations of believers until the time when all—the Mystical Body of which Christ is the head—will be perfect.

Furthermore, is it possible not to see, in the detail of this genealogy, the faithfulness of God that defies centuries and generations, and which cannot be swayed by the vagaries of human history?

The gospel of the annunciation to Joseph has already been read on the Fourth Sunday of Advent, Year A (Matt 1:18-24).[59] It is reconciled here with a prophecy that promises a "righteous shoot" to David, to whose line Joseph belongs (Jer 23:5-8: December 18). Openness to the Spirit is required for all of God's calls, however unexpected they may be. What is occasionally asked of a particular person is frequently required from an entire Christian community, and even more so from the whole Church.

John, the future Baptist, is born, not only of an old woman, but a sterile one (Luke 1:5-25). The gospel of the announcement of his birth is related to another miraculous conception—that of Samson—recorded in the Bible (Judg 13:2-7, 24-25: December 19). In spite of the wealth of scientific knowledge, which explains so many things, the origin of new human life is and always will be a mystery, a "miracle," in the sense that it cannot be reduced to the processes that favor or determine it. All life comes from an "elsewhere" that we give different labels to, but whose meaning always escapes us. Isn't this why some areas of scientific progress tends to upset us when it begins to experiment with genetic manipulation?

The gospel of the annunciation made to Mary (Luke 1:26-38), like the prophecy of the Almah (Isa 7:10-14: December 20), has already been read on the Fourth Sunday of Advent.[60] One day a young woman of Nazareth received a revelation that the messianic joy so often spoken of by the prophets would finally show itself, and that she had been chosen to be the first beneficiary of it: "Rejoice, Mary!" Without hesitation, she accepted this astonishing message and the mission it revealed, even if she did not realize all that was implied by the mysterious proclamation of her maternity. Servant of the Lord, she gave herself to him.

While admiring Mary, we see ourselves perhaps more clearly in Ahaz who, under the pretext of respect for God—by not testing him—rejected his calls, hanging onto his own selfish motives, which were so much more "reasonable." Simple people, more truly humble, are not taken aback by the sudden initiatives of God and his unexpected calls, even if they are not delivered by an angel!

The story of the visitation (Luke 1:39-45: December 21)[61] is gospel, the announcement of the good news of salvation, whose coming was understood by Mary and Elizabeth. The sign the Spirit told them about was there: the mysterious maternity of the virgin and of her cousin, "the sterile woman." Their vocations were certainly exceptional: one gave birth to the Precursor of the Lord, the other to the Lord himself. Nonetheless, both experienced the common condition of faith that involves hope in waiting. "Blest are they who hear the word of God and keep it" (Luke 11:28). For though the gifts and charisms be different, it is the same Spirit who requires that each man or woman accept what God says in forms adapted to his or her own situation.

Along with this Gospel, the Lectionary offers two readings for the price of one. The first is a passage from the Song of Songs, which is used infrequently in the liturgy (Song 2:8-14).[62] This book, which is a song of human love, is open to various interpretations and applications, as the mystics understood it. In particular, they have interpreted it as the quest of the soul for God, and the love of God for all people. During Christmastime, how would it be possible to read it without thinking about the coming of God that fills us with joy and wonder?

The second, taken from the Book of Zephaniah (Zeph 3:14-18), is an invitation to joy addressed to the "daughter of Zion". In it are certain terms and expressions that the angel used when he appeared to Mary: "Rejoice . . . Fear not . . . The Lord is with you."

On December 22 we read the Canticle of Mary (*Magnificat*), which concludes the gospel of the visitation (Luke 1:46-56). This is preceded by a passage from the First Book of Samuel that includes the canticle of Anna, with which Mary's Canticle has much in common (1 Sam 1:24—2:7). Entering into the spirit of these inspired songs is an excellent way to prepare oneself to celebrate the coming of God in Jesus, his Son, the Master—"gentle and humble of heart" (Matt 11:29)—who is to announce to the poor the good news of salvation. In order to appreciate these canticles, one must imitate Mary's sentiments. Praying them, despite all of one's personal obstacles, sets one on the road toward emptiness, the hunger and thirst that God alone can satisfy.

On December 23, continuing our reading of Luke's Gospel, we come to the circumcision of John and the bestowing of his name, almost synonymous with the name given Jesus: John, i.e., "God has been gracious," and Jesus, "God saves" (Luke 1:57-66). The first reading is a prophecy that announces the sending of a messenger charged with preparing the way of the Lord. According to Christian tradition, this prophecy is fulfilled in John the Precursor (Mal 3:1-4, 23-24).[63]

We bear the name "Christian," which means "of Christ," "anointed" by him with the grace of God. A name full of promises but also of responsibilities that we have to assume personally. Perhaps we are not always sufficiently aware of the significance of being called Christians. Nevertheless, it always places us, in the eyes of the world, in a relationship to Christ. At the same time, it makes each of us a precursor of the one who is yet to come into this world.

Finally, on December 24, we read the Canticle of Zechariah (*Benedictus*) (Luke 1:67-79) and the prophecy of Nathan who, speaking for God, promised David that his house would last forever (1 Sam 7:1-5, 8-11, 16).[64]

After the announcement to Mary, her encounter with Elizabeth, the birth of John, and the presentation of Jesus in the Temple, Luke has inserted canticles that express, in a unique way, the meaning of the event. They are always thanksgivings sustained by the Spirit. What else, really, could inspire our praise? Jesus himself will "rejoice in the Holy Spirit" the day he will give thanks to the Father for what he has revealed to the merest children (Luke 10:21).

Giving thanks is the most basic, most profound attitude of a believer before God. It sums up all other professions of faith. Why should we be surprised, then, that it is, under the name of Eucharist, at the heart of the Christian assembly at prayer? It is inseparable from the memorial (anamnesis) of the wonders that God has already accomplished and the invocation (epiclesis) for him to do the same among us, today and tomorrow. It moves inexorably from past to present and future.

David dreamed of a temple in which God would be present. Reality has surpassed his hopes. Zechariah foresees it, but without imagining that the compassionate heart of our God will go forth to make his dwelling among all nations. When, in our turn, we sing the *Benedictus,* we anticipate a fulfillment of the promises that goes beyond all that we dare hope for.

This collection of scriptural texts, designated for the liturgy for the Masses of December 17–24, constitutes an inexhaustible and always fresh storehouse of prayer and meditation during the last week of preparing for the celebration of the nativity of our Lord. If one could retain only one phrase each day, indeed even one word or a single expression, that would be rich nourishment—daily bread—for the journey.

The Psalms can be separated into three groups. In the first are those that have a distinctly messianic flavor. They have in common the evocation of the ideal king whose kingdom will be universal, who will reign with peace and justice, who will be the Chosen One promised by God. His coming is especially awaited by the poor and the weak, the oppressed and the insignificant. The Christian tradition has always applied these psalms to Christ. They are Psalm 72 (December 17, 18), Psalm 24 (December 20), and Psalm 89 (December 24).

Each one echoes the prophetic oracle they follow. The antiphons selected by the Lectionary clearly express their Christological interpretation, in view of the coming celebration of the Lord's nativity.

> Let the LORD enter;
> He is the King of glory!

In recalling the covenant made with David (Ps 89):

> Forever I will sing the goodness of the LORD.

Psalms 71 and 25 are confident supplications:

> For you are my hope, O LORD;
>   my trust, O God, from my youth.
> On you I depend from birth;
>   from my mother's womb you are my strength (Ps 71).

> The sins of my youth and my frailties remember not;
>   in your kindness remember me,
>   because of your goodness, O LORD (Ps 25).

As for Psalm 33, it is a song of joy and thanksgiving.

> Give thanks to the LORD on the harp;
> with the ten-stringed lyre chant his praises.
> Sing to him a new song;
> pluck the strings skillfully, with shouts of gladness.
>
> The plan of the LORD stands forever;
> the design of his heart, through all generations.
> Happy the nation whose God is the LORD,
> the people he has chosen for his own inheritance.
>
> Our soul waits for the LORD,
> who is our help and our shield,
> For in him our hearts rejoice;
> in his holy name we trust.

Inexhaustible praying of the psalms, in which new themes arise in light of scriptural meditation and salvation history—yesterday and today—has never grown tiresome or repetitive, even after so many centuries. Praying the psalms, learning to pray! There seems to be a psalm for every disposition, emotional and spiritual, of a person's soul!

The Liturgy of the Hours

The biblical readings are all taken from what may be called "Second (Deutero-) Isaiah," also called "The Book of Consolation" (Isa 40–55).[65]

At the time when these readings were first compiled, the people had been living in exile for some fifty years! It was certainly a painful time. But, paradoxically, it was also a time when, through severe trials, faith had been reawakened, and people began to look at their history in an attempt to better understand their present situation and to be able to determine their future in light of God's word. Much of the Bible was written at this time. There was a great deal of meditation on the preaching of the prophets—Jeremiah in particular. Once again the ancient texts were taken up. This recollection evoked not only what had happened a long time ago, but it also dealt with past Scriptures in a way that remains exemplary for us today.

The course of both ordinary and extraordinary history can reveal the means by which God will realize his plan. Of course, there is no way to interpret the "providence" of certain people's appearances. But, upon reflection, there are some individuals who can be considered as instruments by which the Lord is served. Cyrus was one of them: he allowed the exiled people to return to their ancestral home. It is the prophet who realizes that God is acting through this conqueror. Hence, the allusions to Cyrus and his deeds alternate with the constant recollection of the almighty power of God (Isa 45:1-13: December 17).

For the Lord is faithful to his covenant. Nothing can hold him back. He is the unshakable king in whom one can and must always trust.

> Hear me, O house of Jacob, all who remain of the house of Israel, My burden since your birth, whom I have carried from your infancy. Even to your old age I am the same, even when your hair is gray I will bear you; it is I who have done this, I who will continue, and I who will carry you to safety (Isa 46:3-13: December 18).

This is a virulent apostrophe to Babylon and, moreover, on the world that pretends to rely only on itself, on its strength, its wisdom, and its shortsightedness. We must read this text in light of our own possible complicity with the world: that we, too, may also rely on things, however important they may be, that can only lead to ruin.

> Go into darkness and sit in silence, O daughter of the Chaldeans, no longer shall you be called sovereign mistress of kingdoms. Angry at my people, I profaned my inheritance, and I gave them into your hand; but you showed them no mercy, and upon old men you laid a very heavy yoke. You said, "I shall remain always, a sovereign mistress forever!" But you did not lay these things to heart, you disregarded their outcome. . .

> Because you felt secure in your wickedness, and said, "No one sees me." Your wisdom and your knowledge led you astray (Isa 47:1, 3-15: December 19).

For paganism is still a temptation against which God constantly guards his own.

> Hear this, O house of Jacob called by the name Israel, sprung from the stock of Judah, you who swear by the name of the Lord and invoke the God of Israel without sincerity or justice, though you are named after the holy city and rely on the God of Israel, whose name is the Lord of hosts. . . .

> Because I know that you are stubborn and that your neck is an iron sinew and your forehead bronze, I foretold them to you of old; before they took place I let you hear of them, that you might not say, "My idol did them, my statue, my molten image commanded them." Now that you have heard, look at all this; must you not admit it?. . .

> For the sake of my name I restrain my anger, for the sake of my renown I hold it back from you, lest I should destroy you. See, I have refined you like silver, tested you in the furnace of affliction. For my sake, for my own sake, I do this; why should I suffer profanation? My glory I will not give to another (Isa 48:1-11: December 20).

With wonderful audacity, the prophet evokes God's sadness when he considers the happiness his people might know but which they ignore. Yet God's tears can give way to a joy that he invites us to share, now that our ordeal is ended.

> If you would hearken to my commandments, your prosperity would be like a river, and your vindication like the waves of the sea; your descendants would be like the sand, and those born of your stock like its grains, their name never cut off or blotted out from my presence.
>
> Go forth from Babylon, flee from Chaldea! With shouts of joy proclaim this, make it known; publish it to the ends of the earth, and say, "The LORD has redeemed his servant Jacob. . . ."
>
> See, some shall come from afar, others from the north and the west, and some from the land of Syene. Sing out, O heavens, and rejoice, O earth, break forth into song, you mountains. For the Lord comforts his people and shows mercy to his afflicted (Isa 48:12-21; 49:9-13: December 21).

God has the heart of both father and mother. His salvation is extended to all the nations. The pagans themselves, one day, will have a share in salvation.

> Zion said, "The LORD has forsaken me; my Lord has forgotten me." Can a mother forget her infant, be without tenderness for the child of her womb? Even should she forget, I will never forget you.
>
> See, upon the palms of my hands I have written your name; your walls are ever before me. . . . Look about and see, they are all gathering and coming to you. . . .
>
> Thus says the Lord GOD: See, I will lift up my hand to the nations, and raise my signal to the peoples; they shall bring your sons in their arms, and your daughters shall be carried on their shoulders. . . . Then you shall know that I am the LORD, and those who hope in me shall never be disappointed (Isa 49:14–50:1: December 22).

To those who may be inclined to forget, God recalls what he has done in the past so that they might experience it: his justice and salvation will always be there, from generation to generation.

> Listen to me, you who pursue justice, who seek the Lord; look to the rock from which you were hewn, to the pit from which you were quarried; look to Abraham, your father, and to Sarah, who gave you birth; when he was but one I called him, I blessed him and made him many. . . .
>
> Raise your eyes to the heavens, and look at the earth below; though the heavens grow thin like smoke, the earth wears out like a garment and its inhabitants die like flies, my salvation shall remain forever and my justice shall never be dismayed.

Hear me, you who know justice, you people who have my teaching at heart: fear not the reproach of men, be not dismayed at their revilings. They shall be like a garment eaten by moths, like wool consumed by grubs; but my justice shall remain forever and my salvation, for all generations (Isa 51:1-11: December 23).

The Lord comes. Arise! The day of joy and feasting is come.

Awake, awake! Put on your strength, O Zion; put on your glorious garments, O Jerusalem, holy city. No longer shall the uncircumcised or the unclean enter you.

Shake off the dust, ascend to the throne, Jerusalem; Loose the bonds from your neck, O captive daughter Zion!

How beautiful upon the mountains are the feet of him who brings glad tidings, Announcing peace, bearing good news, announcing salvation, and saying to Zion, "Your God is King!" Hark! Your watchmen raise a cry, together they shout for joy, For they see directly, before their eyes, the LORD restoring Zion.

Break out together in song, O ruins of Jerusalem! For the LORD comforts his people, he redeems Jerusalem. The LORD has bared his holy arm in the sight of all the nations; All the ends of the earth will behold the salvation of our God (Isa 51:17–52:2, 7-10; December 24).

The Patristic Readings offer five texts on the mystery of the incarnation and three on the Virgin Mary.

On December 17, we read an extract from a letter by St. Leo the Great[66] to the Empress Pulcheria.[67] In his simple and firm manner, this pope, anxious to present orthodoxy clearly, insists on the reality of Lord's humanity, on which the reality of salvation depends.

For unless the new man, by being made "in the likeness of sinful humanity," had taken on himself the nature of our first parents, unless he had stooped to be one in substance with his mother while sharing the Father's substance and, being alone free from sin, united our nature to his, the whole human race would still be held captive under the dominion of Satan. The Conqueror's victory would have profited us nothing if the battle had been fought outside our human condition.

But why has this intervention of God been so long in coming? The *Letter to Diognetus*, written anonymously in the second or third century, and read on December 18, is forced to respond to this objection.[68] It is true, says the author, God seemed to forget us. In reality, though, he was being patient, wanting us to become aware of our inability to attain the kingdom by ourselves. But "when our wickedness had reached its culmination, it became clear that retribution was at hand in the shape of suffering and death. The time came then for God to make known his kindness and power.'' In this way, the superabundance of the love of God and of his kindness toward men are made manifest.

> How wonderful a transformation, how mysterious a design, how inconceivable a blessing! The wickedness of the many is covered up in the holy One, and the wholeness of One sanctifies many sinners.[69]

How could this text not be related to the tone of St. Irenaeus[70] in the hymn of praise to the mercy of God?

> God is man's glory. Man is the vessel which receives God's action and all his wisdom and power. . . .
>
> He is the Word of God who dwelt with man and became the Son of Man to open the way for man to receive God, for God to dwell with man, according to the will of the Father.[71]

St. Hippolytus of Rome[72] insists on the fact that the mystery of God has been made manifest by the incarnation of the Word.

> When the Word was hidden within God himself he was invisible to the created world, but God made him visible. First God gave utterance to his voice, engendering light from light, and then he sent his own mind into the world as its Lord. Visible before to God alone and not to the world, God made him visible so that the world could be saved by seeing him.[73]

Let us rejoice! Let us rise up! In making his only Son ''the Son of man,'' God ''transformed the sons of men into sons of God.''

> Awake, mankind! For your sake God has become man. ''Awake, you who sleep, rise up from the dead, and Christ will enlighten you.'' I tell you again: for your sake, God became man.
>
> You would have suffered eternal death, had he not been born in time. Never would you have been freed from sinful flesh, had he not taken on himself the likeness of sinful flesh. You would have suffered everlasting unhappiness, had it not been for this mercy. You would never have returned to life, had he not shared your death. You would have been lost if he had not hastened to your aid. You would have perished, had he not come.

Let us then joyfully celebrate the coming of our salvation and redemption. Let us celebrate the festive day on which he who is the great and eternal day came from the great and endless day of eternity into our own short day of time.[74]

The Liturgy of the Hours also contains three texts concerning the Virgin Mary. First (December 20) is an extract from a sermon (previously discussed) of St. Bernard (1090–1153).[75] The abbot of Clairvaux gave free rein to his fervent Marian piety. He makes the whole world kneel at the feet of Mary, waiting for the response that she will give to the angel at the annunciation. This imploring is really a meditation on the mystery that God chose to fulfill through the Virgin of Nazareth, for the author knows perfectly well that she said: "Behold the handmaid of the Lord; be it done to me according to your word."

> Why do you delay, why are you afraid? Believe, give praise, and receive. Let humility be bold, let modesty be confident. This is no time for virginal simplicity to forget prudence. In this matter alone, O prudent Virgin, do not fear to be presumptuous. Though modest silence is pleasing, dutiful speech is now more necessary. Open your heart to faith, O blessed Virgin, your lips to praise, your womb to the Creator. See, the desired of all nations is at your door, knocking to enter. If he should pass by because of your delay, in sorrow you would begin to seek him afresh, the One whom your soul loves. Arise, hasten, open. Arise in faith, hasten in devotion, open in praise and thanksgiving.

Thereafter comes a passage from St. Ambrose (339–397) on the visitation (December 21).

> When the angel revealed his message to the Virgin Mary he gave her a sign to win her trust. He told her of the motherhood of an old and barren woman to show that God is able to do all that he wills.
>
> When she hears this Mary sets out for the hill country. She does not disbelieve God's word; she feels no uncertainty over the message or doubt about the sign. She goes eager in purpose, dutiful in conscience, hastening for joy.
>
> Filled with God, where would she hasten but to the heights? The Holy Spirit does not proceed by slow, laborious efforts.

A good pastor, the bishop of Milan always focused on his people assembled in the cathedral: we can have a share in the beatitude of Mary, to whom Elizabeth said "Blessed are you because you have believed."

> Let Mary's soul be in each of you to proclaim the greatness of the Lord. Let her spirit be in each to rejoice in the Lord. Christ has only one mother in the flesh, but we all bring forth Christ in faith. Every soul receives the Word of God if only it keeps chaste, remaining pure and free from sin, its modesty undefiled. The soul that succeeds in this proclaims the greatness of the Lord, just as Mary's soul magnified the Lord and her spirit rejoiced in God her Savior. In another place we read: "Magnify the Lord with me." The Lord is magnified, not because the human voice can add anything to God but because he is magnified within us. Christ is the image of God, and if the soul does what is right and holy, it magnifies that image of God,

in whose likeness it was created and, in magnifying the image of God, the soul has a share in its greatness and is exalted.[76]

As it must, the Liturgy of the Hours offers a patristic text on the *Magnificat*. It is taken from St. Bede the Venerable, a monk of Jarrow in England (c. 672–735). We remember especially his remarks on the thanksgiving that springs from the heart when language finds it impossible to express the greatness of divine favors.

"Mary said: My soul proclaims the greatness of the Lord, my spirit rejoices in God my Savior."

The Lord has exalted me by a gift so great, so unheard of, that language is useless to describe it, and the depths of love in my heart can scarcely grasp it. I offer then all the powers of my soul in praise and thanksgiving. As I contemplate his greatness, which knows no limits, I joyfully surrender my whole life, my senses, my judgment, for my spirit rejoices in the eternal Godhead of that Jesus, that Savior, whom I have conceived in this world of time.[77]

Mary and the Psalter

That Mary is one of the great figures of Advent is clear. The prophetic line of announcement and promise ended with John the Baptist, the summit of the old covenant. In the new covenant, it is Mary who begins and reflects the whole apostolic reception and communication of this promise. John is the voice that announces the advent of the Lord and calls us to repentance because of it. Mary already belongs to this advent, since she is its servant and minister, the first link in the living chain that culminates in the body of Christ.[1]

Why the Psalter?

Why, during Advent, do we link Mary with the Psalter? Because the psalms sung at this time express, better than others, the mystery of Mary? Certainly not. None of the psalms used in this liturgical season are properly called "Marian," though there are those for which the expression may have some meaning.[2] The way in which Jesus and the primitive community after him used scriptural argument should suffice to make us wary. For them, the beginning must be understood in light of the end. The fact that Jesus is the Messiah confers on such and such a passage of Scripture its deepest reality, heretofore unsuspected, discernible only when placed within the framework of the scriptural witness to Christ. The Old Testament says *what* the Christ is, the New Testament *who* he is. It is Christ who makes clear and, in a way, attributes any importance to the witness.

The same thing happens in the liturgy, where the approach to the Bible is "poetic": it encapsulates the totality of the mystery of Christ. From this Christological center we can make connections between texts, figures, events, and persons; their relationship is only revealed because they end in Christ Jesus. The mystery of Mary does not escape this law. The foundation for a Marian reading of Scripture consists in constantly seeing Mary "in light of the resurrection of Christ, itself deeply linked to his incarnation. Quite rightly, the annunciation connects the Virgin to Christ, the source of salvation, as well as to his task of restoring man to the pre-fall condition of Adam, through the resurrection, the crowning act of the passion of God."[3]

Then why the Psalter rather than another book? Because it is the lyrical prayer of Israel. More than any other, the symphony of the psalms evokes the longing, the impatience, the anguish, as well as the joy, of the soul, faithful in bad times to its savior. This is primarily the case with those known as the psalms of "the poor of the Lord," not to exclude many others that reflect the incredible range of people's sentiments in search of interior peace or confronted by the great questions of existence. "Tell me how you pray, and I will tell you who you are." It is especially in contemplating the prayer of the people of the Bible that we come upon the basic fact that inspires whole lives: a covenant between a "Thou" (God) and an "I" (personal or communitarian). The faith behind the great prayers of Israel is based on the One who is not only "the God of all ages" but also "the God of my victory" at the high points of both history and the liturgical life, as well as in the more banal contexts of daily life.[4]

The psalms follow the history of the people of the old covenant. Some psalms are quite ancient; others are from the period of the Exile, and some are even later. The canon of the Psalter seems to determine the end point of the psalms at the Maccabean epoch. Innumerable hands have collaborated, throughout the ages, to transmit its amassed heritage: sages, holy people, priests, simple temple-goers. Most of these people relied on ancient texts, and they emphasize meanings that prove a certain responsible spirituality. If Mary can be seen in a clearer light than what the Bible says about the Daughter of Zion, as well as Israel, Jerusalem, or the Temple itself, may they not be reflected for us in the Psalter, the "mirror" of the Bible, as it is sometimes called?

The Psalms, the Bible, and the Virgin Mary

There are two ways of discovering Mary in the psalms. The first is to look for things that prefigure her, so many rough drafts of which she is the final copy. The second, more interior, way, which conforms to the style of the Psalter, is to uncover the plan of divine benevolence, which step by step creates an example of ideal prayer: the Church, the new Israel, and Mary who is the perfect Daughter of Zion, but also the "Church before the Church," who personally collaborates, without hampering or weakening, with the coming of God in the midst of his people.

The Psalter's complexity clearly indicates these divine forces at work in history. They are recognized throughout the various prayer scenes that the Psalter's literary genres evoke.[5] First come the hymns, those psalms composed for a specific worship setting: they accompanied the morning and evening sacrifice of the holocaust offered in the Temple. But they were also associated with the sacrifices at Passover, Pentecost, and the feast of Tabernacles, commemorating extraordinary events in the national life. Offering praise to God for his manifestations in creation, exalting his mastery and universal lordship over history past, present, and future, these prayers sing also of the sanctuary, the dwelling-place of God, the Temple toward which one faced on the occasion of a pilgrimage or an official feast. The hymns of Israel respond to the need for adoring the One who is greater than all, and who can throw down or raise up whomever he pleases. He is the "Holy One." Therefore, we must show sacred respect before the One Above All, as well as joy, gratitude, and love, since he deigned to become the "Holy One of Israel."

Thanksgiving *(toda)* is the exclusive subject of some other psalms. Following upon Yahweh's benefits, whether for the whole nation or for specific groups or individuals, this thanksgiving accompanies the sacrifice offered *(shelem)* for the grace given, and it expresses the peace *(shalom)*, euphoria, and fraternal communion that result from it. Thus, the whole community is involved in praise when there is a happy event, even though the recipient of the benefit may be an individual or a group.

However, thanksgiving is not limited to happy events. Often enough, it grows out of trials, difficulties, defeats, and days of sorrow. Like a woman in childbirth, Israel has given birth to the Messiah in suffering. This is remembered in the liturgies of expiation that accompany the psalms of lamentation *(qina)*; the one praying weeps, but does not hesitate to ask of God "How long?" One also asks God "to be mindful . . . to raise us up." In prayer, there are numerous cries and questions thrust heavenward.

Other psalms, those described as having a wisdom character, are like so many votive offerings, like the offerings of ancient Egypt that were carried up to the hall of the sanctuaries. The Israelites, the People of the Book, inserted these prayers into the sacred collections, that they might bear witness to religious reflection on certain great questions: the fate of the good and the wicked, the providence of God for Israel, love of the law, the divine justice within the people of God. Some of these psalms often appear to contain short-sighted wisdom. Others echo the eternal questions. Still others, like Psalm 119 (which Pascal saw as the most beautiful of psalms, the one that most strongly foreshadows the mystery of grace), become familiar to us only by degrees, allowing their hypnotic incantation to act upon us.

Some psalms are individual plaints that are more difficult to understand and that defy categorizing. Were they composed for the liturgy or as spiritual canticles for private use? It is often impossible to ascertain whether these psalms involve several different literary genres, including lamentation and thanksgiving, evocation of the past and present, cultural complaints (which inspired the confessions of Jeremiah), and private expressions of individual sorrow, which themselves range between flashes of revolt and acts of faith in God, the final recourse in times of distress. The authors of these works are often looking among the "poor" who, after the Exile, the destruction of the Temple, and the end of the Davidic dynasty, had to purify their faith and find new sources of certitude.[6] This conjuncture of events furnished the occasion for a spiritual leap that caused certain groups to put themselves more readily into the hands of God, to be humble before him, and to be open to his plans. Poverty thus became the ideal for these "faithful of God," this remnant of Israel that began to take form and substance, something already predicted by various prophets.[7] The true Israel now establishes itself with a religion of the heart, with a mysticism aspiring to communion with God in a state of eternal blessedness, with acceptance of the divine gift that evokes a response from everyone.

One day Christ will describe himself as "gentle and humble of heart" (Matt 11:29), a phrase that recalls the spiritual stance evoked and summarized so precisely by the psalmist: "O Lord, my heart is not proud, nor are my eyes haughty; I busy not myself with great things, nor with things too sublime for me . . . " (Ps 131). Just before this, Jesus gave thanks to his Father, "for what you have hidden from the learned and the clever you have revealed to the merest children" (Matt 11:25). Mary will do the same in her *Magnificat*.

The Canticle of Mary (Magnificat)

Luke chooses to place a veil over Mary's soul: "She meanwhile kept all these things in memory" (Luke 2:51). Of her familiarity with the psalms, we know nothing. She abandoned her reserve only once in this humble, confident, and joyful prayer that we call the *Magnificat*. Nevertheless, arising from the depths of the ages and recalling the chant of Miriam, the sister of Moses, who welcomed Israel on the shores of the Red Sea (Exod 15:21), the Canticle of Mary breaks forth in numerous references to the psalms. Without a doubt, it expresses, in some way, the faith of the primitive Christian community and that of the Virgin herself, our "tambourine player," as Claudel called her. She, the first to be full of faith, has she not crossed the Red Sea of the new Exodus in the footsteps of her mysterious Son?

Both a fulfillment and a solemn new beginning, the Canticle of Mary is presented as a song of thanksgiving in a form much like the psalms of thanksgiving.[8] It appears at the end of the long, ardent hope of the "poor of Israel." At the end of a purifying advent, Mary, a child of Israel in the pangs of childbirth, utters through grace the perfect "yes," a word that thereafter will involve all humanity. "Yes" to the blessing that grace brings to birth in our world. "Yes" in blessed ignorance of the ways that God would choose to realize his promise. "Yes" for the whole human family that Mary represents at this moment before God.

Mary's vocation eminently suggests, during this season of Advent, how divine grace needs human soil in which to plant itself, and also how all vocations are revealed ever so slowly, becoming more and more purified, more and more uncovered, to the point where each of us—and the whole Church—can discover in the dim light of our night of faith the dawn of salvation, receiving it in darkness, from the incarnation to Pentecost.

First of the saved, the Virgin receives the Word that from the beginning was with God and that came in the fullness of time and will come again in this world in order to enlighten us. Virgin since her conception, she remains a virgin in her maternity, in bearing Jesus of Nazareth.[9] She submits to her calling early on, even before experiencing what the rigors of a faithful life might portend. Throughout her life, she is asked never to doubt, always to enter clearly into the "yes" of her annunciation, wrapping herself in its profound meaning, from the moment of giving birth to her child to the day when she sees him pass from this world to another, infinitely distant from her.

Mary will be found in the midst of the apostles in the fledgling Church, guiding it in its prayer, shining a light on the mosaic of the psalms so that the destiny of the Messiah may be seen in them. Finally, toward the end of her life, she will entrust some of her memories to the apostles, memories that will become the infancy narratives of the Gospels. With their plots so lacking in concrete details, yet so rich in emotions and sentiments, must not their inspiration come from Mary? As J. Guitton has noted, all elderly mothers tell stories about the joys and sorrows of their child.

New Dawn

From December 17, the Church's strong desire to celebrate once again the coming of the Son of God in our human nature culminates in the solemn chant of the "O" antiphons.[1] Known already at the time of Charlemagne, they distill the pure messianism of the Old Testament into several extremely compact formulas. Did these perhaps trouble the authors of liturgical renewal after Vatican II? The gospel acclamations for the Masses from December 17 to December 23 retain an echo of the old antiphons, like those of the *Magnificat*, noted earlier. It is true that certain allusions are sometimes obscured or lost. It is better to turn to the Latin so that we lose nothing. Therefore we refer to an ancient text that, compared with the newer text, is full of all kinds of biblical references.[2]

O Wisdom, you came forth from the mouth of the Most High (Sir 24:30), and reaching from beginning to end, you ordered all things mightily and sweetly (Wis 8:1). Come, and teach us the way of prudence (Isa 40:14): December 17.

O Adonai (Lord) and Ruler of the house of Israel (Matt 2:6), you appeared to Moses in the fire of the burning bush (Exod 3:2), and on Mount Sinai gave him your Law (Exod 20). Come, and with an outstretched arm redeem us (Jer 32:21): December 18.

O Root of Jesse, you stand for an ensign of mankind (Isa 11:10); before you kings shall keep silence, and to you all nations shall have recourse (Isa 52:15). Come, save us, and do not delay (Hab 2:3): December 19.

O Key of David and Scepter of the house of Israel: you open and no man closes; you close and no man opens (Isa 22:22). Come, and deliver him from the chains of prison who sits in darkness and in the shadow of death (Ps 107:10): December 20.

Rising Dawn, Radiance of the Light eternal (Hab 3:4) and Sun of Justice (Mal 3:20); come, and enlighten those who sit in darkness and in the shadow of death (Luke 1:78): December 21.

O King of the Gentiles and the Desired of all (Hag 2:8), you are the cornerstone that binds two into one (Eph 2:20). Come, and save poor man whom you fashion out of clay (Gen 2:7): December 22.

181

O Emmanuel (Isa 7:14), our King and Lawgiver (Gen 49:10; cf. Ezek 21:32), the Expected of nations and their Savior (Isa 33:22): come, and save us, O Lord our God: December 23.

To give equal attention to each text would take far too long. We will be content here to give a Christian reading of them, i.e., a Christological reading. But first, it is necessary to recall what it is that ties the two Testaments together. Then we will better understand the rightful use of these titles, mostly messianic but sometimes divine, in the liturgy for the vigil of Christmas.

Like Two Halves of a Choir

A "cloud of witnesses" (Heb 12:1) accompanies the march of the pilgrim Church. A great host that sometimes has been compared to two halves of a choir that face each other while looking toward the unique focal point where the historical manifestation of the Emmanuel, God with us, appears. In him the Law and the Prophets are fulfilled (2 Cor 1:20; Rev 3:14). It is he who gives meaning to all the figures of the old covenant who delineate, little by little, the features of his face. Nevertheless, this face is always and everywhere surprising, because it surpasses all that one could imagine. He is the culmination of these figures, and it is their fulfillment in the person of Jesus Christ that helps one to sort out the unfinished rough drafts, to understand what precedes him. The Old Testament is like a letter from Christ opened after his Passover, which alone can make it comprehensible (Rev 5:9).

"Written as a warning to us, upon whom the end of the ages has come," the history of "our ancestors" (as 1 Cor 10:11 says), "serves as an example." We are spiritually Semites. Our Christian roots lie in the soil of Israel's history. It is there that the messianic hope is developed under the influence of the word and action of a God who brought it, in continual tension between promise and fulfillment, to unexpected heights. The divine promises were never seen as being static: whatever event or person that they influenced was accompanied by a dynamism that made people realize that what was proclaimed transcended any particular time.

Why Such Transcendence?

One can explain this perpetual transcendence in two ways. First, by God himself and by Israel's discovery of him. "Truly with you God is hidden, the God of Israel, the savior!" (Isa 45:15). The people of God slowly discovered that to know God consists, essentially, in realizing that he is hidden both in what he is and in what he does. This discovery emerged only bit by bit from a series of experiences to which the only possible response was faith.

Faith in the appearances of God, faith mixed with hope: "The faith I love best, is hope," said Charles Péguy to God.[3] The faith of Israel was always based on hope, open to an unforeseeable future that involved the object of faith as much as its subject. Was it not the Lord himself who had sworn this? Many times Israel had to be reminded that its future was in God's hands. "Remember not the events of the past, the things of long ago consider not; see, I am doing something new!" (Isa 43:18-19). They were told never to measure God by the standards of human wisdom, to allow the future of God to come about and, with it, that of the chosen people.

It was not only God, but also those he called to his service and who seldom lived up to his hope for them. It was they who helped history to be always overreaching itself. The destiny of God's elect usually alternates between rising and falling. The chosen ones triumph when they rely only on the power of God. If they lose this faith, they very quickly stumble, and the Lord no longer considers them his elect. One theme dominates the thread of sacred history: the perfect servant of the covenant has not been found; his place remains vacant. Whether king, judge, prophet, or priest, the chosen one merely passes on, and the task, as well as the title, that falls on this person, waits for still another yet to come. In the Old Testament, the messianic ministry is based, for better or worse, on those who are only provisionally chosen, until they can bow down at the feet of Christ.

The Reality of Jesus Christ

The first theological task of the Christian community was to combine the testimony of the Law, the Prophets, and the psalms with the historical event that was the manifestation of "the benevolence and humanity of God our Savior" (Luke 24:44; Titus 2:11). For it is Jesus Christ who is the "Amen" of God, the "Yes" to all his promises (2 Cor 1:20), the faithful and true Witness (Rev 3:14).

The Old Testament told us *what* the anointed one, i.e., the Christ, was to be; the New Testament announced *who* he was. Together they determine the reality of Christ. In fact, it is because the Old and New Testaments agree in subject that Jesus of Nazareth is the Christ. The name of "Jesus" proclaimed by the inspired authors of the new covenant, apostles, evangelists, and visionaries, is identified with the vocation of the

"Christ," or the "anointed one" of the Old Testament. One is amazed at the way the sacred writers freely chose, from all the writings of the Old Testament, the witnesses that agree with them, simply because Jesus himself chose, in a sense, which of them to fulfill in living out his role.

So each of the two halves of the choir of Scripture continues to play its indispensable role, particularly in "this day" of the liturgy. The easy, almost offhanded way that the texts from the great treasure chest of the Old Testament were chosen indicates that the inspiration of the Holy Spirit was indeed at work in determining what was written down and what was used to promulgate the knowledge of God's miracles.

God Is Spoken in Jesus Christ

How does one speak of God? Above all, how does one name him? Pious people of all religions have tried to do so, even knowing that God defies description and that his name is ineffable. The fact is that when love rules, it wants to bestow a name, even several names, on the beloved. If one cannot utter the secret name that would fully reveal the divine being, at least one can assign qualities to God that express his meaning for us, for example, the words the Moslem mystic uses to invoke Allah: the Clement, the Merciful, the Vigilant, the Patient, the Living One, etc.

In the slow germination of sacred history, the God of the Bible has prepared his response. After being revealed under various and fragmented forms, he has spoken "through his Son, whom he has made heir of all things and through whom he first created the universe" (Heb 1:2). God speaks himself in a child of our race, but this child, in whose blood glory and sorrow are mixed, is the revelation of the eternal Word. The active revelation, so to speak: God is made man that man might become God. To be co-born has here a "poetic" meaning: knowing God in Jesus Christ, we can be born to God by Jesus Christ.

By chanting the titles of the Messenger of God at the vigil of the feast of his birth in our flesh, the Church recalls not only that Jesus Christ is the ultimate Word, the last Word of God about himself. The Church also speaks about humanity, the believers, thus illuminating the Word that dispels the anguish of his precarious existence. For we are of his race, his seed, his future.

O Wisdom from on High!

Throughout the slow development of the human race in a universe held in awe, people have always looked for an explanation of what surrounds them. They have also sought guidance to help them live as best they can as responsible, fully human beings. "Give your servant, therefore, an understanding heart to judge your people and to distinguish right from wrong," asks Solomon, the wise man par excellence (1 Kgs 3:9). Seek a practical wisdom that retains the nostalgia for a lost flavor: the fruit of the tree of life (Gen 2:9; 3:6, 24).

Israel's sapiential books present Wisdom as having been conceived before the ages and abiding with God (Prov 8:22-36): Wisdom is part of God's love for the world. Concerned for all people, Wisdom leaves her royal throne, and comes to Israel in order to save it, as in the days of the Exodus (Wis 18:15). She shows it the love of a "mother," or offers herself as a spiritual "spouse." Resplendent in eternal light, she is the perfect mirror of divine activity (Wis 7). Out of the mouth of the Most High, she wishes to live among the children of Israel, so that those who hunger or thirst for wisdom can satisfy their desire through her, the true tree of knowledge (Sir 24; Prov 9:1-6).

It is Wisdom who presides in the ebb and flow of salvation history. She alone allows one to understand, through depicting the apparent destruction of the divine promises, that a remnant will return, whose faith will know the way of truth (Isa 40:14). For even though "the grass withers and the flower wilts, when the breath of the Lord blows upon it . . . the word of our God stands forever" (Isa 40:8). To discover the transcendence of God's plan over all the world—is that not the summit of wisdom? God's thoughts are not our thoughts, nor are his ways our ways. To be grounded in his word is to abandon oneself to the wisdom that moves the world. "So shall my word be that goes forth from my mouth; it shall not return to me void, but shall do my will, achieving the end for which I sent it" (Isa 55:11).

As in the Gospel of John, Christ is the Word, the divine utterance from the mouth of the Most High (John 1:1-14). According to Paul, he is the divine Wisdom that presides at the new creation (1 Cor 1:24; Heb 1:3). What John expresses in terms of a "new birth" (John 3:3-7), Paul puts in terms of "new creation," of which Christ is the source, the new Adam, and also the creator and redeemer.[4] According to Paul, the mission of divine Wisdom supposes and entails a cosmic dimension of salvation that is tied to the function of Christ as redeemer: all have been created in Christ and for Christ; all have been made heirs of Christ and saved by him and for him (Col 1:15-20).

As for the abundance of divine gifts brought together in Wisdom and the promise that the Lord's spirit would be upon the Messiah (Isa 11:1-2), in Christ it is an abundance that is poured out: ''Of his fullness we have all had a share—love following upon love'' (John 1:16). Paul uses the Greek word *plerōma* (Col 1:19; 2:3; 2:9), an expression denoting that which existed before all else, which is to say that Christ Jesus holds all together and is the principle of the universe and the end of all things. The Christological hymn in the Letter to the Ephesians sings lyrically and enthusiastically of the superabundance of divine grace that is communicated to us in Christ (Eph 1:20ff.). It even identifies the fullness of Christ with the Church (Eph 1:23), the Church that will ultimately attain the adult stature of Spouse (Eph 4:10-16).

In asking the divine Wisdom to show itself once more in the Church, the liturgy appeals to the dynamic mystery of the incarnate Word, the perfect image of the Father, who brings about his universal plan of salvation so that ''God may be all in all'' (1 Cor 8:6; 15:28). ''Come, Wisdom from on high, teach us the paths of truth!''

Once the divine plan for the universe is established, all that remains is the creation of an earth, a people, and a kingdom.

O Lord and Ruler of Israel!

In ancient times, the God of the patriarchs, i.e., the chiefs of nomadic tribes who were united, more or less, by a common race and religion, revealed himself to Moses in the flames of a burning bush. In recalling the promises made to the patriarchs, we see that God revealed himself in shows of strength in the sight of the Hebrews and their enemies (Exod 3:6). After the God of Abraham, the God who led him into unknown lands, we have the God of Moses creating a free people out of a rabble of slaves in flight, a mass of disparate people totally without organization. A covenant and a law will constitute a people of God.[5] Its master and ruler will be none other than the Lord himself. Moses may be able to speak to him face to face in the meeting tent, and therefore hold uncontested authority in the heart of Israel, but he will never be more than an intermediary. He will be like the kings who issue from the root of Jesse, of David's line—mere lieutenants of God, guardians of his heritage and covenant.

O Root of Jesse, O Raised Standard!

Divine Wisdom surely revealed a new part of its plan during David's dynasty. Israel will have a country, a capital, even a temple that will symbolize the divine presence in the midst of the people of the promise. In the person of the king, it also receives a leader, a guarantor of the covenant and servant of the divine will: "It was I who took you . . . to be commander of my people Israel. I have been with you wherever you went" (2 Sam 7:8-9). Even though Israel's unfaithfulness and its kings will earn them a new slavery, David's line will remain a standard, a sign raised to rally the nations as well as the exiles of Israel and Judah. The Chronicler testifies to this in recalling Nathan's prophecy: it has no other purpose than to keep alive the faith of his readers in the promise of God (1 Chr 17:11-14), at a time when hardly anything remained that had been accomplished.

Even in deepest sorrow, Israel maintains enough hope to sing the Songs of the Suffering Servant (Isa 52:15). Isn't it true that in the presence of this suffering and wounded servant— Israel or an individual?—the nations are astonished and the people rejoice? Isn't this proof that this God, who was thought to have died with his people, forever remains the God who works wonders? Once more he will stretch out his hand to redeem the remainder of his people and make known to them his name.

O Rod and Scepter of David!

That he is the only Lord of Israel is suggested by the decadence of the line of David. How did it happen that those kings received universal titles in certain liturgies of enthronement, titles echoed in some of the psalms (Pss 2; 72; 110)? They may have hidden the truth for a while, but the majority of the kings are vilified by the historical books (2 Kgs 17:7-19). Only two kings of Judah receive unreserved approbation (2 Kgs 18:3-6; 22:2). As for the kings of Israel, one tires of the constant refrain: "He did evil in the sight of the Lord."[6] Did not David himself fall into sin? The account given of the last years of his reign is not worth lingering over.

Yet, "my servant David will always have a lamp before me in Jerusalem" (1 Kgs 11:36; Ps 89). Mandate, titles, divine promises will be transmitted further. Thus, the rod and scepter of David's line are transferred, in solemn renewal, to men whose fame and fidelity make one think that their function must be that of mere relays in the race toward the messianic light (Isa 22:15-25).

O Rising Sun, Sun of Justice, O Splendor of Eternal Light!

As the chant of the great antiphons springs forth, the titles attributed to the Messiah become more mysterious, more pregnant with meaning, because they are charged with revealing to the eyes of the faithful the fullness of the messianic task that Jesus will come to fulfill.

"Light is sweet! and it is pleasant for the eyes to see the sun," notes the Sage (Eccl 11:7). There is a natural link between light and life. To be born is to see the day, just as to die is to experience darkness. In order to express the mysterious presence of the living God who gives life, the Old Testament speaks of his action as a decisive presence that dispels darkness. "For you darkness itself is not dark, and night shines as the day" (Ps 139:12). God is the one who distinguishes between light and darkness: he is on the side of light; he is Light. The luminous presence of God is one with his salvation, with the promises of happiness conferred on all those who hope to experience his goodness in the land of the living (Ps 27:1, 13). Certainly, one cannot enter into the splendor of eternal light without trembling. The majesty of a God who wants to reveal himself to all can blind them by the overwhelming intensity of his existence. The darkness that envelops the land of Egypt on the Passover of the Lord becomes one of the signs announcing the Day of God.[7]

But the Day of the Lord is announced as a day of joy and deliverance for all those who hope for salvation: "The people that walked in darkness have seen a great light" (Isa 9:1; 42:7; 49:9; Mic 7:8). How could joy not accompany the dazzling clarity of the endless Day that vanquishes all errors and lies (Isa 30:26; Zech 14:7)? The first and last word of the dialogue that concludes the Book of Malachi (and therefore the Old Testament) shows that judgment, terrible and menacing as it may be, is necessary, the underside of the mystery of salvation that cannot exist without purification (Mal 3:17-21). God's chosen ones will bask in the "sun of justice with its healing rays." When Zechariah salutes the dawn of the messianic day, along with his celebration of John the Baptist's birth, he appeals in his canticle *(Benedictus)* to the "Sun of justice," who is like God and who, in the name of Yahweh, will purify the sons of Levi, harkening to the cry of his people and healing their wounds (Luke 1:78).[8] It is interesting to note that the last prophet of the old covenant evokes the Day of the Lord in the context of the final days, where the messenger, the angel of God, discovers the messianic traits that proclaim Jesus Christ.

O King, O Cornerstone, Savior of the Nations!
As for the cornerstone, it evokes the durable, unbreakable faithfulness of God, the Rock of Israel, but also the work of the Messiah-to-come. Without a doubt, in the Old Testament the title "cornerstone" signifies God himself and the salvation he brings to his people. Is he not the only

fixed point in the universe?[9] This meaning derives from later Judaism which, relying on other citations from Scripture, interpreted the image of the stone in a messianic sense.[10] Toward the beginning of our era, some commentaries—targums—like those concerning the Greek Bible, the Septuagint, did not hesitate to apply certain passages from Isaiah to the Messiah (Isa 8:14; 28:16). The targum discussing Psalm 118 interprets the cornerstone on which God will base the restoration of his people—doubtlessly after the Maccabean revolt—as a son of David, a king and a sovereign. Might he not be a successor of Judas Maccabeus, after the restoration of the Temple and the reconquering of the Greek armies?

It was on the basis of Psalm 118 that the primitive Church attributed to Christ, the vanquisher of death, the synonymous titles "rock" and "cornerstone" (Acts 4:11; 1 Pet 2:4-7).[11] In his work of salvation, Jesus in fact appears as this "stone which the builders rejected, and has become the cornerstone" (Mark 12:10; Matt 21:37-43). The Christological theme of the stone will henceforth become a staple ingredient of the Church's teaching.[12] The letters of Paul, who is anxious to justify the openness of the Christian community to the pagan nations, will also exploit this theme (Eph 2:20).

O Emmanuel, King and Savior!
The great antiphons reach their highest point with the invocation of Emmanuel, the Lord our God, that he might come and save us.

The presentiment that God is not only the Most High, but also the Omnipresent (Pss 119; 148), the creator God present to his work (Wis 11:25), the savior God present to his people (Exod 19:4; Ps 46:8-12), climaxes in the person of Emmanuel, i.e., God-with-us, already obscurely announced in the prophecy of the Almah (Isa 7:14). So the great yearning of faith that longed for Wisdom to dwell among us finally found its fulfillment in the conception of the Son of God, in Mary, by the power of the Holy Spirit (Matt 1:21; Luke 1:28, 35). Concrete presence—in the flesh—of God as man, the actual Word of God, come to pitch his tent among us (John 1:14)! The final, ultimate presence of God, who will remain with the Church forever (Matt 28:20), until the full acceptance by all nations of the One who fills the universe by the power of his resurrection!

Do we think enough about this? Before every prayer, doesn't the Church express the wish "The Lord be with you"? May Christmas help us to understand this, for ever since the feast of the Incarnation, which is also the beginning of the divinization of men and women, the tremendous desire for a salvation is open to all, along with the great desire for God that is offered to all those he loves.

> O God, you are life,
> you are salvation,
> you are health,
> you are immortality,
> you are beatitude,
> you are illumination . . .
> for you take delight
> in nothing other
> than the salvation of mankind.
> (Gregory Narek)

The Season of Christmas-Epiphany

To understand and experience the season of Christmas-Epiphany more fully, it is useful, as we celebrate it today, to recall how the feasts that make up the liturgical year came into being and developed.[1]

A Pagan Celebration Christianized

It is not until the fourth century that a calendar mentions the celebration of the Lord's nativity.[2] This was the Christianization of the pagan feast *sol invictus*—"the invincible sun"—introduced in 274 by the emperor Aurelius (270–275) and celebrated in Rome on December 25. The sun wanes continually from the end of June until the winter solstice, the shortest day of the year. As if to vanquish darkness, however, the sun wins out over the long, dark days by shining a little longer each day until its brightest and most glorious moment at the summer solstice.[3]

The substitution of one feast for another was easy for those who, having once participated in the pagan feast, became Christians. The prophet Malachi had said that one day "the Sun of justice" (Mal 3:20) would arise, and Jesus called himself "the Light of the world" (John 8:12). The true Sun, the "vanquisher of darkness," is the one[4] who has triumphed over sin and death. After the Peace of Constantine (313), the feast of the Nativity of the Lord also supplanted altogether the pagan celebration of the Sun.[5] From the beginning, it also had a definite paschal dimension that is somewhat overlooked today.[6]

About the same time, as a Christianization of the celebration of the winter solstice observed in Egypt and Arabia on January 6, the feast of Epiphany came into being. Epiphany means "showing forth," "manifestation," and as if to refute certain pagan myths, emphasis was placed on the baptism of Jesus, his mission, and on the miracle at Cana by which he revealed his glory (John 2:11). Soon, Epiphany was celebrated throughout the West: we find mention of it as a great feast in Gaul in 361. The East gradually adopted the feast of Christmas somewhere between the end of the fourth century and the first half of the fifth.

Unfolding of the Feast

The earliest celebration of Christmas at Rome was a very simple papal Mass at the basilica. The Mass was no doubt similar to our present Mass at Dawn, with the proclamation of the Prologue to the Gospel of John. In opposition to the Arian heresy,[7] this Mass clearly affirmed that it was celebrating the eternal Word made flesh. This celebration had a decidedly Christological and dogmatic character, including, in 360, a commemoration of the adoration of the magi and the slaughter of the children of Bethlehem.[8]

At Bethlehem, there was a yearly night Mass for Epiphany that was celebrated in the cave of the nativity. From the fifth century on, the night Mass was also celebrated in Rome, this time celebrating Christmas rather than Epiphany. On this occasion, the pope visited the Church of St. Mary Major, built after the Council of Ephesus (313). Here, in a chapel of the basilica,[9] wood from a crèche was customarily placed, hence the phrase that the Mass was celebrated *ad praesepe*, i.e., near the crèche. The reading was the gospel of Jesus' birth at Bethlehem (Luke 2:1-14). The celebration was clearly historical.[10]

But December 25 was also a feast day for the Greek colony in Rome, which assembled in their Church of St. Anastasia (Holy Resurrection). To honor them, the pope went there in the morning to celebrate a Mass before going to St. Peter's. Here, the custom was to celebrate the Nativity by including in the liturgy the reading of the gospel about the announcement of the good news to the shepherds (Luke 2:15-20).

This, then, was the origin of the three Christmas Masses: at night (at St. Mary Major), at dawn (at St. Anastasia), and during the day (at St. Peter).

Today

Besides these three Masses, the Missal contains a Mass for the evening of December 24, the vigil of Christmas: it is rarely celebrated. And Christmas does not have an octave celebration. January 1, however, has been variously consecrated to the motherhood of Mary and to the commemoration of Jesus' circumcision. But in 1969, the liturgical reformers decided in favor of the Solemnity of Mary, Mother of God.

The Sunday after Christmas (or, if there is no Sunday within the octave of Christmas, on December 30)[11] is the feast of the Holy Family, instituted by Benedict XV in 1921; in our country, Epiphany (January 6) is celebrated on the Sunday that falls between January 2 and January 8.[12] Finally, on the following Sunday (or the day after the Sunday of Epiphany),[13] we celebrate the Baptism of the Lord, which closes out the season of Christmas-Epiphany.[14]

Such is the manner in which the present liturgy, the result of the reform of Vatican II, celebrates the Savior's coming (Christmas) and his manifestation in human form (Epiphany, Baptism).

From their beginnings up to today, both in the West and the East, various emphases characterize these feasts. Quite early on, different liturgical traditions crossed paths and influenced one another. Reciprocal borrowing has been the rule. But no matter what has developed since the beginning, and despite all the liturgical formularies, one thing remains: it is impossible to encompass and express in only one liturgy the richness and complexity of the mystery that it celebrates. The "good" liturgies are those that are not limited to one perspective. This accounts for the diversity of scriptural texts that are offered for reading and meditation. They are not as distracting as one might think: they open up, rather, a greater awareness of what is being celebrated. This is also true of the antiphons for the Liturgy of the Hours; there is a certain lyrical quality to them, a poetic compression, whose spirit raises us to a level of contemplation, where we discover the wondrous, infinite horizon of the mystery that gives this season's Liturgy of the Hours a special religious fervor.

> Christ the Lord is born today; today, the Savior has appeared. Earth echoes songs of angel choirs, archangels' joyful praise. Today on earth his friends exult: Glory to God in the highest, alleluia.[15]

> Marvelous is the mystery proclaimed today: man's nature is made new as God becomes man; he remains what he was and becomes what he was not. Yet each nature stays distinct and for ever undivided.[16]

> O marvelous exchange! Man's Creator has become man, born of a virgin. We have been made sharers in the divinity of Christ who humbled himself to share in our humanity.[17]

> Today the Bridegroom claims his bride, the Church, since Christ has washed her sins away in Jordan's waters; the Magi hasten with their gifts to the royal wedding; and the wedding guests rejoice, for Christ has changed water into wine, alleluia.[18]

The Nativity of the Lord[1]

VIGIL MASS

The Light Shines Forth

The Mass suggested for the evening of December 24—either before or after the first vespers of the solemnity—has the liturgical spirit of a Christmas vigil. If this Mass is not celebrated, its readings can be used for prayer and meditation in preparing for the celebration of the feast.[2] "Today you will know that the Lord is coming to save us, and in the morning you will see his glory."[3] It is a quiet waiting that ends with the sudden cry of joy that bursts forth at the beginning of the Office for Christmas Day: "Christ is born for us; come, let us adore him."[4]

The Hour of Celebration Has Finally Come
The first reading for this Mass has a double meaning: historical[5] and liturgical. It is the latter that makes the Book of Isaiah a matter of interest to us (Isa 62:1-5).

It is a kind of poem, probably chanted as part of a celebration and undoubtedly used during a pilgrimage to Jerusalem. "Pass through, pass through the gates, prepare the way for the people; build up, build up the highway, clear it of stones" (Isa 62:10).

The beginning sounds like an invitatory that is well suited to the Christmas vigil: "For Zion's sake I will not be silent, for Jerusalem's sake I will not be quiet, until her vindication shines forth like the dawn and her victory like a burning torch." Yes, the decisive intervention of God is at hand: he will give his people justice and salvation. Make no mistake: justice and salvation here are not limited merely to the granting of an amnesty accompanied by the restitution of confiscated goods. "You shall be called by a new name pronounced by the mouth of the Lord."

Giving a name to someone demonstrates God's all-powerful creativity. The one who receives the name becomes a radically new creature. Out of "Forsaken" and "Desolate," the Lord makes "My Delight," and "Espoused." Out of the dust of the earth, God created a living being whom

195

he called "man" (Gen 2:7). He changes "stony hearts" into "natural hearts" (Ezek 36:26).

To give a name is also to take possession. Here there is a play on words that is untranslatable. "To espouse" can in fact mean "to possess," "to make one's own."[6] Man is the "Lord" of his wife, though this term does not imply any sort of servile subjection. There is a certain daring and power in this way of speaking. The high point is reached in the final verse: "As a young man marries a virgin, your Builder shall marry you; and as a bridegroom rejoices in his bride so shall your God rejoice in you."

This is not the first time that we find this image in Isaiah. "For he who has become your husband is your Maker; his name is the Lord of hosts; your redeemer is the holy One of Israel, called God of all the earth. The Lord calls you back, like a wife forsaken and grieved in spirit, a wife married in youth and then cast off, says your God" (Isa 54:5-6). "I rejoice heartily in the Lord, in my God is the joy of my soul; for he has clothed me with a robe of salvation, and wrapped me in a mantle of justice, like a bridegroom adorned with a diadem, like a bride bedecked with her jewels" (Isa 61:10). The vigil of Christmas is, in a sense, the marriage of God and humanity. In Jesus, the eternal Son of his love, God has concluded with humanity the covenant of his first love.[7]

> For ever I will sing the goodness of the Lord.
>
> I have made a covenant with my chosen one,
>   I have sworn to David my servant:
> Forever will I confirm your posterity
>   and establish your throne for all generations.
>
> Happy the people who know the joyful shout;
>   in the light of your countenance, O LORD, they walk.
> At your name they rejoice all the day,
>   and through your justice they are exalted.
>
> He shall say of me, "You are my father,
>   my God, the Rock, my savior."
> Forever I will maintain my kindness toward him,
>   and my covenant with him stands firm.
> (Ps 89:4-5, 16-17, 27-29)

The Promises of God Fulfilled in Jesus

From the beginning, Christians have always proclaimed that Jesus was the Savior, born of the house of David according to God's promise, and the one to whom John the Baptist bore witness (Acts 13:16-17, 22-25).

It is a similar teaching that gives rise to the ''family record of Jesus Christ, son of David, son of Abraham'' and the story of the announcement to Joseph that is read from the beginning of Matthew's Gospel (Matt 1:1-25).

Biblical genealogy is a particular literary genre whose aim must be understood lest one be misled. To regard these lists as archival documents is to open oneself to endless questions that have no firm answers. They must be read as a way to understand and recapitulate the ancient prophecies, a way of interpreting events rather than merely recounting them. Their value is thus more homiletic than historical. That is why they interest us.

This literary genre, which today has fallen into disuse, is common in the Old Testament.[8] One might remember, for example, that the Genesis account of creation ends with this formula: ''Such is the story [the genealogy] of the heavens and the earth at their creation'' (Gen 2:4).[9]

These genealogies are undoubtedly composed of symbolic elements—coded messages?—that elude our grasp today.[10] We can note, however, that of the four women mentioned in Jesus' genealogy, three are foreigners: Rahab, Ruth, and ''the wife of Uriah,'' who, we are told, gave birth under irregular conditions. Is this a lesson of the universality of grace?

In any case, Matthew decidedly insists on the honorific titles of Jesus: ''son of David,'' ''son of Abraham,'' and ''Christ,'' all three of which evoke divine election and suggest that before all generations, the source of Jesus Christ is to be found in God. The genealogical tree that Matthew outlines ends with ''. . . Joseph the husband of Mary. It was of her that Jesus who is called the Messiah was born.'' Notice, however, that Matthew, evoking the beginning of the genealogy—''Now this is how the birth [origin] of Jesus Christ came about''—quickly recalls that Joseph did not beget this child himself.

The Mission of Joseph, Husband of Mary

The announcement to Joseph is a kind of commentary on the famous prophecy of Isaiah: ''The virgin shall be with child and give birth to a son, and they shall call him Emmanuel, a name which means 'God-with-us' '' (Isa 7:14). The form, which is classical, is that of the announcement of the birth of a protagonist of salvation[11], or the revelation of his mission.[12] God reveals his plan and what he intends as the child's chosen role. Matthew's storytelling is often extraordinary. The story culminates with the bestowal of the child's name and its meaning.

Matthew's genealogy insists on the Davidic line of "Jesus Christ, son of David, son of Abraham." This legitimacy seems to be compromised, since Jesus' origin is directly from Mary. This is not the case, however, since a new protagonist intervenes: the Holy Spirit. Moreover, Joseph, himself a "son of David," must give the name to the child thus conceived and, by doing so, he must integrate him into the line from which he himself descends. Joseph did not beget Jesus. But by giving him the name revealed by the angel and taking Mary into his home to be his wife, he has assumed the role and mission of being the indispensable link to the line of David, to which the Messiah must belong.

In other instances of miraculous conceptions reported in the Bible— Sarah (Gen 17:15-22; 18:4-14), Elizabeth (Luke 1:2-25)— God allowed a couple to become fruitful despite the wife's sterility. The conception of Jesus takes place, however, completely outside the realm of nature. Matthew's teaching is as emphatic on this point as the witness of Luke. But he focuses attention less on Mary than on the role and mission of her husband Joseph.

A Gospel Passage for the Community

However it may appear at first glance, Matthew's beginning does not limit itself to Jesus' origins, his genealogy, and manner of conception. It is truly concerned with the gospel, i.e., with the good news given to the community that Matthew is addressing.

Jesus is the summit toward which past sacred history converges, as does our history, which begins with his birth. From beginning to end, this history is lived out by men and women from generation to generation.

In some way, Joseph and Mary show the road to follow by outlining the general path, which will become specific in the lives of all people according to the way they respond to their vocation. We can recognize ourselves in one or another of Jesus' ancestors, in the sinners that the list mentions; but we are all asked to relate ourselves to Christ, to enter into his line. Salvation history knows no other continuity. It is the duty of each person to find his or her proper place in it. In a way certainly different from Joseph's, but no less real, we have an irreplaceable role to fulfill. God waits for us to do what he tells us, not by the voice of an angel, but by that of Scripture and the Church at first, and later through unexpected situations and people who come into our lives. Jesus receives the name that Joseph gives to him. We have to acknowledge it and pass it on.

Then, "the glory of the Lord will be revealed, and all mankind will see the saving power of God."[13]

"Let the saint rejoice as he sees the palm of victory at hand. Let the sinner be glad as he receives the offer of forgiveness. Let the pagan take courage as he is summoned to life."[14]

Let us rise up, let us go forward with songs of joy. The celebration of Christmas is about to begin.

> The light born of light
> appeared in the night of Judea;
> the eternal Word of the Father
> rouses us with the shepherds.
> Let us go and see in Mary's arms
> God who made himself one of us
> so that we might live with his life.
>
> *"Our Savior is born for us,*
> *Peace on earth and glory to God!"*
>
> The Lord said to me:
> "You are my Son,
> this day I have begotten you."[15]

A Child Is Born to Us

In some countries, people always speak of "Midnight Mass,"[16] even though the Missal simply says "Mass at Night," without further specification. Based on the content of the gospel (Luke 2:8), celebrating the Nativity of the Lord by a Mass held at night in the grotto of Bethlehem was an early tradition.[17] From this beginning, the first Mass for Christmas has kept its character as a celebration "near the crèche."

A Happening Among Us
Little children know by heart the story of Jesus' birth in the manger at Bethlehem. They never tire of hearing it retold. In their drawings of it, they leave out no one: rather they add figures, certainly the result of inspiration and holy imagination. It seems to them quite natural to introduce into the scene people, animals, and objects from their own world. In fact, they often put themselves center stage. Childlike naïveté? Perhaps. But also, it is undeniably a spontaneous understanding of the mystery. Whatever the case, the story of the nativity, as it is read on this night, is not a Christmas fairy tale, but an authentic passage from the gospel (Luke 2:1-14).

All of Luke's writings[18] that are clearly intended to announce something have been written from beginning to end according to certain standards that the author makes known to us: "Many have undertaken to compile a narrative of the events which have been fulfilled in our midst, precisely as those events were transmitted to us by the original eyewitnesses and ministers of the word. I too have carefully traced the whole sequence of events from the beginning, and have decided to set it in writing for you, Theophilus, so that Your Excellency may see how reliable the instruction was that you received" (Luke 1:1-4). This pertains to the events of Jesus' infancy (Luke 1–2), as well as to others.

Luke takes care to place Jesus' birth in a general time-frame by placing it at the time of the census that "took place while Quirinius was governor of Syria."[19] In so doing, Luke makes it clear from the story's first words that the event he is writing about has a particular meaning. This sets the tone for the sacredness of the event.

A Newborn Child in Bethlehem of Judea

It is the census call that requires Joseph to go "from the town of Nazareth in Galilee to Judea, to David's town of Bethlehem—because he was of the house and lineage of David—to register with Mary, his espoused wife, who was with child. While they were there the days of her confinement were completed. She gave birth to her first-born son and wrapped him in swaddling clothes and laid him in a manger, because there was no room for them in the place where travelers lodged." This is why Jesus is born not in Nazareth, where Joseph and Mary lived, but in Judea, in Bethlehem, "the city of David."

The conditions surrounding his birth have an aura of danger and poverty that should not be misunderstood or minimized. True, other women have given birth in conditions that were just as bad, if not worse: for example, all those who have brought a child into the world in a refugee camp, in caves under bombardment, in the midst of war raging all around them. Even so, from the moment of his birth, Jesus experienced a precariousness and insecurity not unlike what we ourselves might experience.[20] In his depiction of the event, Luke displays a characteristic theme of his Gospel.

Could we go further? "Augustus" is the surname of the emperor, and thus evokes the imperial court in all its pomp and power, the kind of power that orders a census of the whole world, and requires everyone to be counted in his native city. And yet, it is to a helpless infant born in misery in Bethlehem that glory belongs. The angels proclaimed it; the paschal enthronement will make it clear. Deprived of all worldly comforts, the child in the manger is the only one to whom the titles of "Savior" and "Lord," titles given to the "divine" emperor "Augustus," truly belong. "Though he was in the form of God" (Phil 2:6), he humbled himself so that we might become rich by his poverty (2 Cor 8:9). What extraordinary paradoxes!

Joseph's behavior is exemplary. With perfect obedience to God, no matter what was asked of him, he took Mary into his home to be his wife; he fled into Egypt with the child and his mother; he returned to dwell in Nazareth (Matt 1:18-25; 2:13-15, 19-23); he gave to Caesar what was Caesar's by humbly submitting to the emperor's edict in calling the census.

Luke is content simply to mention Mary: the readers of the Gospel know quite well that she is the virginal spouse of Joseph, and they know how she conceived this child (Luke 1:26-38). "First-born" evokes the fact of his consecration to the Lord, which will be elaborated upon in the story of the presentation (Luke 2:23), with explicit reference to prescribed Law.[21] In addition, however, this term is full of meaning for Christians: Jesus is the "first-born of all creatures" (Col 1:15), the "first-born of the dead" (Col 1:18; Rev 1:5), the "first-born" in an absolute sense (Heb 1:4). It recalls "the assembly of the first-born enrolled in heaven" (Heb 12:23; Luke 10:20), because God has made of them "a kind of first fruits of his creatures" (James 1:18).[22]

Good News, Great Joy

In Bethlehem, everything happens in silence and humility. In quite extraordinary contrast, and not far from there—"in the locality"—the heavens shine forth with light, while the earth echoes with songs of praise and the glory of the Lord encompasses those whom he loves.

The good news is brought to certain shepherds by "the angel of the Lord," the appointed messenger of salvation (previously sent, for example, to Moses (Exod 3:2–4:17) and Gideon (Judg 6:11-24). The "glory" comes from on high, as it did during the Exodus (Exod 16:10; 24:16-17; Num 14:10) and after the consecration of the Temple (1 Kgs 6:11). The choir of the "multitude of the heavenly host" that sings the praises of God calls to mind those assemblies of worship that glorify the Lord with hymns and psalms. These references, these narrative structures conforming to literary forms of the Old Testament, the use of the language of the Greek Bible—all give the story a sacred character. At the same time, we are reminded of the prophetic promises, which are fulfilled on this night.

Isn't it obvious that this announcement to the shepherds prefigures the apostolic preaching to which Luke consecrated his second body of writing, the Acts of the Apostles? The shepherds are the "merest children" to whom the Father has first revealed his mystery (Luke 10:21), representing the simple and marginal people who will come in great number to receive the words proclaimed by the apostles. The message of joy is, in itself, a gospel: Luke insists so strongly on this point that he is often called "the evangelist of joy."

The Messiah: Savior and Lord

"Savior" is a term typically used in the Hellenistic Churches. Giving this title to Jesus clearly distinguished them from the pagan religions, which spoke of "savior gods." At the same time it sets Jesus in opposition to the pretensions of the Caesars, who thought of themselves as divinized.

Luke is the only evangelist who habitually calls Jesus "the Savior": four-teen times in his Gospel, and at least forty times in Acts. Moreover, he makes frequent use of the word "today" to teach that the acts of salva-tion, though they occurred in the past, are an integral part of each suc-cessive generation.

The shepherds receive a sign that allows them to discover and recog-nize the Savior. "An infant wrapped in swaddling clothes," something seen every day. "Lying in a manger" was probably not a matter of sur-prise to the shepherds. They understood such things. Perhaps they even thought, at the mention of a manger, that this birth concerned them di-rectly, that the child was one of theirs. In any case, in the announcement to the shepherds, Christians can see the image of Christ the Shepherd come to seek out and gather his lost sheep (Luke 15:3-7). Moreover, the sign of the Savior, a tiny little child lying in a manger, is a revelation of the way that God accomplishes his salvation. Having seen the child in Bethlehem, the shepherds "glorified and praised God." Seeing what hap-pened on Calvary and the way in which Jesus, uttering a loud cry, gave up his spirit, the centurion also glorified God (Luke 23:47). Simple people and a pagan: both recognizing the signs of salvation, which Luke offers for the meditation of believers.

Glory and Praise to God, Peace on Earth to Men

We owe to Luke the *Magnificat* of Mary, the *Benedictus* of Zechariah, and the *Nunc dimittis* of Simeon, three canticles of praise that outline the gospel of the infancy. The announcement to the shepherds also ends with a song of praise to God, equally prophetic. It is sung by countless angels, and it is the shortest of all; but it echoes endlessly in the heavens.

In the Old Testament, angels play a liturgical role that is overlooked in today's liturgy. Nevertheless, they are mentioned in the preface to every Eucharistic Prayer, in a way that expresses well the meaning and purpose of their ministry near God, as well as the meaning and purpose of their intervention in our celebrations.

Belonging to the celestial realm, they perpetually sing the praises of the thrice-holy God. Totally and definitively committed to the service of God, the angels are still creatures and, as such, have a role connected to the created universe. By them and with them, our praise is given a cosmic dimension: "Holy, holy, holy Lord, God of power and might! Heaven and earth are filled with your glory. Hosanna in the highest!" In one way or another, this is what the angels, and our liturgy, always say.

This worship is the response of creatures to the gift of God, summarized by the peace promised from the beginning, a gift that the Lord brings about by the mere fact of his birth. It enables us to return, like him, to his Father. Thus we repeat his words in each Eucharist: "Lord Jesus Christ, you said to your apostles: Peace I leave you, my peace I give to you."

The dream of humanity is realized, the promises fulfilled.

The Love of the Lord Has Accomplished This

In the strength of their hope, the prophets foresaw the full realization of the promises, hinted at by the events of their time. Rooted in various historical contexts that we may never truly ascertain, their preaching sheds light on the events of salvation history experienced today. An instance of this is the prophecy of Isaiah that we read on this Christmas night (Isa 9:1-6).

Christians have heard about and meditated on the child born in Bethlehem, the son that God has given us in his "invincible love." "Wonder-Counselor," he who is the Way, the Truth, and the Life. "God-Hero," the "Prince of Peace," who has reconciled us with God. "Father-Forever" is a royal title. It evokes both the paternal and fraternal concern of Christ, who has dwelt among us like a servant (Luke 22:27), who has given his life for those whom he loves (John 15:13), through whom we have been born to life. His coming reveals what will happen for the benefit of all people. This poem on the birth of a royal child involves later revelations and is itself illuminated by them. The reason for including this text in the liturgy of Christmas is not its prophetic character, but rather its teaching on the true scope of the celebrated event: "The zeal of the Lord of hosts will do this!"

But what of the era of peace and justice that the birth of this child is supposed to inaugurate? The yoke still weighs heavily on many people; the rod and whip of their taskmasters have not been broken; the tramping of soldiers' boots and the din of war have not ceased; if the clothes of oppressors and executioners are no longer stained with blood, it is because they can now use "clean" methods to kill. Could the power that rests on the shoulder of the child be illusory? A thought from Pascal comes to mind: "The activity of God, who orders all things most sweetly, is to bring about religion in the mind through reason, and in the heart through grace. But the desire to mold the mind and heart by threats and violence does not bring about religion, but terror—*terrorem potius quam religionem.''*[23] God does not impose peace by force. His reign is born to-day in sorrow. Isaiah's prophecy is an urgent call to praise the one who has sent a savior for the joy and hope of all nations.

> *Today is born our Savior, Christ the Lord.*
>
> Sing to the LORD a new song;
>   sing to the LORD, all you lands.
> Sing to the LORD, bless his name;
>   announce his salvation, day after day.
> Tell his glory among the nations;
>   among all peoples, his wondrous deeds.
>
> Let the heavens be glad and the earth rejoice;
>   let the sea and what fills it resound;
>   let the plains be joyful and all that is in them!
> Then shall all the trees of the forest exult
>   before the LORD, for he comes;
>   for he comes to rule the earth.
> He shall rule the world with justice
>   and the peoples with his constancy.
> (Ps 96:1-3, 11-13)

Epiphany of the Grace of God and Life in the Present World

The second reading for this Mass speaks of the practical implications of "salvation to all" in the manifestation of God's grace. It is a brief passage—four verses—from the Letter of Paul to Titus. The tone and style are more prophetic than epistolary. Moreover, certain formulas make one suspect that they are extracts from a liturgical hymn (Titus 2:11-14).

Each word, each expression, each theme of this beautiful passage de-mands meditation. Salvation is above all an epiphany, a manifestation of the grace and love of God. The coming of "the glory of the great God and of our Savior Christ Jesus" is redemption—liberation—from our faults, a purification of the people of God who are called to do good. The first text among many that come to mind on this theme is "Love, then, con-sists in this: not that we have loved God but that he has loved us and has sent his Son as an offering for our sins" (1 John 4:10).

The epiphany of the love of God is the source of light that guides our lives according to our vocations, "worthy of the gospel" (Phil 1:27). For "to reject godless ways and worldly desires" goes hand in hand with "living temperately, justly, and devoutly in this age." The coming of the Savior, the manifestation of the grace of God, are not merely mysteries to be contemplated from the outside, objects of admiration and faith. They teach us to reject "godless ways and worldly desires."

The Lectionary's translation tries to avoid using words that might be misunderstood. Paul speaks of "impiety" and of lusts or desires of this "world."[24] In order to understand what is really meant by the term "impiety," one must consider its opposite, "piety," of which the Pastoral Epistles often speak.[25] It designates the entire range of interior dispositions that animate the life "worthy of the gospel." It is spoken of along with "justice, faith, charity, patience, meekness." "Impiety" is therefore something other than an element of pagan morality: it is infidelity to the gospel, a real negation of Christ.

The "world," with its desires, lusts, and passions that one must renounce, denotes the source of sin, or impiety. "If anyone loves the world, the Father's love has no place in him" (1 John 2:15). This renunciation is comparable to a crucifixion: "Those who belong to Christ Jesus have crucified their flesh with its passions and desires" (Gal 5:24). Yet, this crucifying ourselves in opposition to the world opens us to the future, to life everlasting. In fact, "the world with its seductions is passing away but the man who does God's will endures forever" (1 John 2:17).

In short, "the grace of God has appeared" so that we may live "temperately, justly, and devoutly" discerning good from evil, and not allowing ourselves to be guided by "worldly desires." It teaches us to bear ourselves as "just" men and women in our relations to those around us, "religious" persons in the eyes of God.

This new life is animated by waiting for "our blessed hope, the appearing of the glory of the great God and of our Savior Christ Jesus."[26] This is a characteristic of Christian faith and living: *Marana tha!* (1 Cor 16:22), "Come, Lord Jesus!" (Rev 22:20). It is at the heart of the liturgy: "We proclaim your death, Lord Jesus, until you come in glory"; "We hope to enjoy forever the vision of your glory, through Christ our Lord, from whom all good things come."

The Dawn of an Endless Day

On Christmas night our eyes are turned toward the manger: "He is born, the divine child!" We should not lose sight of this. On the contrary, it is important to be aware of all that the coming of the Son of God born of a woman implies. However, our guide should be what we hear proclaimed in Scripture more than what we perceive in our imagination and pious sensibility.

Luke is a model for readers looking into the event of Jesus' birth, both by his recognition that it was a definite occurrence in a certain place and in his awareness of its significance for salvation history. "This day" of salvation stretches from the birth of the God-child throughout the life of Jesus from Bethlehem to Easter, and thereafter through the life of the Church. At Christmas, we recognize him as "Savior" and "Christ the Lord," because we confess that he is so always and everywhere.

Our faith is not based solely on the nativity story. Faith is born and develops because of Jesus' presence in all of history, the progressive revelation of his mysterious personality, his message of salvation, his lasting radiance. The revelation of Jesus is a unique event, having happened at a particular time and place; but what took place in the historical past nevertheless has meaning for today. Everyone is called to heed this message. It is a difficult decision because faith involves us completely, demanding that we "reject godless ways and worldly desires," "living temperately, justly, and devoutly in this age as we await our blessed hope, the appearing of the glory of the great God and of our Savior Christ Jesus." Getting to know Jesus, more than any other person, is a tremendous undertaking. It is never complete, but rather a slow process that lasts a lifetime.

For the one who has recognized Jesus as "Savior" and "Christ Lord," the story of the birth in Bethlehem is full of meaning. It clarifies the paradox of the incarnation: poverty and glory. A child born into destitution under a decree of a pagan emperor; childbirth far from home and without any assistance for the mother; honored only by a few shepherds from the region; yet glory proclaimed in heaven by an innumerable heavenly host. An encounter between the misery of humanity and the glory from on high—such is the entry into our history of the Son of God made flesh: a mysterious exchange, an unlikely communion, eternal presence!

> In our heart was lost
> the memory of your face.
> On our faces your image
> burned no longer.
> Lost and alone,
> with no guidance to seek you,
> we went astray in the night.
>
> In your pity, you sent,
> to lift our misery,
> your prophets who delivered
> your promise.

Their words, like a guiding light
on the road of hope,
lead us toward you.

Behold, the Virgin has conceived
and the prophecies are fulfilled.
Your love and truth
shine forth.
Under the veil of flesh,
your unapproachable light
invades our shadow of death.

Not all have seen! We believe,
illuminated by your mystery,
in your Word, we call you
our Father.
Today, end our tears!
Your incorruptible seed
has borne fruit in our hearts.[27]

Behold Your King

The Mass at dawn traces its origin from the feast of St. Anastasia celebrated by the Eastern Church in Rome on December 25.[28] Every community (and every priest) soon wanted to have, in its own church, three Christmas Masses: at midnight, at dawn, and later in the morning. This led to the practice of celebrating, one after another, the Mass at midnight (a solemn or "high" Mass) and the Mass at dawn (less solemn or "low").[29] Eventually, the popularity of the dawn Mass declined in favor of the other two.[30]

The reform of Vatican II put this matter in proper perspective. First, by abandoning the liturgically dubious custom of having two consecutive Masses.[31] Second, by reminding us that it is important for each celebration to take place at its own hour.[32] It is also quite fortuitous that there is no longer any distinction between the Eucharistic celebration of the short low Mass and the high solemn Mass. Another contributing factor is the increased involvement, "full, conscious, and active,"[33] of the "communal participation"[34] at each celebration. The Mass has lost its character as an exercise in "private" piety that it had at one time acquired.[35] Finally, the changing rhythms of life have had their effect. In our country, dawn has ceased to be an appropriate hour for large gatherings, whether liturgical or other.[36]

How should we react to these changes? It would be fruitless to try to reverse what has happened. To allow institutions and formularies to change according to the needs and conditions of a certain time is one of the guiding principles that led the council to undertake liturgical reform.[37] The fact remains that the formulary for the Mass at dawn, transmitted by tradition, is there in the Missal. It shines its light, which should not be ignored, on the mystery of the Lord's nativity and on its celebration.

The Lord Comes, the Earth Exults
The birth of the Son of God made flesh is the dawn of salvation that will shine forth in all its splendor in the glorious manifestation of the Lord— the epiphany in glory—at the assembling of the saved. This light that

bursts forth on Christmas begins our march toward the light of eternity. "See, the Lord proclaims to the ends of the earth" (Isa 62:11-12).

In the phrase "daughter of Zion," to whom the message is ostensibly addressed, we see the image of a new people, still being formed, like a child yet to be born for whom one refuses the names that are given to her: "Holy people," "Redeemed of the Lord." It is the Lord himself who calls her this, because he is the one who sanctifies and redeems her.[38] He comes to lead an immense procession of those he has freed from exile and slavery—his prized ones—into the eternal city.

With the birth of Jesus, God brings history to its end. Salvation history enters into its final phase. Let us enter, singing, into the dawn of this new day.

> *A light will shine on us this day:*
> *the Lord is born for us.*
>
> The LORD is king; let the earth rejoice;
>   let the many isles be glad.
> The heavens proclaim his justice,
>   and all peoples see his glory.
>
> Light dawns for the just;
>   and gladness, for the upright of heart.
> Be glad in the LORD, you just,
>   and give thanks to his holy name. (Ps 97:1, 6, 11-12)

The Shepherds of Bethlehem: The First Evangelists

The Gospel for the Nativity of the Lord does not end with the song of the angelic choir. Luke recounts what the shepherds did after the angels left them (Luke 2:15-20).[39]

These simple folk did not doubt the extraordinary revelation that was given them: "good news," "great joy," "Savior." Nor were they scared away by the light that shone about them. They went to Bethlehem "in haste," as Mary had gone to her cousin Elizabeth's house. They saw for themselves that it was not a dream: they found the "infant wrapped in swaddling clothes . . . in a manger." It was exactly as they had been told. "Once they saw, they understood what had been told them concerning this child." Having been the first to receive the good news, as the first witnesses of the event, they also became the first evangelists.

"All who heard of it were astonished at the report given them by the shepherds." In writing this, Luke is no doubt thinking of all those who have received the gospel message. And who would they be, those who accept the witness of the shepherds, if not simple people like themselves?

Luke feels no need to be more precise: he has seen such things happen in the apostles' preaching. His Book of the Acts of the Apostles emphasizes the point.

People "were astonished." According to Luke, this is a reaction that Jesus frequently inspired, from his first preaching in the synagogue at Nazareth (Luke 22), by his words, authority, and miracles.[40] This reaction may be merely superficial. In any case, it does not foretell what will come of it. Is it not typical that after wondrous sights and events, we often find ourselves quickly returning to our mundane preoccupations? Is this kind of astonishment the trigger that begins our search for the meaning of the event? Will it evolve, much later, into faith? Anything is possible. Even after piously celebrating the feast of Christmas, one follows the same road as before.

Mary's Silence

In contrast with this astonishment, which often defies definition, we find the attitude of Mary. She "treasured all these things and reflected on them in her heart" (Luke 2:19; see Luke 2:51). Doubtlessly, she did not at first perceive the full depth and meaning of her experience. Everyone, including Mary, enters gradually into this mystery, listening attentively to her son's teaching and examining the meaning of his behavior and miracles, beginning with that of Cana. She must confront the "why" of the life of faith, from the day when Jesus remained in Jerusalem because he had to be in his Father's house (Luke 2:41-52) to Calvary where, surrounded by his friends, she watched her son die on the cross (Luke 23:49). The Gospels say nothing about it, but Mary's faith must undoubtedly have come to fruition with the resurrection of the Lord. In any case, Luke mentions her as being among the faithful who were earnestly united in prayer when the Spirit descended on them (Acts 1:14). From that point on, he says nothing more about her. Mary has followed and meditated on the various phases of the mystery. She has seen with her own eyes the vitality of the first Christian community after Pentecost. Nothing remains for her but to enter into glory, to follow her son, to experience at his side the blessedness of those who hear the word and keep it (Luke 11:28).

Though unique, this itinerary of the "privileged of God" maps out the road that all believers must follow. Faith is nourished by listening to Scripture and by meditating on all the events in which God comes to us. But Mary spoke, as well. From whom did Luke receive his information concerning "the whole sequence of events from the beginning" (Luke 1:3), if not from Mary or someone she had told about "the great things God had done for her" *(Magnificat)*?

The Kindness of God and His Benevolence

The wonders that the Lord has accomplished are at the heart of the second reading for the Mass at dawn. The text is similar to the one read at the Mass at midnight, having the same sacred style, the same mention of the showing forth of God's benevolence, similar reference to the salvation brought by Christ the Savior to which, at the end—"eschatologically"—Christian hope is open. Both are doubtlessly part of an ancient baptismal hymn of thanksgiving (Titus 3:4-7).[41]

In the New Testament, the term "benevolence" is the opposite of "severity" (Rom 11:22), and is associated with the expression "heartfelt mercy" (Col 3:12). This "benevolence" is a fruit of the Holy Spirit, as are love, joy, peace, patience, faith, humility, and chastity (Gal 5:22).

"Love" translates the Greek *philanthropon*, a fairly general term with humanistic connotations, somewhat weak in meaning. It is commonly used in Greek texts—kings claimed the title of philanthropist (Luke 22:25).[42] However, it is a truly rightful title for the one God whom Jesus has revealed.[43] The philanthropy of God is a saving love. Renewed by the waters of baptism and the gift of the Spirit, we possess, though only in hope, the inheritance of eternal life promised to the children of God.

In Greek—Paul has clearly sacrificed style for meaning—the four verses of this passage form only one sentence. The English translation must make several propositions out of this one long sentence. Still, it is essential to understand the unity and development in what Paul wrote in one stretch. The Father, from the first moment displaying his benevolence and "philanthropy," accomplishes, through Christ Jesus and the sending of the Spirit, his plan of salvation, which affects each one of us from the moment we are plunged into the waters of baptism.

Glory and Praise to God: Father, Son, and Holy Spirit

The Letter of Paul to Titus recalls in opportune fashion the Trinitarian dimension of the mystery of Christmas, which gives us a share in the eternal life inherited by the saints. As a demonstration of God's love and tenderness, the birth of the Lord can only give birth to praise in heaven and on earth. The story of the Messiah's birth at Bethlehem ends, according to Luke, with a resounding "Glory to God in high heaven" (Luke 2:14).[44] The angels' song at Christmas, which soon became a hymn to the Father, Son, and Holy Spirit, has become the Gloria of our Eucharistic celebrations on Sundays and feasts. This reading for the Mass at dawn is enough to justify such a Trinitarian development. Conceived by the Holy Spirit, the child born in Bethlehem already whispers to us the name of the Father in order to draw us into the communion of love that exists between the three divine Persons, thus prompting our praise.

> We have looked for you, Lord Jesus,
> we have waited long for you,
> we have hungered for your face:
> O only longing of our faith,
> may we gaze on you.
>
> Like a spring gushing forth,
> filling the night with its music,
> you reveal to us the name of the Father:
> Revelation of this Love
> which possessed you since the first day.
>
> What begins there in silence,
> the oblation of grain for the fruit,
> who among us can understand?
> Behold the bread, behold the wine
> already placed in our hands.
>
> Toward what joy do you lead us,
> other than the appearance of the Son
> on the nights of Christmas and Easter?
> Toward the eternal Eucharist
> celebrated in the presence of the God of life.[45]

The Word Is Made Flesh

The tone of the Christmas Mass during the day is in clear contrast to the Mass at midnight, owing, in part, to the respective times of the celebrations. It stems mostly, however, from the two gospels. At midnight Mass, one knows that the story of the birth of Jesus is going to be read, and there are certain popular memories of Christmas that spontaneously accompany the visit to the manger. But the expression of joy is found in greater strength in the Mass during the day. The liturgical texts give us an overview of the mystery from a higher vantage point, so to speak.

The God Who Comes

The first reading is an announcement in the form of a lyrical poem of such extraordinary liveliness that one cannot help being swept up by it. The prophet helps present-day believers to be more aware of the full scope of the event that they now celebrate in joy and thanksgiving (Isa 52:7-10). The good news of salvation and peace resounds throughout all the liturgies of Christmas, reverberating from one Mass to another. We share it with each other in exchanging our wishes: "Merry Christmas!" Do you see the power and novelty of it all? says the prophet. Do you see the coming of the Lord with the eyes of a watchman?

"Your God is King!" or "God reigns!" is a common expression in the Old Testament, used most often in the psalms that we still read.[46] Jesus and the disciples he will send forth will announce the same good news: "The reign of God is at hand" (Mark 1:15; Luke 10:9). He brings salvation to all nations. May our joy in what we see and what we still hope for shine forth everywhere.

> *All the ends of the earth have seen the saving power of God.*
>
> Sing to the LORD a new song,
>   for he has done wondrous deeds;
> His right hand has won victory for him,
>   his holy arm.
>
> The LORD has made his salvation known:
>   in the sight of the nations he has revealed his justice.

He has remembered his kindness and his faithfulness
toward the house of Israel.

All the ends of the earth have seen
the salvation by our God.
Sing joyfully to the LORD, all you lands;
break into song; sing praise.

Sing praise to the LORD with the harp,
with the harp and melodious song.
With trumpets and the sound of the horn
sing joyfully before the King, the LORD.
(Ps 98:1-6)

In These Last Days, God Has Spoken to Us Through His Son

As opposed to dumb idols,[47] God is speech. Creative speech and speech
that reveals God himself, totally and definitively, that gives us the means
for communion with him. If his words remain unuttered, or if we do not
hear them, then chaos will reign; men and women, deprived of their only
sure landmark and guiding light, wander astray in the night, not knowing where they go, unable to avoid obstacles, precipices, and impasses.
God never suffers a loss of memory, but sometimes he keeps his word
in reserve. Yet his silence is still a call. Knowing that our situation has
become intolerable, we end by crying despairingly in the night. Then God,
who cannot long abide these cries of despair, no longer holds back his
speech, and we turn again toward the voice that will give us life, return
us to the right path, and make us go forth in good will, our hope and
longing restored. God's words have never stopped resounding since the
beginning. They echo more and more, adapting their tone and form of
expression to the circumstances and understanding of those who hear.
If their meaning is not perfectly understood, or not at all, God speaks
to us through his actions, i.e., events and happenings whose messages
are easier to understand.

In past times, God's official spokesmen were the prophets, whose written witness we find today in the Scriptures. Through them, God spoke
"in fragmentary and varied ways." Henceforth, "in this, the final age,
he has spoken to us through his Son, whom he has made heir of all things
and through whom he first created the universe."

"This Son" assumes in his person all the functions of the speech of
God. He is the decisive speech, the good news, the Word that saves. This
Word recapitulates all previous words, bringing them to perfect fulfillment. This Word is, in itself, complete. It is the Word in an absolute sense,
to which no other will be added. Truly, these times are the last times.

This Son "is the reflection of the Father's glory, the exact representation of the Father's being, and he sustains all things by his powerful word. When the Son had cleansed us from our sins, he took his seat at the right hand of the Majesty in heaven, as far superior to the angels (and all messengers) as the name he has inherited is superior to theirs." He alone, without the least qualification, is the Son of God.

> Lord, Jesus Christ,
> Lord, blessed Son,
> Creator Word,
> Redeeming Word,
> Jesus, beloved,
> Child, newborn.
>
> We bless you, we glorify you,
> we celebrate you, we adore your glory![48]

The Mystery Contemplated by John

The Christmas liturgy culminates with the Prologue from the Gospel According to John, a text of extraordinary theological and contemplative density.[49] It gives us a gradual understanding of the mysteries of Christ as they are revealed in Jesus' teachings and the "signs" that he worked throughout his life.[50] This great literary and mystical composition is a kind of contemplative hymn to Christ: forever near God, bound to his work of creation, he has been sent into the world, where he has assumed human flesh in order to reveal the Father to all and to communicate to them his own divine sonship. The mystery of the incarnation and all it entails is at the center of John's vision—John, the theological evangelist. Nevertheless, throughout his work, the majesty of his vision is combined with a remarkable realism—"The Word became flesh"—and he does not avoid the practical and concrete implications of the mystery that he contemplates.

John composed a superb prologue to his Gospel, with well-balanced formulas artfully succeeding one another. It is divided into three parts: (1) the Word in relation to God, to creation, and to creatures (vv. 1-2, 3, 4-5); (2) the coming of the light (vv. 6-13); (3) the incarnation of the Word and the new covenant (vv. 14-18). This passage must be read in verse form, the way it is printed in modern Bibles and in the Lectionary.

In the Beginning Was the Word

From the start, John's eagle eye looks as far and high as possible: "In the beginning," to the origin of all things—"the heavens and the earth"—

created by God (Gen 1:1). Beyond that, he comes to God and perceives in God's presence the Word, which has never known a beginning: it simply "was," existing before everything else because it is God. In the same sense, Paul says that the Son is "the first-born of all creatures" (Col 1:15).

"Word" is a term that is well known to us. Many texts from the Old Testament come into play here, especially those that speak of Wisdom personified (Prov 8:23-36; Sir 24:1-22). The Word is the perfect expression of God—his "image" (Col 1:15). All forms of expression try to articulate, as best they can, the inexpressible: the "form of God" (Phil 2:6) possessed by the Son born of the Father before the ages, the perfect "reflection of his glory" (Heb 1:3).

The Word, because of its place "in God's presence" was associated with the work of creation: "Through him all things came into being, and apart from him nothing came to be." Once again, we can think of several passages from the Old Testament that connect creation to the Word of God[51] or to the personification of divine Wisdom.[52] Here, though, it is no longer a question of a personification: the Word is, like God, a Person, equal to the Father yet distinct from him, by whom all things exist and through whom we live (1 Cor 8:6). He is the Life (John 8:12) from which all life springs (1 John 5:12; John 14:6), the Light that one must accept and follow in order to leave darkness and be free from death.

In five verses, John enables us to penetrate to the very threshold of the Word's inaccessible mystery in its unique relation to God, and opens up for us a way of contemplation that imitates his own.

The Word: The True Light Come into the World

In the Bible, there is no discussion of God that is speculative or abstract theology. Rather, there is testimony to the experience of this God who is known by the works that reveal him, beginning with creation. In this creation, the Word-Light has put his stamp on the world.[53] However, humanity as a whole, blinded by sin, has not been able to see it,[54] and so dwells in darkness. Those who, on the other hand, have recognized the signature of the Word in his work, have been elevated to the level of children of God "who were begotten not by blood, nor by carnal desire, nor by man's willing it, but by God."[55]

This rebirth in and through God occupies an important place in John's Gospel. It is the subject of Jesus' conversation with Nicodemus. "Flesh begets flesh, spirit begets spirit." This second birth is the essential requi-

site for entry into the kingdom of God. Jesus invokes all his authority—
"I solemnly assure you" (John 3:1-12)—for this unheard-of revelation that
is at the heart of Christian faith and hope: "See what love the Father has
bestowed on us in letting us be called children of God!" (1 John 3:1).
We are so called because the Son, by becoming one of us, has recreated
humanity and sworn a new covenant that allows us to address God as
Father.

The Incarnation of the Word: The New Covenant

The presence of the Word at the center of creation and in our midst is
not simply a matter of greater awareness on our part: "The Word became flesh and made his dwelling among us." We have "seen with our
eyes . . . touched—we speak of the word of life" (1 John 1:1). Because
of our constant use of these affirmations, they run the risk of losing their
vitality and realism. Nevertheless they make real for us what seems to
be so widely disparate: the Word and flesh, the Word of life and the
senses, the infinite and the finite, what was "in the beginning" and what
exists only temporarily, what was begotten from all eternity and what
lives and dies in history. God is made man;[56] his only Son dwells—pitches
his tent—among us!

The first covenant has not been superseded; it has been extended to
all people and, indeed, to the entire universe. To all of us, for it no longer comes through a particular law and people; it is identified with a Person in whom God and humankind are indissolubly united, from whose
fullness we have received grace upon grace. To the entire universe, for
creation has recovered its full dignity. The Word made flesh invites us
to recognize human value, the treasure of earthly realities washed clean
of the grime of sin by the incarnation of the Son of God.

We have seen the glory by which God, whom "no one has ever seen,"
manifests his presence in the world. John sees this manifestation primarily
in the paschal event (John 13:21; 17:2-5), but also in the "signs"[57] that
Jesus accomplished (John 2:11; 11:40) and in the unity of the disciples
(John 17:22-23).

The Prophets: Witnesses to the Light

John, the contemplative and mystic, is still an apostle. He wrote his Gospel
so that its readers might believe that Jesus is the Messiah, the Son of God,
and that because of their faith, they may have life in his name (John 20:31).
He knows that the good news must be announced and preached unstintingly, but also that personal witness is indispensable as a guide to the

encounter with the Lord. He remembers very precisely the day and hour when John the Baptist, with two of his disciples, saw Jesus walking along the banks of the Jordan, and said: "Look! There is the Lamb of God."[58] The two disciples, hearing this exclamation, followed Jesus, staying near him throughout that day (John 1:35-39). It is impossible to forget such an experience.

The mission of John the Baptist was certainly unique. He was chosen, sent by God to prepare the way of the Lord (Luke 1:76), to bear witness to the light in whom all must believe. He fulfilled his role admirably when he proclaimed, "It is he of whom I said: 'After me is to come a man who ranks ahead of me, because he was before me.'" A true precursor, he was never tempted to allow himself to be mistaken for the Messiah, to thrust himself between his own disciples and the one who was to come. Far from being the least bit chagrined by the success of Jesus' preaching, he drew great joy from it, a joy that satisfied him perfectly. "He must increase, while I must decrease" (John 3:22-30). It was important for the evangelist to recall this.

Still, the conduct and witness of John the Baptist is a valuable example for every believer and for the Church itself. Without witnesses, the Light remains hidden, and discovering it becomes difficult. Each of us, at some moment in our lives, has experienced this. It is impossible to say what would have happened, what we would have become, what we would have lost, if. . . . One thing it certain: the personal witness has been critical, decisive for each of us. Happy those men and women of whom one can say, "There was a man, a woman, sent by God for me." This need for witnesses, with which Christ cannot dispense, heightens the realism of the incarnation.

In Our Present Time

The liturgy for the Mass during Christmas Day raises us to the heights of heaven, not just to fill our minds with lofty things, an escape into piety from the responsibilities and exigencies of daily life. Rather, it is meant to free us from any narrow perspective we might have of those things that may be too much with us.

The child born in Bethlehem in an obscure stable is the Word of God, the Light of the world. To really understand this paradox and its significance, we must return to "the beginning," in the presence of the God who is now made man that all might become children of God. A new relationship has been instituted between God and humanity. This new covenant is gained—one might say made—through the person of Jesus. It is available to everyone who seeks such a relationship.

Everything is acted out "in this, the final age." It is in this world that the Light confronts darkness in a gigantic battle, the result of which is certain, a fact that makes it no less difficult. No one can remain firm in an attitude of neutrality; we must choose sides. The message of the good news is spread throughout the world, announcing peace and salvation.

The Lord's nativity and its celebration cannot be dissociated from the rest of the mystery of salvation. The prophets, "in fragmentary and varied ways," announce the decisive intervention of God. The birth in flesh of his own Son strikes these promises home to us in an unfathomable way. God's Son is born to make known to us the unseen God. He is to die on the cross, be gloriously resurrected, and communicate to us the fullness of his life.

To grasp the meaning and importance of the Christmas event and to enter into its dynamism, we must try to encompass, in one great overview, the whole history of salvation, from the beginning, when God created the heavens and the earth, to the end, when all who are saved will be assembled in the heavenly Jerusalem.

> The Son of God, the King of Glory,
> wished to be born among us;
> he came on our earth
> and left the mark of his love.
>
> Those who walked in darkness
> have seen their night dispelled,
> and on the people in distress
> a light has shown.
>
> In our night arises the dawn
> of his justice and peace:
> God sends his deliverance,
> and he will never abandon us.
>
> He has shown us the way,
> he is laden with our sorrows;
> and we march toward his Promise,
> his love shining in our faces.
>
> When the Holy City will appear,
> when the new heavens will open,
> we will relish life without end
> before the throne of the Lamb.
>
> *"Today, your kingdom is at hand,*
> *Come among us, Lord Jesus!"*[59]

Sunday After the Nativity

The Holy Family [1]

Among the celebrations taking place during the season of Christmas-Epiphany, that of the Holy Family is a peculiar case: its origin is not really liturgical; it has been on the calendar for a little more than seventy-five years; during this short time, its date has changed four times.

Various groups devoted to the Holy Family have appeared in different Western countries since the seventeenth century. Toward the end of the nineteenth century, family life and morality were in a state of crisis, and laws concerning marriage were undergoing change. The state assumed more responsibility, and legal requirements regulating civil marriage were made independent of the Church. Divorce was sanctioned. This evolution began and developed in a climate of confrontation between those who held for the pluralistic character of social life (anticlericalism was also a factor) and the Church. Also, it was becoming gradually more obvious that Western countries had ceased to merit the label "Christian." But acknowledging this fact did not imply approval. On the contrary, papal teachings of the time were aimed at curbing this kind of decadence, and the Church fought to recover what it considered lost ground. [2]

Groups like those of the Holy Family associations seemed capable of playing an important role in combating these modern developments. Accordingly, Pope Leo XIII recognized their potential and centralized them, giving them full Church approval and establishing regulations to foster their activity. [3] On June 14, 1893, he instituted a feast of the Holy Family for the Third Sunday after Epiphany. But this celebration—with its own Mass and Office—remained optional, having been placed into the liturgical calendar only in those dioceses that requested it.

In 1914, Pope Benedict XV transferred the feast to January 19 and allowed it to be a kind of votive celebration. But on October 21, 1921, he moved it to the First Sunday after Epiphany, and what was more important, he entered it into the universal calendar of the Roman Church, which meant that it was to be celebrated everywhere.

The Roman Calendar published on March 21, 1969, in accordance with the liturgical reform of Vatican II, finally designated it for the Sunday after Christmas (or on December 30 if there is no available Sunday between December 25 and January 1). The formulary of the Mass comprised three readings for the Sunday celebration.[4] However, the first two were the same each year, though there was a different gospel for each year, A, B, and C.[5] In 1981, the feast was granted a complete cycle of readings for the three years.[6]

The gospels tell us all we know about the Holy Family: the flight into Egypt and the return from exile (Matt 2:13-15, 19-23: Year A); the presentation of Jesus in the Temple (Luke 2:22-40: Year B); what happened when Jesus, twelve years old, made the Passover pilgrimage to Jerusalem with Mary and Joseph (Luke 2:41-52: Year C).

The first readings are not directly related to the gospels. The texts for Year A, which are the ones most tailored to the origins of the feast, speak of the duties of children toward their parents (Sir 3:2-6, 12-14) and familial virtues (Col 3:12-21). Year B recalls the miraculous birth of Isaac (Gen 15:1-6; 21:1-3) and the eulogy of the faith of the patriarchs in the Letter to the Hebrews (Heb 11:8, 11-12, 17-19). In Year C, after the story of Anna's maternity and the consecration of her son to God (1 Sam 1:20-22, 24-28), we read an exhortation to the children of God to obey the commandments of the Lord (1 John 3:1-2, 21-24).

God Among Us,
Jesus the Savior

Honor Your Father; Glorify Your Mother

Respect for parents and their authority is a fundamental rule of all societies whose core is the family. Insistence on the duties owed a father and mother varies according to the dominance of one (patriarchate) or the other (matriarchate) in the family system.[7]

"Honor your father and your mother" is the fourth commandment of the Decalogue (Exod 20:12; Deut 5:16). The Old Testament often refers to it, giving examples of its application, commenting on it, etc.[8] The New Testament cites it five times with no additions.[9] Yet, on the occasion of the controversy with the Pharisees and scribes, Jesus, reminding them that this commandment is a "word of God," condemns as hypocritical, "useless practice" all tradition and doctrine opposed to it (Matt 15:1-9; Mark 7:8-13). As for Paul, in the brief tract on domestic morality in the Letter to the Ephesians (5:21–6:9), he says that this commandment is "the first to carry a promise with it" (Eph 6:2), which means that he considers it a commandment of primary importance.

"To honor"[10] implies veneration and respect not only in word, but in deed, i.e., reverential obedience. The duty of loving one's parents is not explicitly indicated. But are they not the ones closest to their children? Love for parents thus comes from the second commandment, which is like the first (Lev 19:18; Matt 22:39).

Asking to be steadfast, Ben Sirach addresses a beautiful prayer to God as "Father and Master of my life, Father and God of my life" (Sir 23:1, 4). This is surely seeing in God the source "from whom every family in heaven and on earth takes its name" (Eph 3:15). Inversely, the behavior of a father toward his children can mirror the manner in which God behaves toward us. Jesus, too, readily speaks of a father in those parables where he reveals the love, compassion, tenderness, and mercy of God toward humankind. Our duties toward parents are rooted in God. The honor we show them reflects on God and determines, so to speak, his behavior toward us. "He who honors his father atones for sins." "Kindness to a father will not be forgotten." Likewise, "he obeys the Lord who brings comfort to his mother."

The text of the sage Ben Sirach is a kind of brief variation on the theme of the fourth commandment, which comes from God and in which we find the foundation for the duties owed to our parents throughout their life. To observe this precept is to walk according to God's ways, to act like those who dwell in the house of the Lord, who have the good fortune to be part of his family.

> *Happy are those who fear the Lord and walk in his ways.*
>
> Happy are you who fear the LORD,
>   who walk in his ways!
> For you shall eat the fruit of your handiwork;
>   happy shall you be, and favored.
>
> Your wife shall be like a fruitful vine
>   in the recesses of your home;
> Your children like olive plants
>   around your table.
>
> Behold, thus is the man blessed
>   who fears the LORD.
> The LORD bless you from Zion:
>   may you see the prosperity of Jerusalem
> all the days of your life.
> (Ps 128)

Family Relationships in the Lord

From culture to culture, from age to age, many factors affect the condition of people—men, women, and children—and their relationships in society and in the family. These are not small matters. Some developments can be interpreted as progress, but not all. To appreciate this, we must get beyond our own perspective. Paul was a man of his time. He did not try to question it; what would be the sense? Paul's interest lay elsewhere. The apostle was attempting to remind his correspondents and readers of certain principles, both general and particular, of Christian morality (Col 3:5-25). This morality is theological: it does not consist in observing precepts of a code that is completely outside the purview of the one who acts by it; it has its source in God himself, toward whom we move by adopting his own ways of acting (Col 3:12-21).

Even as he deals with conduct between neighbors, and especially between family members, Paul focuses on divine favor. God has made

Christians "his faithful and beloved." Those whom God has loved first must "clothe themselves with heartfelt mercy, with kindness, humility, meekness, and patience." In other words, they must allow God to create in them a new heart.[11] The basis for Christian morality is the radical transformation of men and women, through divine grace. From this flows everything else. There is no room for equivocation. Only one thing matters: to act "like the Lord," "in the name of our Lord Jesus Christ," "in the Lord." The form of relationships between couples, between parents and children, can change, and they have in fact, since Paul wrote this letter. Nevertheless, in every situation, the general principle that our relationships should be "in Christ" must be of primary importance. "The peace of Christ," "perfect unity," produces its precious fruit in all seasons.[12]

The Daily Eucharist of Family Life
The theological dimension of Pauline morality—especially in dealing with familial relations in the Lord—is such that the apostle speaks of this life in terms of worship, or at least in relation to worship.

To be sure, this is not surprising, coming from Paul. In fact, in the Letter to the Romans, he writes: "The God I worship in the spirit by preaching the gospel of his Son . . . " (Rom 1:9). A little while later, he gives thanks that God has made him "a minister of Christ Jesus among the Gentiles, with the priestly duty of preaching the gospel of God" (Rom 15:16). Elsewhere, the apostle clearly considers the whole Christian life to be an act of worship given to God.[13]

The "substance" of this worship is all that one says and does "in the name of our Lord Jesus Christ." that is to say, by virtue of one's being united with him in faith and charity, insofar as "the word of Christ, rich as it is, dwells in us." This life is one of endless thanksgiving, a eucharist at every moment. The summit to which it leads and the source from which it flows is the liturgy.[14] There, our awareness and thanksgiving are made explicit "in psalms, hymns, and inspired songs."

Jesus, Mary, and Joseph on the Road to Exile
In a simple "Life of Jesus," the precipitous flight of the Holy Family into Egypt, the return to their own country, to Nazareth, the story tells us so little that our appetites are whetted for more information and we are bothered on more than one point. We would like to know a little more, for example, about the conditions this poor couple with its newborn child

experienced in Egypt, how long they dwelt in this foreign land, etc.[15] In addition, the insistence of the evangelist on the appearance of the angel of the Lord, who visits Joseph three times in order to tell him what to do, bothers us a little. We may also be tempted to think that the Holy Family went through this easily, with hardly any problems. But to think this way is to forget that this is a gospel and must be dealt with as such: an announcement of the good news and revelation of the mystery of Jesus, Son of God made man, Savior and Lord. "The reality of this mystery is 'historical,' but its historicity surpasses and always will surpass the apparent words and deeds that it contains."[16] The twice-repeated formula— "In this way what was said through the prophets [prophet] was fulfilled"—invites us to read the passage in the perspective in which it was written (Matt 2:13-15, 19-23).[17]

This is a well-structured composition, the two parts of which have the same literary scheme: setting ("After the astrologers had left . . . After Herod's death . . . "); "the angel of the Lord appeared in a dream to Joseph"; then the immediate execution of the directive and a quotation from the prophet.

Moreover, both of these texts are part of a triptych: announcement to Joseph (Matt 1:18-25); flight into Egypt (Matt 2:13-15); return to Galilee (Matt 2:19-23). Note the recurrence of the verb "to call" in the three fragments: "You shall call him Jesus," the child who is going to be born (Matt 1:21); "Out of Egypt I have called my son" (Matt 2:15); "He shall be called a Nazorean" (Matt 2:23). Each time—the intervention of the angel of the Lord leaves no doubt—it is God who takes the initiative for the fulfillment of his plan. This is not simply just an episode in the life of the Holy Family and Jesus, but an *event* in the strongest sense. The meaning is unfolded by those discrete redactional details that the Christian reader can easily decode.

Jesus, the Liberator of the People of God

"Out of Egypt I have called my son" is a quote from the prophet Hosea (Hos 11:1), which says that the true history of the people of God began with the Exodus. For God had said to Jacob: "Do not be afraid to go down to Egypt. . . . Not only will I go down to Egypt with you, I will also bring you back here." So Jacob went there with his family and possessions (Gen 46:2-5). Likewise, Joseph was told that his family's sojourn in Egypt would not be long, and he went "taking the child and his mother" (Matt 2:13-14).

To this first parallel is added another that is quite striking. When he told Moses to return to Egypt in order to deliver his people, God said to him, "Go back to Egypt, for the men who sought your life are dead." So "Moses took his wife and his sons, and started back to the land of Egypt" (Exod 4:19-20) Matthew uses practically the same terms: the angel of the Lord said to Joseph: "Get up, take the child and his mother, and set out for the land of Israel. Those who had designs on the life of the child are dead." He got up, took the child and his mother, and returned to the land of Israel" (Matt 2:19-21).

This double connection that Matthew obviously intends us to make lets us decode the message.

The history of the new people of God begins with Jesus' departure into Egypt and his return to the land of Israel. This pilgrimage is similar to the one Jacob made.

Jesus is the instrument of the freedom that God initiated, hinted at by the freedom for which Moses was protagonist.

The path of God's grace is hence turned upon itself. "God remembers forever his covenant" (Ps 105:8).

"He Shall Be Called a Nazorean"

Like his departure into Egypt, Jesus' return from exile fulfills "what was said through the prophets." As a matter of fact, we do not know what prophecy Matthew is alluding to. No matter; the fact remains that, by saying this, the evangelist suggests that we be attentive to his text, for it includes a message.

Moses died in the desert without entering into the Promised Land, which he was able to see only from the top of Mount Nebo (Deut 34). Jesus is greater than he. Moreover, there it was a matter of entering into a country for the first time; here it is a question of returning to one's own country. It is a definitive return, the three stages of which are clear: "the land of Israel," "the region of Galilee," "a town called Nazareth."

Jesus has made the small town of Nazareth famous—"his own country" (Mark 6:1; Luke 4:16); its name will forever be attached to his. There is no scriptural prophecy on this subject. Perhaps Matthew wants to teach from the beginning that all the promises are definitively fulfilled after Nazareth, which Jesus left to live in Capernaum and preach the good news (Matt 4:13, 17). The "region of Galilee" is where he manifested himself to the crowds. It was there that the resurrected Christ summoned together the eleven apostles in order to show himself to them one last time and to send them on their mission (Matt 28:16-20). The very mention of this region strikes a responsive chord in the hearts of Christians who read these Gospel verses. It is while traveling around Galilee that Jesus proclaims his teaching (Matt 4:23). It is in Galilee that the Sermon on the Mount (Matt 5:1-7:29) is heard. And finally, it is on a mountain in Galilee that he says to us: "And know that I am with you always, until the end of the world" (Matt 28:20).

Matthew edited this portion of his Gospel with great care, in the light of his faith, his experience of Jesus' ministry and teaching, the life of the Church, and long reflection on the mystery of salvation through Jesus of Nazareth, a mystery that is an established part of history—which is absolutely necessary as a basis for faith—but a part of history that is not limited to scholarly interest.

We must interpret Matthew's Gospel according to the clues he has given us. But of no lesser importance is our own interpretation, made in the light of our own faith and Christian experience and the faith and experience of the Church yesterday and today.

And the Holy Family?

One might say that the feast of the Holy Family is a celebration with a double perspective. Without explicitly saying so, the first part of the Liturgy of the Word (Old Testament and Second Reading), by recalling the fourth commandment and the theological dimension of familial "morality," hints that we should look for a model; and where may one be found, if not in the Holy Family—Jesus, Mary, and Joseph? It is a model that no family can equal, for none is comparable to it: Joseph "the upright man," Mary the virgin mother, and the only Son of God! It remains a model precisely because there is an ideal relationship between persons, based on a perfect relationship with God, that reaches its highest attainment in the Holy Family. It is a model despite the paradox of these relations: the Son of God made flesh was submissive to Mary and Joseph; this incomparable couple provided the family milieu where Jesus grew steadily "in wisdom and age and grace before God and men" (Luke 2:51-52).

Like all other families on this earth, the Holy Family experienced its own special situations, difficulties, and anxieties. It was burdened with trials and subjected to the winds of fortune: an emperor's edict forced the Virgin, about to give birth, to leave for Bethlehem, where she laid her newborn son in a manger; a king's cruelty forced Mary, Joseph, and the child to flee into Egypt; fear of Herod's successor made them settle in Nazareth of Galilee. Throughout all this, they placed themselves in the hands of Providence, subject to the will of God, who frequently revealed it to their eyes of faith. The Word dwelt among them in all its fullness and—how could anyone doubt it?—they lived in a state of thanksgiving (Second Reading); Mary never stopped singing her *Magnificat*, she who "treasured all these things and reflected on them in her heart" (Luke 2:19).

Along with Mary and Joseph, Jesus experienced, from his infancy, certain events whose meaning sets an example for family life. Among them is the flight into Egypt and the return to Israel, recounted by Matthew in a story full of teachings and revelations concerning the mystery of Jesus.[18] We should not minimize its importance just to make it fit neatly into the context of praising those virtues that make families holy.

This celebration takes place at Christmastime, indeed just a few days after the solemnity. Its prayers certainly petition God to "help us to live as the holy family, united in respect and love";[19] they appeal to Mary and Joseph's prayer that God will "unite our families in peace and love,"[20] they petition God to grant us "to live as Jesus, Mary, and Joseph, in peace with you and one another."[21] The Eucharistic Prayer opens with a preface of the Nativity, and the communion antiphon also attracts our attention: "Our God has appeared on earth, and lived among men." Which is to say that after the gospel, the celebration takes a turn. Without undoing what happened before—even less, renouncing it—the celebration firmly places the mystery of the Holy Family within the context of the incarnation.

The Son of God is truly made man: born of a woman, he grew "in age and wisdom" in a family. He has experienced all human conditions, including being subject with his parents to the rulers of this world, to the perils of human existence. But throughout all this, in fact because of it, he accomplished the will of his Father and the work of salvation. It is to the plan of the incarnation that the Son of God voluntarily submits himself. It is this same plan that defines the means to salvation for all who come into this world. It is not a question of fleeing reality, breaking all human ties, rejecting them in order to seek and find God and be saved. "God is at work in this age"[22] not elsewhere. "We do not await the end of days to find him. . . . Nor do we imagine that he is everywhere except where we die"[23] and where we are caught up in the vicissitudes of human existence.

In the highest degree of perfection, the Holy Family experienced the mystery of the incarnation and its lesson for us.

> Nazareth is a kind of school where we may begin to discover what Christ's life was like and even to understand his gospel. Here we can observe and ponder the simple appeal of the way God's Son came to be known, profound yet full of hidden meaning. And gradually we may even learn to imitate him.
>
> Here we can learn to realize who Christ really is. And here we can sense and take account of the conditions and circumstances that surrounded and affected his life on earth: the places, the tenor of the times, the culture, the language, religious customs, in brief everything which Jesus used to make himself known to the world. Here everything speaks to us, everything has meaning. Here we can learn the importance of spiritual discipline for all who wish to follow Christ and to live by the teachings of his gospel.
>
> How I would like to return to my childhood and attend the simple yet profound school that is Nazareth! How wonderful to be close to Mary, learning again the lesson of the true meaning of life, learning again God's truths.[24]

The feast of the Holy Family is certainly not just another devout votive celebration, just a minor addition; rather it is a major contribution toward helping us to understand the mystery of the Lord's nativity.

Blessed Be the Name of the Lord Who Comes!

After the nativity and the adoration of the magi, Matthew's Gospel tells us of only one event concerning the infancy of Jesus: the flight into Egypt and the return to Israel with the Holy Family's settling in Nazareth. This incident is read for Year A of the feast of the Holy Family. For years B and C, the readings are taken from Luke, who relates the stories of the presentation of Jesus in the Temple and of the three days he remained there when, at age twelve, he accompanied his parents on a pilgrimage to Jerusalem.[25]

Both of these episodes concern Jesus, Mary, and Joseph. The parents presented their newborn child in the Temple to fulfill the prescription of the Law; when they discovered that he was not with the caravan returning to Nazareth, they found him seated among the doctors of the Law. In both these stories attention is focused on Jesus himself. This is the child about whom Simeon and Anna spoke and prophesied. At twelve years of age, he takes the initiative. Moreover, the evangelist recounts Jesus' first speech, which Mary and Joseph, in their puzzlement, did not understand. The liturgy of years B and C gives the feast of the Holy Family a different orientation, one more explicitly centered on the person of Jesus and his mission.[26]

Abraham Begat Isaac, Son of the Promise

"For my eyes have witnessed your saving deed displayed for all the peoples to see: a revealing light to the Gentiles, the glory of your people Israel." These words of Simeon help us to understand the choice of the first reading (Gen 15:1-6; 21:1-3).

This reading is made up of only nine verses out of a total of 159 verses found in six chapters (Gen 15:1–21:7) that tell of the promise of a son to Abraham in his old age and the realization of this promise.

This is a good time to consider just how liturgical texts are chosen. The liturgy selects from the Bible, perhaps from only one story, what is well suited to a particular celebration. More precisely, it chooses what texts, along with others, will contribute to the composite structure of a Liturgy of the Word. It is pointless to deal with it in any other context. In some cases, it would even be rather misleading.[27]

The first reading recalls that with Isaac—the son of the promise—the long line of heirs to the covenant begins. The liturgy uses this text because Jesus is the fulfillment of this line, this promise, this covenant that culminates in his person. That is also why the Christian assembly sings Psalm 105.

> Give thanks to the LORD, invoke his name. . . .
> He remembers forever his covenant
>   which he made binding for a thousand generations—
> Which he entered into with Abraham
>   and by his oath to Isaac.
> (Ps 105:1, 8-9)

Thanks to Faith

From beginning to end, the covenant rests on the initiative and faithfulness of God. He has chosen Abraham and is solemnly sworn to him. By giving him a son, God assured him of an unending line of heirs to the promise. However, in order to benefit personally from the "great reward" of this covenant, one must devote oneself to God in steadfast faith, of which Abraham is still the model. The brief passage from the Letter to the Hebrews this Sunday is particularly valuable for comprehending the nature of this faith (Heb 11:8, 11-12, 17-19).

The author recalls, successively, Abraham's journey from his homeland to a place that God promised him, the birth of his son Isaac, and the subsequent demand to sacrifice his only son. Abraham, the "father of believers," went along with it all. In these three situations, Abraham gave proof of his complete confidence in God and his word. He left his country "not knowing where he was going," but with the assurance that at the end of his wandering—a prefiguring of the Exodus—he would enter into possession of the promised inheritance. He had no heir "born of his blood," but when God announced that he would have one, he did not doubt, in spite of his and his wife Sarah's advanced age. When God demanded that he offer his son in sacrifice, he set about to obey this absolutely devastating command that would, it appeared, put an end to the promised line of descendants once and for all.

Faith, therefore, is totally and completely placing oneself in the hands of God, not in blind obedience, but with the assurance of having a bond with him. It establishes a communion with God, wherein God's promise and the destiny of the one who believes in his word are intertwined and will always be so, no matter what happens. It allows one to walk in the right direction with humble—sometimes painful—confidence, as if one could see the Invisible. Finally, faith consists in recognizing that the living God will even raise the dead in his desire for his own to have a share in the life of which he is the source. His promise extends from age to age, from generation to generation, to all those who, with Abraham, respond "Ready!" to the call of God (Gen 22:1).

Jesus' Entry into the Temple

From first to last, the life of Christ is obedience to the Father. Coming into the world, he declared: "I have come to do your will" (Heb 10:9). "Born of a woman, born under the law, to deliver from the law those who were subjected to it, so that we might receive our status as adopted sons" (Gal 4:4-5). He was circumcised on the eighth day after his birth and, in the following month, his parents took him to Jerusalem to present the prescribed sacrifice to the Lord.

By making this journey, Mary and Joseph conformed to the prescriptions of the Law: "Every first-born male shall be consecrated to the Lord."[28] Mary and Joseph knew their duty here, fully aware that their child belonged to God! Luke reports this episode for its prophetic value. In his Gospel, it is at this point in the Temple where Jesus' manifestation begins and ends.[29] In some sense, he is enthroned by his parents at the presentation. There, he is recognized as "the Anointed of the Lord" by two old people—a man and a woman—symbols of all those who live in hope of "the consolation of Israel."

Nunc Dimittis

This brief canticle of Simeon proclaims that the mystery of salvation is already accomplished. Like the *Magnificat*, it is woven with biblical memories that hark back to Isaiah's "Book of Consolation."[30] Simeon begins by recognizing that the Lord has kept his promises: "Now, Master, you can dismiss your servant in peace; you have fulfilled your word." Up till then, God was preparing his salvation: the whole of sacred history is thus evoked. "Now" salvation is given, and even the pagans will participate in it. Jesus, "light of the nations," has come to bring them this revelation: his mission[31] will later be taken over by the apostles.[32]

"The child's father and mother were marveling at what was being said about him." Astonishment is, in the Bible, the normal reaction to revelation: Luke has already noted this in the story of the annunciation (Luke 1:29). Its absence signifies either that one is blind to the presence of divine mystery or, because it has been heard or celebrated so often, that it has become rather blasé.

Until that time, Jesus had only been hailed as the Messiah for Israel (Luke 1:31-33, 43; 2:11). It is another matter to recognize him as the salvation of the pagans. Luke, in his Gospel and in Acts, insists on this point; he knows that it goes against the grain to acknowledge this universalism and put it into practice. Peter's hesitation is a matter of record in Acts (Acts 10–11); one day, it will be struck down by Paul, who will openly oppose Peter (Gal 2:11-14). Luke seized the occasion to show that the extension of salvation to the pagans was acknowledged at Jesus' infancy by a man who was the model witness of Israel in waiting.

A Sign of Contradiction

After his prophetic song, Simeon turns to Jesus' parents in order to bless them and to give thanks to God for what he has done and will do for and through them. This benediction is in the form of a "beatitude," similar to what Elizabeth used to address Mary (Luke 1:42). But that is not all. Simeon suddenly sees in the child a sign of division: he will cause the fall and rise of many in Israel; foundation for the edifice of salvation (Isa 28:16), he will be a stumbling block (Isa 8:14-15) for some, as the First Letter of Peter says:

> For Scripture has it: "See, I am laying a cornerstone in Zion, an approved stone, and precious. He who puts his faith in it shall not be shaken." The stone is of value for you who have faith. For those without faith, it is rather, "A stone which the builders rejected that became a cornerstone." It is likewise "an obstacle and a stumbling stone." Those who stumble and fall are the disbelievers in God's word; it belongs to their destiny to do so (1 Pet 2:6-8).[33]

Speaking directly to Mary, Simeon says: "and you yourself shall be pierced with a sword." What is the personal trial of which he speaks? Some have thought of it as a test of faith that Jesus' mother would undergo before his death. Others, following St. Augustine, see it as the sorrow of a mother and a believer who is present, though powerless, at the sufferings of Jesus on the cross. Still others think that Simeon was talking about Mary's involvement in the trials of her son, who was so harshly opposed during his mission, the object of slander, misunderstanding, etc. Let us look at it in context.

Simeon said that Jesus will become "a sign to be contradicted." Mary the believer (Luke 1:45) is troubled (Luke 1:29); she wonders (Luke 2:33), she is astonished (Luke 2:48), and she questions (Luke 1:34); she does not understand (Luke 2:50), and she reflects and meditates on the mystery (Luke 1:29; 2:19, 51). The sword that cleaves the people of God asunder has struck this daughter of Zion personally.[34]

The story ends with Anna's intervention. She approaches and "the praises of God" sung by the angels at Jesus' birth resound in the Temple as Jesus is about to enter. Then Anna, "a prophetess," takes over, so to speak, from the shepherds at Bethlehem, and begins to speak of the child "to all who looked forward to the deliverance of Jerusalem." The presentation of Jesus at the Temple is truly the feast of Encounter, as the Eastern Church calls it. "O God, we ponder your kindness within your temple. As your name, O God, so also your praise reaches to the ends of the earth" (Ps 48:10-11).

Return of the Holy Family to the Hidden Life

"When the pair had fulfilled all the prescriptions of the Law of the Lord, they returned to Galilee and their own town of Nazareth." A long period of silence begins for the Holy Family. They will lead a humble and hidden existence that has never been revealed. The Gospel reports only that "his parents used to go every year to Jerusalem for the feast of the Passover" and what happened when "they went up for the celebration as was their custom" when he was twelve (Luke 2:41-52).[35] Luke contents himself with noting that "the child grew in size and strength, filled with wisdom, and the grace of God was upon him."[36]

Once again, we can see here the parallelism between Jesus and John the Baptist that characterizes Luke's infancy narrative. About John he writes: "The child grew up and matured in spirit. He lived in the desert until the day when he made his public appearance in Israel" (Luke 1:80). The differences between these two accounts are significant. Jesus, conceived by the Holy Spirit, is "filled with wisdom." Wisdom, understood in its primary scriptural sense,[37] truly belongs to Jesus. Luke repeats this several times (Luke 2:52; 11:31; 21:15). Is it not in harmony with the Spirit (Acts 6:10)? Again, while John goes into the desert early on, Jesus remains with his family, sharing the life of the people of Nazareth until the very beginning of his ministry. Unlike John, he does not wait for someone to come to him: he announces the good news on the roads and in public places, in synagogues and houses.

The One We Wait for Is Here Among His Own

In Year B, the liturgy for the feast of the Holy Family shows the child Jesus borne in the arms of Mary, accompanied by Joseph. Simeon and Anna, two old people, are enlightened by the Holy Spirit and recognize this child as the Messiah for whom they have waited. No angelic intervention is involved here, but rather a man and a woman animated by intense longing. It is enough: their eyes see the coming of God, the object of their lifelong hope.

This year's focus does not bear directly on the example of familial virtue suggested by the Holy Family, but primarily on the fact that faith and the Spirit allow one to recognize the presence of the Lord among us, however humble and inauspicious it may appear.

Another fact needs our attention. The encounter of Simeon and Anna with Jesus took place on the occasion of his presentation. Mary and Joseph made this journey in order to satisfy a prescription of the Law. They planned to go to the Temple in Jerusalem, make the customary offering, and then return home. Imagine their astonishment when they saw this stranger approach, an old man who took the child in his arms, blessed them, and said the most extraordinary things. Their surprise no doubt increased when they saw Anna the prophetess approach proclaiming the praises of God. Their situation was ordinary enough, a journey made by hundreds of other families without anything unusual happening. Then all of a sudden the unforeseen and the unforeseeable come to light. An encounter takes place. A word, indeed a revelation, is given that God clearly intends for us. At the same time it allows others to perceive the hidden Lord.

Exceptional grace belonging to exceptional people? Certainly not, for it is God who guides our steps and those of others. We have nothing, it is true. But the One who gave an aged Abraham a posterity can bring the most extraordinary bounty out of our simplest actions. Faith and obedience to God can work wonders, often when we least expect it.

> I am the most certain for I am improbable
> I come from farther off than your despair
> I draw near and I appear
> as ripe or green fruit
> according to my pleasure
> to display my spring
> I need your branches
> by knowing my name
> you learn your own but I am the Wholly Other.[38]

Surprising Wisdom in a Twelve-year-old Child

The story of Jesus' discovery in the Temple is part of the celebration of the Holy Family, Year C, because it is the third episode that we read in the infancy narratives of the Gospels. Jesus had been taken to the Temple several times since his birth. Perhaps he had accompanied his parents on their annual pilgrimage to Jerusalem. However, if this is so, the Gospel says nothing about it. Instead, Luke thought it important to add to his "sequence of events" (Luke 1:3) the story of what happened at Jerusalem when Jesus went there for Passover at the age of twelve. The essential purpose, to be sure, is that we may render an account of the certainty of the teachings that we have received (Luke 1:4). In addition though, the Church believes, rightly enough, that there is a lesson here for family life.

The Child Given by God Belongs to the Lord
The first reading is a short piece from the First Book of Samuel, which tells why the child Samuel, once he was weaned, was consecrated to the service of the Lord (1 Sam 1:20-22, 24-28).[39]

According to the etymology used in the Lectionary, "Samuel" means "God granted."[40] In fact, this child, born after many years of sterility to a woman who had never stopped asking God for the favor of becoming a mother, was truly the answer to a prayer.

We are a little surprised that Hannah did not go up to the sanctuary with her husband Elkanah and the rest of the family, "to offer the customary sacrifice to the Lord and to fulfill his vows." But it is true that presentation of the child was not required by the Law. In any case, Hannah's abstention from making the ritual pilgrimage does not mean that she was unwilling, and she says so to her husband. Instead of going to offer "the customary sacrifice," Hannah would wait till the child was weaned and then present him as one consecrated to God from before his birth, a Nazirite. But in his mother's mind this consecration is not partial, i.e., limited to the observance of certain rules for a specific way of life.[41] She wanted Samuel to be consecrated to the Lord forever and to remain in the service of the Lord in the sanctuary for his entire life. When she went up after having weaned the child,[42] she took her son to Shiloh so that he would live in the sanctuary "all the days of his life."

After reading such a story today, the question may arise, "Why should this concern us?" We have become extremely sensitive to questions of personal liberty, even for a child, sometimes so far as to be obsessed with everything that might even remotely affect his or her future.[43] In any case, the practice of offering a little child as a religious oblate is no longer allowed.[44] Nevertheless, the fact remains that the child is and always will be a gift of God: he or she does not really belong to the parents. We must also note that God's plan for a child's vocation surpasses all. Moreover, the search for God must animate one's whole life, determining all choices. This is what Psalm 84 expresses. In God alone—in his "dwelling-place"— are found the only true blessings.

> *How lovely is your dwelling place,*
> *O Lord of hosts!*
>
> My soul yearns and pines
>   for the courts of the LORD.
> My heart and my flesh
>   cry out for the living God.
>
> Even the sparrow finds a home,
>   and the swallow a nest
>   in which she puts her young—
> Your altars, O LORD of hosts,
>   my king and my God!
>
> Happy they who dwell in your house!
>   continually they praise you.
> Happy the men whose strength you are!
>   their hearts are set upon the pilgrimage.
>
> O LORD of hosts, hear my prayer;
>   hearken, O God of Jacob!
> O God, behold our shield,
>   and look upon the face of your anointed.
> (Ps 84:3-6, 9-10)

Children of God in the Image of His Son

The search for God is not a quest that is valuable in and of itself, i.e., in the goodwill and perseverance with which it is followed, since we know that God is and always will be inaccessible. We can neither force open the doors of his dwelling-place nor assume the right to have them opened. But the love of God has fulfilled us beyond our wildest hopes and dreams: he has admitted us into his family. The second reading for this Sunday expresses this fact (1 John 3:1-2, 21-24).

"We are God's children now." This extremely strong affirmation may be understood in the proper meaning of the words and expressions that compose it: "now," "we are," and "children of God." It certainly remains on the level of faith: we must wait for the appearance of the Son of God so that by seeing what he is, what we are—"now"—will become clear. And because faith alone reveals our true identity, the world can neither discover nor know God. Do not think, however, that to say "this comes from faith," indicates merely a personal, subjective conviction. On the contrary, it is a truth that comes from God and finds its guarantee in him.

What necessarily follows is fidelity to the commandment given by Jesus Christ: to recognize that he is the Son and to love one another. This fidelity, which we achieve with the help of grace, is the guarantee, in a concrete and immediate way, that we dwell in God and God in us.

John often uses the verb "to dwell," particularly in the discourses after the Last Supper (John 14–17). Throughout his work this verb has a very real meaning. In God alone is life because he alone has life in full. Our dwelling in God and God in us denotes a mutual communion of life beyond all imagination. In order to fully grasp this, one must wait until God reveals himself, that one may see him as he is.

John adds that we will recognize him "from the Spirit that he gave us." It is a matter of communion with the intimate life of the three Persons of the Trinity, i.e., admittance into the family of God.

The First Manifestation of Jesus' Wisdom

At the end of the story of the presentation, Luke notes that Jesus was "filled with wisdom" from his infancy. Later, he recounts the first manifestation of this wisdom, which took place in the Temple, where Jesus excited the admiration of those learned in the Law. This last passage of Luke's infancy narrative is a serious and solemn finale to the infancy account. While rich in psychological and human detail, it remains an lively and natural redaction that is also of great theological importance. It ends the introduction to the Gospel history (Luke 2:41-52).

It is at the Temple that the twelve-year-old Jesus manifests his wisdom; and it will be at the Temple where he will end his teaching ministry (Luke

19:41–21:38). Now the legal scholars "are amazed at his intelligence and his answers"; later they will oppose him. But the people will not tire of listening to him, and they will be "hanging on his words" (Luke 19:48).

During the Christmas season the liturgy enables us to contemplate, like the evangelist, the One who speaks of God and the things of God with an authority that no doctor of the Law ever had. His keen insight is not simply that of an exceptional intelligence, a sign of a naturally gifted child. It comes from a unique relationship with God.

"I Had to Be in My Father's House"

At first glance, the story of what happened to the Holy Family after one of its pilgrimages to Jerusalem appears to be rather banal. Mary and Joseph could not find the young Jesus, already twelve years old, on the evening of their return journey to Nazareth. Worried, they retraced their steps, looking for him. All ended well. They found him in the Temple. Even in their relief, they couldn't refrain from reproaching him for his conduct: he should have warned them, and realized that by staying in Jerusalem without saying a word to anyone, he had caused them great anxiety. Taken thus, we can look at the story in several ways: the attitude of the parents of an unusual adolescent; the problem posed by such surprising conduct in a young boy, in all other ways a model of submissiveness to his parents; the inevitable conflict of duties between obedience owed to parents versus the call of God; etc. But such a reading misunderstands the nature and clear intention of the Gospel. It is not a collage of historical events meant to move or edify us; it is a narrative of salvation events in which the person and personality of Jesus are revealed. A naïve reading does not deal with what Jesus said to his parents. Not only is this response the summit toward which the story moves; it has a profound meaning that must be discovered, i.e., Mary and Joseph's complete stupefaction and incomprehension clearly point to this.

Jesus, a child like others, obeying his parents, yet clearly possessing an incomparable wisdom, has a mysterious relation with the Father. The mystery of his person is only revealed, little by little, through his obedience to the will of God. The veil will not be completely lifted until Easter, which is already on the horizon. It will not escape the attentive reader that Jesus is found—reappears—on the third day after his absence, as it will be three days between his death and resurrection. The incomprehension of Mary and of Joseph evokes that of the disciples, whom the resurrected Jesus reproaches by saying to them: "What little sense you have! . . . Did not the Messiah have to undergo all this?'' This manner of speaking and arranging the story tends to make us believe that Luke wants us to refer to the story of the disciples on the road to Emmaus (at the end of his Gospel: Luke 24:13-33), the moment when ''what is now hidden will be made clear.''[45]

Keeping All These Things in Her Heart

''His mother meanwhile kept all these things in memory.'' Luke repeats here, in an abbreviated form, what he had already said at the end of the story of the nativity (Luke 2:19). This is for our benefit. We must meditate constantly on the Gospel of the infancy and the texts used in the celebration of the Holy Family. They illuminate the rest of the Gospel, the increasing revelation of the mystery of Jesus, the meaning of his mission in light of the fulfillment of the ancient promises, the end when Christ will be all in all.

Mary and Joseph traveled this road of faith before us. Joseph is no longer mentioned after the last episode of the of the infancy narrative. But isn't he the model of the ''upright man,'' humbly submissive to the word, faithful in carrying out his role regarding Jesus? Mary will be mentioned only briefly and intermittently, though her place in the story of the miracle at Cana, her silent witness at the cross, and her presence on the day of Pentecost will not be ignored.

Beyond preaching about familial virtues, about the relations that must exist in the Christian community, the feast of the Holy Family celebrates the Christ who is revealed in daily realities because he is the Son of God, a man among us all.

> He came among his own,
> the Messiah of the poor,
> he came, the child
> promised for centuries!
> He took flesh on our earth.
>
> He comes to us in these days,
> the resurrected Christ of Easter,
> he comes to us, the Lamb,
> The first-fruit of another age!
> He gives life to all his brethren.
>
> He will return at the last day,
> the Lord of glory,
> he will return, the King,
> conqueror among the angels!
> He will bring us to his Father.[46]

Mary, Mother of God

"From earliest times [Mary] has been honored under the title of Mother of God. . . . Hence from the Council of Ephesus [431] onward the devotion of the people of God toward Mary wonderfully increased in veneration and love. . . ."[1] The solemnity of Mary, Mother of God, is the oldest of all Marian celebrations.[2] The new Roman Calendar of 1969 places it on January 1.[3] Consequently, it is on the octave of the Christmas. We do not lose sight of this date being the first day of the year in every country that follows the Gregorian calendar.[4]

The celebration of Mary, Mother of God, is exemplary, insofar as it perfectly expresses the justification and object of the Marian cult in the Church.

> Devotion to Mary as it has always existed in the Church, even though it is altogether special, is essentially distinct from the worship of adoration paid equally to the Word incarnate, the Father, and the Holy Spirit. For the various forms of Marian devotion sanctioned by the Church, within the limits of sound orthodoxy and suited to circumstances of time and place as well as to the character and culture of peoples, have the effect that as we honor the Mother we also truly know the Son and give love, glory, and obedience to him, through whom all things have their being (see Col 1:15-16) and "in whom it has pleased the eternal Father that all fullness should dwell" (Col 1:19).[5]

The way the Christian assembly enters into the celebration of Mary, Mother of God, proclaims why the Church venerates the Virgin Mary and celebrates this solemnity on the octave of Christmas.

> A light will shine on us this day, the Lord is born for us: he shall be called Wonderful God, Prince of peace, Father of the world to come; and his kingship will never end.
>
> Hail, holy Mother! The child to whom you gave birth is the King of heaven and earth for ever.[6]

The same is true for the prayers addressed to God on this day: they evoke the role of Mary in the accomplishment of salvation. The Mother

of God is the perfect model of the reception of grace. The Church asks
for her intercession.

> God our Father,
> may we always profit by the prayers
> of the Virgin Mother Mary,
> for you bring us life and salvation
> through Jesus Christ her Son.
> (Opening Prayer)

> God our Father,
> we celebrate at this season
> the beginning of our salvation.
> On this feast of Mary, the Mother of God,
> we ask that our salvation
> will be brought to its fulfillment.
> (Prayer Over the Gifts)

> Father,
> as we proclaim the Virgin Mary
> to be the mother of Christ and the mother of the Church,
> may our communion with her Son
> bring us to salvation.
> (Prayer after Communion)

The Son of God Born of a Woman

The Virgin Mary is Mother of God "because she bore according to the
flesh the Word of God made flesh." This affirmation of the Council of
Ephesus (431) rightly makes the divine motherhood of Mary the corollary of the incarnation of the Son of God.[7]

The most explicit expression of faith in the incarnation, professed by
Christians since the beginning, is still that of St. John: "The Word became flesh" (John 1:14).[8] The Letter to the Galatians testifies that the announcement of this mystery, which is not the object of philosophical or
theological discussions, is due to faith in the preaching of the apostles.
Christians have made it part of their faith that "God sent forth his Son
born of a woman, born under the law" (Gal 4:4-7).

But it is one thing to assent to the truth of this faith, reaffirming it readily
each time we say the Creed, and something else to perceive the actual
consequences of it. By taking flesh, the Son of God partakes fully in the
human condition, subject to the same constraints as any human, although
he frees them and makes them "sons of God." To each of us St. Paul
says: "You are no longer a slave but a son! And the fact that you are
a son makes you an heir, by God's design."

"God has sent forth into our hearts the spirit of his Son which cries out 'Abba!' " This is how all Christians address God each day when they repeat the only prayer that "we have received from the Lord": "Our Father, who art in heaven." This is the prayer that assembles them and that they can say again and again "united in the Spirit."

Proclaimed on the first day of the new year and in the light of Christmas, this short text from the Letter to the Galatians is particularly significant. It reminds us of our human condition, our greatness as sons and daughters of God, our freedom acquired by Jesus and perpetually realized by his Spirit.

We cannot foresee what the new year will hold for us, or even if we will see its end. Each day that we are given to live must be illuminated by this certitude: "The fact that you are a son makes you an heir, by God's design." Only one thing is of real importance: to become day after day what we really are.

Jesus and Mary

The gospel for the solemnity of Holy Mary, Mother of God, repeats almost exactly what was read at the Mass at dawn on the Nativity. But instead of stopping after the departure of the shepherds, it continues: "When the eighth day arrived for his circumcision, the name Jesus was given the child, the name the angel had given him before he was conceived" (Luke 2:16-21).[9]

According to Luke (1:31), the angel told Mary to give the child this name.[10] Actually, there are a number of biblical figures who are named Jesus or Joshua.[11] There is nothing extraordinary about the name in itself, and Luke apparently did not think it worthwhile to note that it means "God saves." Again, this is not the first time in the Bible that a name is given to a child because it has been received from on high, on the day when his birth was announced: one need only recall the case of John, the son of Zechariah and Elizabeth (Luke 1:13, 60, 63). As for the "circumcision on the eighth day," it was prescribed by the Law in the preamble to the "purification" of the mother (which was to occur after thirty-three days: Lev 12:3-4). This short note is a simple reminder of Mary's obedience to all that the angel said to her and to all the prescriptions of the Law that Jesus was "subject to," as Paul puts it (Gal 4:4-6). But Christians who hear this Gospel know that to give the child the name of Jesus tells us who he is, what his mission will be, and that his power is the power of salvation. This is certainly what Luke wants them to understand.

The disciples that Jesus sends out expel demons and work miracles in his name (Luke 10:17). Some, who are not among the disciples, do likewise, and Jesus insists that they not be deterred (Luke 9:49-50). The power of the name of Jesus is made ever more clear after the resurrection (Acts 3:6; 4:7-12). But it cannot be used with impunity. The exorcists of Ephesus found this out most painfully. They "tried to invoke the name of the Lord Jesus over those who were possessed by evil spirits, saying, 'I adjure you by the Jesus whom Paul preaches.' But the evil spirit answered, 'Jesus I recognize, Paul I know; but who are you?' Then the man with the evil spirit sprang at them and overpowered them all. He dealt with them so violently that they fled from his house naked and bruised" (Acts 19:13-17).

This is not simply an anecdote that Luke tells us in order to liven up the story or to show, by this example, that not just anyone can appropriate the power of the name of Jesus. To invoke, to pronounce this name, is to appeal humbly to the one whom we recognize as the Lord and in whom we place our faith. It is to receive the Savior who frees from evil. To say "Jesus" is to be open to salvation, like the man condemned to death for his crimes who says, "Jesus, remember me when you enter upon your reign," and to whom Jesus responds, "I assure you: this day you will be with me in paradise" (Luke 23:39-43). We must hold the name of Jesus in our hearts and meditate on it constantly, just as we meditate on the name of Mary, his mother.

Like every mother, she must have wondered what her child would become. But she knew that he would be great, be called Son of the Most High, that the Lord would give him the throne of David his father, that he would reign always over the house of Jacob, and that his reign would be without end (Luke 1:32-33). How? This was not revealed by the angel. She had not asked for it. She was content to say, "I am the servant of the Lord. Let it be done to me as you say" (Luke 1:38). Despite her virginity, Mary, by saying "yes" to become the mother of the one whom the angel announced to her, consented to God's mysterious plan for her and her child. That is the basis of her incomparable greatness. But we should not forget that Mary, too, had to always renew and deepen her faith.

As Jesus grew up, Mary drew back in silence, a silence respected by the evangelists, and she gradually discovered that her son was indeed the Lord. She still "treasured all these things and reflected on them in her heart," but she remained silent throughout Jesus' preaching, his death on the cross, his resurrection, and on the day of Pentecost.

246 JANUARY 1 — MARY, MOTHER OF GOD

There is here a wondrous and great interplay between a woman, the Mother of God, and the Son of God made flesh, whom she brought into the world!

> See the shimmering dew
> illuminating the night!
> The barren land becomes fertile.
> Mary accepts, dazzled,
> the Son of God.
>
> See the new flower
> from the rod of Jesse!
> God's promise is kept.
> He comes, the prophesied child,
> the Son of God.
>
> See, the burning bush
> is not consumed!
> Oh! what blessedness for a woman!
> The Virgin holds in her arms
> the Son of God.
>
> See the wondrous exchange
> when the Word takes flesh,
> when the body is praise!
> Life contends with death
> for the sons of God.[12]

May the Lord Bless You and Keep You!

"Blest are you among women" (Luke 1:42). In its simplicity, Elizabeth's exclamation expresses all that we can say on the subject of the Mother of God, which we constantly repeat when we pray to her: "Hail Mary, full of grace."

In the language of our day, benediction evokes primarily, if not exclusively, the consecration of a thing or a person. In the Bible, it is an action of God that leads to happiness and fulfillment. "Blessed," then, is the one who has the favor of God, whom divine grace inhabits and leads; by definition, that person is also just, because he or she participates in the justice and sanctity of God, who is himself the Blessed One in the absolute sense of the term.

For the celebration of Holy Mary, Mother of God, on the first day of the year, the liturgy uses the most solemn benediction that can be found in the Old Testament (Num 6:22-27):

> "The Lord let his face shine upon you!" May his light shine upon you, may he smile upon you, may he envelop you with his luminous presence.

"The Lord look upon you kindly!" May he receive you and be favorable to you, may he pardon you and draw you toward him.

"The Lord give you peace," the greatest gift, the condition for all the others which come with it. Peace of Christmas and of Easter morn, when Jesus, resurrected, revealed himself to his disciples and said to them "Peace be with you!" Peace in which we are led to the passover of our death.

The solemnity of Mary, Mother of God, is a celebration of extraordinary theological and spiritual richness. It enables us to contemplate in Mary the humble servant of the Lord elevated by the grace of God to an inconceivable majesty because she brought into the world the one who was, for her first of all, "God saves," Jesus.

In her we salute the one who is blessed among all women, perfect model not only of all the blessed of God, but of the whole Church, of which she is the greatest icon.

In bearing the Savior, she gave us the one who makes us sons of God, heirs by the grace of the kingdom, who cry out to the Father by calling him "Abba!"

The wish that ends the liturgy and which we exchange among ourselves before Communion takes on, in this day of grace, its full meaning:

Go in the peace of Christ!
Thanks be to God.

Second Sunday After Christmas

Light for Today

In most countries, the solemnity of the Epiphany is celebrated on the second Sunday after Christmas. But when the feast is set for January 6, there is a formulary that is an extension of the Christmas Mass during the day. It is the same for Years A, B, and C.[1]

The liturgy opens with a beautiful antiphon that, in Latin, was one of the great prayers of the repertoire.[2]

> When peaceful silence lay over all, and night had run half of her swift course, your all-powerful word, O Lord, leaped down from heaven, from the royal throne.

We can see in it an invitation to prolong our meditation on the mystery of Christ, as Mary did. To speak of the night that "had run half of her swift course" cannot be reduced to merely saying that Jesus was born at midnight, the hour when the deepest silence reigns! Rather, the antiphon alludes directly to darknesses other than those of the nocturnal hours, which we experience daily, namely, those of a world where the light of God does not shine.[3] This night is joined with that formidable silence that does not give rise to the creative and redemptive Word of God, and with the silence of creation and of a humanity that holds its breath in expectation of the Word that will restore everyone to courage and life.[4] Silence, thus, has many varied meanings, but throughout all of them runs a great hope. It is the silence of adoration at the appearance of God.

This is what happened at Christmas. The silence was broken by a word of God transmitted by a prophet: the Word himself came down from heaven, the Word of God was made flesh and dwelt among us. Dialogue has been finally renewed through the initiative of God. He reopens our lips, and we find ourselves able to address him with the confidence of children: Abba! We discover the words "peace" and "brothers and sisters" in our vocabularies. We can speak to one another of the marvels of God, and announce to all the good news of salvation.

The Wisdom of God Dwells Among Us

The first reading has the same atmosphere of peaceful and silent meditation as the opening antiphon. It is a short excerpt from the Book of Sirach that meditates on Wisdom, which the author personifies (Sir 24:1-4, 8-12).

This Wisdom, which is a common theme of those books of the Bible that are called the "Wisdom literature,"[5] has nothing in common with the humanistic style of living that bases itself on personal reflections on experience. It is, rather, the personified manifestation of God, of his Word. Reread in the light of later revelation, the many Wisdom texts allow us to interpret Wisdom as Christ, the Word of God. This interpretation, which expands the meaning of these pages, is solidly rooted in the New Testament and has been a traditional part of the Church since the patristic period. In fact, one could read the text chosen for this Sunday replacing "Wisdom" with "Word." In any case, this is the proper understanding in the context of a Christmas season liturgy.

Wisdom, says the text, has been associated from the beginning with God's work, which it reveals. Christ, we read in the New Testament, is "the image of the invisible God, the first-born of all creatures. In him everything in heaven and on earth was created. . . . He is before all else that is. In him everything continues in being" (Col 1:15-17). And, "This Son is the reflection of the Father's glory, the exact representation of the Father's being" (Heb 1:3). At the end of the parable of the capricious children, Jesus, speaking of himself, said that God's wisdom is vindicated by all who accept it (Luke 7:35). From his infancy he demonstrated a wisdom that astonished and often surprised those who heard him (Luke 2:52; Mark 6:2). He extended invitations and calls that were expressed like those of the sages and of Wisdom: "Come to me . . ." (Matt 11:28); "No one who comes to me shall ever be hungry, no one who believes in me shall ever thirst" (John 6:35); "If anyone thirsts, let him come to me; let him drink who believes in me. Scripture has it: 'From within him rivers of living water shall flow'" (John 7:37-38).[6] Jesus has been made "our wisdom and also our justice, our sanctification, and our redemption" (1 Cor 1:30). He has been sent to dwell among us.

The Word of God became man, and lived among us.

Glorify the LORD, O Jerusalem;
    praise your God, O Zion.
For he has strengthened the bars of your gates;
    he has blessed your children within you.

He has granted peace in your borders;
  with the best of wheat he fills you.
He sends forth his command to the earth;
  swiftly runs his word!

He has proclaimed his word to Jacob,
  his statutes and his ordinances to Israel.
He has not done thus for any other nation;
  his ordinances he has not made known to them.
Alleluia.
(Ps 147:12-15, 19-20)

Give Thanks to God for His Son

The Letter to the Ephesians begins with an extraordinary thanksgiving, the quality and liturgical style of which is echoed by the best of the prefaces today (Eph 1:3-6, 15-18). We must read this text aloud during this Eucharist. Whether or not it came from the pen of Paul the Apostle, it transmits to us an echo of the apostolic liturgies.

> Praised be the God and Father of our Lord Jesus Christ, who has bestowed on us in Christ every spiritual blessing in the heavens! God chose us in him before the world began, to be holy and blameless in his sight, to be full of love; he likewise predestined us through Christ Jesus to be his adopted sons—such was his will and pleasure—that all might praise the glorious favor he has bestowed on us in his beloved.

> It is in Christ and through his blood that we have been redeemed and our sins forgiven, so immeasurably generous is God's favor to us. God has given us the wisdom to understand fully the mystery, the plan he was pleased to decree in Christ, to be carried out in the fullness of time: namely, to bring all things in the heavens and on earth into one under Christ's headship.

The Prayer of an Apostle for All the Faithful

Immediately following is the prayer of the apostle for the Christians and the community. It is first and foremost a thanksgiving for the gifts received by the Ephesians and the way in which they responded to them, living in faith and charity. He asks that "the God of our Lord Jesus Christ, the Father of glory" grant them "a spirit of wisdom and insight to know him clearly"; that he may open their hearts "to know the great hope to which he has called them, the wealth of his glorious heritage to be distributed among the members of the church."

Each of these formulas holds our attention. They witness, in fact, to an extraordinary theological orientation of the prayer. Paul always has the mystery of salvation before his eyes, embracing it fully; he sees everything in its light—his ministry and each of the ecclesial communities, with its strengths and weaknesses, its struggles and victories. At the center is Christ, the gift that God gives us, and the call to participate in his glory. And always, in one way or another, the reprise of the trilogy of faith-hope-charity.

The prayer of the apostle is a model, and it surprises us because it is expressed spontaneously in the framework of a letter written to a Christian community. May it lead us to pray like him and to give thanks "always and for everything" (Eph 5:20)!

The Word: True Light Come into This World

For the second time in several days, the liturgy proclaims the Prologue to the Gospel According to John (John 1:1-18).[7]

In the context of this Sunday's liturgy, we are suddenly confronted by the image of the Word of God as a Light come to enlighten us all. This is what the first reading suggests. There is no longer a forced personification here: the Word of God made flesh is in his person the Light which was always near God and which now dwells among us, having pitched his tent here.

Henceforth, knowledge of God is not the object of a more or less uncertain quest, but rather illumination, i.e., grace given us by the only Son, who is in the bosom of the Father. No longer is it only the prerogative of wise men; on the contrary. "I offer you praise, O Father, Lord of heaven and earth, because what you have hidden from the learned and the clever you have revealed to the merest children. Yes, Father, you have graciously willed it so" (Luke 10:21-22).

> The face of the Kingdom
> is today uncovered:
> a child teaches us
> of the eternal infancy of God,
> and God, at our door,
> waits to be welcomed
> like a child.
>
> From whence comes, in Mary's eyes,
> this light of tenderness?
> What is the source
> of this dazzling sight?
> The Virgin contemplates the eternal light
> sleeping in her arms.
>
> On the first day
> the universe sprang from the Word;

and you, Christmas Day,
you see the Word rise out of the universe,
proclaim the final day
when the universe will be consumed in the Word.[8]

The Epiphany of the Lord

After the Nativity of the Lord and the solemnity of Mary, Mother of God, comes the third major celebration of Christmastime, which closes with the feast of the Baptism of the Lord.[1]

What the Western Church celebrates on Epiphany—a term of Greek origin—is expressed at the beginning of the Mass:

> The Lord and ruler is coming; kingship is his, and government and power. (Entrance Antiphon)[2]

> Father,
> you revealed your Son to the nations
> by the guidance of a star.
> (Opening Prayer)

It is therefore a question of the universal kingdom of Christ, of his manifestation—which is what "epiphany" means—to the pagans. We typically speak of the magi as the first fruits of the nations. The liturgy is not concerned with such matters. It does not fasten its gaze on the magi in order to proclaim thereafter what they represent. We might even say that it doesn't see these mysterious personages as coming from the East. In any case, it does not distinguish them from the countless multitudes of nations to which, later, the only Son will be revealed. It already sees those nations following the star. Moreover, the liturgy proclaims what happens "today."

It is not simply a matter of imaginative ways of speaking or of poetic and lyrical style. The liturgy refers to facts situated in time and which, as such, are never repeated. But they are events in the history of salvation in which God holds the initiative and in which, though invisible, he is the principal protagonist. These events, happening once and for all, transcend the time to which they belong in a special way. As revelation of God and of his plan of salvation that they accomplish, they bear fruit that does not perish. The liturgy re-presents them, that is to say, it makes them present and active "today." Not in their material components, but in their power—their grace—of salvation.

Furthermore, these two opening texts of the Epiphany Mass are calls to understand the biblical readings that follow: as the announcement of a mystery, of the good news, of what is and will be.

Toward the Full Epiphany of the Glory of God

The first reading of the Liturgy of the Word opens up the enormous panorama of the mystery and its various levels of fulfillment (Isa 60:1-6).

Quite often—if not always—prophetic oracles are founded in facts, situations, real events to which the prophet is a witness either by personal involvement or through recollection in meditation. Under the power of the Spirit, prophets are able to fathom the depths of meaning in God's plan for today and tomorrow. Often enough, the eye of the prophet is so perceptive that it reaches to the horizon of time. The prophet perceives, more or less confusedly, the fulfillment of all things. In light of the prophet's experience, descriptions are rendered in images that belong to the poetic genre, the most apt language for describing such visions. It has a universal character that makes it comprehensible in all times. Accordingly, this type of language continues to have an impact on us today.

When we hear the prophets read over and over throughout the years, the meaning of their announcements and visions gradually becomes clearer to us. We seem to view God's plan anew, especially in light of the mystery of Christ and the Christian faith. The liturgical context of these texts helps to make clear their entire meaning and importance. This is particularly true of Isaiah's prophecy that is proclaimed on Epiphany.

The prophet's gaze focuses on Jerusalem, toward which he sees a long and joyous procession of her children who ''come from afar,'' i.e., from the Exile from which God has delivered them. On the summit of Zion, the newly reconstructed Temple blazes with the light of candelabra. What a marvelous and glorious spectacle!

Some earlier prophetic texts are certainly brought together in its spirit. One of them, in particular:

> One moment yet, a little while, and I will shake the heavens and the earth, the sea and the dry land. I will shake all the nations, and the treasures of all the nations will come in, and I will fill this house with glory. . . . Greater will be the future glory of this house than the former . . . and in this place I will give peace (Hag 2:6-9).[3]

Thus, in his ecstatic view, all is changed. The city appears to him brightly illuminated, ablaze with the glory of the Lord upon it, while the rest of the world remains in darkness. Toward this glittering light, it is no longer the throng of exiles or the procession of the feast of Tabernacles that is marching up, but the countless multitudes of nations and kings from every land. They bear their offerings—gold, incense, riches—while singing the praises of the Lord. The prophet sees this transfigured Jerusalem, and he lets us see what looms beyond the horizon of history, the point toward which all eyes look, the assembly place for all the nations marching toward the full manifestation—Epiphany—of the Lord.

Isaiah didn't dream this; he was not the victim of a mystical hallucination. Throughout the Exodus, particularly after the theophany at Sinai, the glory of God was manifested with clarity (Exod 24:16-17). It was announced that one day all would see it at the same time (Isa 40:5: Second Sunday of Advent, Year B). What the prophet contemplated was the realization of this promise.

Later on, St. John had a similar vision. In the Book of Revelation (Apocalypse) he described the heavenly Jerusalem in the same terms—radiant with the glory of God. He added, though, that the Lamb now occupies the place of the lamp (Rev 21:10, 23-26).

Nevertheless, this Epiphany is not some kind of mirage that moves farther off the closer one comes to it. When the Word was made flesh and dwelt among us, ''we have seen his glory: the glory of an only Son coming from the Father'' (John 1:14). From the beginning of his ministry, at Cana, by the many signs that he accomplished, Jesus, ''the light of the world'' (John 8:12), revealed his glory, which is that of God.[4] For a moment, the darkness of the passion appeared to veil it; yet it shone forth again when Christ was raised from the tomb. The preaching of the gospel spread it to the four corners of the world and made it burn brightly in the hearts of believers (2 Cor 4:6).

The mystery of the Epiphany—the showing forth—of the glory of God is both a present reality and an object of hope. Seers in the Old and New Testaments were able to briefly contemplate the splendor of the Jerusalem-to-come so that with this vision before our eyes we might join the multitude of nations marching toward the full epiphany of the Lord while singing, with them, of our faith and hope.

Lord, every nation on earth will adore you.

O God, with your judgment endow the king,
  and with your justice, the king's son;
He shall govern your people with justice
  and your afflicted ones with judgment.

Justice shall flower in his days,
  and profound peace, till the moon be no more.

May he rule from sea to sea,
  and from the River to the ends of the earth.

The kings of Tarshish and the Isles shall offer gifts;
  the kings of Arabia and Seba shall bring tribute.
All kings shall pay him homage,
  all nations shall serve him.

For he shall rescue the poor man when he cries out,
  and the afflicted when he has no one to help him.
He shall have pity for the lowly and the poor;
  the lives of the poor he shall save.
(Ps 72:1-2, 7-8, 10-13)

Magi from the East in the Time of King Herod

Matthew is the only one of the evangelists to report the episode of the magi who came from the East to give homage to "the king of the Jews," whose star they "observed at its rising" (Matt 2:1-12).

It requires serious attention to read and meditate on this story, trying not to be misled by popular presentations and folklore, e.g., the fairy tales of Christmas that it evokes. It is a passage from the Gospel, very carefully constructed and edited to tell of a mystery—not to give free rein to the imagination (even though inspired by piety).[5]

After the genealogy of Jesus, which is a kind of introduction (Matt 1:1-17), Matthew's Gospel concerning the infancy contains five episodes that refer to five prophecies of the Old Testament: (1) the virginal conception of the Lord (Matt 1:18-25; Isa 7:14); (2) the adoration of the magi (Matt 2:1-12; Mic 5:1-3); (3) the flight into Egypt (Matt 2:13-14; Hos 11:1); (4) the slaughter of the children of Bethlehem and the surrounding area (Matt 2:16-18; Jer 31:15); and (5) the return to Nazareth (Matt 2:19-23: evocation of what had been said by the prophets—"He shall be called a Nazorean"[6]). The evangelist suggests that we read these different stories in the light of the Old Testament prophecies,[7] thus revealing the presence of a particular literary genre. One must not read these pages as if they are simply collections of anecdotes[8] or as if they were the strict and unbiased telling of facts, their only concern being material exactitude. This is the gospel, the good news of salvation in Jesus Christ. In order to announce this, Matthew has recourse to a variety of elements taken from biblical literature, various traditions, symbols, etc.[9]

Consequently, the story of the adoration of the magi is to be understood in this literary context: artificial, certainly, but profoundly theological, although we do not mean that it is purely legendary and without any historical basis.[10] One might speak of it as a history overheard at the door of Scripture and faith.[11]

According to the Scriptures

Matthew does not tell of the Lord's nativity or of the annunciation to Mary.[12] Christians today are familiar with these events and even celebrate them before the feast of Epiphany: they are in no danger of being forgotten;[13] the celebration actually reminds us of them. But it draws attention to the fact that the birth of Jesus in Bethlehem is far from being fully explained, despite the fact that we know there was a census ordered by Caesar Augustus (Luke 2:1). Jesus was destined to be born in Bethlehem, because the Scriptures had announced that Bethlehem would be the Messiah's birthplace. The evangelist cites an oracle from the prophet Micah to support this: "But you, Bethlehem-Ephrathah, too small to be among the clans of Judah, from you shall come forth for me one who is to be ruler in Israel" (Mic 5:1).

Closer examination of the Bible[14] will show that this text does not correspond exactly to that of the Book of Micah. Matthew says "Bethlehem of Judea" instead of "Bethlehem-Ephrathah." But this is only a detail to distinguish one town from another with the same name in Galilee and to turn attention to the city of David, symbol of the Messiah.

In the text of Micah, Bethlehem is called "too small to be among the clans of Judah." Matthew writes that this does not fit, but does not really contradict the prophet. Micah chose to juxtapose Bethlehem's tiny size with the greatness of its mission: "From you shall come forth for me one who is to be ruler in Israel." For Matthew and for all Christians, Bethlehem is great and renowned among all cities because the Lord was born there, even though it is still considered, by its sparse population, a relatively small village.[15]

At the end of the quotation, the evangelist makes his own modification. In place of "one who is to be ruler in Israel" (Mic 5:1), he writes: "a ruler who is to shepherd my people Israel." This title comes from the Second Book of Samuel. When the tribes of Israel rallied to David, they reminded him that the Lord had said to him while Saul was still king: "You shall shepherd my people Israel and shall be commander of Israel" (2 Sam 5:2; Christ the King, Year C). This interpretation is completely in line with Matthew and the Christian tradition: Jesus is the new David. At the same time, it suggests that Jesus, "the king of the Jews," must surely have been born in Bethlehem.

This example of a reading from the Old Testament is certainly worthwhile, especially a reading from the Prophets. Much of the Old Testament sheds light on the writings and events of the New Testament, most of all on Christ himself: his person, his mystery, his teaching. The full meaning of the Old Testament is discovered in the light of the New Testament. Moreover, because God is the principal author, the inspiration for all the sacred writers—Scripture explains Scripture.[16] Finally, we cannot neglect other sources of interpretation, each with its own authority: the magisterium of the Church, the patristic tradition, the studies of the exegetes, and the diverse commentaries, including for the Old Testament the Jewish commentaries called "midrash" and "targum,"[17] to which Matthew refers in his story of the adoration of the magi.

A mere academic knowledge of Scripture is practically worthless, as Matthew illustrates with his example of the chief priests and the scribes. They quote the prophecy of Micah about the birthplace of the Messiah from memory, but they do not seem the least bit interested in it.[18] Herod alone[19] takes the information seriously, which is not to say that he apprehends its true value. He understands the title "king of the Jews" in a purely temporal sense, imagining that the newborn child is a threat to his throne.[20] Lest we be amazed at his short-sightedness, we must realize that the same thing happens today, that some Christians understand and apply the prophecies in a very similar way, the result of regarding them merely as predictions of verifiable fact. Disputation becomes their primary function: "Well has it been said of you!" Reduced to this, the Old Testament prophecies become no longer really interesting; they shed no light on the events of salvation history, and the reason they are continually cited is incomprehensible. The importance that Matthew accords them in his announcement of the gospel is just the opposite.[21]

Magi from the East Follow a Star

The persons who came from the East to give homage to the newborn "king of the Jews" are still shrouded in mystery.[22] The Gospel says nothing about their home country, their status, their religion, their number, and believe it or not, their names. All that can be said about these matters is conjecture, i.e., ideas originating outside the Gospel.

They are supposed to have been kings, but this stems from a very literal translation of a psalm verse: "The kings of Tarshish and the Isles shall offer gifts" (Ps 72:10). Ancient depictions of them never involved symbols of royalty, but simply the Phrygian cap and garments of noble Persians. One document[23] reports that the Persian soldiers of Chosroes II, who in 614 destroyed all the sanctuaries of Palestine, spared the basilica of Bethlehem. When they saw the mosaic of the adoration of the magi, they thought it was a picture of their countrymen.

If they were Persians, they would have belonged to a caste of sages of the Zoroastrian religion, a caste that believed in the coming of the Messiah.

Ancient traditions disagreed about their number: two,[24] three,[25] four,[26] eight,[27] or even twelve.[28] The number three prevailed, undoubtedly because of the three presents (gold, incense, and myrrh) or the belief that they represented the three races: Semite (Shem), Black (Ham), Indo-Germanic (Japheth).

The traditional names of the magi—Melchior, Caspar, and Balthazar—are found in a ninth-century Italian manuscript.[29]

But what does all this matter? Matthew tells us that all we need to know is that from the time of his coming into the world, the Lord was manifested to people who came from distant lands. God made the good news of this birth known to them by a suitable sign, which guided their journey. But it was necessary for the chief priests and scribes to supply the Scriptures to the strangers so that they might reach "the house" where they would find the one for whom they were looking. One day in Athens, St. Paul, addressing the members of the Areopagus, an academic body, said to them: "What you are thus worshiping in ignorance I intend to make known to you. . . . the Lord of heaven and earth does not dwell in sanctuaries made by human hands. . . . They were to seek God, yes to grope for him and perhaps eventually to find him—though he is not really far from any one of us" (Acts 17:23-27).

The missionary Church never ceases to proclaim this message. It cannot forget the last words that Jesus spoke before returning to his Father: "Full authority has been given to me both in heaven and on earth; go, therefore, and make disciples of all the nations. Baptize them in the name 'of the Father, and of the Son, and of the Holy Spirit.' Teach them to carry out everything I have commanded you. And know that I am with you always, until the end of the world!" (Matt 28:18-20). The Church pursues this mission, knowing that for everyone, today as yesterday, God raises up a "star."

What was this sign for the magi? We can not say for certain.[30] But consider the fresco in the cemetery of Priscilla at Rome (see Acts 18). This picture witnesses very simply to a remarkable awareness of the mystery of Epiphany and the star. Near the Virgin, who is holding the child Jesus on her knees, is a person who is pointing to a star. According to common interpretation, this person is Isaiah, whose book contains the prophecy about the birth of Emmanuel (Isa 7:14), and who proclaims the day of Epiphany (Isa 60:1-6). Under one form or another, God, by the signs he gives and the preaching that reveals their meaning, invites all people to seek and find the Savior.

Gold, Incense, and Myrrh

The magi who have come from the East to give homage to the newborn "king of the Jews" offer him presents. When the queen of Sheba came to Jerusalem, drawn by the wisdom of Solomon, she offered him "a large amount of gold and precious stones" and an abundance of spices, the like of which has never been seen since (1 Kgs 10:2, 10). To the one who is greater than Solomon (Matt 12:42), the magi offer "gifts of gold, frankincense and myrrh."

The important thing is not the detail of the offerings; what Matthew wants us to understand is the way in which this homage expresses the fulfillment of the messianic prophecies.

> The wealth of nations shall be brought to you. . . .
> All from Sheba shall come
>   bearing gold and frankincense,
>   and proclaiming the praises of the LORD (Isa 60:5-6).
>
> The kings of Tarshish and the Isles shall offer gifts;
>   the kings of Arabia and Seba shall bring tribute.
> All kings shall pay him homage,
>   all nations shall serve him.
> (Ps 72:10-11)

The Christian tradition very quickly attributed additional meaning to these presents. Thus, St. Irenaeus (c. 135-202): "Myrrh signified that he, for our mortal human race, would die and be buried; gold, that he was the King whose reign would be without end; incense, that he was God who came to make himself known in Judea, and to show himself to those who had never sought him."[31] The myrrh prefigures what Nicodemus brought for Jesus' burial (John 20:39-40).

The Magi Depart by a Different Route

Matthew says nothing about what may have happened to the magi after their visit except that "they received a message in a dream not to return to Herod, so they went back to their own country by another route."

God, who sees into the hearts of everyone, knew that Herod, when he commissioned the magi to "get detailed information about the child" and to return when they had found him, was thinking of anything but paying him homage. He did not allow the magi to give Herod the information that would have allowed him to quickly suppress "the king of the Jews," whose birth had been announced by a "star."[32] Through his intervention with the magi, God foiled the plans of the tyrant.[33] But is there more we can learn?

The distance between Jerusalem and Bethlehem is not great. One can hardly imagine the suspicious Herod relying solely on the goodwill of strangers to obtain the information he needed to suppress a rival. He had plenty of guards and informers to shadow the magi. Moreover, how could they have escaped his vigilance and left clandestinely by another route? To pose such questions is to treat Matthew's story like a document subjected to historical criticism, from which one can ruthlessly rip out everything that appears to be unlikely. The Gospel of the infancy is more than a simple recitation of facts. The way that Matthew presents these events "is colored by the faith which enlightened the evangelist when he wrote his work; it expresses and clarifies the faith of the Church at the time; he intended it to be an aid to the faith of those Christians for whom he wrote. But faith is not simply a matter of acknowledging that Jesus is Messiah, Lord and Son of God. It involves obedience to him, now. The Gospel is not only 'kerygma,' that is to say, proclamation of faith; it is also 'catechesis,' instruction on how to unify one's faith and life. This part of the message is especially stressed in Matthew."[34]

This "part of the message" in Matthew comes out at the end of his Epiphany story. God's order to the magi to return to their country "by another route" actually suggests that there must be a change in our ways after we encounter the Lord in faith. This last lesson is all the more clear when we can disentangle it from all the distracting anecdotes. The magi disappear as mysteriously as they appeared: Matthew says nothing of what became of them. All encounters with the Lord, to whom we give homage,[35] to whom we offer presents—in the sense of liturgical action—involve taking "another route" back to our own "country," back to our daily occupations.

The Announcement of the Gospel: Epiphany of Mystery

The Church does not celebrate Epiphany as a past event—the recognition of the Savior by a few pagans from the East—but as a living reality of salvation in today's world and in the Church, which has been given the mission of announcing it and opening the way to it. No one is more clearly conscious of this than Paul, the apostle to the Gentiles. Look at what he wrote to the Ephesians about the apostolic ministry (Eph 3:2-3, 5-6).

The mystery of Christ is a revelation made "now by the Spirit to the holy apostles and prophets." It is a question of an epiphany: Paul did not use that word, but spoke instead of "revelation" and "knowledge," which are related terms.

The point of this manifestation is that "the Gentiles are now co-heirs with the Jews, members of the same body and sharers of the promise." It is accomplished "through the preaching of the gospel."

The missionary activity of the Church is not taken lightly, nor is it limited by circumstances. Even to say that it is a matter of life and death doesn't fully grasp the point. For in this activity we discover the mystery of God and Christ, his epiphany. The Church would be disavowing its Lord if it were not missionary: May the Church forever say with Paul: "I am ruined if I do not preach the gospel."

For the Church, this requirement involves the stringent duty to constantly reform, "to adapt more suitably to the needs of our own times those institutions that are subject to change; to foster whatever can promote union among all who believe in Christ; to strengthen whatever can help to call the whole of humanity into the household of the Church," as the Second Vatican Council said at the beginning of the first constitution it promulgated.[36] In addition, in one of the last conciliar documents we read:

> The Church, which has been sent by Christ to reveal and communicate the love of God to all men and to all peoples, is aware that for her a tremendous missionary work still remains to be done. There are two billion people—and their number is increasing day by day—who have never, or barely, heard the gospel message; they constitute large and distinct groups united by enduring cultural ties, ancient religious traditions, and strong social relationships. Of these, some belong to one or other of the great religions, others have no knowledge of God, while others expressly deny the existence of God and sometimes even attack it. If the Church is to be in a position to offer all men the mystery of salvation and the life brought by God, then it must implant itself among all these groups in the same way that Christ by his incarnation committed himself to the particular social and cultural circumstances of the men among whom he lived.[37]

The whole Bible witnesses that God's plan is to bring together all people and indeed all things into unity.[38] Only then will God be fully manifested.

In the meantime, the history of the world and the Church is that of a developing epiphany and therefore a mystery that is revealed each day.

> Behold, in the depths of the night,
> under our eyes a Star appears.
> Someone leads us step by step
> toward the source of light.
>
> Abraham the believer
> took this route before us;
> joyous, we go toward the Child
> whose new Day we have seen.
>
> The call from a distant rendezvous
> rings in our heart,
> the Father will secretly, up till the end,
> lead us toward his Son.
>
> Already the city of David
> appears before our eyes;
> the quest in our hearts we follow
> in your light, Lamb of God.[39]

The Liturgy and the Sacraments: Mysteries of Epiphany

The liturgy not only celebrates the mystery of the Epiphany: it *is* the mystery of the Epiphany in act. This is also true for all sacraments, collectively and individually. Christ is present there and recognized in faith as the Lord of glory. Elevated to the presence of the Father, he acts for the sanctification of all, the Church and the world, by his humanity and by the Spirit he sends.

When we celebrate the liturgy and the sacraments, we do not bring gifts of gold, incense, and myrrh, but our personhood and our hearts.[40]

In each celebration of the liturgy and the sacraments—all the way from baptism, i.e., "illumination," to anointing, which is received just before entering into eternal light—we proceed toward a clearer vision of the splendor of God.[41]

Finally, when the assembly is dispersed, it is "by another route"—that of conversion—that each return home "in the peace of Christ."

> God has called you out of darkness
> into his wonderful light.
> May you experience his kindness and blessings,
> and be strong in faith, in hope, and in love.
>
> The wise men followed the star,
> and found Christ who is light from light.
> May you too find the Lord when your pilgrimage is ended.[42]

The Lectionary for the Week

Throughout this period, from the beginning of day to the end of night, the Lectionary for the week celebrates the coming of the rising Sun, the Light from on high that comes to those who lie in darkness and in the shadow of death. The readings help us discover the divinity of our Brother and the humanity of our God, the incredible interchange that happened in the incarnation of the Word. Joy predominates, but seriousness also has its place.

From December 29 to Epiphany, the episodes in the gospels of the infancy and the first chapter of the Fourth Gospel go from darkness to light. As for the various "epiphanies" that mark the beginning of Jesus' ministry, read during the week following his manifestation to the magi, they are so many signs of the drama that will be unified at the end of the earthly ministry of the Messiah sent by God. And what can we say about the Gospels for the feasts of the saints after Christmas? Stephen the first martyr, the Holy Innocents, John, apostle and evangelist, are so many witnesses that remind us of the incomparable love of God, and that there is no greater love than to give one's life for one's friends.

The First Letter of John is offered for continuous reading during this brief time. Tirelessly, it tells us over and over of the love that God bears for us in his Son Jesus, born in our flesh. To believe in the love that God will always have for us is to be compelled to love the brothers and sisters that he gives us in Jesus Christ.

The end of the first century in the primitive Church was a time of intense theological and spiritual reflection. Coming out of the pagan world to which the Church opened itself, the Gnostic tide was in danger of submerging the gospel: the Gnostics preached a special, personal, religious "knowledge" that one might attain by avoiding the temporal and carnal realities of the faith, and by being open to the direct and personal illumination of the Spirit. There was a great danger of bypassing the revelation of Christ, becoming indifferent to the fundamental features of Christian mystery, misconstruing the reality of the incarnation, the resurrection, and the Eucharist. How could we remain humble before God when such a stress was being placed on the possibility of actually understanding the divine mysteries? How could one avoid succumbing to a merciless indifference to others when personal enlightenment was the source of salvation? Such were the kinds of questions to which the author of the letter was responding.

It is not often that the liturgy will prescribe the reading of an entire letter within a particular liturgical season. What we have here is a particularly appropriate teaching for Christmas-Epiphany.

The True Gnostic Is the Believer

Faced with the seduction of Gnosticism, John wants to create certainty in the hearts of his readers: the true believer is the one who knows without a doubt that he is born of God, that he is from God, and that he knows God in an intimate and personal way, since God dwells in him and he in God (1 John 5:18-21). This is why the author has written his Letter: "to make you realize" (1 John 5:13). True knowledge is definitely the key to understanding the letter. Witness John's frequent use of the terms "knowing" and "knowledge" (23 times). The author insists on this, even appearing to be saying the same thing over and over again (1 John 2:3-4), all with a skillful use of language. For him, there is a Christian dimension to knowledge, a way of knowing that has to do with being born in the Lord. Far from merely arriving at a knowledge of God after a purely intellectual journey, he wants to obtain an awareness of God so vital that it is truly mystical: an experience of the heart (in the biblical sense of the term), where the believer, with his or her whole being, penetrates further into the utterly gratuitous revelation of the mystery of God, discovering in thunderstruck joy the love of which he is the object.

True Gnostics Live What They Know

One true test of Christian knowledge is the behavior of the believer. Those who are born of God can no longer sin (1 John 3:9-10). The letter thus presents a remarkable model of mystical realism with a perfect joining of heart and mind.

That Christians must live out who they are and what they know is central to the author. He says it in a variety of arguments that frame the work. Each time, he starts with an affirmation of a divine quality in order to find its match in the behavior of a believer. Does a person live what he or she confesses? Only then can they claim to be true knowers. Thus John repeatedly says that God is light (1 John 1:5-7), pure and holy (1 John 3:3-7), that God is love (1 John 4:8, 16). Does the so-called Christian live in conformity with this lifestyle, this light, this love? In that case, Christians know by experience that they are from God, that they are born of God, i.e., they live a life of intimacy with him that is expressed by such words as "union" (1 John 2:5), "abide" (1 John 2:5, 6, 24; 3:6, 24; 4:13, 15, 16), "begotten" (1 John 2:29; 4:7), "to know" (1 John 3:6; 4:7).

The Spiritual Knowledge of the True Gnostic

The "knowledge" of which John speaks is an extension of the biblical notion of "knowledge." It is essentially a matter of experience. The First Letter of John speaks of a spiritual presence of the one in the other, like a diamond thrust into a ray of light which then becomes light itself. It is a dynamic presence as well, for God is first and foremost the giver of life (1 John 5:11-12): it is from him that we have received through Christ a "seed" of new life (1 John 3:9) whose power needs to be felt throughout existence. It is also the presence of the Spirit whom Christ, faithful to his promise, has given us (1 John 3:24; 4:13): God is the One who guarantees his active presence in us and the experience of it that forms all moral living.

This transformation is first verified on the level of knowledge and faith (1 John 2:20-27). The anointing of the Spirit is the principle of faith and allows one to confess Jesus as the Son of God. Whoever confesses the divine mystery of the incarnate Word by the power of the Spirit can be sure that God is with them and dwells within them (1 John 3:24–4:2). But the active power of the divine presence is also exhibited on the level of neighbor-love. For if God is love, and if he has shown himself to us by sending his Son to save us (1 John 4:8-16), we must also translate the active character of this love into love for one another. Another pious saying? Not at all. It is rather the real substance, the solid nourishment of the dynamic presence of God loving in and through us. Consequently, just as confessions of faith can be made only in the power of the Spirit, so all true love comes only from God. Love of one another is, therefore, a sure sign of the divine presence in the heart of believers (1 John 4:12; 3:17).

The New Covenant

A close look at the ever-present theme of the knowledge of faith and love that the divine presence excites in believers makes one think that perhaps John is saying something else, i.e., to show that it is Christ Jesus who has come to fulfill the new covenant previously announced by the prophets.[1] The renewal of the inward person by the Spirit of God is accomplished, thanks to the passion of Christ (1 John 5:6-12).

The connections between this letter and the prophecies of Jeremiah— perhaps Ezekiel's even more—are evident.[2] Each emphasizes how the

Spirit of the new covenant will develop, in those who receive it, an intimate knowledge of the things of God, an ability to "walk" in his paths, to "keep" his commandments, to "practice" justice.[3]

Since the new covenant aims at restoring the right relation between everyone and God, John's Letter unhesitatingly affirms that sin will disappear with this last covenant. Not that sin becomes impossible for the Christian (1 John 1:7-10; 5:13-17), but insofar as knowing God in faith and love, the believer acts under the influence of the dynamic, divine presence; the Christian now acts in line with what he or she has become—a child of God.

Such is the message that the first reading for the week of Christmas-Epiphany offers us: as Pope St. Leo insisted, we must be aware of our dignity as Christians[4] and we must come to grips with our knowledge of the faith that is based on our experience of Christ, who has taken on our flesh. To deny the reality of his incarnation (1 John 4:3) is to watch all of Christianity fall into ruin, for then there is no redemption, no true knowledge of God, and no true love.

The Gospels
A quick glance at the gospels for the week of Christmas-Epiphany shows that they are grouped in three series: on December 29 and 30 and January 1 we read Luke 2:16-40; on December 31 and from January 2 to 7, before Epiphany, we read John 1:1–2:12; the week after Epiphany, we read several texts taken from the Synoptics and the Fourth Gospel, which define and prolong the manifestation of the Lord celebrated on the feast of Epiphany.

The Reality of the Incarnation and Reactions of Believers
The three gospels that make up the first series (Luke 2:16-40) recount, successively, the visit of the shepherds to the manger, the circumcision and presentation of the child in the Temple, and the return to Nazareth, where Jesus would secretly grow great in the strength and wisdom of God. The liturgy is not terribly concerned with chronology, since the visit by the shepherds and the circumcision are retold on January 1, while on December 29 and 30, the stories concerning the presentation in the Temple and the acknowledgment of the Messiah by Simeon and Anna have already been told. The concern must therefore lie elsewhere.

The three stories combined bring the reality of the incarnation to light. The narration of the events surrounding the birth of Jesus is made up of contrasts. First, the contrast between poverty and glory: the Messiah is an ordinary child with no trappings of majesty, born in peril, but already celebrated by the angels as Lord and Savior. Laid in a humble manger, he is first revealed to those living on the fringe of society, to shepherds scorned by the privileged people of the time.

Secondly, there is a contrast in the fact that the King of glory for whom Israel waits submits himself to the Law, thus being perfectly obedient from the beginning. It is in the weakness of humanity that the glory of God shows itself, as the mystery of Christmas tells us. Jesus is ''born of a woman, born under the Law'' (Gal 4:4).

Each gospel underscores the different reactions of people who enter into the story. Their immediate and unreserved faith is surely a wonderful example for the liturgical community today. The shepherds' faith has a missionary dimension: after having seen the awaited child lying in a manger, they hasten to spread the news of what the angel told them about the child. Good news is meant to be shared! As for Simeon and Anna's faith, it involves recognition and acceptance: both are prophets, for Scripture is for them a living word that allows the present to be understood and the future to be foreseen. And what about Mary's faith? Very little seems to be said about it at first glance, but much more is said if we look more closely. Her faith is deepened by meditation: ''Mary treasured all these things and reflected on them in her heart'' (Luke 2:19).

A typical reaction of these simple people is that of admiration and astonishment, leading to thanksgiving. This is another liturgical characteristic of Luke's story. Amazement is not enough. All those who were astonished at the shepherd's story sustained the thanksgiving of believers. To be amazed before the manger suggests that we go beyond this attitude by proclaiming and living our faith and making it known, much like the shepherds who, as beneficiaries of this grace, overflowed with thanksgiving and, in returning, returned everything, so to speak (Luke 2:20). What about the astonishment of the child's father and mother (Luke 2:33)? Mary received the full blow of the prophecy concerning the Messiah as a sign of contradiction in addition to her association with his martyrdom. Her astonishment occurred before this prophecy, however, with Simeon's confirmation that Jesus is truly the light of the nations. Mary had to arrive slowly and sorrowfully at an understanding of the second part of the prophecy before being able to comprehend the praise.

The introduction of Simeon and Anna puts the seal of divine authenticity on the episode of the presentation in the Temple and justifies their behavior. Both prophesied, and their double witness, required under the Jewish penal code,[5] confirms that the coming of the Messiah has universal impact: Jesus will be the "light for the nations" destined to shine for all peoples (Isa 49:6, 9; 52:7-10; 60:1-3). To the "benediction" given by Simeon, Anna adds a praise that completes the narration and shows that "all who looked forward to the deliverance of Jerusalem" (Luke 2:38; cf. vv. 26, 29) are, at the same time, both supplicants and witnesses who share in their joy.

The Revelation of the Mystery in the Fourth Gospel
The Lectionary for the week offers six texts from the Fourth Gospel.[6]

From the moment believers open the Fourth Gospel, John directs their gaze toward Christ: it is he who establishes the fate of the universe and the destiny of humanity. Isn't he the one whom the Book of Revelation calls Alpha and Omega, the Beginning and the End (Rev 1:8)? In the eyes of the evangelist, the Christian mystery is not just an abstract ideology having no roots in the real world. Christianity is the history of salvation. Things and people do not follow paths to nowhere, moved by blind necessity or meaningless chance. John believes in a creation where God expresses himself. In Jesus, he sees the Word born of God who comes to renew creation. In the eyes of the evangelist, his prologue is a kind of overture, rather than an introduction, to a symphony of a new world (John 1:1-18); it outlines the great themes that will be developed through the rest of the book, especially in the story of the first week of Jesus' ministry, as if John wanted to establish a provocative parallel between the first week of the beginning of the world and that of the new creation, the work of the incarnate Word. The sign at Cana, which closes this first section, thus represents a summit.

The Eagle Eye of St. John the Evangelist
The place occupied by the prologue (John 1:1-18) in the liturgy for the last day of the year recalls the place it occupied at the end of the Eucharistic celebration in the ancient liturgy. In a few lines, the whole Gospel is summed up and the essential themes are brought together. From the start, John evokes the great confession of faith proclaimed at Christmas, with all its aspects, its richness, and its theological consequences encompassing space and time. In Jesus, God enters the world and its history in order to bring it to an end and save it. That is the key for understanding the work of Jesus, the incarnate Word.

So from the beginning, our gaze is set on the eternal Word of God, whose person and manifestation sink their roots into the world of God and the history of humankind. He is, before all things, turned toward God, near God, God himself. From the beginning, he is the creative Word, the divine Wisdom and the source of life who calls forth the world.[7] But he is also the Word who makes the new creation, who offers to everyone life and illuminates our existence, who makes the presence of God descend into our midst by coming "to pitch his tent," his dwelling place, among us. Life, light, truth: they are the words charged with so much meaning, words that reveal God and who he is and that sum up and fulfill our deepest longings. The Word reveals the divine meaning of existence.

But this light does not recklessly assert itself: it asks for acceptance, and it can be refused. This is the conflict that is always possible between people and the Word who gives them their meaning, the struggle between light and darkness. In this matter, John the Baptist plays an important role: did he not come to announce to "his own," that is, to Israel, the coming of the One who is their hope for the fulfillment of all the promises of salvation? In Jesus, and in him alone, the very Word of God is made flesh, becomes human, so that the life of God himself may be present in the midst of all creation. Following the people of the old covenant, everyone must make choices in the face of truth. To accept God in our lives is to receive in faith the very light and strength that enables us to receive it.

Therefore, no one other than Jesus Christ is able to give us salvation. There is no other mission or revelation to wait for. Jesus is the key to the Old Testament: the Law was "written large in Christ" (St. Augustine). More than a new Moses, Jesus makes the old covenant give way to the new, the definitive covenant. Christ is not merely the last of the messengers of God; he is the unique and exceptional one. He breaks the mold once and for all, the prototype of the new creation. It is because he the Son is like the Father, and because in him God forever speaks his last word, the one that completely expresses and reveals his plan of salvation for the world. He gives meaning to all human speech because in him we have received grace upon grace, because he has made God the Father known to us.

Such are the three great proclamations of the prologue of John's Gospel.

The First Week of Jesus' Ministry

Even if the division into seven days is simply a literary construction, it seems that John has adopted it for a reason: to symbolically establish a parallel between the first creation of the world by the Word of God and the new creation, realized by the same Word, incarnate. It is a question of "theological time" that can be outlined as follows: the witness of the Baptist to the "Jews" (vv. 19–28); the witness of the Baptist to his disciples (vv. 29–34); the calling of Andrew and another (vv. 35–39); of Simon Peter (vv. 40–42); of Philip (vv. 43–46); of Nathanael (vv. 47–51); the wedding at Cana, Jesus' first sign (2:1-12).

As one can see, two sections concern the witness of the Baptist, four are accounts of how Jesus chose his disciples, and the last, on the seventh day, is the first sign by which Jesus manifests his glory and prompts his disciples to belief. The first week foreshadows the conclusion of the Fourth Gospel, written, says John, "to help you believe that Jesus is the Messiah, the Son of God, so that through this faith you may have life in his name" (John 20:31).

The Witness of the Baptist

John the Baptist first addresses the Jewish authorities who came to interrogate him (vv. 19–28), then his disciples. In both cases, his role is more that of witness than preacher or baptizer.

When the "Jews" sent an embassy to question him about his claims, John first said what he was not: neither the Christ, nor Elijah, nor Moses, nor the prophet. Then he defined himself: a voice, a term that hearkens back to Isaiah 40:3 and suggests that the Baptist merely prepares the way of the Messiah, his voice being strictly dependent on the Word. He then alludes to his baptizing by water in order to focus attention on the baptism of the Spirit by "one among you whom you do not recognize," yet who is present in their midst. The Christ is characterized by his hidden presence, an important factor to consider. At least this is what the Fourth Gospel says when it first speaks of him.

"The next day" (v. 35), this time in the presence of two of his disciples, John's witness is more explicit. He clearly affirms who Jesus is: "The Lamb of God [who] was before me." In other words, the One, scorned among men (Isa 53:7ff.), who is greater than all, for he is close to the Father from all eternity (John 1:2). At the same time, the Baptist defines his role a bit more clearly. He helps to bring about, by baptizing Jesus in the water, the manifestation of the One who will baptize in the Spirit. The Baptist has seen the Spirit descend and rest on Jesus. Thus "the chosen one of God" (Isa 42:1) is the sacrificial Lamb who will baptize in the Spirit.

Four Accounts of the Call to Discipleship

Again, the scene is divided in two parts, each one introduced by the same expression of time: "the next day" (vv. 35, 43).

The first group of disciples is recruited in Judea, across the Jordan, among the disciples of the Baptist (vv. 35–42). The first is Andrew, the second is anonymous, though it could be John himself, who is never named in the Gospel. It is at this "tenth hour" that he would have encountered Jesus and "seen where he was lodged" (v. 39). The Fourth Gospel contains the fruit of this contemplation, which is based on "seeing" and "dwelling." Note the intermediary role played by the Baptist, who points out the Lamb of God: out of free choice, one can "follow" Jesus by an act of faith that involves one's fate.

Nothing is reported of what is said or seen: as far as the evangelist is concerned, very few conditions are necessary for becoming a disciple of Jesus: a witness to open the way; the Master who calls and goes on ahead; and the journey, which involves following him and leads to dwelling with him "that day" (v. 39), i.e., henceforth. But this is not the end, for Andrew communicates his joy to his brother Simon, becoming a kind of baptist in order to lead Simon into Jesus' presence. There, the tone changes: not only does Jesus know the identity of his visitor, but he looks at him and changes his name, thereby changing his life and destiny. Jesus recruits a second group of disciples, but this time they do not include the Baptist's disciples.

We move on to Galilee. Philip follows Jesus without hesitation and immediately thereafter testifies on his behalf to his friend Nathanael: he has met "the one Moses spoke of in the Law—the prophets too" (v. 45). But Nathanael is more hesitant; he seems not as open as the others to Jesus' call. Doubtlessly, this is why Philip tries to convince him by speaking of the Scriptures, having recognized in them the humble identity of Jesus, "son of Joseph, of Nazareth." Nathanael must know the Scriptures well: he knows that the Messiah must be born in Bethlehem. He remains skeptical. Philip then says to him to "come, see for yourself," i.e., to ascertain by personal experience who Jesus is, which is what Nathanael will do.

Jesus sees in Nathanael "a true Israelite," one who by his righteous conduct was capable of discovering the Messiah, of seeing in him the Son of God. Just as Jesus "saw" him in his most secret privacy (v. 48), it was given to Nathanael to see in Jesus "the king of Israel" (v. 49). The supernatural knowledge displayed by Jesus opens Nathanael to faith, so that a vision of the future will be given to him: the dream of Jacob, father of the Israelites, at Bethel will become real: the Son of man will establish himself as the definitive connection between God and all people on the day when heaven will open up, when the divine glory will show itself in the total and definitive triumph of Jesus (vv. 50–51).

We can see a clear progression in the titles that the first disciples gave to Jesus: first they called him "Rabbi" (v. 38), then "Messiah" (v. 41); then he is presented as "the one spoken of by Moses and the prophets" (v. 45); and finally they call him "the king of Israel" (v. 49), while Jesus defines himself as the "Son of Man" (v. 51).

The Wedding at Cana

At the end of the first week of Jesus' ministry is the wedding at Cana. This story, at the beginning of the Gospel, can be understood only in relation to the crucifixion, at the end. In both cases, "his mother was there" (John 2:1; 19:25). Through her, humanity is granted the salvation it so ardently desired. But how can we speak of salvation at the wedding at Cana (John 2:1-12)?

"The wine ran out" (John 2:3), and just when the feast is getting underway. Mary tells her son about the problem. She is cautious and discreet, and her mien clearly shows that she is not about to be rebuffed (John 2:5). But her Son knows only one need: that his "hour has not yet come" (John 2:4): it is still only the third day (John 2:1). The hour has been fixed by the Father and Mary cannot change it. This is why Jesus is content to satisfy earthly demands in this situation, but in such a way that his action becomes a "sign" that will make those who witness it aware of the true gift to come (John 2:11). He will not yet pour himself out, since he is one stone water jar short of seven, the number that symbolizes completeness (John 2:6). Thus the wine at Cana is not yet the wine of the eternal wedding feast.

What is the meaning of this "sign"? The fifteen to twenty-five gallons capacity of each container denotes a fullness to come; for, as the steward of the feast humorously remarks, without knowing the true meaning of the event, "You have kept the choice wine until now" (John 2:10). What is happening here? To understand that, we must look at the cross and see the fulfillment of all that God has promised us from the beginning. Since the baptism of Jesus, "the Spirit rested upon him" (John 1:33), so that one day he might give of it unstintingly (John 3:34). That day, when he will be "lifted up . . . from his side will flow rivers of living water" (John 7:38). When he is glorified, he will send his "Spirit" (John 7:39).

Out of his fullness we will receive "love following upon love" (John 1:14-16).

What is ultimately bestowed by Jesus is not the Law as it was given previously through Moses (John 1:17); nor is it a "purification" such as the Jews tried to achieve (John 2:6). What comes to us through Jesus Christ is "enduring love" (John 1:17). In the miracle of Cana, Jesus tells us who he is: the one in whom the glory of God is made manifest, and for whom the glory of God consists in achieving our salvation. Because he is at the same time giver and gift, Jesus presents himself as both the true steward of the feast and the "good wine": he gives himself and contains all the best that humanity can hope for. Not only does Jesus give salvation completely, but he is himself the personification of salvation.

Some "Manifestations" of the Lord

The apparent disparity between the gospels for the week after Epiphany is overlooked by virtue of being read in liturgical context, i.e., in a way that prolongs the manifestation of Jesus celebrated on January 6. Taken from the four Gospels, the chosen texts summarize all the "manifestations" of Christ, each one of which announces a salient aspect of his messianic activity.

The first manifestation takes place in Galilee (Matt 4:12-17, 23-25; Monday). It announces his manifestation in pagan lands and the universality of his mission. For Galilee is the geographical and theological frontier of the people of the first covenant. There, after the arrest of the Baptist, says Matthew, Jesus begins his preaching to a mixed population, partly pagan.

The First Gospel sees the fulfillment of a prophecy (Isa 9:1-6), taken in a universal sense, about the birth of a royal child whose birth we have celebrated at Christmas. For the Church, the marginalized people who make up the true Israel have been born on the outskirts of the heavenly city. Today, the light of the One who is proclaimed "the light of the world" (John 8:12) shines upon it.

Jesus comes to inaugurate the last phase of salvation history: "Reform your lives! The kingdom of heaven is at hand" (v. 17). Preaching the gospel always turns one outward, to wherever the Church encounters the world, at the risk of becoming lost in it, but with the desire to raise up the signs of full and real liberation among us: "He cured the people of every disease and illness" (v. 23).

We are still in Galilee, on the shores of the lake where Jesus is going to appear before the crowds who have come because they have heard of his preaching. He has also gathered his disciples around him (Mark 6:34-44: Tuesday).

Jesus sees an emptiness in the people, a lack of religious sensibility that needs to be filled. With his disciples' help, he will bring about a sense of community by sharing a meal that he miraculously brings into being. It is a special kind of nourishment. Note that it is Jesus' idea to create this feeling of community (v. 34), as it is his idea to "give them something to eat" (v. 37).

Note also that Jesus makes his disciples move from a somewhat disinterested attitude (v. 37) to one of responsibility, having to do with the gift that each possesses, even if it is small: "How many loaves have you? . . . Five, and two fish" (v. 38). The miracle brings about the birth of a diverse people who bring to mind the people of the Exodus[8]: a satisfied people who already proclaim something of the reality of the Eucharist and of the messianic feast of the last times.[9]

Jesus' next manifestation is aimed directly at his disciples who "had not understood about the loaves" (Mark 6:45-52: Wednesday). Jesus then "insists" that his disciples leave him for a while and he himself "dismisses" the crowd (v. 45). He then wants a lifting up, through prayer, to commune with the source of his being (v. 46).

Next, walking on the waves, Jesus tries to reveal himself to his disciples as the one in whom the divine power dwells, the power that in the beginning ruled the primordial waters. This demonstration is accompanied by an invitation to believe in him: "Get hold of yourselves! It is I. Do not be afraid!" (v. 50). When Jesus is in the boat (the Church) with his followers, all fear disappears, if one has faith.

But the disciples have yet to understand such phenomena, because they are confused by the frightening nature of Jesus' actions, the apparent dichotomy between Jesus' simple humanity and his true spiritual essence. But they see that he alone can calm the wind and the sea.

Jesus' preaching reputation spread throughout Galilee, and Jesus goes next to Nazareth "where he had been reared" (Luke 4:14-22: Thursday, v. 16). He observed the custom learned in his youth of going to the synagogue on the Sabbath, the place where the Law was read and discussed. Matt 13:53-58 and Mark 6:1-6 simply report the event without emphasizing the audience's uneasy reaction. Luke cites several lines from Isaiah (Isa 61:1-2 and 58:6) in which the prophet speaks of one moved by the Spirit of God and anointed for a mission: to announce the good news to all, beginning with the poor, and to proclaim a year of favor, i.e., benefits granted by the Lord.

It is an "appealing discourse" that Jesus announces (v. 22), for he chooses to limit the quotation's meaning by avoiding any mention of "the day of vengeance for our God." The congregation sees this and speaks favorably of him. The people are amazed. But amazement is not faith!

The "today" that is accomplished in the preaching of the word is first of all Christmas (Luke 2:11), then the baptism in the Jordan (3:22), the miracles of Jesus throughout his ministry (5:26), the conversion of Zacchaeus (19:9), and finally the cross, the response to the hope-against-hope of all penitents (Luke 23:43). And, to be sure, it includes all liturgies celebrating the mystery of salvation.

A passage from the Law will help us to understand the meaning of Jesus' encounter with a leper in an unnamed village (Luke 5:12-16; Friday). The leper is the outcast par excellence, not only because of the fear of physical contagion, but because of the leper's religious condition: he is impure, and one could go so far as to surmise that he is a sinner. Isaiah (Isa 53:3-10) describes a mysterious man of sorrow, similar to a leper, pierced for our offenses and offering his life in expiation. For Luke, this is an encounter of mercy and misery, of grace and sin. In healing by a single word, as opposed to the unusual artifices of Elisha (2 Kgs 5), Jesus is seen as infinitely powerful with regard to sin, at least when he encounters faith: "if you will to do so, you can . . ." (v. 12).

The extraordinary popular success of Jesus never kept him from acting in accordance with his custom: going into the desert to pray.

The sixth manifestation is addressed to John the Baptist's disciples and through the Baptist's mediation (John 3:22-30: Saturday). Jesus is in Judea and, through his disciples, he gives a baptism of purification reminiscent of that of the Precursor. Told of this by a "Jew" (i.e., someone opposed to Jesus, according to John the Evangelist's language), the Baptist's disciples are offended by such competition, and they believe that they should stop it: "The one about whom you have been testifying is baptizing now, and everyone is flocking to him."

John refuses to assume more power than what God has given him: he is not the Christ, and if the Messiah is now at work, the Precursor need only to remain in the background. It is enough for him to be there, to hear the voice of the Bridegroom and to rejoice in it, a perfect joy that does not feel the slightest sting of envy: it is enough for him to be a listener and hear the word. His mission is finished: he has only to disappear before the One whom he preceded.

Of People, Places, and Things

The "manger" at Bethlehem to which the shepherds hastened after hearing the words of the angel; the "house" where the magi from the East, guided by a star, bowed down in homage to the child; the "Temple" of Jerusalem, where two elderly people welcomed the Messiah of God: these are so many realities that lend themselves to liturgical spirituality. They may seem insignificant to us in comparison with the central object of the mystery of Christmas. Nevertheless, they play modest secondary roles, united in a drama where everything leads to thought and prayer.

And then there is the imagination. We need not point out that religious folklore has added so many details to the gospel stories that the events, once shrouded in mystery, have now become gilded legends. How can we abide this in the name of pure faith? Insofar as the Christmas liturgy has caught the fancy of Western peoples, its roots are now planted in human soil from which it cannot be uprooted without taking something away from popular religion and whatever faith it implies. Pure faith may not have soiled hands, but then again, it doesn't have hands at all. Its function is to delineate, to be aware of extraneous and so-called revelations. But gradual window dressings, so to speak, express nothing less than the sentiments aroused in the Christian people by the mystery of Christmas.

The Crèche, the Shepherds, and the Angels at Bethlehem

The Gospel According to Luke is the only one to say that Jesus was laid in a manger by his parents after his birth "because there was no room for them in the place where travelers lodged" (Luke 2:7). John will later say: the Word was in the world, and "his own did not accept him" (John 1:11). Was it just negligence or selfishness on the part of the people of Bethlehem who could have made room for a woman about to give birth? Was it perhaps a certain reserve on the part of his parents, who did not wish to cause a fuss and were content to rest anywhere as weary travelers? Let us not be too sentimental: before Mary and Joseph, many others had been forced to find refuge in the caves surrounding Bethlehem. It was shelter considered good enough for the poor, and travelers used to the fortunes of the road seemed resigned to it. And the idea of an ''unknown Messiah'' is fascinating, especially in light of the Jewish tradition in Jesus' time that expected a messiah who would be hidden to the point of being unrecognizable.

The crèche evokes popular Western piety. It serves as the dwelling place of the newborn, a place where different people witness his birth or come to do him homage. As an expression of devotion to Jesus' infancy, interest in the crèche seems to have existed very early in the Church. Around the year 150, St. Justin speaks of it as being in a cave, relying on a rather liberal reading of Isaiah.[1] Though it is true that the Gospels never speak of a cave, Justin's witness is no less valuable: having been born in Palestine, he would have known about the place. It is through Justin that this detail entered into Christian literature.

Whereas popular piety speaks of a crèche and freely pictures it in a cave, the biblical text uses various words related to the Hebrew term *'urvâh*, a term so general that it can signify manger, stall, stable, or even the food that was thrown into the trough for the cattle. The liturgical Lectionary uses the word ''manger.''

In the sixth century, the cave of the nativity was reconstructed at Rome in a small oratory hollowed out of the side of the Church of St. Mary Major. For the veneration of the faithful, it erected a manger out of five pieces of wood, thus making a connection between the wood of the crèche and wood of the cross. In 248, Origen described the birthplace of Jesus, the cave at Bethlehem, as containing a manger for the animals, doubtlessly made of hardened clay. More economical and easier to work than wood, clay was widely used for this purpose in Palestine and Egypt. St. Jerome appeared to confirm this in a famous sermon, given around 400 in Bethlehem: he wished that he had placed in the cave a manger of gold rather than of clay.[2] So much for the symbolism of the cross! But like St. Jerome, we admire ''the creator of the world who did not desire to be born in gold or silver, but in a crèche of clay.'' As if he wanted to emphasize his condition as the Son of man, a descendant of Adam who was formed out of the clay of the earth by his creator (Gen 2:7).

Bethlehem and the manger were very soon related to the altar of the Eucharist. Is it not a kind of crèche? Bethlehem means ''the house of bread.'' And doesn't Jesus describe himself as ''the bread of life'' (John 6:35, 51)? The early Fathers did not neglect this source of inspiration. There are many, both in the East and the West, who like to think of the altar as a crèche that is approached so that one may be nourished by the bread of God offered to men and women.[3]

At a Christmas celebration in Greccio in 1223, St. Francis of Assisi restored this ancient tradition. The Poverello placed in a cave a crèche filled with straw, around which were placed an ass and a cow. Mary, Joseph, and the child were not depicted in this reconstruction, as if Francis wanted to turn from the merely physical event to the meaning that it symbolized. In fact, the Mass was celebrated over the crèche. Only later would a fixed altar replace the provisional one.

The Ass and the Cow. Luke does not mention the ass and the cow, however, and had nothing to do with their fame. Popular imagination cannot conceive of a crèche without an ass and a cow to breathe on the newborn child to warm him. And what about the twenty-fifth of December? True, just like the presence of the ass and the cow, this date has no historical basis. In order to find the source for including the two animals, we must go to Isaiah, as did Origen, who seems to have started the whole thing: "An ox knows its owner, and an ass, its master's manger; but Israel does not know, my people has not understood" (Isa 1:3).

The religious souls of the common people have always understood. Finding inspiration in the Old Testament rather than in Luke's story, they wanted, instinctively, to associate the homage of animal creation with the birth of the One who, by restoring peace of Paradise, would be the benefactor of all creation (Isa 11:6; Hos 2:20-24; Amos 9:13; Joel 4:18).

The Shepherds Are Not Imaginary. It is very likely that they were at the crèche, the first to go and adore the child. The region of Bethlehem is bleak and hilly. In the spring the ground is covered with grasses that sheep and goats can graze upon. It is a land of steppes, desolate areas, and scrub-growth.

What a curious coincidence! God calls them all together by the mediation of the angels! This is their home, this land where God had chosen his servant David to make him the shepherd of his people Israel:

> And he chose David, his servant,
> and took him from the sheepfolds;
> From following the ewes he brought him
> to shepherd Jacob, his people,
> and Israel, his inheritance.
> And he tended them with a sincere heart,
> and with skillful hands he guided them.[4]

As a young boy, David tended the sheep in what was called the desert, and what could be termed "pasture land" (1 Sam 16:11). As far as we know, in those times the people of the Bible were shepherds. Abel kept lambs, and Jabal is called "the ancestor of all who dwell in tents and keep cattle" (Gen 4:2, 20). The patriarchs were shepherds: Abraham, Isaac, and Jacob, who complained about the hard way of life (Gen 13:7-8; 26:20; 29:18; 30:31; 31:40), a way of life that was not highly esteemed in the eyes of the world. "All shepherds are abhorrent to the Egyptians" (Gen 46:35).

The establishment of the Hebrews in Canaan brought about a progressively more settled life. Nevertheless, the collective memory remembered the nomadic origins of the chosen people, those distant days when God was Shepherd par excellence (Gen 48:15; Ps 23:1) and Israel his flock, his inheritance (Pss 28:9; 80:2). The development of the messianic hope would therefore naturally be expressed in pastoral terminology, which, as a matter of fact, seems to parallel the royal vocabulary of the East: the king was thought to be the shepherd of his people. The rulers of Israel would also be regarded as shepherds, though always depending on God (Ps 77:21). They were often so faithless to their mission that he would seek to replace and punish them (Jer 3:15; 23:1-4). After the return from the Babylonian Exile, the royal line would not be reestablished, and God alone would be the Shepherd of Israel (Isa 40:9-11; Ezek 34; Zech 10-11).

Does Luke allude to this theme? Not likely. In his time, shepherds were poor, weak, and shunned: they did not know the Law, nor could they live by its rigorous standards. That is why God himself called them first. But there would be a divine subtlety in the choice of this social class, this "people of the land," as great and wise men disdainfully called them? Luke knows very well that Jesus is the Good Shepherd who searches for the lost sheep (Luke 15:2-7), the Great Shepherd who will give his life in order to lead his flock along the road of the new Exodus. Who better than these simple folk gathered around the crèche in response to the divine call could understand and live the mystery of grace in joy, praise, and thanksgiving?

Others will be called after them. They will have to conduct themselves as examples to the flock (1 Pet 5:1-4), going in their turn to the lost sheep of the house of Israel (Matt 10:6). Yet, in their joy, the shepherds of Bethlehem have already become the first missionaries of the good news: sharing their happiness, they repeat all that was told them about this child.

The Angels Are Omnipresent. Their praise gives way to the shepherds' thanksgiving, joining the angels in unceasing praise and anticipating the worship of the Church. For liturgical action, of which praise and thanksgiving are the essential elements, is the normal response of the creature to the gift of God.

Yet, there is great contrast in this picture of radiance and joy between the angels' role in the old covenant and that which they will perform in the new! According to Paul and the tradition of late Judaism, it was they who transmitted the Law at Sinai, thus playing a strong intermediary role in the life of humankind. That is why they alone can travel between heaven and earth in the story of Jacob's ladder (Gen 28:12-18; John 1:51). The heavens open and the angels ascend and descend a ladder that reaches to heaven: all this is fulfilled in a theophany of God himself, in the glory of the Father and in his Son become flesh of our flesh. There is no longer any need for an intermediary when the Father acts directly through his Son; when this Son, present on earth, does everything according to what he sees, hears, and knows of his Father.[5]

Henceforth, the angels are no more than the escort of the Son of God on earth. They are present because they have a share in the celestial glory that illuminates God's mystery, this mystery into which "the angels long to search" (1 Pet 1:12). But it is the glory of the incarnate Word that they serve, which eclipses all other light because, in the mystery of the incarnation, "heaven has visited earth." They announce the social nature of this kingdom of God that will transform the whole universe.

Thus they appear above the crèche, in the wake of a mystery that has come down from heaven to earth, like the fringe of a heavenly garment that at the ascension will appear as the radiant rising of the Son into the bosom of the Father. But they will withdraw themselves when Jesus speaks and acts in the maturity of his own power. Even in his form as a slave, Jesus is not under their power (Heb 1:7–2:9).

But at Christmas, we still see the angels hovering around this Word, so helpless in his earthen cradle. Are they not "the first degree of the Terrible" (R.M. Rilke), charged with announcing to us the presence of the Wholly Other? Near the crèche at Bethlehem, they once more get our attention to remind us that God is near. It is the angel of the Lord, an anonymous figure, almost a fixture in the Old Testament, who announces the good news to the shepherds, as he did previously to Hagar, to the mother of Samson, to Moses, and to Gideon (Gen 16; Judg 13; 6:11-24; Exod 3:2-4:17). With a transcendence unknown till then, the heavens

break forth in celestial glory. Soon a multitude of angels appears, as they
had suddenly appeared previously in the exceptional circumstances of
a mysterious epiphany of God.[6] Doubt is no longer possible; this is the
dawn of salvation.[7] "A multitude of the heavenly host," the whole celestial army is there to relay the joyous message "Glory to God in high
heaven, peace on earth to those on whom his favor rests" (Luke 2:13-14).

Glory to God where he already reigns, in the mysterious transcendence
which is his forever and which is brought near to us in his Son. Glory
to God! the greatest hymn of our liturgy. For the first time, the angels
act out their liturgy around the Son of God made man, a liturgy that is
preeminently theirs.[8] In the midst of this epiphany of God's Word, they
join us to their song, to his song, and to the liturgy that takes place before the face of God.[9] Isn't this always set before us as we celebrate the
feast of joy and hope that is Christmas? The idea of being gloriously united
with them is presented to us throughout the liturgical year in the various
prefaces of the Mass.

The House, the Magi, and the Star

The Gospel According to Matthew is one of those books that must be
read beginning at the end. We must read the two last verses: "Make disciples of all the nations . . . . And know that I am with you always"
(Matt 28:19-20). Then we can go back to the beginning: in the announcement to Joseph, Jesus is presented as "God-with-us" (Matt 1:23), while
the coming of the magi reveals the child of Bethlehem as God for the pagans (Matt 2:1-2).

In Luke, the birth of Jesus is set among the poor, who visit other poor
refugees in a temporary shelter. Apart from heaven and the angelic host,
few people are aware of the event. Matthew's story speaks of wise men
coming from afar to adore a royal child, of King Herod's disquiet, and
all Jerusalem with him—the elite of the Jewish religious world. Luke uses
two events to teach about Jesus: first, his reception by the poor people
at the crèche; then, the incident in the Temple, where he is welcomed
as the light who shines for the world. Matthew, on the other hand, puts
everything into one scene: the adoration of the magi, where places, kings,
and attitudes are opposed to one another, under the light of a star that
is at once a sign and a symbol.

Without reviewing the details of a well-known story, we will point out
some obstacles or contradictory elements in a text whose theological significance seems evident. Interestingly, each obstacle is highlighted by re-

course to scriptural argument, which Matthew handles with consummate artistry.

Jerusalem Against Bethlehem.[10] According to Luke, the events that surround the birth of Jesus happen near the crèche at Bethlehem, whereas Matthew speaks of "the place where the child was," a "house" that the magi entered in order to adore him (Matt 2:9, 11) at the end of a long journey. The whole thing (Matt 2) is presented as a dramatic travelogue that leads us from Bethlehem to Jerusalem, then, with the magi, to Bethlehem again, followed by the flight into Egypt, and finally ending at Nazareth. The editor (final redactor) has deemed it necessary to present this itinerary in order to justify something and to place it in a certain context.

To justify. He must justify the fact that the one who is called "Jesus of Nazareth" is nonetheless the Messiah: not a Galilean by birth, but born in Judea in the city of David, according to the prophecy of Micah (Mic 5:1ff.). From then on, he meticulously notes the displacements of a royal child, born at Bethlehem but, because of a king's murderous plans, forced to flee his birthplace and to look for a more secure place. Each displacement is justified by reference to a scriptural argument, especially those texts that speak of a "son" or a "child." The Messiah deserves nothing less, even if the argument occasionally leaves something to be desired (Matt 2:23).

It seems that Matthew is also preoccupied with contrasts. The duality of Bethlehem-Nazareth is extended by a still more significant contrast between Bethlehem and Jerusalem, the "house" (Matt 2:11) where the people can adore the child presenting itself rather like a midpoint between the two cities, the capital of Judaism and the city where David was born. "Coming from the East"—for a Judean, this means from some point beyond the Jordan—the magi arrive in Jerusalem to find out where the king of the Jews is to be born. At first Herod is upset and summons a meeting of the Sanhedrin, composed of Israel's most worthy representatives. The response they give the king has a great deal of authority, since they quote the words of a prophet and reinforce them with a historical book of Scripture (though for a Jew, history itself is prophetic). Not only must the Messiah be born in Bethlehem (Mic 5:1ff.), but he will be the shepherd of Israel (2 Sam 5:2). The argument appears to be decisive for Matthew, since it is the only explicit quotation from Scripture he offers in the story: elsewhere he makes use of allusions. What is important here is that the information is supplied by the Sanhedrin: it is as if Matthew wants to tell his reader that he did not make it up, that it was produced by the authorized theologians of Judaism.[11]

The contradistinction drawn between the place where knowledge and power reside (Jerusalem) and where the awaited Messiah is born and dwells is reinforced by the fact that neither the Sanhedrin nor Herod does what one would expect, namely, hasten to the place where they might find the newborn child. Herod plots and conceives dark designs. As for the Sanhedrin, the solemn testimony it gives at Herod's request prefigures, in some way, the verdict of condemnation that it will give thirty years later on the night of Passover (Matt 26:66).

What can we make of the fact that the adoration of the magi takes place "in the house" and not at the crèche (Matt 2:11; cf. Luke 2:16)? Let us trace the path with the magi, whom Herod sent, in spite of themselves, to play into his hand. They leave Jerusalem, the place where Matthew first introduced them to us. They have found some information there that will help them on the remainder of their journey. They do not trust their own powers or only the information given them by Herod. The star that has led them this far is still there; it has not abandoned them but precedes them, stopping "over the place where the child was" (Matt 2:9). Full of joy, they enter "into the house" (Matt 2:11) and prostrate themselves. In a way, one could say that their quest is over, even if they must return to their country "by another route" (Matt 2:12). In any case, they do not return to Herod in Jerusalem.

In going from Jerusalem to Bethlehem, the journey of the magi prefigures the turnabout that will occur on the day when God, because of the chosen people's lack of belief, will direct his plan of salvation in another direction, toward this "Galilee of nations" where Jesus himself, after the circuitous path traced by Matthew, will end up, settling in Nazareth.[12] Having been born at Bethlehem, according to the prophecies, Jesus was known as "the Nazorean." The primitive Christian community seems to have seen in this fact justification for the missionary work of the Church and its expansion from its Jewish center toward the frontiers of the world and of other nations. From its grounding in the Jewish tradition to going beyond it, according to God's plan, the trip from Jerusalem to Bethlehem and beyond appears as a sign. Though Jerusalem is not to be neglected, one can neither stay there or return to it; one must turn to Bethlehem in order to recognize "on entering the house" the one who is at the center of all the promises. Life then takes on a different meaning, and one can substitute for the place where he or she orginally dwelt by taking "another route."

Can we conclude that "the house" where one discovers "God-with-us" may be the Church, henceforth detached from Jerusalem and from its religious authority, and open to all those who, in search of the Messiah, enter into it and take on a new life?[13] The flow of the text seems to support this typical example of Matthew's theology, but lexicographical examination does not warrant such a conclusion. Numerous presumptions are no basis for certainty. Perhaps, however, they allow the text to strike responsive chords in a heart that listens; in the house of the Church, which the pagans may freely enter, Matthew would readily assert that since the birth of Jesus, a gulf is opened between Jerusalem, hearing and keeping the letter of the Scriptures, and Bethlehem, symbol of openness, with its house that furnishes an end to one quest and begins another.

Kings in Contrast. We think we know the magi: kings coming from the East, traveling on camels, in order to adore the Son of God made flesh. There are three of them: a Black, an Arab, perhaps a Chinese, each of them bringing a gift. Their names? Melchior, Caspar, and Balthasar.[14] One tradition even claims that their tomb is in Cologne, the ways of God being mysterious and the roads taken by relics being subject to all sorts of historical mishaps!

Let us return, rather, to the simplicity of Matthew's account: the evangelist does not overflow with details. Is it because of his deplorable silence on the subject of the mysterious magi that folklore and literature have felt the need to fill the void? Matthew is not the kind of storyteller to satisfy the imagination of devotees of legend. If he reports something, it is with a very specific goal in mind, i.e., as a theologian who wishes to prove that Jesus, waited for by the Jews at first, has finally been received as the Messiah, especially by the pagans.

The magi belong to a type of figure well known in the pagan literature of the age (see Philo of Alexandria and, before him, Herodotus). Their abilities class them among the intelligentsia of the time: they are presented as the best of the wise men of antiquity. Among various testimonies on the subject, two recurring beliefs hold sway, both encountered east of Palestine in Media, Persia, and Babylonia. The magi are the capable and official interpreters of extraordinary events and natural phenomena, as well as dreams (Dan 2:2; 4:15; 5:7). Moreover, their coming to Bethlehem after discovering a new star and their subsequent role there is very understandable according to the traditions of ancient culture.

But Matthew depicts them even better by referring to Scripture, especially the associations that come to mind if one thinks of the ascent of the pagans toward Jerusalem, which is found in certain strands of Jewish apocalyptic literature. Numerous texts from Isaiah evoke sights that are recapitulated in the gospel story. Is it not first at Jerusalem that the magi discover the "illuminating" information that directs them toward Bethlehem (Isa 2:2-3)? Is not the pilgrimage of pagans processing toward the messianic light verified in the adoration of the child by the magi and the splendid gifts that they bring to his cradle (Isa 45:14; 60:1-6; Ps 71:10-15)? This is not a skeleton story that folklore devotees have decided to embellish by identifying the magi with kings and by describing their splendid accoutrements as they travel toward the holy city. Where Matthew's story is surprising and innovative is in the contrast between Herod, the suspicious and motionless king, and the pilgrim magi who find themselves led toward Jerusalem, though only in order to pass through it, to go farther beyond.

Their visit recalls another wisdom theme that Jesus has undertaken. At one point in his ministry, he dares to draw a parallel between the wisdom of Solomon and what he himself offers his listeners (Matt 12:42; 1 Kgs 10:1). By so saying, the parallel is completed by a prophetic evocation of the coming of the pagans to the one who is "greater than Solomon": they will have a share in the feast of the kingdom of heaven, while the subjects of the kingdom will be cast out (Matt 8:11-12).

Looked at in another way, we see that the pilgrimage of the magi, whose objective is to go first to Jerusalem, ends up in Bethlehem in the house of the child, so that they themselves are in contrast to King Herod, from whom they are detoured. They prostrate themselves, pagans and yet wise men, before the king of kings, while Herod believes that he surpasses them in authority and in the political realm. He is ready to be served by these pagans in order to assure his dominance, but they only wish to serve the one whom they recognize and honor as the one true king. In view of the unavoidable conflict of kings that will soon come to pass, the Christian community affirms its reliance on the victory that will elevate the Anointed One of God over all those kings who conspire against him (Ps 2; Acts 4:25-28).

A Star in Heaven. "We have observed his star at its rising and have come to pay him homage" (Matt 2:2). The justification the magi give for their journey could only make Herod more upset. The magi have caught the fancy of many. Let us not leap too quickly at the chance to explain away the star as some Halley's Comet, scrutinizing the astronomical table for the appearance of it at the presumed time of the nativity. It could perhaps have sent these magi-astrologers on their way, but in the tradition of ancient culture, the appearance of a star at the time of the birth of a great person is a well-known phenomenon, even a conventional one. If each of us is "born under a favorable [or unfavorable] star," wouldn't we take for granted that the birth of the Messiah was announced by the timely appearance of a wondrous star? The literature of the age, both Jewish and pagan, readily reports the occurrence of such natural phenomena on the occasion of the birth of a person whose destiny will fall outside the ordinary: Alexander, Caesar, Abraham, the Messiah awaited by the Qumran community, and others.

In Matthew's story, various terms refer quite freely to the legend reported by the Book of Numbers (Num 22–24). The king of Moab sent Balaam, a prophet of the East, to confront Israel, which was trying to force its way into the Promised Land. Far from cursing the chosen people, as he had been ordered to do, Balaam was constrained by God not to obstruct the way of the invaders. He prostrated himself and, in a vision, discerned a star coming out of Jacob and a scepter, a sign that Israel would, in the future, rule over the land of Canaan. The Greek tradition was bound to personalize the oracle: it spoke of a man who would rise up out of Israel. In this way the prophecy acquired an indisputably messianic dimension.

Matthew is freely inspired by this legend. That is why he gives the star a slightly different role: it will guide the magi toward the dwelling place of the Messiah. In Luke, the angels in heaven proclaimed the glory of God. In Matthew, the star fills the heaven of the pagans and plays a providential role for them: the magi see a sign from God, a sign that points clearly to the object of their desire.

By so reinterpreting the Scriptures, Matthew shows how sincere pagans, with the natural knowledge they possess, can advance, God willing, to an encounter with the messianic light. Must not Jesus, the true Lion of Judah (Gen 49:9-10), become the king over all nations? The royalty of Jesus of Nazareth can shake empires: he is the heir to the throne of David and the promises attached to it. In rereading this text, we see that Matthew's Judeo-Christian community discovered, with a greater joy than that of the magi, the realization of these promises, which are extended to all those who hunger for salvation and who long for a sure light to guide their lives.

Undoubtedly, Matthew's apologetic concerns are revealed here: the star that burns bright over Judah ends up leading the pagans out of Jerusalem to the house (Church) where "God-with-us" begins to reign. After their return from Egypt, the Holy Family settles in Galilee (Matt 2:22), the land of the pagans (Matt 4:15), the messianic light clearly taking over the role of the magi's star. The natural elements must now step back before the reality, frail though it may appear, of a child-king who holds the promise of salvation. Somewhat less peaceful than Luke, Matthew says only this at the end: peace to those whom God loves, even if they are pagans!

Jerusalem, the Temple, the Law, and the Prophets

Matthew's interest in Galilee is well documented: that is where his Gospel begins and ends. Luke's attention is focused rather on Jerusalem: his story opens and closes at the Temple. The infancy gospels do not escape the special emphases of their redactors. Luke's infancy narrative begins in the Temple with the announcement of the birth of John the Baptist to Zechariah. It ends with two episodes that involve Jesus at the Temple: his presentation there by his parents, forty days after his birth (Luke 2:22-38); and his discovery there, at age twelve, by Mary and Joseph, in the midst of the doctors of the Law (Luke 2:41-50). The two references to the hidden life at Nazareth are not enough to deflect interest from what happens at Jerusalem (Luke 2:39-40, 51-52).

The story of the purification and the presentation is typical in this regard. In a liturgical atmosphere, the Anointed One of the Lord takes possession of his sanctuary in order to fulfill the Law and the Prophets, to substitute his own offering for the old practice of multiple sacrifices. The literary framework is that of the community of Israel, defined by the Temple as the center of worship, by observance of the Law of Moses, and by prophetic witness.

The Temple of Jerusalem. Each of the two episodes that conclude Luke's Gospel of the infancy plays a Christological role. Thus the finding of Jesus in the Temple brings to light the relationship between Jesus and his Father (Luke 2:41-50). The story of the purification and the presentation, forty days after Christmas, concerns the relationship of the Messiah to his people: it is to the messianic people that the promises of the purification (v. 22) and the redemption (v. 38) are brought, while the two prophecies attest to the importance of the event (vv. 33–38).

Note that, for Luke, purification and presentation are one and the same messianic manifestation: as we will see, he has consciously combined the two rites. Both take place in the Temple, at the heart of Jerusalem, always referred to here by its sacred name of Ierousalem. "If Ierousalem is the holy city, the place of messianic revelation and the working of salvation, Hierosolyma is the secular city, but also the guilty city, which denied its Lord and which, for that very reason, is faced with ruin."[15]

If Jerusalem appears here as the center of salvation history and of the Israel who waits for the Messiah,[16] the Temple is the place where we see the "glory" (1 Kgs 8:11; Isa 6:1-5), sign of the divine presence among the chosen people. Jesus comes into the Temple as the one who embodies glory (v. 32), i.e., one who expresses the holiness and grandeur of God himself. The Temple becomes the sacred place of encounter between the Anointed One of God, in whom divine glory is vested, and the faithful Israel that awaits purification and deliverance.

In fact, neither Jesus nor his mother (who is not named once in the whole passage) requires purification and deliverance: that is the prerogative of the chosen people. This explains the anonymity of those who present the child to the Lord. The explanatory gloss of the liturgical Lectionary distorts the text, which is content with a very general "they" (v. 22). In the mind of the redactor, it is the faithful, each of us, who offer the child in the Temple, thanks to a bounteous purification and deliverance.

Yet very shortly, Jesus will leave Jerusalem to return to Nazareth, and the divine presence will go with him. Later, he will drive out of the Temple the merchants who furnish the pilgrims with doves and pigeons for the redemption of the firstborn. Jesus will thus serve notice of what belongs to him so that he may manifest in his person the divine glory and the salvation he brings to the chosen people. Immediately afterward, Luke will show the Master teaching daily in the Temple, as if he were the authoritative voice that leads to salvation (Luke 19:45-47). After the sacrifice of his Passover, he will rise to heaven while blessing his followers, like the high priest who parts the veil and passes through into the holy of holies (Luke 24:50).[17]

Later Christian tradition will continue its reflection by proclaiming Jesus as the new Temple of God in whom we encounter the Father (John 2:12-22; 1 Cor 3:16-17), the only High Priest of the new Law who has gained access for us to the sanctuary (Heb 9:6, 12, 24; 10:5).

The Law of the Lord. The first verses of the story use a vocabulary that deals with the offerings for worship prescribed by the Law. It speaks of "purification," and "presentation" (v. 22), "consecration to the Lord" (v. 23), "offering in sacrifice" (v. 24). Luke seems anxious to show that Jesus' parents complied with all the ritual prescriptions of Judaism. But if he emphasizes Mary and Joseph's faithfulness, it is less the exactitude of their observance than the prophetic value of the old Law to which he gives homage.[18]

If we hold to what Luke says, the presentation ceremony took place "when the day came to purify them according to the law of Moses" (Luke 2:22). This presents a problem. Set for forty days after the birth of a male child, the rite of the mother's purification is accompanied by the offering of two turtledoves or two young pigeons (Lev 12:3, 6, 8). However, there is no trace in the Bible of a prescription involving a customary presentation of a newborn child to the Lord. Someone will object by pointing to the case of the child Samuel, which Luke seems to have taken as a literary model (1 Sam 1:19-28; Luke 1:46 and 1 Sam 2:1-10). But Samuel is presented in Shiloh in order to be consecrated *(nazir)* to the Lord and to live in the sanctuary: this is not the case with Jesus, who returns to Nazareth. Some people suggest that it was a pious custom, but the hypothesis is utterly gratuitous.

It is more likely that Luke is alluding to the sacrifice of the firstborn of Israel, a prescription resulting from the first Passover in Egypt (Exod 13:15; 34:20; Num 18:15; Lev 27:11-12, 27). Remembering the passage of the Lord sparing Israel's firstborn, every male firstborn child must be redeemed, for they are owed, consecrated to the God of the covenant. But our difficulty remains, for the redemption must be made "when he is one month old" (Num 18:16) and not after forty days. Also, it is accompanied by an offering of five shekels of silver, something Luke never mentions.

We must conclude that Luke is dealing here with allusions and approximations. Rather than precise rites, he goes to the scriptural texts that give meaning to the first coming of Jesus to the Temple. The "holy offspring," whose birth the angel announced to Mary (Luke 1:35), has no need for himself to be purified, any more than his mother. Neither has he to be redeemed. But because he is the Anointed One of the Lord, he can, according to the prophecy of Malachi 3:1-3, come into his Temple to purify the sons of Levi "that they may offer due sacrifice to the Lord." Is there also an allusion to Daniel 9:24? According to one Palestinian tradition, Jesus' entry into his Temple would coincide with the end of the prophecy of the seventy weeks that would see "the most holy be anointed." In this case, the eschatological significance of the event would be reinforced and the child's entry into the Temple would also announce that "guilt will be expiated, everlasting justice will be introduced, vision and prophecy ratified." All things will be realized in the Passover of the Son of God.

Whatever scriptural influences may have been involved in the redaction of Luke's story, how could one ignore the Letter to the Hebrews? Not only does it say that we have in Christ "a merciful and faithful high priest, to expiate the sins of the people" (Heb 2:17), but it does not hesitate to put on the lips of the incarnate Word the words of the psalmist: "Sacrifice and offering you did not desire, but a body you have prepared for me; holocausts and sin offerings you took no delight in. Then I said, 'As is written of me in the book, I have come to do your will, O God'" (Heb 10:5-7; Ps 39:7, 9).

By submitting himself as a young human being to all the legal obligations that proceed from being a male, the Anointed One of the Lord becomes capable of transforming the Law by fulfilling it through his perfect obedience.

The Prophets. By entering the Temple, Jesus comes to fulfill the Law, but he also receives the witness of prophecy in the person of a man and a woman who have no official or hierarchical authority.

As is common in Luke, scenes and people appear in pairs, and in a play of parallelism and interrelationship,[19] Simeon and Anna, both prophets, appear. Their welcoming of the child takes up the theme of the *Benedictus:* their eyes have seen salvation (Luke 1:67, 71, 77; 2:30). To the humble shepherds of Bethlehem, the first to receive the good news, are added the representatives of pious people, the "poor of Yahweh" who live in the shadow of the Temple.

Simeon and Anna are the personification of faithful Israel, which waits for its Savior with all its heart. Through them, Christ encounters the "remnant," already represented by Mary, the daughter of Zion. All the features that characterize them recall the circle of the poor who have never despaired. Both wait for the coming of the consolation of Israel with justice and piety (Luke 2:25), with prayer and fasting (Luke 2:37). Both are moved by the Spirit of God and given the gift of prophecy (Luke 2:27-28, 36). Simeon recognizes in the child he takes into his arms his deepest mystery, his glory and messianic future. As for Anna, in her own way,

292 OF PEOPLE, PLACES, AND THINGS

she plays the role of the shepherds at the crèche: she "talks" of the child, proclaiming in inspired terms the meaning of the event (Luke 2:38). Thus, to the fulfillment of the Law by the firstborn succeeds the fulfillment of the prophecies by the Spirit. For from now one, it is important to be able to interpret the Scriptures on the subject of Jesus "beginning with Moses and the prophets, . . . every passage which referred to him" (Luke 24:27).

Apart from the "symbolic" cases of Simeon, Anna, and Mary, the daughter of Zion who receives the revelation of the division that will rend the heart of the Israel (Luke 2:34-35), one could say that human beings really have no place in this story. It says nothing about either the parents or the priests who are usually in charge of the rites. Even the angels of the nativity remain unseen. The Lord himself has become the subject, with the child, the actor at once passive yet most perfect, and the Spirit acting in the shadow where he delights. Mary herself, named only once, parts with her son, giving him into the arms of another as a sign foreshadowing the new order where Jesus will pass from hand to hand. As for Simeon, he is witness to the fact that our hands and arms can express meaning. So near to death, he bears in his arms the hope of the world, the hope of pagans as well as of Israel.

In receiving into his arms the Word of fulfillment, Simeon, representing the old world, receives the youth of the world, the One who will be the Consolation (v. 32) for all men, their assembly, their return from captivity, so to speak.[20] The Canticle of Simeon, sung in Ierousalem, the holy city, is properly revelatory. The voice of Anna, on the other hand, assures the missionary dissemination of the good news to all those who hope in the benevolence of God. The parents of Jesus, the first to be amazed and enlightened, are not the last beneficiaries of this Gospel. Thanks to the light of prophecy, all are asked to grow and be strengthened in their faith.

Why two witnesses? Why this man and this woman? Does this interpretation point to the fact that, according to the prescription of the Law, two witnesses are required for a reliable testimony (Deut 19:15)? The prophets are always alone when they prophesy. Could it be that Anna's role at Simeon's side is rather "that of woman accompanying man,"[21] symbolic of the human race—male and female—witnessing the new Adam (Luke 3:38)?

Don't they represent what and who we are—believers— children of God led by the Spirit?

Simeon comes to the Temple under the guidance of the Spirit of God (Luke 2:27). You too, if you wish to hold Jesus in your hands and earn your release from judgment, are able to do what you can to submit yourself to the guidance of the Spirit and come to the Temple of God. See, even now you are in the Temple of the Lord Jesus, i.e., his Church, the Temple made of living stones. You are the Temple of the Lord when your life and conduct are truly worthy of the name that defines the Church. If it is in this spirit that you come to the Temple, you will find the child Jesus. You will lift him in your arms and say: "Now, Lord, you may dismiss your servant in peace, according to your word!"[22]

The factors that have produced the liturgical atmosphere of the infancy gospels, i.e., the ordinary people, places, and things, are neither the gifts of the magi nor the parents of the child, nor the lights of heaven or the Temple, nor the pastoral humility of the shepherds, nor the hymns or canticles of angels and people. Even less are they the subtle arguments of the theologians, based on what was for them the dead letter of Scripture, or the abundance of various rites that vanished before the reality that gave them meaning.

The liturgical importance of these stories, more elaborate than one can imagine, is due above all to their Christological emphasis, to the omnipresence of the Spirit who accomplishes all sanctification, to the mystery of Easter that shines through all things, to the dynamic power of a living salvation, and to the missionary dimension that they involve. Finally, it is due to the mystery of the Church, the people of God coming from all races and tongues, who assemble, through the praise that encompasses their whole life, in order to adore the Father in spirit and in truth by symbolic gestures, which always compel a deepening of faith.

Here, heaven and earth are joined in praise. They proclaim, without ignoring the shadows that are still present, the light of the new Jerusalem, this "image of the crossroads"[23] whose living stones are made of regenerated men and women, transfigured in Jesus Christ, here and now mere servants, nevertheless important in their own way, later on becoming free worshipers of the Father and companions of the incarnate Word, the center of Scripture and the liturgy.

Sunday After January 6[1]

The Baptism of the Lord

The feast of the Baptism of the Lord is of relatively recent origin in the Roman Church,[2] and its Liturgy of the Word is still tentative in the sense that of the three series of biblical texts prescribed (Years A, B, C), the first two readings of Year A can be used each year.[3] However, it is important not to have too narrow a view of the mystery. This will happen if we limit ourselves to the fact that Jesus submitted himself to the baptismal rite that John the Baptist practiced in the waters of the Jordan. Each of the four Gospels has transmitted some recollection of what happened.[4] Matthew recounts it in detail; Mark and Luke are content to merely mention it. John does not speak explicitly of the baptism but only of the Baptist's attesting that he had seen the Spirit descend on Jesus, "the chosen one of God."[5] One must refer to the Synoptic Gospels.

All three have in common their corroboration that the Spirit came over Jesus, and that a voice was heard.[6] The event is therefore a theophany that happened on the occasion of Jesus' baptism. This explains why the Eastern Church celebrates the Baptism of the Lord on Epiphany, for it was the manifestation of his status as the chosen one, the Son of God. In the Latin Church, the feast of the Baptism of the Lord has the same focus, as the entrance and communion antiphons clearly state:

> When the Lord had been baptized, the heavens opened and the Spirit came down like a dove to rest on him. Then the voice of the Father thundered: This is my beloved Son, in whom I am well pleased.
> (Entrance Antiphon)

> This is he of whom John said: I have seen and have given witness that this is the Son of God. (Communion Antiphon)

Yet, one can not dissociate the baptism of Jesus from that which he himself instituted in order to be given to those who believe in him. Not only because of the similarity of the rites, but because of the witness of the Baptist reported by the Fourth Gospel:

> The one who sent me to baptize with water told me, "When you see the Spirit descend and rest on someone, it is he who is to baptize with the Holy Spirit (John 1:33-34; see Luke 3:16).

294

In fact, the liturgy places Christian baptism in the perspective of the divine manifestation that took place upon the baptism of Jesus by John.

> Father, all-powerful and ever-living God,
> we do well always and everywhere to give you thanks.
> You celebrated your new gift of baptism
> by signs and wonders at the Jordan.
> Your voice was heard from heaven
> to awaken faith in the presence among us
> of the Word made man.
>
> Your Spirit was seen as a dove,
> revealing Jesus as your servant,
> and anointing him with joy as the Christ,
> sent to bring to the poor
> the good news of salvation.
>
> In our unending joy we echo on earth
> the song of the angels in heaven
> as they praise your glory for ever.
> (Preface)
>
> Almighty, eternal God,
> when the Spirit descended upon Jesus
> at his baptism in the Jordan,
> you revealed him as your own beloved Son.
> Keep us, your children born of water and the Spirit,
> faithful to our calling.
> (Opening Prayer I)[7]

As the manifestation—epiphany—of the Lord, the baptism of Jesus proclaims the baptism that elevates believers to the status of sons and daughters of God. It is a salvation event, a mystery and not an anniversary, that the last liturgy of the Christmas season celebrates. A mystery that must be meditated upon and lived in the light of the Scriptures, both of the Old and New Testaments. It is a mystery whose unfathomable depth can be seen in the rhythm of the celebrations that unfold in a kind of triptych. The central panel belongs successively to Matthew, Mark, and Luke. On the left panel, we read a different prophecy from Isaiah each year.[8] On the right panel there is a text of the Book of Acts (Year A) and an excerpt from the First Letter of John (Year B) or a passage from the Letter of Paul to Titus (Year C).[9] Before lingering over each of them, the community assembled for the liturgy turns itself toward God.

> Father,
> your only son revealed himself to us by becoming man.
> May we who share his humanity
> come to share his divinity. (Opening Prayer II)

The One Whom the Prophets Announced

Here Is My Servant, My Chosen One

The Scriptures witness to Christ: in order to be fully aware of this, one must read them in light of the message of the New Testament, keeping in mind the one whom they speak of without naming, who fulfills them beyond all hope. Proclaimed in the context of the liturgy and in the celebration of a particular mystery, a prophecy amplifies, in a certain manner, what the gospel says, by accentuating its most important aspects. It is like a melody, a recitative that is enriched with harmony. At the same time, the prophet invites us to fix our attention on the one whose features and mission he himself has seen from afar, more or less distinctly.

Throughout so many prophecies, the Christological aspect is constantly identified and enriched. See, for instance in the Book of Isaiah, the so-called "Servant-of-the-Lord oracles."[10] The first of them is used for the liturgy of this day (Isa 42:1-4, 6-7).

This text was too well known for Jesus to ignore. He must have heard it read in the synagogue and, by meditating on it, recognized it as the divine expression of his vocation: "To open the eyes of the blind, to bring out prisoners from confinement, and from the dungeon, those who live in darkness." Moreover, at the beginning of his ministry, during a service in the synagogue in Nazareth, he found in the book that was handed to him one day a similar oracle: "The spirit of the Lord God is upon me, because the Lord has anointed me; he has sent me to bring glad tidings to the lowly, to heal the brokenhearted, to proclaim liberty to the captives and release to the prisoners, to announce a year of favor from the Lord" (Isa 61:1-2). After having closed the book, he sat down and said: "Today this Scripture passage is fulfilled in your hearing" (Luke 4:1-21).

To the Christians gathered today to celebrate the Baptism of the Lord, the prophet shows Jesus: "Fix your eye on the Chosen One of God to whom belongs all his joy, on whom the Spirit rests. He is the meek and humble Master, the faithful Servant, whom no one nor nothing can force to yield, because God is with him. He fulfills the expectation of the nations, of whom the magi are the first-fruits. In him, in his person, I have made my Covenant.''

When this prophetic voice stops resounding, how can we possibly not fall to our knees in homage?

> *The Lord will bless his people with peace.*
>
> Give to the LORD, you sons of God,
>   give to the LORD glory and praise,
> Give to the LORD the glory due his name;
>   adore the LORD in holy attire.
>
> The voice of the LORD is over the waters,
>   the God of glory thunders,
>   the LORD, over vast waters.
> The voice of the LORD is mighty;
>   the voice of the LORD is majestic.
>
> The voice of the LORD twists the oaks
>   and strips the forests,
>   and in his temple all say, ''Glory!''
>
> The LORD is enthroned above the flood;
>   the LORD is enthroned as king forever.
> (Ps 29:1-4, 9-10)

Jesus of Nazareth Anointed by the Spirit

The one whom the prophet points to without knowing his name is Jesus of Nazareth, who has come for all men and women without exception, the Lord of all. Today these assertions seem rather commonplace. But do we always truly understand the meaning of the good news, sufficiently conscious of what is understood by reference to the Lord's person? Peter's experience sheds light on this.

The Book of Acts reports two speeches addressed by the leader of the apostles to the people of Jerusalem, and two others that he made before the Sanhedrin.[11] He proclaims with strength and assurance the lordship of Jesus whom God has raised from the dead. But while he could have made a similar discourse to the pagans, the intervention of God was required to overcome his initial reticence (Acts 10:1-33). Moreover, the Holy Spirit had to descend on the pagans for Peter to baptize them (Acts 10:44-48). Then, on his return to Jerusalem, he could justify his conduct to those brethren who took him to task (Acts 11:1-18). This whole affair is recapitulated in the second reading (Acts 10:34-38). But these few lines from the Book of Acts mean a great deal when heard in the context of the feast of the Baptism of the Lord, especially after Isaiah's prophecy. Peter says: "God anointed [Jesus] with the Holy Spirit and power." It seems that the apostle is content here with few words because he pronounces them with an eye to the prophet, on the opposite panel of the triptych, and is saying in effect: "You know well what I want to say. Remember what the prophet wrote in his first Song of the Servant (Isa 61:1), which Jesus read in the synagogue in Nazareth. In him, God has fulfilled what he had announced through the mouths of his prophets (Acts 3:18). Yes, as he promised, God anointed his chosen one with the Holy Spirit and granted him power. I wish to say that the presence of the Spirit allowed Jesus to do good everywhere he went, to heal all those who were under the power of the devil, to sanctify you who, today, celebrate this mystery."

The dialogue thus begun between the prophet and the apostle is nowhere near being finished; we must continue to hear it in our personal meditation. But the liturgy forces our attention to the center panel of the triptych, painted this year by Matthew.

Coming from Galilee, Jesus Came to John

Matthew's Gospel of the infancy ends with the Holy Family's return from Egypt and settling in a town of Galilee called Nazareth (Matt 2:19-23). Matthew then speaks of John the Baptist's preaching, his first mention of the Baptist (Matt 3:1-12). He brings Jesus into the scene by saying very simply: "Jesus, coming from Galilee, appeared before John at the Jordan to be baptized by him." This is the gospel read today (Matt 3:13-17).

This manner of shifting abruptly[12] to the public ministry of Jesus, without saying anything about his hidden life at Nazareth, confirms that the first two chapters of Matthew are truly gospel, not merely tales of Jesus' infancy. This is also true of what follows, although one can divide the central part of the book into "narrative" and "discourse."[13]

"Jesus came to John to be baptized by him"! As if he had to repent because of the nearness of the kingdom of heaven (Matt 3:2) and, by yielding to this rite, express his conversion! John, as we know, "tried to refuse him with the protest, 'I should be baptized by you, yet you come to me!'" To this objection, which we make as well, Jesus responds: "Give in for now. We must do this if we would fulfill all of God's demands." It is useless to resort to pious explanations signifying that Jesus wished to share in the sinners' condition. No, there is no dissembling on his part. His mission is placed alongside that of the Precursor, as Matthew will remind us at various times (Matt 4:12; 11:11-15; 17:12-13; 21:25-27).[14] His action in some way authenticates the baptizing by John. It also situates his own mission in line with the will of God, beyond the perspective of temporal power. Above all, in being baptized by John, Jesus came, in the humility of his human condition, to the encounter that God had ordained for him on the banks of the Jordan, where the voice of the last prophet reverberates with the promise that will be accomplished without delay. Jesus can now take up the message of John: "Reform your lives! The kingdom of heaven is at hand," while giving it an absolutely new meaning because his baptism has shown that he is—in person—the good news of the kingdom, the fulfillment of the Scriptures.

The Holy Theophany of the Baptism of Jesus

"After Jesus was baptized, he came directly out of the water." It is at this moment that the theophany takes place, the manifestation of God, the revelation—epiphany—linked to the baptism of the Lord.[15] This theophany is decidedly lacking in sobriety.

"The sky opened" or was rent: there is no other way of evoking the heavenly origin of what happens. In the Bible, the dove is an unusual symbol for the Spirit. However, certain rabbinic texts represent the form of a dove as "the breath of God" that moved over the waters when the earth was a formless wasteland (Gen 1:2). In any case, the gospel tradition—as well as iconography—uses this symbolism.

The Spirit of God descends and comes to rest on Jesus. Isaiah's prophecies (Isa 42:1; first reading; and 61:1) abound here.[16] Consequently, this is a messianic investiture in which Jesus solemnly receives from God the mission for which he was sent, in conformity with the promises that were made through the prophets. For it is Jesus who "saw the Spirit of God descend like a dove and hover over him." Matthew says, moreover, that immediately afterward Jesus was led into the desert by the Spirit, where he wrestled with Satan, whose dominion he had come to destroy (Matt 4:1-16), that he then began to preach, calling his first disciples (Matt 4:17-22), and ". . . toured all of Galilee. He taught in their synagogues, proclaimed the good news of the kingdom, and cured the people of every disease and illness." Matthew adds: "As a consequence of this, his reputation traveled the length of Syria. They carried to him all those afflicted with various diseases and racked with pain: the possessed, the lunatics, the paralyzed. He cured them all. The great crowds that followed him came from Galilee, the Ten Cities, Jerusalem and Judea, and from across the Jordan." The Christian cannot contemplate the icon of Christ, with the Spirit descending and resting on him, without thinking about what he did shortly after his baptism. What immediately follows, according to Matthew, is in fact the best and most indispensable commentary on the meaning and importance of the solemn investiture of the Lord that took place on the banks of the Jordan.

As usually happens in theophanies, a voice coming "from the heavens" imposes itself: "This is my beloved Son. My favor rests on him." Curiously, in Matthew's Gospel, the voice is not addressed to Jesus. But there is no reason to regard this as an anomaly or some verbal disorder that would have escaped the redactor: the evangelist expresses what at all costs must be understood. The "voice" does not reveal to Jesus, as if he had been previously ignorant of who he is, the "beloved Son" on whom God's "favor rests." It is for us that the "voice" makes itself heard, for *we* must recognize—through Christian faith—who Jesus is, in the real sense of the word—the "Son of God."[17]

From the Baptism of Jesus to Christian Baptism

The feast of the Baptism of the Lord celebrates first and foremost the manifestation—the epiphany—of his dignity as Son of God, beloved of the Father. But Matthew discreetly invites us to reflect on the baptism that the Lord instituted and the order that he gave to his disciples to "make disciples of all the nations. Baptize them in the name 'of the Father, and of the Son, and of the Holy Spirit' " (Matt 28:19). In any case, how could one not make the connection between this final command of the risen Christ and his first action, his undergoing baptism by John? The practice of baptism in the Church is reflected in the very elaborate formulation of the Lord's command, just as the faith of the Church leaves no doubt about the meaning of "Son of God," according to which we understand all that is revealed to us after the Lord's baptism. Later theological developments are based on this connection. For, coming out of the baptismal water, one confesses Jesus Christ as the only Son of God,[18] receives the Spirit that rests upon him or her "as it rested on Jesus"[19] and is elevated to the status of an adopted child of God, whom we have the right to call "Father."[20] An icon or some other representation of Jesus' baptism is quite appropriate in a baptismal chapel or over the baptistery.[21]

> The Son of God comes out of the Jordan,
> on him the Spirit rests
> and he is glorified by the Father:
> baptized in water and fire,

we become children of God:
now, the heavens are opened.

Jesus, beloved Son,
the love of the Father dwells in you.

For you, I consecrate myself,
you will be consecrated in Truth.

Jesus, beloved Son,
the love of the Father dwells in you.

The Father has given me a glorious name,
and I call you my friends.

Jesus, beloved Son,
the love of the Father dwells in you.

I am with you till the end of time,
be my witnesses over all the earth.

Jesus, beloved Son,
the love of the Father dwells in you.[22]

The Baptism of the Lord—Year B

Beginning of the Gospel

All Are Called to the Covenant

Once again, the Liturgy of the Word opens with a prophecy from the Book of Isaiah. This time it is a three-part text that is remarkable for its dramatic development (Isa 55:1-11).[23]

The prophet begins by extending, on behalf of God, a ringing invitation: "Come to me heedfully, . . . I will renew with you the everlasting covenant." A striking invitation, and how enticing! To those who have no money, he offers himself for their free acquisition. To those who have all the goods they want but are still dissatisfied, he promises nourishment that will satisfy them once and for all. The perfect end for an insatiable and ravenous desire! May all come to be satisfied with "good things"! The prophet enumerates them breathlessly, from the simplest—water—to the most costly—rich fare—by way of milk and wine.

One must not understand these "good things" in a vulgar, material sense; but neither should they be solely understood as metaphor. They evoke not only what allows us to survive but also what enables us to live, to be strong.

The point is really to "listen, that you may have life." The one who invites—"Come to me"—will himself take the initiative that will ensure the possession of all goods: "I will renew with you the everlasting covenant." If we come, if we hear, if we listen, this mutual confidence will be established. Yesterday, there was uncertainty about tomorrow: now, we can be confident of the future, since the covenant will be eternal. Gradually, unity between all people will be established "because of the Lord, your God." The covenant made previously with David will take on a new, unheard-of extension. The radiant manifestation of the "splendor" of God will shine upon us.

It is hard to be indifferent to a call formulated in this tone and with such emphases. Imagine an auction in the marketplace. One voice dominates all the others. It invites the passers-by to stop, to think of their most vital needs, to consider what is offered them. It is worth infinitely more than anything that could be found elsewhere. It is exactly what everyone has always looked for in vain. And lastly—what luck!— everything is free.

God: So Far and Yet So Near

The goods of life, indeed life itself, cannot be bought with money: rich and poor alike experience this truth. God alone gives these gifts, and he gives them freely, because he alone owns them and has the power to dispose of them, as he does to those who trust in his covenant. Toward him we must turn, in a journey called "conversion." Through the voice of the prophet, God moves all those who wish to live toward committing themselves resolutely and without delay: "Let the scoundrel forsake his way, and the wicked man his thoughts; let him turn to the Lord for mercy; to our God, who is generous in forgiving."

This call is similar to what is learned from Jeremiah, of whom the redactor of the second part of the Book of Isaiah is doubtlessly a disciple.

> When you look for me, you will find me. Yes, when you seek me with all your heart, you will find me with you, says the Lord, and I will change your lot; I will gather you together from all the nations and all the places to which I have banished you, says the Lord, and bring you back to the place from which I have exiled you (Jer 29:13-14).

Imagine being so near to a God who invites us to search for him and lets himself be found, though he is beyond all! "For my thoughts are not your thoughts, nor are your ways my ways, says the Lord. As high as the heavens are above the earth, so high are my ways above your ways and my thoughts above your thoughts."

Paradoxically, this transcendence of God is revealed in his immense capacity for love and pardon, his kindness that nothing can hold in check.

> For as the heavens are high above the earth,
>   so surpassing is his kindness toward those who fear him.
>
> As far as the east is from the west,
>   so far has he put our transgressions from us.
>
> As a father has compassion on his children,
>   so the LORD has compassion on those who fear him.
> (Ps 103:11-13)

This is what the prophet Hosea expressed in unforgettable terms:

> My heart is overwhelmed,
> my pity is stirred.
> I will not give vent to my blazing anger, . . .
> For I am God and not man,

the Holy One present among you.
(Hos 11:8-9)[24]

The Word of God Is Real and Effective

Certainly, it is the Word who gives us the most direct experience of the transcendence and the nearness of God. The word of God is certain, because the one who pronounces it is infinitely beyond the human condition of hesitancy, uncertainty, changeability, in spite of itself. But this sure word is expressed and expresses itself with human words. It teaches us the language that lets us speak to God, and God to us, in the intimate dialogue of I and Thou.

The efficacy of the word of God is such that it acts, it brings into being what it says, as opposed to the word of humans, who can only say that which is or express wishes, intentions, desires, which is only vanity. God comes to us with his Word that gives us our very being and allows us to grow.

The word of God directs history, the most human reality there is. The second part of the Book of Isaiah (40–55) never ceases to express this firmly. It begins with an affirmation: "Though the grass withers and the flower wilts, the word of our God stands forever" (Isa 40:8). In its conclusion, the beautiful text proclaimed today echoes it:

> For just as from the heavens the rain and snow come down and do not return there till they have watered the earth, making it fertile and fruitful, giving seed to him who sows and bread to him who eats, so shall my word be that goes forth from my mouth; it shall not return to me void, but shall do my will, achieving the end for which I sent it (Isa 55:10-11).

God invites us to enter into his covenant. The goods that he offers he gives us, as he said. His word strikes at the heart of each and every person. Joy and thanksgiving!

> With joy you will draw water
> at the fountain of salvation.
>
> God indeed is my savior;
> I am confident and unafraid.
> My strength and my courage is the Lord,
> and he has been my savior.
>
> Give thanks to the LORD, acclaim his name;
> among the nations make known his deeds,
> proclaim how exalted is his name.
>
> Sing praise to the LORD for his glorious achievement;
> let this be known throughout all the earth.

Shout with exaltation, O city of Zion,
> for great in your midst
> is the Holy One of Israel!
(Canticle of Isaiah 12:2-6)

Recognizing That Jesus Is the Son of God

After the prophecy of Isaiah, the liturgy of the Baptism of the Lord proclaims, this year, one of the great texts of John's letters (1 John 5:1-9).[25]

The richness and profundity of this passage can in some measure "discourage," and its composition may embarrass us. We are used to developments that happen in sequence, i.e., gradually, step by step. This is not John's way. His thought develops and progresses in spiral fashion around a central idea enunciated in various ways. "Everyone who believes that Jesus is the Christ has been begotten of God. Now, everyone who loves the father loves the child he has begotten." Love of God consists of keeping his commandments; this faithfulness verifies the true love for the children of God. To recognize that Jesus is the Son of God is to participate in his victory over the world, i.e., over the sin and death that exist in it.[26] It is on the witness of the Spirit—which is truth—and the Father that faith in Jesus as the Son of God stands. In the context of the celebration of the Baptism of the Lord, the movement of the text finds its apogee: we believe that Jesus is the Son of God because God himself witnesses to him.

Jesus Christ, Son of God: The Good News

The baptism of Jesus occurs at the beginning of Mark's Gospel. One could even say that it *is* the beginning. In a phrase that would make a good title for this text, we are told that Jesus himself is the gospel: "Here begins the gospel of Jesus Christ, the Son of God" (Mark 1:1).

This introduction is followed by the presentation of John the Baptist. The messenger sent "before" the Lord to prepare his way, "proclaiming a baptism of repentance which led to the forgiveness of sins." This "baptism in water" announced the baptism "in the Holy Spirit" that will be given by the one whom the Baptist describes as "more powerful than I" (Mark 1:2-8).

After this introduction, Mark proceeds to tell us what he has prepared us to hear: "During that time, Jesus came from Nazareth in Galilee and was baptized in the Jordan by John. Immediately on coming up out of the water he saw the sky rent in two and the Spirit descending on him like a dove. Then a voice came from the heavens: 'You are my beloved

Son. On you my favor rests.' " This is the gospel read this day (Mark 1:7-11).[27]

In Mark's presentation, the baptism of Jesus is truly the inaugural event of the Gospel. This event is situated in line with the prophecies that announce the coming of John as the Precursor to the coming of Jesus. Clearly, it is a key to the comprehension of the whole Gospel of Mark that is read in the course of Year B.[28]

"Jesus came from Nazareth in Galilee and was baptized in the Jordan by John." Mark quickly disposes of incidental material in order to draw attention to what took place "on [Jesus'] coming up out of the water"[29]: the theophany from which he had benefited "immediately."

"He saw the sky rent in two." Mark chose the word "rent" instinctively, because it is the kind of evocative word he readily employs. But whoever reads it today recalls that the Book of Isaiah says: "Oh, that you would rend the heavens and come down" (Isa 63:19–64:3). Note also that at the moment of Jesus' death "the curtain in the sanctuary was torn in two from top to bottom" (Mark 15:38). Mark's Gospel mentions "rending" when Jesus breathes his last. Intentional or not, the coincidence is striking.

Here the theophany is directed to Jesus himself. It is he who sees the Spirit descend, and he again who hears the voice say, "You are my beloved Son. On you my favor rests." But we are no less involved. Yes, God has descended, and in Jesus we recognize the Son of the Father who has clothed himself in our humanity.

Again, two Old Testament texts come to mind. That of Isaiah: "Here is . . . my chosen one with whom I am pleased" (Isa 42:1)—read in Year A—and that of a psalm: "The Lord said to me, 'You are my son; this day I have begotten you,' " (Ps 2:7). We could also note that Isaac, a figure of Christ, is called the "beloved" son of Abraham (Gen 22:2, 12, 16).

At any rate, this theophany proclaims the unique and intimate relationship that unites Jesus to God whom he calls to in his agony: "Abba [O Father]" (Mark 14:36). In addition, the coming of the Spirit on Jesus invests him, so to speak, in view of his mission.

> Children of the Word,
> exiles of the Kingdom,
> formed from glory and dust,
> molded from silver and light,
> rescued from water and darkness,
> Jesus restores you to his Father.

See the Son of man
baptized in the Jordan
where the angels of heaven adore
the Lord!
See the Son of the Father
conqueror in the desert
where the angels serve him!

Come, sons of men
torn from the night:
May heaven and earth adore
the Lord!
Come, children of the Father
filled with the Holy Spirit:
May the Church serve him![30]

Anointing and Investiture of the Messiah

Here Is Your God, the Lord God

The first reading for the celebration of the Baptism of the Lord, Year C, is the beginning of "The Book of Consolation," a text already encountered on the Second Sunday of Advent, Year A (Isa 40:1-5, 9-11).[31]

What marvelous good news! God, the Lord God, comes. He is here. He brings his people pardon and liberation. He arises like a victorious but peaceable king. He leads like a shepherd guiding his flock. He gathers the lambs to his bosom. He takes special care of the weak ones. His coming inaugurates an era of grace and peace. One is reminded here of the other prophecy of Isaiah—"The spirit of the Lord . . . has sent me to bring glad tidings to the lowly" (Isa 61:1)—about which Jesus himself says: "Today this Scripture passage is fulfilled in your hearing" (Luke 4:14-21).

"Today": the occasion of this feast of the Baptism of the Lord, when the Lord Jesus came to the banks of the Jordan and was henceforth elevated into the glory of the Father, assembles his faithful ones, who follow him in song.

> *Water and Spirit give witness to you,*
> *Lord of glory!*
>
> You are clothed with majesty and glory,
>   robed in light as with a cloak.
> You have spread out the heavens like a tent-cloth;
>   you have constructed your palace upon the waters.
>
> You make the clouds your chariot;
>   you travel on the wings of the wind.
> You make the winds your messengers,
>   and flaming fire your ministers.
>
> How manifold are your works, O Lord!
>   the earth is full of your creatures;
> The sea also, great and wide,
>   in which are schools without number
>   of living things both small and great.

They all look to you
  to give them food in due time.
When you give it to them, they gather it;
  when you open your hand, they are filled with good things.

If you hide your face, they are dismayed;
  if you take away their breath, they perish
  and return to their dust.
When you send forth your spirit, they are created,
  and you renew the face of the earth.
(Ps 104:1-4, 24-25, 27-30)

The Grace of God Is Manifested

The second reading—two extracts from the Letter of Paul to Titus—takes up the theme of splendor, thereby without losing contact with the daily realities for which believers are responsible (Titus 2:11-14; 3:4-7).[32]

Salvation—this era of grace of which Isaiah speaks (Isa 58:6)—is the grace of God for all, a completely gratuitous gift, the sovereign initiative of God, the manifestation—epiphany—of his extraordinary mercy. Accordingly, he is, above everything else, the good news, a revelation to be welcomed.

Nevertheless, it is not a matter of some sort of decree of general amnesty that God grants out of his goodness and that nullifies the effects of condemnation without really changing anything about the condemned. The fact that "the grace of God has appeared, offering salvation to all" makes them "just." A redemption "from all unrighteousness" affects only the present by wiping out the past, without giving any guarantee about the future. The grace of God "trains us to reject godless ways and worldly desires, and live temperately, justly, and devoutly in this age." Moreover, it forms those ransomed into a people "eager to do what is right."

Epiphany of the Benevolence and Love of God

The other half of the reading (Titus 3:4-7) has the look of a hymn to the "kindness" and "love" of God that have been manifested.

"Kindness" is a strong theme in the New Testament and particularly in Paul, as can be seen, among other places, in a passage from his Letter to the Colossians: "Clothe yourselves with heartfelt mercy, with kindness, humility, meekness, and patience" (Col 3:12). "Heartfelt mercy" translates what signifies "entrails of mercy." "Kindness" is thus a sentiment that has its very deep roots Paul's being, and takes hold of him completely.

What is here called the "love" of God for all—often associated with "benevolence"—the Greeks called "philanthropy," a weak enough word today in English, but one the Greek Fathers considered an attribute of God.[33]

This "benevolence" and "love" of God shown by Jesus Christ for everyone has been freely given by him and the Holy Spirit. "This Spirit he lavished on us . . . that we might be justified by his grace and become heirs, in hope, of eternal life." In the passage, Paul recalls that "he saved us through the baptism of new birth and renewal by the Holy Spirit."

In this long sentence,[34] we can distinguish three levels of the development of Paul's thought: the salvation accomplished by the Father at the time of epiphany of his "benevolence" and "philanthropy"; the realization of this plan of salvation by Christ; and the effusion of the Spirit.

A People in Waiting

It is striking how the evangelists, without contradicting each other, report the same event with nuances that give a particular character to each account. Such is the case with the story of the Lord's baptism. Luke's account contrasts sharply with Matthew's and Mark's (Luke 3:15-16, 21-22).

Luke has spoken at length about the announcement of John's birth (Luke 1:5-25, 57-80), then of his youth. He has told of his coming into the region of the Jordan and his preaching (Luke 3:1-14). He shows him now in the midst of a people "full of anticipation" who ask if he is not the Messiah. John, not unaware of these unasked questions, addresses himself to all of them: "I am baptizing you in water, but there is one to come who is mightier than I. I am not fit to loosen his sandal strap. He will baptize you in the Holy Spirit and in fire" (Luke 3:15-16).

In the framework of this day's celebration, there is no room to dwell on what John means by baptism "in the Holy Spirit and in fire."[35] Instead, we retain his witness concerning the one who comes, the one who is "mightier" than he. Above all, we will note that Luke insists on the fact that Jesus' manifestation takes place in the midst of a people reaching toward the epiphany of the Messiah.[36]

As Jesus Prayed

The second remarkable thing in Luke's Gospel is that the theophany is not tied to Jesus' baptism, but to his prayer. Jesus came to be baptized "when all the people were baptized," incognito, so to speak, in the midst of the people who were coming to John.

In the biblical tradition, prayer precedes divine revelation.[37] According to Luke, it is connected with the gift of the Spirit[38] and occupies an important place in the life of Jesus.[39] Consequently, we can understand why the evangelist attaches the divine intervention of which Jesus will be the beneficiary not to his baptism in the Jordan but to the prayer that he made "after having been baptized."

Jesus Anointed and Consecrated by the Holy Spirit

In the Gospel According to Luke, the trappings of revelation, which are somewhat unwieldy in Matthew and Mark, have disappeared. Everything is extremely simple, as in the celebration of a sacrament where liturgical simplicity is a virtue.

Jesus himself is said to be "anointed" by the Spirit (Luke 4:18). He receives it here under a sacramental form. The Spirit descends on him "in visible form." A declarative voice is heard: "You are my beloved Son. On you my favor rests."[40]

Immediately thereafter, Luke has inserted the "genealogy" of Jesus, "son of Adam, son of God" (Luke 3:23-38). Peter, on the day of Pentecost, will proclaim: "God has made both Lord and Messiah this Jesus whom you crucified" (Acts 2:36). In other words, the meaning of the inaugural investiture of Jesus is fully understood in the light of the paschal experience. But is it not with this Easter faith that Christians celebrate the mystery today?

One could speak of a "Pentecost for Jesus" that took place after his baptism, "at prayer." In fact, it is also when the disciples were at prayer that the Spirit came upon them in material form: "Tongues as of fire appeared which parted and came to rest on each of them" (Acts 1:14; 2:3).

The messianic investiture of Jesus, consecrated and anointed by the Spirit, does not have to do only with his ministry, therefore, but also with his presence in today's Church and world.

Through the Prism of the Gospels

However carefully prepared we are, we must enter into the celebration with a sufficiently free and festive spirit in order to be ready to receive the new, indeed the unforeseen, in the liturgy. This is certainly the case for the feast of the Baptism of the Lord. What we remember is usually a mixture of what is read in Matthew, Mark, and Luke. The celebration of each of the years of the cycle centers around only one of these Gospels. Besides, the two other readings vary as well from year to year. We therefore celebrate the same mystery, which is seen through the prism of the

Gospels, from three different angles, each with its own particulular emphases. It would be a serious error to ignore this opportunity to deepen our knowledge of, and improve the way we experience, what it is that we celebrate.

Year A emphasizes the fulfillment of the Scriptures by Jesus, who "appeared before John at the Jordan to be baptized by him." Moreover, it is in Matthew's story that reference to the Christian baptism is most marked.

In *Year B* we read Mark. Jesus, the good news, is recognized by believers as "Christ, Son of God." The Lord's baptism is the inaugural scene of the Gospel. The heavens are rent asunder. The Savior is here. The promised covenant is offered to all by a God who is at the same time transcendent and near. Those who recognize Jesus as messenger are born of God. Borne by faith and love, they participate in the victory of Christ over the world.

Year C, finally, we celebrate the anointing of Jesus by the Spirit, his royal investiture and his eternal birth in God (Ps 2; Luke 3:38). By coming into the world, he has shown "the kindness and love of God." Believers have a share in the gift of the Spirit received by the Lord. Having become just, they henceforth form "a people of his own, eager to do what is right," who wait with confidence for the manifestation of "the glory of the great God and of our Savior Christ Jesus."

> Church, Spouse of Christ, who by his blood has freed you from error, idolatry, and the worship of demons, give praise and thanksgiving to the Son who has wedded you in water and who, by his baptism, has purified you and given his body for your food, and for spiritual beverage the blood, thanks to which you are daily made one with his children. Give honor and thanksgiving to the Son who has saved you.

> The Church is the Spouse of the Most High, who has chosen her among the nations to wed her to his Son; out of his love he has given her, for her dowry, his hidden and marvelous mysteries. Adam has descended into the Jordan and has been washed clean of his defilement. He has come out of it spiritually pure, and he has been fed with the body of the one who gives us life, who is raised up to heaven and is seated at the right hand of the one who sent him. He has called the Church to everlasting life in the eternal kingdom. With Christ, she is happy at all times and raises her songs toward the Son who has made her free.[41]

Mysteries of Epiphany

> Three mysteries mark this holy day:
> Today, the star leads the magi to the infant Christ;
> Today, water is changed into wine for the wedding feast;
> Today, Christ wills to be baptized by John in the
> Jordan River to bring us salvation.

This ancient antiphon of Eastern origin is sung in the Roman Liturgy of the Hours on the evening of Epiphany.[1] It expresses admirably what has been celebrated throughout the liturgical season just completed, and it introduces what was begun on the day following the feast of the Baptism of the Lord.[2] But because it is so full of valuable lessons, one should study its composition.

"Three Mysteries Mark This Holy Day"

Each liturgical celebration of the season that has just ended has its own clearly marked theme and purpose in the Western liturgy: the Nativity of the Lord, Epiphany, and the Baptism of the Lord.[3] But these distinctions are not discrete. On the contrary. At Christmas, as at the adoration of the magi and the baptism of the Lord, it is a question of the mystery of his manifestation to the people (shepherds) of the country where he is born and to those from afar (magi). "The Word became flesh and made his dwelling among us, and we have seen his glory: the glory of an only Son coming from the Father, filled with enduring love. . . . No one has ever seen God. It is God the only Son, ever at the Father's side, who has revealed him" (John 1:14-18).

The reminder of the wedding at Cana may be surprising: this event is not commemorated during the season of Christmas-Epiphany, and the antiphon mentions it between the adoration of the magi and the Lord's baptism![4] Nevertheless, we admire this correct interpretation of the liturgy, when we recall the end of the Cana story: "Jesus performed this first of his signs at Cana in Galilee. Thus did he reveal his glory, and his disciples believed in him" (John 2:11). The "sign" of water changed into wine is truly a "mystery of epiphany." To remember it is to open oneself to an acknowledgment of the other "signs" performed by Jesus—

313

all manifestations of his glory. The greatest among them must give way to the passion-resurrection. From then on, and especially after Pentecost, the Lord will be preached to all the nations, who will recognize him as the Christ, Son of God, the Savior. They will drink the new wine of the kingdom in celebrating the Eucharist. The mention of the epiphany of Cana in Galilee appropriately evokes the paschal dimension of the mystery of the incarnation.[5]

Finally, the mystery of the Son of God made man is that of the espousal of God with humanity, in which Jesus' mealtaking, particularly that of the wedding feast at Cana, are so many parables in deed, and of which the Eucharist is the sacrament: "Happy are those who are called to the supper of the Lord," to "the wedding day of the Lamb" (Rev 19:17), and happy is "he who eats bread in the kingdom of God" (Luke 14:15).

"Today"

The liturgy is never simply a commemoration of a past event, revived only in the memory of those who celebrate its anniversary on a certain date. "In the course of the year, moreover, [the Church] unfolds the whole mystery of Christ from the incarnation and nativity to the ascension, to Pentecost and the expectation of the blessed hope of the coming of the Lord."[6] All liturgical celebration is at once "memorial," and "participation" in the mystery made present and active by the sacrament, which is "anticipation" and announcement of the glory to come.[7] This "today" must be understood in the strongest and most direct sense of a true mystery that has happened once and for all historically, and in which we participate in our time.

Another Epiphany antiphon proclaims this by evoking these three mysteries:

> Today the Bridegroom claims his bride, the Church, since Christ has washed her sins away in Jordan's waters; the magi hasten with their gifts to the royal wedding; and the wedding guests rejoice, for Christ has changed water into wine, alleluia.[8]

We must spiritually experience this present reality of "today" when we celebrate not only the feast days but the Sundays of Ordinary Time as well.

NOTES

The Sacrament of the Liturgical Year—Pages 1–19

1. The First Sunday of Advent falls at the earliest on November 27 (when Christmas is a Sunday); at the latest on December 3 (when Christmas is a Monday). Thus, the liturgical year ends on the Saturday between November 26 and December 2.

2. P. de Ronsard (1524–1585), *Prières retranchées.*

3. The solar calendar is far from having supplanted the lunar calendar used in Islam. We ourselves often reckon by the moon and its phases. The moon affects a number of natural cycles.

4. The Bible often speaks of these rhythms in our lives: in addition to Eccl 3:2-8 ("a time to be born, and a time to die," etc.: second Friday of the Twenty-fifth Week in Ordinary Time); Gen 38:27; Ezek 8; Lev 15:25; 1 Kgs 11:4; 15:23; Ps 72:9; Job 33:25).

5. Astrology, which claims that the stars influence the character and fate of humanity, is almost certainly as old as the world. Whatever else may be said about it, the status it enjoys today, in our country, indicates a certain fear of responsibility and a desire to act on the basis of certainty. As result, most newspapers feel obliged to publish horoscopes.

6. We know very well that past peoples have divinized the sun, the moon, the stars. An extraordinary number of things have been linked to their cycles, not the least of which is the fertility of the earth and its creatures!

7. These no longer exist in this form in our age, but they haven't disappeared entirely in our mind-sets, as witnessed by certain customs and practices. We have already mentioned the prevalence of astrology and horoscopes that tell us not to oppose the stars or fight against their influence How many other superstitions and "rites" could we name? "Celebration" of the new year; "promises" to be made in certain circumstances or at certain times? The practice of placing the first fruits of the year on the table has but recently been abandoned. Let us not forget those rites that are tied to biological rhythms—rites of birth, the first tooth, adolescence, etc. Even among people without religion, reference to "something beyond us" is very common.

8. That is, feasts of the new moon.

9. The Jewish calendar numbers years from the date of creation. Thus, 1989–1990 of the Christian era is year 5750 of the Jewish era (1989–1990 because their year begins in the fall: September 30 in 1989, September 20 in 1990, etc.).
The Moslem era begins with the Hegira, the flight of Mohammed to Medina. August 13, 1989, of our era begins (Muharram 10) year 1409 of the Hegiran calendar.

10. Constitution on the Liturgy, n. 10.

11. Ritual of Viaticum.

12. Prayers for the Dying.

13. Let us be clear about what we mean by "strong times." It is not a question of opposing these periods to times that might be called "weak," but of particularly significant "times" that require especially active participation because of all they entail. Ordinary Time is so-called not because it is of no real importance, requiring only partial attention. Isn't it in

315

Ordinary Time that there is a particular need to "stay awake," keeping oneself in readiness? In addition, it involves a real sense of rushing toward an end in sight.

14. Some feasts are celebrated at different times according to the discretion of the various countries: Ascension, for example, is not the Thursday after the Sixth Sunday of Easter, but the following Sunday.

15. One ought to refer to other books that explicitly trace this history. One such, very accessible, is A.-G. Martimort, *The Church at Prayer* IV (Collegeville: The Liturgical Press, 1986) 9-150: "Sunday and the Week" and "The Year" (P. Jounel).

16. Nisan: Hebrew name of Babylonian origin for the first month of the year beginning in the spring: it corresponds to March-April (see Neh 2:1; Esth 3:7; 8:9).

17. There were two ways of fixing the date. The Asian Churches celebrated the Christian Easter on the day of the Jewish Passover (14 Nisan): others—particularly the Church of Rome—on the following Sunday. There were also various ways to calculate when 14 Nisan would occur in the solar calendar. Eventually, the Council of Nicaea (325) determined that Easter should be celebrated the Sunday following the new moon after the spring equinox, therefore between March 22 and April 25.

In 1582, Pope Gregory XIII (1572-1585) reformed the Julian calendar, which was in use until that time. He decided that October 15 (it was on the night of October 4[15] that Theresa of Avila died). Now, the Gregorian calendar is thirteen days ahead of the Julian calendar, which is still used by some Churches. This is why our Easter only rarely coincides with that of the Eastern Church: sometimes they are as much as a month apart.

18. Constitution on the Liturgy, n. 102.

19. *Ibid.*, n. 107.

20. Here are the earliest and latest dates possible for each of them. Advent: November 27/December 3-December 24; Christmas Epiphany: December 25-January 9/13; Lent: February 4/March 10-March 21/April 24; Easter: March 22/April 25; Eastertime: March 22/April 25-May 10/June 13.

Ordinary Time is divided into two sections: from the Baptism of the Lord to Ash Wednesday, then from the Monday after Pentecost to the Saturday of the thirty-fourth week. The first section covers, depending on the year, January 8/14 to February 3/March 9 (it lasts for six to eight weeks). The second goes from May 11/June 8 to November 26/December 2 (covering 24-29 weeks).

21. Accordingly, Epiphany is celebrated between January 2 and 8.

22. These three Sundays do not use the formulary for Ordinary Time.

23. In some countries, Ascension is celebrated the following Sunday (seventh after Easter).

24. It is usually the case, for instance, that after the solemnity of the Body and Blood of Christ, one cannot take up the series of Sundays of Ordinary Time where one left off before Lent. There are only six exceptions between 1989 and 2006: 1989, 1995, 1996, 2000, 2001, 2006.

25. Calendars are available from many publishers. Some missals intended for the use of the faithful contain the dates of Sundays and feasts for several years.

26. Particularly for the school calendar and the divisions of classtime and vacations.

27. Declaration of the Second Vatican Council on the Revision of the Calendar, appendix 1 to the Constitution on the Liturgy, Vatican II.

28. It is perfectly natural to want to retain the traditional computation that, in spite of differences in calculation, is clearly associated with the Jewish Passover celebrated by Jesus. Moreover, the differences of the Eastern Church are no longer due only to the fact that they still use the Julian calendar, revised by Gregory XIII (October 4-15, 1582).

29. Declaration of the Second Vatican Ecumenical Council on the Revision of the Calendar n. 2, *ibid.*

30. History begins with the written and transmittable testimony of human life. Prehistory is before that time.

31. Text by D. Rimaud (Chant F 47).

32. Antiphon for Epiphany vespers.

33. The last gospels of the liturgical year—from Wednesday through Saturday of the Thirty-fourth Week in Ordinary Time—each begin with the phrase: "Jesus spoke to his disciples about his coming" (Luke 21:12-19; 21:20-28; 21:29-31; 21:34-36).

34. Matt 24:42, 44 (Year A); Mark 13:33-37 (Year B); Luke:36 (Year C).

35. Text by D. Rimaud (Chant T 50).

36. Eucharistic Prayer IV.

37. According to the thesis of B. Standaert (*L'évangile de Marc. Composition et genre littéraire* (Bruges: Zevenkerken, 1978), Mark's Gospel was meant to be read at one time in the framework of a Christian celebration, more precisely, during the Easter vigil (pp. 541-516 and 624). The apostolic letters addressed to a particular community were undoubtedly read when that community came together for the assembly.

38. See A.-G. Martimort, *The Church at Prayer* I (Collegeville: The Liturgical Press, 1987) 133ff.

39. Constitution on the Liturgy, n. 51.

40. For all these, see Th. Nève, "Les structures du nouveau Lectionnaire," in *Assemblées du Seigneur*, second series, n. 1 (Paris: Cerf, 1969) 7-29.

41. It is convenient that Year C always falls on a year that is divisible by three, which happened for the first time in 1971. We read Matthew during Year A, Mark during Year B, and Luke during Year C. However, since Mark's text is somewhat shorter than the others, it is completed by readings taken from John.

The Fourth Gospel traditionally occupies a special place in the cycle: for several of the great feasts—Lent, Eastertime.

42. References to the various texts may be found in the tables of most popular missals for the faithful.

43. Constitution on the Liturgy, n. 106.

44. *Ibid.*, n. 108. In fact, there are now only nine feasts that can take precedence over a Sunday if they happen to coincide: the Presentation of the Lord (February 2), the Birth of St. John the Baptist (June 24), the solemnity of Sts. Peter and Paul (June 29), the Transfiguration of the Lord (August 6), the Assumption of Mary (August 15), the Triumph of the Cross (September 14), All Saints (November 1), the Commemoration of all Souls (November 2), and the Dedication of St. John Lateran (November 9). The two other solemnities in the calendar—St. Joseph (March 19) and the Immaculate Conception (December 8) that occur each year, one in Lent and the other in Advent, are celebrated on March 20 and December 9 if their particular date falls on a Sunday. It is only during the week that we celebrate the feasts of the saints.

45. From the decree on the Roman Calendar, Vatican II, Typis Polyglottis Vaticanis, 1969, pp. 65-83.

46. Constitution on the Liturgy, n. 111.

47. *Ibid.*

48. One must add that during Lent, "obligatory memorials" become "facultative."

49. I.e., the extracts from each book are taken in order, although they may not directly follow one another.

50. See the two Prefaces of Holy Men and Women.

51. We will deal in more detail with the cult of the saints in Volume 7.

52. This reading is not exegetical; it does not deal with an explanation of the texts. When a detail must be given in order to prevent a possible mistaken meaning, or to specify the

importance of a term, the necessary explanation will be found in a note. But the liturgy is not the place for exegetical study. It is a question of reading—of hearing the texts read— so that they are present outside of their literary context. This is particularly the case during Advent, Christmas-Epiphany, Lent, Eastertime, and for the Old Testament during the Sundays of Ordinary Time. During this latter period, the situation of the gospel is rather different. Actually, we read the Synoptics "continuously." Therefore it is necessary to relate each passage of the gospel to those that preceded it. This is why, for Ordinary Time, we will suggest the grouping of several Sundays into "sequences."

Finally, we are not trying to "modernize" the texts, always attempting to link them to our situations today. We are trying instead to perceive their present meaning. Isn't this what the evangelists did when they reported these words and deeds of Jesus? Those for whom Matthew, Mark, Luke (and John) wrote did not live at the time of Jesus or travel in his entourage. Most—those who came over from paganism—didn't even have a biblical culture similar to ours.

53. Constitution on the Liturgy, nn. 9, 10.

The Season of Advent—Pages 21-30

1. See J. Hild, "L'Avent," in *La Maison-Dieu 59* (1959), 10–24. More briefly, P. Jounel, "Advent" in A.-G. Martimort, *The Church at Prayer* IV (Collegeville: The Liturgical Press, 1986) 90–96.

2. Forty days, according to the Eastern way of reckoning, i.e., five days in a week, excluding Saturdays and Sundays.

3. Even today the weekdays from December 17 to 24 are directly oriented toward the immediate preparation for Christmas (*Calendarium romanum 1969*, n. 42).

4. It was already traditional that a day of baptism was preceded by a period of preparation, with which the community associated itself in prayer and fasting. But in the West, Epiphany was not a day of baptism.

5. An Advent hymn (C.F.C., E 201) begins thus: "Behold the long-awaited time."

6. First Sunday of Advent, Office of Readings, in *The Liturgy of the Hours* (New York: Catholic Book Publishing Co., 1975) 139.

7. *The Rule of St. Benedict*, chapter 41. The Lenten fast, however, is more rigorous, since one can eat only after Vespers, whereas it is after None at other times of the year.

8. *Ibid.*, chapter 49.

9. Even though the vigil of Christmas was a day of fasting in northern Italy and Africa in the fourth century.

10. See: I.-H. Dalmais, "Le temps de préparation à Noël dans les liturgies syrienne et byzantine," in *La Maison-Dieu 59* (1959) 25–36.

11. This orthodox faith was successively attacked by Nestorianism, which distinguished two persons in Christ, man and God (condemned at the Council of Ephesus, 431), then by Monophysitism, which claimed that the human nature was absorbed by the divine nature (condemned at the Council of Chalcedon, 451). According to the orthodox faith, there are two natures (divine and human) but only one person. More concretely: Jesus is God and man.

12. Troparia of Sunday morning: I.-H. Dalmais, *op. cit.*, pp. 27–28.

13. *Ibid.*, p. 28.

14. *Ibid.*, p. 29.

15. *Calendarium romanum*, 1969, n. 39.

16. Monday of the first week; Tuesday of the third week, Wednesday of the first, sec-

ond, and third weeks; Thursday of the second and third weeks; Friday of the first, second, and third weeks; December 21, 24.

17. Tuesday of the first week.

18. The entrance antiphon and the prayers are the same for each Sunday of each year (A, B, C).

19. "Arise, the Lord is coming" (E 235); "Come soon, Savior of the world" (E 157); "A voice travels the earth" (E 202); "The day will come when God will reveal himself" (E 115); "Light for men today" (E 61); "O come Jesus, O come Emmanuel" (E 147); "Behold the time so long awaited" (E 201); "The peace of God" (E 124); "May the just come like the dew" (E 191); "God is working in this age" (T 50); "The one who must come" (E 193); "May the dew come onto the earth" (ELH 103); "You who come to save us all" (E 68); and the Latin hymn *Conditor alme siderum* with its translation "O Jesus, eternal light" (*Prière du temps présent*, pp. 1–12).

20. Above all, when it is a question of prayer celebrated in the night or at dawn, as in the monasteries. It is dominated by waiting for the definitive and glorious appearance of the Lord, the rising Sun "to shine on those who dwell in darkness" (*Benedictus*).

21. Catechetical instruction, *The Liturgy of the Hours* (New York: Catholic Publishing Co., 1975) 142–144.

22. *Ibid.*, pp. 152–153.

23. *Lumen gentium*, n. 48, *ibid.*, pp. 219–220.

24. *Dei verbum*, n. 3–4, *ibid.*, pp. 294–295.

25. They will be quoted when they occur.

26. "The peace of God" (E 124), in *Prière du temps présent*, p. 6.

FIRST WEEK—Pages 31–65

1. This is the translation of the traditional Latin antiphon from the Missal: *Ad te levavi animam meam, Deus meus, in te confido, non erubescam. Neque irrideant me inimici mei, etenim universi qui te exspectant non confundentur.* In *Le Psautier, version oecuménique, traduction liturgique*, Paris, Cerf, 1977, these three verses of Psalm 25 are translated: "To you I lift up my soul, O Lord, my God. In you I trust; let me not be put to shame, let not my enemies exult over me. No one who waits for you shall be put to shame; those shall be put to shame who heedlessly break faith."

2. J. Daniélou, *Essai sur le mystère de l'histoire* (Paris: Seuil, 1953) 331.

3. Of the nine texts from the Old Testament read on these Sundays, seven are taken from Isaiah. There are an additional sixteen in the Weekday Lectionary.

4. The Temple of Jerusalem was downhill with respect to the adjacent land, especially in relation to the Mount of Olives, which dominated it. This conception of God dwelling and revealing himself in the highest mountains is found throughout religious history. Psalm 48:3 says: "Mount Zion, 'the recesses of the North,' is the city of the great King."

5. Cl. Duchesneau, *Comme un ami* (T 58).

6. Text by D. Rimaud (T 50).

7. Chapters 56–66 belong to the third part of the Book of Isaiah, which is made up of the oracles of the great prophet (chs. 1–30) reread and completed by first one disciple (chs. 40–55), then by a second.

8. God "the *go'el* of his people" is an expression that runs throughout the second part of the Book of Isaiah (Isa 41:14; 43:14; 44:6, 24; 49:7; 59:20).

9. This is still the case today. We speak, for example, of being "in the dark" when we no longer comprehend our situation, when doubt or anguish engulfs us, etc.

10. However, "night" in the Bible has another meaning. It can be the time of feasting (Isa 30:29), of prayer and encounter with God (Gen 15:5, 17; 26:24; 28:11-13), of visions and supernatural interventions (Acts 12:6; 16:9). When God "in the beginning created the

heavens and the earth," "darkness covered the abyss." But, very properly, the first thing he creates is light (Gen 1:1-3). It is during the night that the Lord delivers his people from their slavery in Egypt. But a pillar of fire guides them (Exod 11:4; 12:8, 12, 31; 14:20-21).

11. This letter can be dated the spring of 56.

12. B. Pascal, *Oeuvres*, ed. J. Chevalier (Pléiade, 1939) 1060.

13. *Commission Francophone Cistercienne, Tropaires pour les dimanches* (Dourgne: Livres d'Heures d'Encalcat, 1980) 101 (E 239).

14. See the synopsis of the gospels and the study of J. Dupont, *Les trois apocalypses synoptiques: Marc 13; Matthieu 24-25; Luc 21* (Paris, Cerf, Lectio divina 121, 1985).

15. Eucharistic Prayer IV.

16. On messianic hope, see the short (64 pp.) work of J. Coppens, *L'espérance messianique, ses origines et son developpement* (Louvain: *Anal. Lov. Bibl. Orient.* IV/2, 1964) and also (80 pages), S. Amsler, *David, Roi et Messie* (Neuchâtel: *Cahiers théologiques 49,* 1963).

17. Contrary to what one reads ten chapters earlier (Jer 23:5-6). This is what the line of David has become: it can be called a "seed of justice." Consequently, the institution of messianism is referred to as the City to come.

18. Trans. of *The Jerusalem Bible*, reprised in Chant K 39.

19. The literary genre of apocalyptic writing appears in the Bible with the Book of Daniel and certain chapters of Isaiah (24-27). It was developed before Christ in a certain number of noncanonical books: Enoch, Assumption of Moses, Secrets of Enoch, Apocalypses of Elijah, Zephaniah, and Abraham. After the destruction of Jerusalem (A.D. 70) came the Apocalypses of Esdras and Baruch.

20. The apocalyptic genre was prefigured in rough form by the last prophets (Ezek 40-48; Isa 24-27; 34-35; Joel; Zech 9-14). But the differences are notable. The prophetic books are collections of sporadic preaching. The prophets take personal responsibility for their words. Finally, if they speak of the Judgment of God, they do not spend much time describing it; they are fixed in the present, and they preach conversion. The apocalypses, by contrast, are works written according to particular literary conventions. Their authors hide under the name of some famous figure of the past. They are most interested in the future and, with great detail, they describe the events of the end of the world.

21. See Luke 12:35-46 (the parables of vigilance) and 17:22-36 (the Day of the Son of man).

22. This temptation is evoked several times: Luke 12:45; 1 Thess 5:6-7; Rom 13:13.

23. Explanation of the parable of the sower (Luke 8:14); discourse on dependence on Providence (Luke 12:22-31); discourse on the Day of the Son of man (Luke 17:27-28).

24. Every commentator remarks on the place that prayer occupies in Luke's Gospel. See, for example, A. George, *Pour lire l'Evangile selon saint Luc* (Paris: Cerf, Cahiers Evangile n. 5, 1973) 42-54.

25. *The Rule of St. Benedict*, ch. 11.

26. Antiphon of Psalm 93, the Sundays of Advent.

27. Constitution on the Liturgy, n. 9.

28. *Ibid.*, n. 10.

29. Text by D. Rimaud and music by J. Berthier, *Choristes* (Lyon 1983).

30. *Prière du temps présent* does not contain the Office of Readings, which combine a scriptural and a patristic text with their response.

31. Even without participating in daily Eucharist, one can read, in the Weekday Missal, the texts for the day and a brief commentary. See: N. Berthet-Gantoy, *Chaque jour ta Parole. Le Lectionnaire de semaine. Notes de lectures, textes pour la prière,* 7 volumes, each of 110-116 pages (Paris: Cerf—Publications de Saint-André, 1979).

32. With the Sunday Missal and the Weekday Missal, the Bible and *Prière du temps présent* (in lieu of the four volumes of *The Liturgy of the Hours*), constitute the basic books of the Christian library.

33. The two biblical readings (Old Testament and Gospel) with the responsorial psalm, and the opening prayer change each day. There is one entrance antiphon, one prayer over the gifts, one communion antiphon, and one prayer after communion for each day of the week, that is repeated on Monday, Tuesday, etc. for the first three weeks. The fourth week—from December 17 to 24—each part of the formulary is particular.

34. Isa 4:2-6 (Year A) or 2:1-5 (Year B): Monday; 11:1-10: Tuesday; 25:6-10: Wednesday; 26:1-6: Thursday; 29:17-24: Friday; 30:19-21, 23-26: Saturday. From the Exile on, many of Isaiah's prophecies took on new importance because of their frequent (forty-two times) use of the expression "on that day." The prophecies open up a distant, indefinite future that belongs to God alone, but which one can be assured will arrive.

35. Matt 8:5-11: Monday; Luke 10:21-24: Tuesday; Matt 15:29-37: Wednesday; Matt 7:21, 24-27: Thursday; Matt 9:27-31: Friday; Matt 9:35—10:1, 6-8: Saturday.

36. *The Rule of St. Benedict*, ch. 9, testifies to this.

37. First week: Isa 66:1-13 (Sunday); Isa 1:21-27; 2:1-5 (Monday); Isa 2:6-22; 4:2-6 (Tuesday); Isa 5:1-7 (Wednesday); Isa 16:1-5; 17:4-8 (Thursday); Isa 19:16-25 (Friday); Isa 21:6-12 (Saturday). However, in the plan for readings over a two-year period, there are five texts from Ruth (1:1-22; 2:1-13; 2:14-23; 3:1-18; 4:1-22) from Monday of the second week to Sunday of the third; one passage from 1 Chronicles (17:1-15) on Monday of the third week; four texts from Micah (4:1-7; 4:14—5:7; 7:7-13; 7:14-20) from Tuesday through Friday of the third week.

38. See above, p. 27.

39. *Catéchèse* 15:1-3, *Patrologie grecque* 33, col. 869–873.

40. *Homélie pour l'Avent*, 5:1-3, *Edition cistercienne* 4, 1966, pp. 188–190 (Wednesday).

41. *Proslogion* I, in *Opera omnia*, Edimbourg, t. I, pp. 97–100, 1946 (Wednesday).

42. Commentaire sur l'Evangile concordant 18:15-17, in *Sources chrétiennes* 121 (Paris: Cerf, 1966) Thursday.

43. "Les avantages de la patience," 13, 15, in *Corpus scriptorum ecclesiasticorum Latinorum*, 3, pp. 406–408 (Saturday).

44. Lettre pastorale, in *Acta Ecclesiae Mediolanensis*, Lyon, 1683, vol. 2, pp. 916–917 (Monday).

45. Homélie 45 pour la Pâque, 9:22, 26, 28, in *Patrologie grecque* 35, col. 633–636, 653, 657, 661 (Tuesday).

SECOND WEEK—Pages 67–95

1. See First Week above, n. 7 on the composition of the Book of Isaiah.

2. The spiritual tradition affirms this. Thus it is that St. Benedict often appeals to the perspective of judgment. "The fear of judgment" is an "impulse to good works," arising from "spiritual skill" (*Rule*, ch. 4). He recalls it four times to the abbot (chs. 2 and 3), and to the cellarer (treasurer) of the monastery (ch. 31). To which one must add the evocation of the rendering of accounts, which the abbot again must bear in mind (ch. 2, three times; ch. 3; ch. 63; ch. 64; ch. 65) as well as the cellarer (ch. 31).

3. We read the same apostrophe in Luke's Gospel (3:7-9). There, however, John is not speaking to the Pharisees and Sadducees (as in Matthew), but "to the crowds."

4. On all this, see J. Dupont, "L'Evangile de saint Matthieu: quelques clés de lecture," in *Communautés et liturgies* 57 (1975), pp. 3–40, particularly "III. Un enseignement à mettre en pratique," pp. 21–25.

5. One must reread the parable of the wedding banquet (Matt 22:2-14), and that of the weeds, especially its explanation (Matt 13:37-43); the beginning of chapter 18, which invites us to imitate the little children, to avoid anything that would scandalize them; chapter 24, which speaks of the problems that arise within the community, in addition to those which come from outside persecutions; etc.

6. *Commission Francophone Cistercienne* (C.F.C.) Chant E LH 118.

7. The end of Mark (16:9-19) "is part of inspired Scripture and regarded as canonical. This does not necessarily mean that it was authentically edited by Mark. In fact, whether or not it belongs to the redaction of the Second Gospel is questionable." (Note *d* of *The Jerusalem Bible*).

"A later author, probably during the second century, edited an addendum to Mark's text. He compiled the traditions reported by the other evangelists. Mark, who originally had the flavor but not the form of a drama, was thus brought in line with the other gospel stories. His finale received a concluding narrative from them, which was especially modeled on that of Luke" (B. Standaert, *L'évangile selon saint Marc. Commentaire* (Paris: Cerf, Lire la Bible 61, 1983) 114).

8. Rom 15:33; 16:20; 1 Cor 14:11; Phil 4:9; Eph 2:14-17; 1 Thess 5:23; 2 Thess 3:16; Heb 13:20.

"Peace be with you" is the greeting of the resurrected Christ who manifests himself to his disciples (Luke 24:36; John 20:19, 21, 26). It is also the greeting said by those whom Jesus sent out, upon entering a house (Matt 10:12; Luke 10:5).

9. Surely we can't have forgotten this query of Pope John Paul II at Bourget, June 1, 1980: "France, what have you done with your baptism?"

10. Text by M. Scouarnec (Chant E 130).

11. St. John also speaks of the preaching of John the Baptist: "I am a voice in the desert, crying out. . . . There is one among you . . . the one who is to come after me—the strap of whose sandal I am not worthy to unfasten." But this is in another context, namely John's response to the interrogation of the priests and Levites: "Who are you? . . . Why do you baptize?" (John 1:19-28; January 2). Moreover, Luke reports what John the Baptist responded to those who asked him: "What ought we to do?" (Luke 3:10-14; third Sunday C).

12. This text was doubtlessly composed by the final redactor at the beginning of the second century B.C., or it was inserted into this book at that time.

13. It is extremely uncommon for God to be called "the Eternal" in the Bible. Of the nine times it does occur, eight are found in the Book of Baruch, more precisely, in this poem (Bar 4:10, 14, 20, 22, 24, 35; 5:2). The other instance is Daniel 12:7.

14. This was done for Abraham (Gen 17:5), Sarah (Gen 17:15), and Jacob (Gen 32:29).

15. In Hebrew, what we translate in this way can be said in one word, which is composed of several roots.

16. See R. Gantoy, "L'assemblée dans l'économie du salut," in *Assemblées du Seigneur*, first series, n. 1 (Bruges: Publications de Saint-André, 1962) 55–80; on assembling around the word of God, pp. 67–70; R. Swaeles, "Rassemblement et pèlerinage des disperses, *ibid*, n. 78, 1965, pp. 37–61.

17. "Traditional" because it is found in Matthew (3:3), Mark (1:2-3) and John (1:20).

18. When one reads Luke's Gospel, one must never forget that it is the first of two parts, the second of which is the Acts of the Apostles.

19. Eucharistic Prayer II.

20. Text by D. Rimaud, in *Choristes*, 1983.

21. We read successively: Isa 35:1-10 (Monday); 40:1-11 (Tuesday); 40:25-31 (Wednesday); 41:13-20 (Thursday); 48:17-19 (Friday); and Sir 48:1-4, 9-11 (Saturday).

22. Psalms 85 (Monday); 96 (Tuesday); 103 (Wednesday); 145 (Thursday); 1 (Friday); 80 (Saturday).

23. Luke 5:17-26 (Monday); Matt 18:12-14 (Tuesday); Matt 11:28-30 (Wednesday); Matt 11:11-15 (Thursday); Matt 11:16-19 (Friday); Matt 17:10-13 (Saturday).

24. In *The Liturgy of the Hours* and *Prière du temps présent*, the psalter is spread over four weeks. Some communities say the entire Book of Psalms in two weeks; others, less numerous, in only one.

25. After Isa 22:8-23 on Sunday; Isa 24:1-18 (Monday); 24:19-25:5 (Tuesday); 25:6-26:6 (Wednesday); 26:7-21 (Thursday); 27:1-13 (Friday); 29:1-8 (Saturday).

26. *The Jerusalem Bible*, note c, which continues: "This is doubtlessly one of the latest sections of the Book of Isaiah; it cannot be placed before the fourth century." See also *Cahiers Evangile* n. 23 (1978).

27. Saturday, Office of Readings, responsory.

28. *La montée du Carmel*, 34-35, ed. H. Hoornaert (Paris: DDB, 1936) 154-161

29. *Sur le psaume 109*, 1-3.

30. *Traité contre les hérésies* 5:19:1; 20:2; 21:1 (Friday).

31. *Homélie pour l'Assomption*.

32. *Ibid.* (Saturday).

33. Vatican II, *Lumen gentium*, n. 48 (Tuesday).

THIRD WEEK—Pages 97-130

1. See First Week above, n. 7 and n. 33.

2. This solidarity is often expressed in the Bible, particularly in the psalms: "Tabor and Hermon rejoice at your name" (Ps 89:13); "Let the heavens be glad and rejoice . . . let the plains be joyful and all that is in them" (Ps 96:11-12); etc. "The earth mourns and fades, the world languishes and fades" (Isa 24:4).

3. One readily imagines the desert as an uninhabited and inhospitable region (Jer 2:6), desolate, without the least vegetation (Deut 32:10), arid (Hos 13:5), even terrifying (Jer 2:6, 31).

Today, it is surprising when, for example, one goes to the Sinai desert and sees the camels grazing on the meager vegetation, visits the encampments of the Bedouin, or discovers the monastery of St. Catherine and its oasis, where monks have lived since the fourteenth century.

4. One often finds several words in the psalms that have the same meaning.

5. Exod 14:1-2; Num 10:11-12, 13-28. The story of the fall of Jericho is recounted like a true liturgical procession (Josh 6).

6. One finds these same images in Isa 13:7 and Job 4:3-4.

7. See Matt 11:5; Luke 7:22.

8. See the notes of *The Jerusalem Bible* and *Traduction oecuménique de la Bible: Edition intégrale (TOB)*, which testify to the difficulty of translating the nuances of the original Hebrew.

9. The New Testament often speaks about the robust character of the faith, which is not only an object of exhortation, but of prayer as well: Luke 22:32; Acts 18:23; 1 Thess 3:2; 1 Pet 5:10.

10. Exod 34:6; Ps 86:15; 103:8; Nah 1:3; 1 Pet 3:20; Rom 2:4; 9:22; 1 Tim 1:16; Matt 18:26. See the article "Patience" in *Vocabulaire de théologie biblique* (Paris: Cerf, 1970) col. 921-924.

11. There, as the *TOB* comments, it is a matter of "a cento of passages from Isaiah: 26:19 (dead); 29:18 (deaf); 35:5-6 (blind, lame, dumb); 61:1 (good news to the poor)."

12. The Lectionary translates simply by "men" the expression *les enfants des femmes* = "the children of women" (*The Jerusalem Bible*) and *ceux qui sont nés d'une femme*" = "those who are born of a woman" (*TOB*).

The traditional way the Bible speaks of "men" brings out the humility of their earthly condition: those "born of woman" are weak (Sir 10:18), subject to sin (Job 15:14; 25:4), born to a brief life (Job 11:2, 12; 14:1).

Used here—certainly intentionally—this expression contrasts with what is said in the second part of verse 11.

13. John the Baptist is named in the preface for Advent II; he has a preface proper to both the feasts of his birth (June 24) and his martyrdom (August 29).

14. It goes without saying that it would be absurd to admire him to the extent of being dissatisfied with the gifts and charisms that one has received, for the vocation and mission

to which one has been called. Just refer to what St. Paul says: "Men should regard us as servants of Christ and administrators of the mysteries of God. . . . I have nothing on my conscience. But that does not mean that I am declaring myself innocent. The Lord is the one to judge me, so stop passing judgment before the time of his return. . . . At that time, everyone will receive his praise from God" (1 Cor 4:1-5).

15. Text by the *Commission Francophone Cistercienne* (Chant E 202).

16. This question is debated by exegetes. See, for example, F. Festorazzi, in *Assemblées du Seigneur*, second series, n. 12 (Paris: Cerf, 1969) 34–39.

17. The Church "exercises the divinely conferred commission and mystery of watching over and interpreting the Word of God" (Vatican II, Dogmatic Constitution on Divine Revelation *(Dei verbum)* n. 12).

18. Psalms 10, 11, 22, etc. See the article "Poor" in *Vocabulaire de théologie biblique*, col. 928–929; A. Gelin, *Les pauvres de Yahve* (Paris: Cerf, *Temoins de Dieu* 14, third ed., 1962, 182 pp.).

19. That is, these "poor" are not only those who are materially destitute. On the beatitudes, the basic study is that of J. Dupont, *Les Béatitudes* (Paris: Gabalda, 3 vol., 387, 426, 743 pp., 1958, 1969, 1973). More generally accessible: "Le message des béatitudes," in *Cahiers Evangile* 24 (Paris: Cerf, 1978, 65pp.).

20. See A. Gelin, *op. cit.*, chapter VI: *"Marie et son chant de pauvreté,"* pp. 121–132.

21. St. Ambrose (339–397), Traité sur l'Evangile de Luc, II, 27, *Sources chrétiennes*, 45bis (Paris: Cerf, 1971) 83–84.

22. Col 1:19; 2 Thess 1:11; Eph 1:16-20; Phil 4:6.

23. No other selection from chapter 14 of the First Letter to the Corinthians has been retained in the Lectionary.

24. Even today. It may indeed be surprising to an age marked by skepticism that such phenomena, readily proclaimed as "supernatural," could be such a success with the masses. Apparitions, self-styled prophets or visionaries, draw a great deal of attention.

This is not to say that all "seers" are imposters, guided by whatever perverse intentions or concerns.

25. According to St. Justin (first-century martyr), *Dialogue with Trypho*, VIII, 3, this was the opinion in certain Jewish milieus.

26. See R. Swaeles, "Jésus, nouvel Elié, d'après saint Luc," in *Assemblées du Seigneur*, first series, n. 69 (Bruges: Publications de Saint-André, 1964) 41–66.

27. See J. Dupont, "Es-tu celui qui vient?" in *Assemblées du Seigneur*, first series, n. 4 (Bruges: Publications de Saint-André, 1961) 36–37.

28. The identification "Bethany of the Transjordan" or "across the Jordan" is problematic. Some manuscripts say "Bethabara," a name that suggests "place of passage" or "ford." This led Origen to believe that the Gospel begins where the people, freed from slavery, crossed the Jordan to enter into the promised land. Perhaps there was a Bethany, unknown today, other than the one where Martha and Mary lived. We know, however, that the topographical details of the Fourth Gospel are generally accurate.

29. Text by Cl. Bernard (Chant E 193).

30. As in *The Jersualem Bible* or the *TOB*.

31. See canticle AT 20 in *Le psautier, version oecuménique, texte liturgique* (Paris: Cerf, 1977) 296.

32. Before Vatican II, this epistle was read each year on the Third Sunday of Advent, which was called "Gaudete Sunday."

33. The Lectionary's translation is not inaccurate, but it must be understood in this way: the Christian's joy comes from his or her union with Christ; it is not simply participation in the joy of the Lord.

34. This is not to be construed as explaining the causes of various states of depression. These are maladies that should not be considered in judging people or their relation to God.

35. The Fathers, because of the story of Pentecost (Acts 2:3), often thought that this refers to the fire of the Spirit. But this interpretation does not take account of the description of judgment that immediately follows.

36. Responsory of the Office of Readings, season of Advent, Monday I, in *The Liturgy of the Hours.*

37. Num 24:2-7, 15-17 (Monday); Zeph 3:1-2, 9-13 (Tuesday); Isa 45:6-8, 18, 21-25 (Wednesday); Isa 54:1-10 (Thursday); Isa 56:1-3, 6-8 (Friday).

38. In fact, there are three representations of Balaam, but the one from the frescoes is the best known and the most legible. This is the one that is usually reproduced. See F Cabrol and H. Leclercq, *Dictionnaire d'archéologie chrétienne et de liturgie,* t. 2/1 (Paris: Letouzey, 1925) col. 133.

39. Other passages judge Balaam severely, making him responsible for the faithlessness of Peor, the area where he prophesied (Num 25; 31:8, 16; Josh 13:22). The New Testament retained this negative appreciation (2 Pet 2:15-16; Jude 11; Rev 2:14).

40. There are no readings given for Saturday of the third week, because each year it falls between December 17-24, which days each have their own readings.

41. Matt 21:23-27 (Monday); Matt 21:28-32 (Tuesday); Luke 7:18-23 (Wednesday); Luke 7:24-30 (Thursday); John 5:33-36 (Friday).

42. The passages that follow in Matthew (Year A: Volume 4 of this series) and Luke (Year C: Volume 6) will discuss this teaching.

43. This is signified by the fact that since the reform of Vatican II, a selection from the Old Testament is read during the liturgy every Sunday, not only during the week. The exception of Eastertime, where texts only from the New Testament are read (with passages from the Book of Acts for the first reading), proves the rule.

44. Isa 29:13-24 (Sunday); 30:18-26 (Monday); 30:27-33; 31:4-9 (Tuesday); 31:1-3; 32:1-8 (Wednesday); 32:15–33:6 (Thursday); 33:7-24 (Friday).

45. *Sermon* 293:3. Bear in mind that St. Augustine addressed this to the faithful of Hippo, an assembly of simple people whom he thought could understand and appreciate such material.

46. *Sermon on Psalm* 37:13-14.

47. *The Imitation of Christ,* 2:2-3.

48. William of St. Thierry, Cistercian abbot (c. 1085-1148), La contemplation de Dieu 9–11, in *Sources chrétiennes* 61 (Paris: Cerf, 1959) 91–97.

49. St. Irenaeus, Contre les hérésies, IV, 20:5, in *Sources chrétiennes* 100, t.2 (Paris: Cerf, 1965) 640–641.

50. Vatican II, Dogmatic Constitution on Divine Revelation *(Dei verbum),* 4.

51. Text by D. Rimaud, in *Choristes,* 1983.

JOHN THE BAPTIST—Pages 131–36

1. Cf. R. Laurentin, *Les évangiles de l'enfance du Christ. Vérité de Noël au-delà des mythes* (Paris: Desclée-Desclée de Brouwer, 1982) 25–26. By the number of verses that are included in each sequence, Luke suggests that Jesus differs greatly from John.

2. J. Steinmann, *Saint Jean Baptiste et la spiritualité du desert* (Paris: Seuil, Maîtres spirituels 3, 1955).

3. A conviction echoed by Matthew and Mark. As for Luke, see R. Swaeles, "Jésus, nouvel Elié, dans saint Luc." See Third Week above, n. 26. Luke omits Jesus' remarks on whether John the Baptist may be the new Elijah. For Luke, John ceased to exist, theologically, after the appearance of Jesus, (Luke 3:20), and it is Jesus who appears as the great prophet of the last times, the new Elijah full of the Spirit.

On the remnant of the baptists in the New Testament, see Acts 18:25; 19:3-4.

4. The stereotypical formula of Luke 3:2 is reconciled with Jer 1:1 *(LXX)*; Luke 3:20 is reconciled with Jer 39:3 *(LXX)*; 32:3 (Hb).

5. St. Augustine, Sermon 288:4; PL 38, col. 1306.

6. Cf. J. Daniélou, *Le Mystère de l'Avent* (Paris: Seuil, 1948) 77.

7. J. Daniélou, *op. cit.*, p. 78, who quotes Origen, Homélies sur saint Luc, IV, the text of which can be found in *Sources chrétiennes* n. 87 (Paris, Cerf, 1963) 135.

8. O. Clement, *Questions sur l'homme* (Paris: Stock, 1972) 119.

FOURTH WEEK—Pages 137–76

1. Preface of Advent II for every Mass from December 17 to 24.

2. Some years, this Sunday falls on December 24 (e.g., 1989, 1995, 2000, 2006, etc.).

3. The first translation conveys the original sense of the Hebrew. That of the Greek Bible (Septuagint) and the Latin Vulgate are in parentheses. The Hebrew word *'almah* does not signify a virgin, but a young woman who is already married: thus it is used in the most ancient texts, including those that are not part of the Old Testament. The Septuagint, the work of Alexandrian Jews before our era, translates it *parthenos* (virgin), a translation not found in Matthew's quotation of Isaiah (1:23). The Christian interpretation of Isaiah 7:14 is based on the Septuagint. But it is not tied, *sine qua non*, to the translation of the term *'almah*. St. Jerome, in controversial instances, usually preferred the Hebrew rendition: he spoke of the *veritas hebraica* ("truth of the Hebrew"). We simply point out that *'almah*, like the translation "young woman" or "young girl" *(neanis* in certain Greek translations) is indefinite, referring to a woman—a young girl—whether or not she is a virgin.

4. "Look at me and the children whom the Lord has given me: we are signs and portents in Israel" (Isa 8:18). Isaiah walking around naked and barefoot for three years is a sign (Isa 20). The sign given to Hezekiah: "This year you shall eat the aftergrowth, next year, what grows of itself; but in the third year, sow and reap, plant vineyards and eat their fruit" (Isa 37:30), the sign given to the king so that he might believe Isaiah when he announced the king's recovery: "See, I will make the shadow cast by the sun on the stairway to the terrace of Ahaz go back the ten steps it has advanced" (Isa 38:7-8).

5. As Gideon did (Judg 6:36-40).

6. Exod 17:2; Deut 6:16 cited by Matt 4:7 and Luke 4:12; Ps 79:17-18. Jesus will reproach "this evil and unfaithful age" for demanding a sign (Matt 12:38).

7. The formula "will be with child [will conceive] and will bear a son" is a classical one: "You are now pregnant and shall bear a son; you shall name him Ishmael" (Gen 16:11); "You will be with child and will bear a son (Samson)" (Judg 13:5, 7). And in the story of the annunciation: "You shall conceive and bear a son and give him the name Jesus" (Luke 1:31).

8. The Bible itself is full of examples of such reinterpretation, not only with previous texts but also with past events: the Exodus, for one, and the Book of Isaiah which, in addition to the oracles of the great prophet, integrated the interpretations of his disciples.

The same thing happened in the New Testament: the evangelists themselves reinterpret many words of Jesus in the context of their time and community. Such reinterpretation continues in the Church under the guidance of the Holy Spirit and the care of the magisterium. This is the question of the relation between Scripture and Tradition about which Vatican II spoke several times: the Dogmatic Constitution *(Dei verbum 1965)*, 130–133 in particular.

9. Not long ago it was read at the Vigil Mass.

10. One should reread at this point the great discourses from the Book of Acts, beginning with that of St. Peter on the day of Pentecost: Acts 2:14-36; 3:12-26; 7:1-54. In addition: Acts 8:35; Rom 1:17; 2:24; 3:4, 10; 4:3, 17, 23; 8:36; 10:5; 1 Cor 15:1, 3-5; etc.

11. The common translation is "on the part of" God and Jesus Christ. This is acceptable, as long as it is understood that there is no third person mediating between God or Jesus Christ and men and women.

12. Acts 2:29-32; 13:22-23.

13. "A family record of Jesus Christ, son of David, son of Abraham" (Matt 1:1).

14. In the Old Testament, the line of descent continues only through the father.

15. It is not helpful to psychologize this passage from the Gospel: it doesn't deal with Joseph's sentiments or "state of soul." There is no room here for our imaginations: the purpose of God's silence, which would have given free reign to Joseph's suspicions, including the possibility of Mary's infidelity; Mary's silence in saying nothing to Joseph, etc. In short, nothing more should be read out of the text than what the evangelist clearly intended.

For further thought on the subject: A. Paul, *L'Evangile de l'enfance selon saint Matthieu* (Paris: Cerf, Lire la Bible 17, 1968); X. Léon-Dufour, "Le Juste Joseph," in *Nouvelle revue théologique* 91 (1959), pp. 225-231; A. Bouton, "C'est toi qui lui donneras le nom de Jésus," in *Assemblées du Seigneur* n. 8 (Paris: Cerf—Publications de Saint-André, 1972) 17-25.

16. Remember Paul's way of speaking: "I know a man in Christ who, fourteen years ago, whether he was in or outside his body I cannot say, only God can say . . . was snatched up to Paradise to hear words which cannot be uttered . . . " (2 Cor 12:2-4).

All those mystics who have received personal revelations have had the same difficulty describing the experience. Matthew says "in a dream." (See the article "Songes" in *Vocabulaire de théologie biblique* (Paris: Cerf, 1970) col. 1245-1247. One can read, in the *Dictionnaire encyclopédique de la Bible* (Paris: Brepols, 1987) 1216-1217, this admirably concise account: "The whole Near Eastern tradition testifies to the experience of the divinity speaking to his faithful, particularly during the night. Dreams, therefore, are an especially appropriate means for this communication. Later, authors began to use dreams as literary clichés designed to emphasize the divine origin of some received message."

17. Trans. of X. Léon-Dufour, *art. cit.* "Without doubt" and "but" (translation of two Greek particles), clearly indicate the opposition between the two halves of the sentence; on the one hand ("without doubt"), Mary has conceived by the Holy Spirit; on the other hand ("but"), it is Joseph's duty— such is the will of God—to give a name—this name—to the child.

18. *Commission Francophone Cistercienne, Tropaires des dimanches* (Dourgne, Livre d'Heures d'Encalcat, 1980) 8 (Chant U LH 95).

19. An example from biblical history, note Jeroboam's building of the sanctuaries at Bethel and Dan in order to keep people from going up to Jerusalem (1 Kgs 12:26-33).

But the history of the colonial age gives other examples: cathedrals constructed to affirm the presence and domination of one country over another, where the majority of people are non-Christian. This may also be the case with the establishment of missions in another country. How do we reconcile this with the mandate of evangelization?

20. See Y. Congar, *Le mystère du Temple* (Paris: Cerf, Lectio divina 22, 1963).

21. Among countless pictorial representations, the "truest" or those that seriously evoke the ineffability, the interiority, the mystery. One that comes to mind is the stirring fresco by Fra Angelico (1387-1455) at the convent of St. Mark in Florence.

22. In several passages of the Septuagint—which especially inspired Luke's infancy narrative—the "daughter of Zion," i.e., Jerusalem, is invited to rejoice, because God is either in her midst or is coming (Zeph 3:15; Joel 2:27; Zech 9:9).

23. The Latins translated this participle *gratia plena*, which, like the translation of *chaire* by *ave*, had more to do with theological deductions than proper exegesis. Consequently, we have imagined this to refer to sanctifying grace, and we have speculated that Mary possessed it to a degree greater than anyone except Jesus. These thoughts are not false, but

are more connected to a derivative reading than a literal one" (P. Benoit, "L'Annoncia-tion," in *Assemblées du Seigneur*, second series, n. 8 (Paris: Cerf, 1972) 41.

24. Some of the Fathers spoke of this as a gesture of modesty on seeing a young man entering her house. Such a commentary has nothing to do with exegesis and relies on an overly anthropomorphic image of the angels. Other people have spoken of this reaction as humility, a humility that would allow her to take as personal eulogy these words of the angel, which may or may not contain such a meaning.

25. Announcement of the birth of Ishmael (Gen 16:11), Isaac (Gen 17:19), Samson (Judg 13:5-7), and Emmanuel (Isa 7:14).

26. Nevertheless, in the strongest sense of the Christian faith, this is not enough to af-firm the divine sonship of Jesus.

The Bible calls "Son of the Most High," "Son of God"—in a metaphorical sense—whoever lives in an intimate relationship with God: angels (Ps 29:1; Job 1:6), the chosen people (Wis 18:13; Hos 11:1), the pious Jew (Eccl 4:10; Wis 2:13), and above all the Messiah (2 Sam 7:14; Ps 2:7; 89:7).

This metaphorical way of speaking also occurs in the New Testament; according to Luke: "Love your enemy. . . . You will rightly be called sons of the Most High" (Luke 6:35).

27. The Apocrypha—books that have no canonical authority—tried to depict, without al-ways exhibiting good taste, what Mary's life must have been like, as well as the child Jesus'. Mary, the daughter of a couple almost at the age of sterility—Joachim and Anna—was at a very early age offered (presented) at the Temple. When she was twelve years old, she was engaged to Joseph, an old widower—91 years old in some accounts—so that her vir-ginity would be safeguarded. A certain popular piety makes use of such legends. Iconog-raphy has also (alas!) exploited them, especially in the pictures of St. Joseph, the elderly protector of Mary and Jesus.

The liturgical feast of the Presentation of Mary (commemorated November 21) originated in the dedication, in 543, of the basilica of *Sainte Marie Nouvelle*, near the Temple in Jerusa-lem. Although this building was destroyed, the feast of the Presentation of Mary was cele-brated throughout the East. Added to the calendar of the Papal Chapel in Avignon in 1373, suppressed by Pius V in 1568, it was reintroduced to the Roman calendar in 1585 *(Calendar-ium romanum*, Cité du Vatican, 1969) 108-109). Thus it is a devotional feast that certainly has its legitimacy, but is assumed to have little or no historical basis.

28. To indicate the parallelism of the two verbs, one would have to translate it: "The Holy Spirit will come over you and the power of the Most High will cast its shadow over you." In Greek, each verb begins with the preposition *epi-* (on or over).

29. Pss. 17:8; 36:8; 57:2; 63:8; 91:4.

30. Opening prayer reprised in the Angelus: "That we, to whom the incarnation of your Son was made known by the message of an angel, may by his passion and cross be brought to the glory of his resurrection."

31. The genealogy given by Matthew (Matt 1:1-17) begins with Abraham and ends with "Joseph the husband of Mary. It was of her that Jesus who is called the Messiah was born." Immediately afterward, the First Gospel moves to "the birth of Jesus Christ," whose mother "was found with child through the power of the Holy Spirit" (Matt 1:18-25).

32. See X. Léon-Dufour, "Adam," in *Vocabulaire de théologie biblique*, second ed. (Paris: Cerf, 1970) col. 19-19.

33. Thus to Gideon, the sign of the fleece (Judg 6:36-40); to Ahaz, the sign of the Em-manuel (Isa 7:10-16); to Zechariah, his dumbness (Luke 1:18-20).

34. St. Bernard, *Homélie a la louange de la bienheureuse vierge Marie*, 4:8-9, in the Office of Readings for December 20.

35. It is found in this form in various passages: Jer 32:17; 32:27; Mark 10:27; Luke 18:27. But there are countless texts that refer to God's ability to do anything.

36. P. de la Tour du Pin (Chant L 49).

37. *Commission Francophone Cistercienne, Tropaires des dimanches* (Dourgne: Livre d'Heures d'Encalcat, 1980) 9.

38. "The virgin shall be with child and give birth to a son" (Isa 7:14; Matt 1:23). "Out of Egypt I have called my son" (Hos 11:1; Matt 2:15). "A cry was heard at Ramah . . . " (Jer 31:15; Matt 2:18). "He shall be called a Nazarene" (Matt 2:23). "Land of Zebulun, land of Naphtali . . . " (Isa 8:23-9:1; Matt 4:14). "It was our infirmities he bore . . . " (Isa 53:4; Matt 8:17). "I will open my mouth in parables" (Ps 78:2; Matt 13:35). "Your king comes to you . . . " (Isa 62:11 and Zech 9:9; Matt 21:5). "They took the thirty pieces of silver . . . " (Zech 11:12-13 and Jer 32:6-15; Matt 27:9), etc.

39. This results from the structure of the rather short Book of Micah (7 chapters, 105 verses). It alternates between two kinds of prophecies: 1) reproaches directed at the people and denunciation of their crimes, which will be punished by the destruction of Jerusalem (chs. 1-3); 2) promises of deliverance, of happiness, of a "Messiah" (chs. 4-5); 3) a trial between the Lord and his people (6:1-7:8); 4) celebration in hope (7:9-20). The different kinds of prophecies have different contexts. The people became aware of the emptiness in which they lived, they opened themselves to God's grace, they returned from exile. But that isn't the end of the story. Though they were freed, they still awaited their full liberation.

40. In Isaiah 60:22 one can see a similar contrast: "The smallest shall become a thousand, the youngest, a mighty nation."

41. The verb "to come forth" evokes the Exodus, but also the action of a shepherd who leads his flock to the fields. The same idea is found in John, where there is an association between the images of the shepherd and the gate. Jesus is the "gate" by which one enters the sheepfold and through which one leads the lambs, who follow the shepherd because they know his voice; the gate by which one enters and leaves (John 10:1-18).

42. Might we go so far as to say that the Bible itself witnesses to an endless rereading of the ancient prophecies?

43. Luke often uses the expression "thereupon" or "at that time." It means "in those very days," as, for example, when he writes that at the passion of Jesus, Herod "happened to be in Jerusalem at the time" (Luke 23:7).

44. Preachers often interpret it in this sense. The bishop of Lourdes, speaking one day at the grotto to the cyclists of the Tour de France, told them that if she had been able to, Mary would have ridden a bicycle to Elizabeth's home in order to get there more quickly.

45. Rom 12:8, 11; 2 Cor 7:11-12; 8:7-8, 16; Heb 6:11; 2 Pt 1:5; Jude 3. Likewise Dan 3:24 (91); 6:19 (20).

46. The verb is *skirtaô*: "You mountains, [why do] you skip like lambs?" (Ps 114:6); "Yes, rejoice and exult, you that plunder my portion; frisk like calves on the green" (Jer 50:11); "You will gambol like calves out of the stall" (Mal 3:20); "On the day they do so, rejoice and exult" (Luke 6:23). Also: "Rebekah became pregnant. But the children in her womb jostled each other so much . . . " (Gen 25:21-22).

47. Again, the translation "cried out in a loud voice" weakens the sense.

48. The text does not say explicitly that John was filled with the Spirit as well. It is true that Luke reports that the angel said to Zechariah: "He will be filled with the Holy Spirit from his mother's womb." But it is not a matter of an emotional outburst.

49. The evangelist does not pretend to report the exact words of Elizabeth. It would be presumptuous to say that the gift of the Holy Spirit had allowed Elizabeth to realize that Mary was with child (and that her son would be the Messiah), that she had received the announcement of it from heaven, that she had responded in faith, and that Elizabeth's own son would be the precursor to Mary's. It would also have been a little too soon to speak about "the fruit of your womb" and "the mother of my Lord," when Mary had only just conceived. In short, one ought not imagine that Elizabeth acted as if she had already read

and meditated on the Gospel! Elizabeth's greeting was not extraordinary. If one is waiting for the Messiah, one always says such things, inspired by messianic hope, to a pregnant woman. Even today, this is not uncommon among fervent Jews.

50. Deut 7:14; 33:24; Judg 5:24; Jdt 13:18, etc.

51. "Blessed among (above all) women" is to be taken in an absolute sense.

52. The first canon of the Council of Ephesus reads: "If anyone does not acknowledge that Emmanuel is in truth God, and that the holy Virgin is, in consequence, *Theotokos*, for she brought forth after the flesh the Word of God who has become flesh, let him be anathema" (G. Dumeige, *La foi catholique* (Paris: Ed. de l'Orante, 1961) n. 295 = H. Denzinger, *Enchiridion symbolorum*, n. 113).

53. Constitution on the Liturgy, n. 10.

54. *Commission Francophone Cistercienne, Guetteur de l'Aube* (Paris: Desclée, 1976) 34 (Chant E 146).

55. Exceptions: 1989 and 1990, when the Fourth Sunday of Advent falls, respectively, on December 24 and 23.

56. Thus in 1989, 1995, 2000 and 2006: Third Sunday: December 17, Fourth Sunday: December 24.

57. Gen 49: 2, 8-10 (December 17); Jer 23:5-8 (December 18); Judg 13:2-7, 24-25 (December 19); Isa 7:10-14 (December 20); Cant 2:8-14 or Zeph 3:14-18 :(December 21); 1 Sam 1:24-28 (December 22); Mal 3:1-4, 23-24 (December 23); 2 Sam 7:1-5, 8-11, 16 (December 24).

58. In the same way that we are not bothered by the differences between the genealogy of Jesus claimed by Matthew and that which Luke establishes (Luke 3:23-38).

59. See the text, pp. 142–43.

60. See above, Years A and B.

61. See above, Fourth Sunday of Advent, Year C.

62. Never on Sundays or regular weekdays. In the Sanctoral: St. Mary Magdalene, July 22 (3:1-4); St. Bernard, August 20 (8:6-7); and the Common of Virgins (8:6-7). Among the texts proposed for marriage (2:8-10, 14, 16; 8:6-7, 8-14). For the Mass for the Consecration of Virgins (8:6-7). Finally, in the Common for the Masses of Holy Men and Holy Women. Note that the same text (8:6-7) reoccurs five times. In Judaism, on the other hand, the whole Book is read during the week following Passover.

63. At the time of Jesus, the coming of a messenger who would precede the Messiah was expected. Because of the way in which it was prophesied (v. 23), some people even thought that the messenger would be Elijah himself (Matt 6:15; 8:28; 9:11-13).

64. Above, Fourth Sunday of Advent, Year B.

65. "Second Isaiah," because we recognize in this part of the Book of Isaiah the work of one of Isaiah's disciples writing two centuries later—therefore from the sixth century B.C. "Book of Consolation," because of the first words of this section—"Comfort, give comfort to my people" (Isa 40:1)—and the principal theme of these fifteen chapters. See the introductions to *The Jersualem Bible*, the *TOB* (pp. 735-740), and *Cahiers Evangile* n. 20, "*Le Deuxième Isaë*" (Paris: Cerf, 1977) Cl. Wiener. During this week we read successively: Isa 45:1-13; 46:1-13; 47:1, 3-15; 48:1-11; 48:12-21 and 49:9-13; 49:14–50:1; 51:1-11; 51:17–52:2, 7-10.

66. Pope from 440 to 461.

67. Letter 31:2-3.

68. This writing comes to us from the Henri Estienne edition of 1592. Ostensibly, it is the response of a Christian to a pagan who questioned him about the origin, character, and efficacy of Christianity, and why Christ's coming took so long. The addressee—Diognetus—is as unknown as the author. The date of the letter is still uncertain, but was probably before 190 or at the beginning of the third century?

69. Lettre à Diognète, 8:5–9:5 (December 18). See *Sources chrétiennes*, n. 33bis.

70. Bishop of Lyon, c. 135–202.

71. Traité contre les hérésies, 3:20:2-3. See *Sources chrétiennes* n. 211, pp. 374–382 (December 19).

72. Curious person, this Hippolytus. Undoubtedly of Greek origin, well educated, he was a priest in Rome, where Origen, one day in 212, heard him preach. His literary output was considerable. A great attacker of heresies, he wasn't able to avoid falling into those errors directly opposed to the ones he was denouncing. Elected bishop of Rome by a handful of partisans, for several years he played the part of an antipope. The schism came to an end shortly before or after Hippolytus was deported to Sardinia, "the isle of the dead," with the former pope Pontian. Both died in 235. Their bodies were returned to Rome August 13, 236 or 237. Both were recognized and venerated as martyrs, one at the cemetery of Callistus, the other at the cemetery of the Via Tiburtina, which bears his name. A famous third-century statue of Hippolytus, with a list of his works and an Easter calendar was discovered in 1551. It has stood at the entrance to the Vatican Library after a fire at the Lateran Museum forced it to be relocated. See J. Quasten, *Initiation aux Pères de l'Eglise*, vol. 2 (Paris: Cerf, 1957) 193–249.

73. *Traité sur l'hérésie de Noët*, 9–12.

74. St. Augustine (354–430), *Sermon 185* for Christmas (December 24).

75. *Homélie à la louange de la Vierge Marie*, 4:8-9.

76. *Homélie sur l'Evangile de Luc*, II, 19:22-23, 26-27. See *Sources chrétiennes*, n. 45.

77. *Commentaire de l'Evangile de Luc*, 1:46-55 (December 22).

MARY AND THE PSALTER—Pages 176–80

1. On this point, see Y.-M.J. Congar, *Le Christ, Marie, et l'Eglise* (Paris: Desclée de Brouwer, 1955) 20–21.

2. In the sense that certain psalms are usually used in the celebration of Marian feasts, the expression has some justification. It is inappropriate, however, to think that a single verse of the Psalter, *a fortiori* a whole psalm, is prophetic of the Virgin Mary or could allude to her in any literal sense. Thus J. Gelineau, "Marie dans la prière chrétienne des psaumes," in *La Maison-Dieu 38* (1954), p. 30.

3. Ch. Moeller, *Mentalité moderne et évangélisation* (Bruxelles: Editions Lumen Vitae, 1962, p. 225. *Lumen gentium* 103 confirms this interpretation: the council saw in Mary the eschatological icon of the Church, as such always dependent on Christ and the Church, and prefigured by other Old Testament realities: Israel, Jerusalem, the Daughter of Zion, etc.

4. On all this, see A. Gelin, *L'âme d'Israël dans le Livre* (Paris: Fayard, Je sais-Je crois 65, 1958) 46–68.

5. The works of H. Gunkel, among others his *Einleitung in die Psalmen* (Göttingen: Vandenhoeck-Ruprecht, 1933) have exercised considerable influence here. The classifications that he proposed can vary somewhat, but they are still universally valid. See A. Descamps, "Pour un classement littéraire des psaumes," in: *Mélanges Bibliques en l'honneur d'André Robert* (Paris: Bloud et Gay, Travaux de l'Institut Catholique de Paris 4, 1957) 187–196.

6. On this point, see A. Gelin, *Les Pauvres de Yahvé* (Paris: Cerf, Témoins de Dieu 14, 1953, reedited under the title: *Les pauvres que Dieu aime* (Paris: Cerf, Foi Vivante 41, 1967). Compare with J. Dupont, "Les pauvres en esprit," in: *A la rencontre de Dieu. Memorial Albert Gelin* (Paris-Lyon: X. Mappus, *Bibliothèque de la Faculté de Théologie de Lyon*, vol. 8, 1961) 265–272.

7. Thus in Zeph 2:3; 3:12, but also in the short catechism of Mic 6:8, whose insistence on the duty of "walking humbly with your God" recalls the teaching of Isaiah.

8. Among the psalms evoked by the *Magnificat*, one can cite Psalms 9:9; 34:2-4, 11; 35:9; 89:11; 98: 1, 3; 99:3, 5, 9; 102:18; 103:17; 105:8-10; 111:9; 113:7-8; 149:4; etc. On the enormous bibliography devoted to the Canticle of Mary, note among others: J. Dupont, *Les Béatitudes* (Paris: Gabalda, *Etudes Bibliques*, t. III, 1973) 186–193, followed by: "Le Magnificat comme

discours sur Dieu," in *Nouvelle Revue Théologique 102* (1980), 321–243; I. Goma Civit, *El Magnificat, Cantico de la Salvacion* (Madrid: BAC, 1982); A. Valentini, *Il Magnificat. Ricerche contemporanee. Struttura. Esegesi* (Rome: Institut biblique pontifical, 2 vol., 1982). But the *Magnificat* is also in some way a reprisal of the Canticle of Anna (1 Sam 2:1-10).

9. For I. de la Potterie, "Il parto verginale del Verbo incarnato: Non ex sanguinibus . . . sed ex Deo natus est (John 1:13)," *Marianum 45* (1983), pp. 127–176, the unusual plural does not signify, as some have understood it, the mixing of "bloods" between the father and mother or merely the coming of Christ into the world. It is a question here of virgin birth: the author teaches that there was no menstrual impurity in the birth. The same is the case in Luke 1:35 and the expression "the holy offspring," i.e., without any stain of blood.

NEW DAWN—Pages 181–90

1. On their origin, see the few details set out, for example, in A.-G. Martimort, *The Church at Prayer*, IV (Collegeville: The Liturgical Press, 1986) 95.

2. Here is the Latin text from the old Breviary: *O Sapientia, quae ex ore Altissimi prodiisti, attingens a fine usque ad finem, fortiter suaviterque disponens omnia: veni ad docendum nos viam prudentiae* (December 17).

O Adonai, et Dux domus Israel, qui Moysi in igne flammae rubi apparuisti, et ei in Sina legem dedisti: veni ad redimendum nos in brachio extento (December 18).

O Radix Iesse, qui stas in signum populorum, super quem continebunt reges os suum, quem gentes deprecabuntur: veni ad liberandum nos, iam noli tardare (December 19).

O Clavis David, et sceptrum domus Israel; qui aperis, et nemo claudit; claudis, et nemo aperit: veni, et educ vinctum de domo carceris, sedentem in tenebris et umbra mortis (December 20).

O Oriens, splendor lucis aeternae, et sol justitiae: veni, et illumine sedentes in tenebris et umbra mortis (December 21).

O Rex gentium, et desideratus earum, lapisque angularis, qui facis utraque unum: veni, et salva hominem, quem de limo formasti (December 22).

O Emmanuel, Rex et legifer noster, exspectatio gentium, et Salvator earum: veni ad salvandum nos, Domine, Deus noster" (December 23).

3. C. Péguy, *Le porche du mystère de la deuxième vertu* (Paris: Gallimard, 1935) 20–22.

4. Rom 8:14-17; Gal 3:26-27; 6:15; 2 Cor 5:17-18; Eph 2:15; 4:24. See 1 Cor 15; Rom 5:12, 18.

5. See J. Leenhardt, *La parole et le buisson de feu. Les deux sources de la spiritualité chrétienne et de l'unité de l'Eglise* (Neuchâtel: Delachaux et Niestlé, 1962). The author rightly characterizes Abrahamic spirituality and Mosaic spirituality as the two forces that make up the mystery of the Church.

6. 1 Kgs 16:25, 30, 33; 21:15; 2 Kgs 9:18, 24, 28; 17:2, 7, 23.

7. See Isa 13:10; Jer 4:23; 15:16; Ezek 32:7; Amos 5:18-20; 8:9; Joel 2:10; 3:4; 4:15.

8. See Isa 9:6; 11:3, 5, 9; 30:26; 60:17; 61:3, 10; 62:2.

9. Deut. 32; 1 Sam 2:2; 2 Sam 22:47; 23; Isa 30:29; 44:8; Hab 1:12; Ps 18:3; etc.

10. Gen 28:18; Dan 2:34; Zech 4:7, 10.

11. The development of the Christological theme abundantly illustrated by the quotations taken from all of Scripture is reminiscent of an exegetical chain, a kind of anthology of texts. The discoveries at Qumran allow us to verify the existence and probable use of them by the primitive Christian community. Such is the case from Exod 17:6; Isa 8:14; 28:16; Ps 118, which is alluded to, for example, by Rom 9:33; 1 Cor 10:4-11; 1 Pet 2:4-8.

12. See J. Betz, "Christus-Petra-Petrus," in *Eglise et Tradition* (Lyon-Paris-Le Puy, X. Mappus, 1963) 23.

The Season of Christmas-Epiphany—Pages 191–241

1. See A.-G. Martimort, *The Church at Prayer*, IV (Collegeville: The Liturgical Press, 1986) 77–96; J. Lemaire, *La manifestation du Seigneur* (Paris: Cerf, *Lex orandi 23*, 1957) 23–64.

G. Hudon, "Noël dans la tradition latine," in *Assemblées du Seigneur*, first series (Bruges: Publications de Saint-André, n. 10, 1963) 75–92; "L'Epiphanie chez les Pères latins," *ibid.*, n. 13, 1962, pp. 63–78; O. Raquez, "Les saintes Théophanies dans le rite byzantin," *ibid.*, n. 13, 1962, pp. 7–13.

2. This calendar is called "Chronography of 354." See A.-G. Martimort, *op. cit.*, pp. 78, 80, 91.

3. Even today, the winter solstice is celebrated in Nordic countries by feasts that mix some surviving elements of paganism and traditional folklore, even including a reference to the feast of St. Lucy on December 13.

4. See John 1:5, 9.

5. This was, in part, the result of Emperor Constantine's policies. He tried to make pagans and Christians celebrate the "rebirth" of the *sol invictus* and the birth of Christ, the Light of the world, in the same places and on the same feast days, whenever possible.

6. See P. Danet, "Noël et Pâques, mystères de paix" in *Assemblées du Seigneur*, first series (Bruges: Publications de Saint-André, n. 10, 1963) 93–103. Remember that the early Church had only one celebration, that of the yearly and weekly Easter; it was from this that the liturgical year slowly developed. See above, pp. 7–9.

7. Named for Arius, an Alexandrian priest (c. 280–336), Arianism was condemned at the councils of Nicea (325) and Constantinople (381). It constituted, especially in the East, one of the most serious crises the Church has ever known, spreading itself so rapidly under various guises that the Christian world, according to St. Jerome (c. 347–420), suddenly found that it was Arian. After many strange twists of fate, compromises, ambiguous symbols, etc., orthodoxy triumphed at the second ecumenical council of Constantinople (381). But Arianism continued to spread among the Goths and held sway for a long time. By then, however, its impact was more political than religious.

8. A homily of Optatus, bishop of Milevis in Numidia (c. 360) testifies to this. See G. Hudon, *art. cit.*, p. 75.

9. It was said later that it was a relic from the crèche at Bethlehem.

10. Soon enough, moreover, December 25 was thought to be the exact date of the birth of Jesus. See J. Gaillard, "Noël, memoria ou mystère?" in *La Maison-Dieu 59* (1959), pp. 37–70; G. Hudon, "Le mystère de Noël dans le temps de l'Eglise d'après saint Augustin," *Ibid.*, pp. 60–85.

11. When Christmas falls on a Sunday, as in 1994 and 2005. Then, there is no free Sunday between December 25 and January 1.

12. In this case, the formulary for the Second Sunday after Christmas is never used.

13. When this Sunday is the seventh (1990, 1996, 2001, 2007) or the eighth of January (1989, 1995, 2006).

14. The Eastern Churches commemorate this Baptism (Investiture and Manifestation of the Lord) on Epiphany.

In the West, at the end of the eighth century, when an octave of Epiphany—January 6—was instituted, the gospel of the Baptism of Jesus was read on January 13. This feast was included in the Roman Calendar in 1960, then ratified in 1969.

15. Nativity of the Lord, antiphon of the *Magnificat*.

16. Mary, Mother of God, antiphon of the *Benedictus*.

17. *Ibid.*, *Liturgie monastique des Heures*, first antiphon for Lauds.

18. Epiphany, antiphon of the *Benedictus*.

NATIVITY OF THE LORD—Pages 195-220

1. The continuous celebration of the three Christmas Masses—a longstanding custom—or the celebration of the Mass at dawn immediately following that of the night was an abuse. The three celebrations initially took place at Rome in three different sanctuaries: St. Peter, St. Anastasia, and St. Mary Major, where the faithful came at different times (see text, p. 192). The monastic custom was that after the solemn Mass at night, the three Christmas Masses were celebrated "in private" by each priest, followed by the celebration, by the whole community, of the Masses for dawn and the day. All six(!) took place with joy and great piety, certainly. But objectively speaking, concelebration has allowed these customs to be put to rest.

2. It could also be put to good use as a preparation for an eventual Christmas Vigil.

3. Entrance antiphon.

4. Invitatory refrain.

5. The historical context is that of the return from the Exile, following the decree of Cyrus (539). The exiled people had never stopped dreaming of this promised return—like a new, triumphal Exodus. The initial reentry silenced them. They found Jerusalem destroyed. They were met with hostility by those living in the country. The situation thus created was deplorable and resulted in turmoil. All fought to establish their own claims, to rebuild their own houses, etc., without bothering about anyone else or with the fact that the Temple lay in ruins. It was an atmosphere of discouragement and grave disappointment: "This is what God promised? Then his arm isn't long enough!" The prophet's oracle is meant to encourage the people, to reawaken their hope.

6. This sense is familiar to us as we speak, for example, of espousing someone else's ideas.

7. See D. Rimaud, "Au Dieu de toute Alliance," in *Les arbres dans la mer* (Paris: Desclée, 1975) 57: "C'est en lui, le Fils éternel de ta tendresse, que tu as conclu avec l'humanité l'Alliance de ton premier amour."

8. 1 Chr 1:1-34; 2:1-15; 3:59; 5:27-29; 6:18-32; Ezek 7:15; 8:2; Neh 7:61, 64; Ruth 4:18-22.

9. *The Jerusalem Bible says:* "l'histoire" ["the history"]; the *TOB:* "la naissance" ["the birth"]. But both note that the Hebrew word used here commonly signifies the act of giving existence to something.

10. Matthew insists on the fact that there are, in total, three sets of fourteen generations. Note that the consonants of the name of David have numerical values of 4 (*daleth*) and 6 (*Waw*), which total $4 + 6 + 4 = 14$. Note also that $3 \times 14 = 7 \times 6$ or six times the value of a week. The Bible frequently refers to this unity of time in the apocalypses, as in the story of creation. (See the notes of the *Bible de Jerusalem*, p. 1422 K, and the *TOB*, Nouveau Testament, p. 44d). But there are only six series of "weeks," not seven (the perfect number). Is Matthew suggesting that the ages before Christ were times of nonfulfillment? Such observations are interesting, but let us not give them more importance than they deserve.

11. Ishmael (Gen 16:7-12), Isaac (Gen 17:15-22; 18:4-14), Samson (Judg 13:1-25).

12. Charge of Solomon announced to David (1 Chr 22:8-10).

13. Communion antiphon.

14. St. Leo the Great (pope from 440–461), Homélie pour Noël 1:1 (*Sources chrétiennes* 22bis, p. 67), from the Office of Readings, December 25.

15. Text C.N.P.L. (Chant F 147-1).

16. Often, it does not begin until the bell has tolled twelve times. By contrast, there was a tendency to move the hour of the Easter Vigil forward since, by tradition, it was to last until dawn.

17. See text, p. 192.

18. The Gospel and the Acts of the Apostles.

19. Even though the accurate determination of this date is a problem for historians today.

20. It is useless to add to what the Gospel says, for example, by bringing in the character of a hotel-keeper who refused to make room for a poor couple, the wife of which was about to give birth. Luke simply says: "There was no room for them in the place where travelers lodged," whether an inn or house (Matt 2:11).

21. Exod 13:2, 12, 15; 34:20; Num 18:15-16; Lev 12:8.

22. Isa 6:3; Job 38:7; Ps 29:1-2; 103:20-21; 148:1-2; etc. See C. Vagaggini, *Initiation théologique à la liturgie*, 1 (Paris: Bourges, 1969) 233-245.

23. "La terreur plutôt que la religion." B. Pascal, édition Brunschwicg, n. 185.

24. Thus it is translated in *The Jerusalem Bible* and the *TOB*.

25. 1 Tim 2:2; 3:16; 4:7, 8; 6:3, 5, 6, 11; 2 Tim 3:3; Titus 1:11.

26. This is a beautiful formula, but it must be understood that "our blessed hope" denotes the object of our waiting. The "manifestation" is itself, in another sense, the object of this waiting (which is called the "parousia").

27. *Commission Francophone Cistercienne, La nuit, le jour* (Paris: Desclée-Cerf, 1973) 66-67 (Chant F 160).

28. See text, p. 192.

29. Not long ago—and this accentuated its status as a "minor" celebration—in most churches, only a portion of the faithful who had participated in the previous Mass stayed for this one.

30. When they were each celebrated at different times and in different places, each had an equal "chance." Remember also that in Rome, at the beginning, there were only the three Masses for Christmas, each celebrated by the pope, to which every Christian in the city was urged to go.

31. In the same way and for the same reason, there has been a suppression of the celebration, on November 1, of the first Vespers for All Souls after that of All Saints.

32. This principle was enunciated regarding the Liturgy of the Hours (Constitution on the Liturgy, n. 14). It has led, since 1951, to the cessation of the aberrant custom of celebrating the Easter Vigil on the morning of Holy Saturday.

33. Constitution on the Liturgy, n. 14, 19, 30.

34. *Ibid.*, n. 27.

35. Not so long ago, Eucharistic piety, which is not to be disparaged, as it has been the source of genuine sanctity, and a certain theology—which is more contestable—led to the proliferation of Masses that were curiously called "devotional."

36. Very few orders other than the Trappists and certain Benedictines still rise at dawn to celebrate the first Office of each day.

The shifting of our hours of activity is due mainly to the quality of our public and domestic lighting. Previously, one had to be in one's own house at nightfall, which meant that all of one's activity took place as the day allowed: even solemn ceremonies—religious or otherwise—took place at what would today be regarded as rather extraordinary hours. Even today, however, in certain regions, in Africa for example, especially in the bush, people rise and go to sleep with the sun.

37. Constitution on the Liturgy, n. 1.

38. The importance of the imposition of a new name is well known.

39. The liturgical splitting up of the story of the Nativity into two parts (Luke 2:1-14 and 15-20) presupposes participation in both the night and dawn Masses.

40. Luke 8:25; 9:43; 11:14; 20:26; 24:12, 41.

41. The first part of verse 5—"he saved us; not because of any righteous deeds we had done, but because of his mercy"—seems to be added to the text of a primitive hymn. In fact, it is certainly a stereotypical phrase from Paul's preaching (see 2 Tim 1:9).

42. The liturgical translation of Luke 22:25 says "benefactors."

43. See N. Egender, "La philanthropie de Dieu chez les Pères grecs," in *Assemblées du Seigneur*, first series, n. 57 (Bruges: Publications de Saint-André, 1965) 53–66.

44. Similar hymns are often found in Luke: Luke 5:25-26; 7:16; 13:13; 17:15; 18:43; 19:37; 24:53; Acts 2:47; 3:8-9; 4:21; 11:18; 13:48; 21:20.

45. *Commission Francophone Cistercienne, La nuit, le jour* (Paris: Desclée-Cerf, 1973) 68.

46. Pss 47:8-9; 93:1; 96:10; 97:1; 99:1.

47. "They have mouths but speak not; they have eyes but see not; they have ears but hear not; they have noses but smell not; they have hands but feel not; they have feet but walk not; they utter no sound from their throat" (Ps 115:5-7).

48. An extract from "Veilleurs dites-moi," D. Rimaud, *Les arbres dan la mer* (Paris: Desclée) 115 (Chant F 270).

49. Among many commentaries: P. de Surgy, in *Assemblées du Seigneur*, first series, n. 9 (Bruges: Publications de Saint-André, 1964) 31–52; *Ibid.* second series, n. 10 (Paris: Publications de Saint-André—Cerf, 1970) 68–79.

50. In spite of the title by which it is currently known, this first page is anything but a mere "prologue" to the Gospel According to John.

51. Pss 33:6, 9; 147:15-18; Isa 40:26; 48:3; Wis 1:3.

52. Prov 8:27-30; Wis 7:12; 8:4; 9:9.

53. John uses the word "world" in two different senses: the universe and the "world" of sinful humanity.

54. The Old Testament speaks of the refusal of Wisdom: Bar 3:10-14, 23, 31; Prov 1:2; 4:1; 9:10; 30:3; Sir 6:27; 18:28.

55. In some versions and patristic citations, the verb is in the singular. Hence the translation: "who was born not out of human stock or urge of the flesh or will of man but of God himself" *(JB)*.

56. "Flesh" denotes the whole human person: flesh and spirit.

57. This is the precise meaning of the term used.

58. See this expression in *Vocabulaire de théologie biblique*.

59. Text by J. Chrestien (Chant F 59).

THE HOLY FAMILY—Pages 221–41

1. If Christmas is a Sunday, there is no free Sunday and this feast is celebrated on December 30. Such is the case in 1988, 1994, 2005, 2011, 2022.

2. See *Les enseignements pontificaux. La mariage* (Paris: Desclée, 1955).

3. Letter *Neminem fugit*, June 14, 1892.

4. There is only one reading before the gospel if the celebration takes place on a weekday.

5. The first two readings: Sir 3:2-6, 12-14 and Col 3:12-21. Gospels: Matt 2:13-15, 19-23 (Year A), Luke 2:22-40 (Year B), Luke 2:41-52 (Year C).

6. Decree of the Congregation for the Sacraments and Divine Worship, dated January 21, 1981. However, the new readings for Years B and C are facultative. Those from Year A can still be read every year. See *Notitiae* 17 (1981), p. 358, n. 5 and 420–421; *Ordo lectionum missae. Editio typica altera*, 1981, p. 13, n. 17.

The addition of the first two readings *ad libitum* for each celebration was also done for the Baptism of the Lord, Ascension and Pentecost: *Notitiae, ibid.; Ordo lectionum*, n. 21, 58, 62. (For these last two celebrations, the first reading is still the same each year.)

7. The people of the Old Testament were patriarchal, hence the insistence on duties toward the father and particularly the obedience owed to him. In the Old Testment, the word "father" occurs 1,187 times, "mother" 251. Therefore it should not be surprising that the father is named here twelve times and the mother only six.

Generally speaking, it is important to avoid anachronistic judgment on texts like these or a complete rejection of them, because they were situated in social contexts rather different than ours.

8. Thus "He will be put to death who strikes (Exod 21:15) or curses (Exod 21:17) his father or mother"; "He who mistreats his father, or drives away his mother, is a worthless and disgraceful son" (Prov 19:26); "He who defrauds father or mother and calls it no sin, is a partner of the brigand" (Prov 28:24); "Woe to him who asks a father, 'What are you begetting?' or a woman, 'What are you giving birth to?'" (Isa 45:10); etc.

9. Matt 15:4; 19:19; Mark 10:19; Luke 18:20; Eph 6:2.

10. "To glorify" has the same meaning here.

11. It would suffice to refer to the eighteen other Pauline instances of the verb in order to realize that "to clothe" has, for Paul, a strong enough sense to let him write, in particular, "put on Christ" (Rom 13:14; Gal 3:27), "that new man created in God's image" (Eph 4:24), "incorruptibility" and "immortality" (1 Cor 15:53-54; four times).

12. Fairly often today, women cannot bear to hear or read these lines that say the wife must be submissive to her husband. Some go so far as to call Paul an awful antifeminist. Such a reaction betrays an extremely petty and reductionist reading of the text. The father, husband, and master of the house would have been in authority in Paul's time. But he admonishes that this relationship of authority must henceforth be lived "in the Lord." Again, he adds that the husband must love his wife and not act in an offensive manner to her; that parents must keep watch over their children, but not to the point of aggravating them. How, then, is it possible to accuse Paul of supporting the idea of a wife's slavery or parents' tyranny?

13. Rom 12:1; Phil 2:17; 3:3; 4:18; Acts 13:2; 2 Tim 1:3; 4:6. Same idea: Heb 9:14; 12:28; 13:15; 1 Pet 2:5.

14. Vatican II, Constitution on the Liturgy, n. 10.

15. The apocryphal writings benefited from the lack of information in the canonical Gospels; they could freely imagine what actually happened, resulting in stories so circumstantial as to border on the impudent.

16. A. Paul, "La fuite en Egypte et le retour en Galilée," in Assemblées du Seigneur, second series, n. 11 (Paris: Cerf-Publications de Saint-André, 1970) 28.

17. Verses 16-18, omitted here, recount the slaughter of the children of Bethlehem, which Jesus escaped.

18. The same is true in the other two episodes of Luke's infancy Gospel: the presentation of Jesus in the Temple (Luke 2:22-39) and his "escapade," when he stayed in Jerusalem for three days (Luke 2:41-52).

19. Opening prayer.

20. Prayer over the gifts.

21. Prayer after communion.

22. D. Rimaud, "Dieu est à l'oeuvre en cet âge," in Prière du temps présent, 1980, p. 7 (Chant T 50).

23. Idem., "Puisqu'il est avec nous," ibid., p. 698 (Chant P 79).

24. Paul VI, "Homélie prononcée à Nazareth le 5 janvier 1964," in La Liturgie des Heures, 1980, p. 251 (Office of Readings for the Holy Family).

25. Luke quickly notes (Luke 2:21) Jesus' circumcision and the imposition of his name at the end of the story of the Nativity. This verse, omitted on Christmas (Mass at dawn), is read when Luke's Nativity story is taken, in part, from the solemnity of Mary, Mother of God (Years A, B, C). The Roman calendar of 1969 therefore suppressed the feasts of the Circumcision of Our Lord and the Holy Name of Jesus, previously celebrated on January 1 and the Sunday between the Circumcision and Epiphany (or January 2), respectively.

26. This "bigger picture" is due to the fact that now there is a three-year cycle of read-

ings for nearly every feast that can be celebrated on a Sunday. We certainly ought to be pleased with this end result of the liturgical reform, and profit from it.

27. An analogous experience would be that of a group of people looking at a montage made up of pictures taken in a place that they all know. Instead of attending to the "message" of the montage, to what it is meant to express, they are easily distracted because they are trying to recognize places and people, as if it were a documentary.

28. Lev 5:7; 12:8; Num 18:15; Exod 13:2, 13; 34:20.

29. Luke 2:41-52; 4:9-13; 19:31, 51; 13:22; 17:11; 20:37-38. The Temple was also the place where the apostles began their mission: Acts 2:40; 3:1-26; 5:20, 25; without even counting Peter's address on Pentecost, delivered to the pilgrims who came to Jerusalem for the feast (Acts 2:5).

30. Isa 40:5 (cited also in Luke 3:6); 52:10; 49:6 (cited also in Acts 13:47); 46:13 or 45:25.

31. The *Benedictus* (Luke 1:76-77) likewise ends with the proclamation of John the Baptist's mission.

32. In fact, Luke applies the same prophecy to the apostles' mission (Acts 13:47).

33. See also Rom 9:32-33.

34. This personification of Mary as Daughter of Zion is well summarized in *Vocabulaire de théologie biblique*, second ed. (Paris: Cerf, 1970) col. 716: "For Luke, Mary is not simply a Jewish woman. In the annunciation and the visitation, he presents her as the Daughter of Zion, in the Old Testament sense, the personification of the people of God. The 'rejoice' of the angel is not a common salutation; it evokes the promises of the coming of the Lord to his holy city. The title 'highly favored,' object par excellence of divine love, recalls the bride in the Song of Songs (Cant), a very popular traditional figure of the chosen people. These literary indications correspond to Mary's role in these scenes: she receives, in the name of the house of Jacob, the announcement of salvation; she accepts it and makes its fulfillment possible. In her *Magnificat*, she quickly goes beyond her own gratitude in order to join her voice to that of Abraham's race, in gratefulness and joy."

35. This passage from the Gospel is read for the Holy Family, Year C.

36. This note occurs again, in a more developed form, after the episode of Jesus discovered at the Temple, which closes the infancy Gospel according to Luke (Luke 2:51-52).

37. See the article "Sagesse" III, in *Vocabulaire de théologie biblique*, col. 1173–1176.

38. Sr. M.-P. Faure, "Oracles," in *Prières aux quatre temps*, coll. Vivante liturgie 101 (Paris: Publications de Saint-André—Centurion, 1986) 206.

39. The first three chapters of this book are particularly engaging, with lively narration, moving passages, and picturesque elements: Hannah's humiliation by her husband's concubine and her sorrow over her sterility; her urgent prayer at the sanctuary of Shiloh, when the priest Eli thought she was drunk, because though he saw her lips move, he couldn't hear her say anything; her beautiful canticle, in which one finds many elements in the *Magnificat*; the wickedness of Eli's sons; the calling of the young Samuel.

40. According to popular etymology, this name can also signify "He who is with God."

41. The nazirite had to abstain from wine (Amos 2:11-12; Judg 13:4-5, 7, 14), let his hair grow (Judg 13:5; 16:17; 1 Sam 1:11), etc. This consecration, at first for life, became a temporary vow with codified requirements (Num 6:1-21). Some rites were ordained for the end of the period of consecration, before the return to normal life. Paul, having made such a vow, ended his nazirite period at Cenchreae (Acts 18:18). He also went to the Temple with four nazirites in order to perform the sacrifices required to terminate their nazirite vows (Acts 21:23-26).

42. At that time, as in certain countries today, children were weaned quite late.

43. This is what some people argue concerning baptism, saying that one cannot choose for a child, that he or she will have to make his or her own decision later on.

44. This is still a longstanding practice: children promised by their parents to espouse religious life, for example, or promised to someone in a marriage decided for them while they are very young. Are these practices of primitive society intolerable violations of personal responsibility? We cannot give simple answers to these questions without dealing with more fundamental issues. What is freedom? Education, the teaching of values—and faith—are they necessarily constraints?

45. A very pertinent remark from Origen, recalled by J. Dupont: "Jésus rétrouvé au Temple," in Assemblées du Seigneur, second series, n. 11 (Paris: Publications de Saint-André—Cerf, 1970) 51.

46. M. Coste, in Prières aux quatre temps (Paris: Centurion, coll. Vivante liturgie 101, 1986, p. 28.

MARY, MOTHER OF GOD—Pages 242-47

1. Vatican II, Lumen gentium, n. 66.

2. It is celebrated on December 26 in the Byzantine and Syrian rites; January 16 in the Coptic Rite.

3. Formerly, the Motherhood of the Virgin Mary was celebrated on October 11. This feast was instituted by Pius XI in 1931 on the fifteenth centenary of the Council of Ephesus (431-1931). Both the feasts of the Circumcision of Our Lord (January 1) and the Holy Name of Jesus (Sunday between January 1 and 8, or January 2) were abolished in 1969.

4. The formulary for this Mass—readings included—is the same for each of the three years (A, B, C) of the liturgical cycle.

5. Lumen gentium, n. 66.

6. The Missal offers a choice between these two entrance antiphons. The first is from the Mass at dawn; the text is inspired by both Isa 9:1-5 and Luke 1:33.

7. G. Dumeige, La foi catholique, Paris, Orante, 1961, n. 295, p. 191. The Church, endangered by the teaching of Nestorius (died c. 440), who distinguished two persons in Jesus (one human, one divine), called the Council of Ephesus in order to define faith in Jesus Christ as true God and true man. One consequence of Nestorianisn was that Mary was the mother only of Christ the man, to which the Person of the Word was joined. For this reason, the council began with the affirmation that Mary is the mother of God.

8. One might wonder how some theologians, such as those of the Alexandrian school or Arius, bishop of Constantinople, came to be heretics. Actually, they denied neither the humanity of Christ nor his divinity. But their philosophical theories about nature and "person" led them to speak of a man—Jesus, the Christ—who was united to a divine Person through a unique grace. The Christian people would probably have been unaware of the controversy had not Arius, in his public preaching, directly confronted the faith by refusing Mary the title Mother of God (Theotokos), claiming that she was only Mother of Christ (Christotokos), i.e., mother of the man who was only later united with the divinity. "Only one Lord, Christ and Son" and at the same time God and man.

9. The (now abolished) feasts of the Circumcision and the Holy Name of Jesus both used this sentence from Luke's Gospel (2:21).

10. Matthew, who recounts no annunciation to Mary, says that this name was revealed by an angel to Joseph (Matt 1:21).

11. Jesus: Sir 1:7; 50:27; 51:30; Luke 3:28-29; Col 4:11. Joshua: Deut 3:21; Judg 2:8; 1 Chr 1-2; etc.

12. Text by St. M.-P. Faure, in Prières aux quatre temps (Paris: Publications de Saint-André—Centurion, coll. Vivante liturgie 101, 1986) 30. (Chant E LH 130).

SECOND SUNDAY AFTER CHRISTMAS—Pages 248-52

1. The centerpiece is in fact the Prologue to the Gospel According to John (John 1:1-18) read on Christmas for Mass during the day.

2. *Dum medium silentium tenerent omnia, et nox in suo cursu medium iter haberet, omnipotens Sermo tuus, Domine, de caelis a regalibus sedibus venit.*

3. See the article "Lumière et ténèbres," in *Vocabulaire de théologie biblique*, second ed. (Paris, 1970) col. 684–690.

4. See the article "Silence." *ibid.*, col. 1237–1238.

5. Under this title are grouped Job, Psalms, Proverbs, Ecclesiastes (Qoheleth), the Song of Songs, Wisdom, and Sirach (Ecclesiasticus).

6. Compare these lines with Sir 24:19-22 and Isa 55:1; Prov 9:1-6.

7. See above, Mass during the day for Christmas, p. 214.

8. *Commission Francophone Cistercienne, Guetteur de l'Aube* (Paris: Desclée, 1976) 39.

THE EPIPHANY OF THE LORD—Pages 253-63

1. See above, pp. 191-93, regarding the formation of this cycle. A.-G. Martimort, *The Church at Prayer*, IV (Collegeville: The Liturgical Press, 1986) 77–90, with a bibliography. In the East, Epiphany celebrates the manifestation of the Lord at his baptim. Only the Armenian Monophysite Church has but one feast, January 6, that celebrates together the nativity, the adoration of the magi, and the baptism. See O' Raquez, "Les saintes Théophanies dans le rite byzantin," in *Assemblées du Seigneur*, first series, n. 13 (Bruges: Publications de Saint-André, 1962) 7–18.

2. The antiphon is inspired by Mal 3:1 and 1 Chr 19:12.

3. The whole of Isaiah 60 seems to repeat this brief oracle, applying it to the holy city in light of Isa 49:14-26 and 54:1-17.

4. The Fourth Gospel underlines the relationship between the "signs" and the manifestation of the divine "glory" of the Messiah: John 2:11; 11:4; 12:41; etc.

5. These remarks are not meant to call for a debunking of the legends about Christmas, its folklore, and the countless various pictorial representations of the adoration of the Lord. But they must be read and interpreted in light of the gospel, not the other way around.

6. It is not certain to what text the evangelist is referring. See the notes of *The Jerusalem Bible* and the *TOB*.

7. Throughout his Gospel, Matthew insists on the fulfillment of the prophecies.

8. The apocryphal gospels of the infancy, by contrast, are merely anecdotes.

9. It is striking, for example, to note the curious coincidences between the story of Jesus' infancy in Matthew and the stories of Moses' infancy in the Book of Exodus and in midrashic literature. The "midrash" is a rabbinic commentary on the Old Testament, most often an edifying paraphrase enriched with elements taken from what might be called "gilded" legends.

The births of both children are announced by a dream and a prophecy. They cause great fear in a king and his followers (Herod and his court, Pharaoh and his people). Herod consults his scribes, Pharaoh his astrologers. Both describe a massacre of children from which these two escape. Finally, in both cases, the person is returned to his own place because "those who had designs on the life of the child are dead" (Matt 2:20; Exod 4:19).

10. See further on.

11. Cf. the maxim "the epic is history listening at the door of legend."

12. After the genealogy of Jesus (Matt 1:1-17) comes "the birth of Jesus Christ," and the annunciation to Joseph (Matt 1:18-25) is immediately followed by the visit of the magi (2:1-12).

13. That Matthew does not speak of them does not signify that he had not heard of them, but simply that he has his own way of presenting Jesus' birth. Likewise, one should not

conclude that the first readers of Matthew had not learned what Luke relates (Luke 1:25-56; 2:1-21), where there is no mention of the magi.

14. Either of the Bible or the Missal, Fourth Sunday of Advent C, where Mic:1-4 is read.

15. Today, Bethlehem has 20,000 inhabitants, while Jerusalem and its environs have 160,000, and Tel Aviv nearly 400,000.

16. From thence comes the legitimacy and the usefulness of what are called "biblical themes." The first series of *Assemblées du Seigneur*, Publications de Saint-André, 68 volumes, 1962–1968, published 67 of them. Likewise, most of the articles of *Vocabulaire de théologie biblique*, second ed. (Paris: Cerf, 1970) are often outlines, quite thorough, of biblical themes.

17. See the Dogmatic Consitution of Vatican II on divine revelation, particularly chapter 3, "Sacred Scripture: Its Divine Inspiration and Its Interpretation."

The definition of midrash was cited above (note 9). Targum is a translation-interpretation of the Old Testament, long transmitted in oral form and similar to midrash.

18. According to John, expectation of the birth of the Messiah at Bethlehem was widespread among the people. One day while Jesus was teaching in the Temple, "Some in the crowd . . . began to say, 'This must be the Prophet.' Others were claiming, 'He is the Messiah.' But an objection was raised: 'Surely the Messiah is not to come from Galilee? Does not Scripture say that the Messiah, being of David's family, is to come from Bethlehem, the village where David lived?' " (John 7:40-42).

19. We must distinguish between the two Herods who reigned during the time of Jesus. The first, Herod the Great (37-4 B.C.) was king during the Nativity and ordered the massacre of the children of Bethlehem. He was a great builder, who left his country many memorials: the palaces of Jericho and Jerusalem, the fortresses of Masada and the Herodian Machaerus, the Temple of Jerusalem, the tomb of the patriarchs at Hebron, etc. The other, Herod Antipas (4 B.C.-A.D. 39) is the one who had John the Baptist killed and was at Jerusalem during Christ's passion.

20. From what we know about the last year of Herod the Great's life and his last stay in Jerusalem, which he left seven or eight months before he died, we can conclude that Jesus was born at least four or five years before our era. See S. Munos Iglesias, in *Assemblées du Seigneur*, second series, n. 12 Paris: Cerf—Publications de Saint-André, 1969) 22-23.

21. Matthew often invokes the fulfillment of prophecies: Matt 1:23; 2:15, 17, 23; 8:17; 12:17; 13:35; 21:4; 26:54, 56; 27:9; etc.

22. See below, pp. 282-87.

23. Synodal letter of the Council of Jerusalem (836).

24. Fresco at the cemetery of Sts. Peter and Marcellus.

25. Sarcophagus at the Lateran Museum in Rome.

26. Cemetery of Domitilla in Rome.

27. Vase in the Kircher Museum.

28. Syrian and Armenian tradition.

29. In a Parisian manuscript of the seventh century, they are named Bithisarea, Melichior, and Guthaspa.

30. See above, pp. 258-60.

31. St. Irenaeus, *Contre les hérésies*, 3:9:2, in *Sources chrétiennes* (Paris: Cerf, 1974) vol. 211, p. 107.

32. Herod is remembered as a cruel monster. He killed Aristobolus, his brother-in-law, whom he had made high priest; Joseph, the husband of his sister Salome; Marianne, his first wife, and her children; Alexandra, his mother-in-law; Antipater, one of his sons suspected of plotting against him; even the servants of his household and a good number of his subjects. A suspicious man, he built several fortresses, such as Masada (with its three elevated villas), Macheronte, and the veritable eagle's nest known as Herodium, several

kilometers from Bethlehem, where he could retreat in the event of difficulties with his subjects.

33. The flight of the Holy Family into Egypt—also prompted by a dream—had the same result. The journey of three poor people must have easily escaped the notice of Herod's police.

34. J. Dupont, "L'évangile de saint Matthieu: quelques clés de lecture," in *Communautés et liturgies* 57 (1975), p. 21.

35. J. Dupont, *art. cit.*, pp. 9–11, points out two verbs in Matthew that characterize the attitude of people before Jesus: they "advance toward" him (this verb occurs fifty-two times); or they "prostrate" themselves (ten times, three of which occur in the episode of the magi: 2:2, 8 and 11).

36. Constitution on the Liturgy, December 4, 1963, preamble.

37. Decree on the Church's missionary activity, n. 10.

38. R. Swaeles, "Rassemblement et pélerinage des disperses" (biblical theme), in *Assemblées du Seigneur*, first series, n. 78–79 Paris: Cerf—Publications de Saint-André, 1955) 37–61. See also, R. Salaun, "Le Christ est-il manifesté aujourd'hui à tous les hommes?," *ibid.*, first series, n. 12 (Paris: Cerf, 1969) 68–77, a reflection on what is involved today in being "missionary."

39. *Commission Francophone Cistercienne, La nuit, le jour*, (Paris: Desclée—Cerf, 1973) 74 (Chant P 122).

40. Epiphany Mass, prayer over the gifts.

41. *Ibid.*, opening prayer.

42. *Ibid.*, solemn benediction.

THE LECTIONARY FOR THE WEEK—Pages 264–76

1. See Jer 31:31-34; 24:7; Ezek 36:25-28.

2. 1 John 5:17-20 and Jer 24:7; 1 John 2:27 and Jer 31:33; 1 John 3:23; 4:13 and Ezek 36:27; 37:14; 1 John 3:9; 5:18 and Ezek 36:27.

3. 1 John 1:5-7; 2:6, 9-11; 2:3-5; 3:23; Ezek 36:25-28.

4. St. Leo (pope from 440 to 461); "Homélie pour Noël"; 1:3, in *La Liturgie des Heures*, vol. 1, p. 235.

5. Deut 19:15; Matt 18:16; John 8:17; 2 Cor 13:1; etc.

6. John 1:1-18 (December 31); John 1:19-28 (January 2); John 1:19-34 (January 3); John 1:35-42 (January 4); John 1:43-51 (January 5); John 2:1-12 (January 7).

7. See Gen 1:1; Prov 8:30.

8. Exod 18:21, 25; Num 31:14; Deut 1:1.

9. Isa 25:6-8; 55:1-2; Matt 8:11; Mark 14:22.

OF PERSONS, PLACES AND THINGS—Pages 277–93

1. Justin, *Dialogue with Trypho*, 78 and 70, which clearly alludes to Isa 33:16. See also, around the same time, the *Protévangile de Jacques*, 18.

2. See Origen (c. 185–253), *Contre Celse*, 1:51 (Paris: Cerf, (*Sources chrétiennes* 132), 1967) 214; Jerome, *Homilia de Nativitate Domini, PLS* 2, 183.

3. Among others, Ephrem of Nisibis, Evagrius Ponticus, Gregory of Nyssa, John Chrysostom, Cyril of Alexandria, Zeno of Verona, Ambrose of Milan, Gregory the Great, Aelred of Rievaux, Walfrid of Pisa, etc. All of these references are given by C. Van Hust, *art.* "Crèche," in *Dictionnaire de spiritualité*, t. 2, II, col. 2520–2524.

4. Ps 78:70-72.

5. Cf. H. Urs von Balthasar, *La Gloire et la croix*, t. 1 (Paris: Aubier, *Théologie* 61, 1965) 572–574.

6. Exod 16:10; 24:16-17; Num 14:16; 1 Kgs 8:11.

7. Ezek 43:1-12; Isa 40:5; etc.

8. Isa 6:3; Job 38:7; Ps 29:1-2; 103:20-21; 148:1-2.

9. On all this, see P. Grelot, "Il vous est né aujourd'hui un Sauveur," in *Assemblées du Seigneur*, second series, n. 10 (Paris: Cerf, 1970) 58–63. On the liturgical role of angels, C. Vaggagini, *Initiation théologique à la liturgie*, t. 1 (Bruges: Biblica, 19) 233–245. Let us not forget the excellent little book of E. Peterson, *Le livre des anges* (Paris: Desclée de Brouwer, 1953).

10. We take this subtitle from A. Paul, "L'Evangile de l'enfance selon saint Matthieu" (Paris: Cerf, Lire la Bible 17, 1968) 97, of which the account of both of them is particularly enlightening. See also A.-M. Denis, "L'adoration des mages vue par saint Matthieu," in *Nouvelle Revue Théologique*, t. 82 (1960), pp. 32–39.

11. Matthew (2:6) does not hesitate to reinforce the witness of Micah concerning Bethlehem: "You . . . are by no means least among the princes of Judah. . . . "

12. Cf. Ch. Perrot, "Les récits de l'enfance de Jésus," in Cahiers Evangile, n. 18 (November 1976), p. 53.

13. Cf. J. Radermakers, *Au fil de l'évangile selon saint Matthieu, 2. Lecture continue* (Bruxelles: Ed. de l'IET, 1972) 41.

14. The details concerning the number and condition of the magi are found already in the sixth century in an apocryphal writing: *Le Livre arménien de l'enfance*, 5:10.

15. Cf. I. de la Potterie, "Les deux noms de Jérusalem dans l'évangile de Luc," in *La Parole de grâce. Etudes lucaniennes à la memoire d'A. George*, collected by J. Delorme and J. Duplacy (Paris: Recherches de Science Religieuse, 1981) 70. The city is first mentioned under its profane name (v. 22), then, under its sacred name (vv. 25, 38, 41-43, 45).

16. The connection made between "the consolation of Israel" and "the deliverance of Jerusalem" (vv. 25 and 38) testifies to this.

17. In Luke 17:15, we already see an indication of this: the Samaritan who is healed of his leprosy presents himself to Jesus and not to the priests.

18. See R. Laurentin, *Les évangiles de l'enfance du Christ. Vérité de Noël au-delà des mythes* (Paris: Desclée-Desclée de Brouwer, 1982) 247 s.; Ph. Bossuyt-J. Radermakers, t. II, 1981, pp. 122-124; A. George, "La Présentation de Jésus au Temple," in *Assemblées du Seigneur*, second series, n. 11 (Paris: Cerf, 1970) 29–39.

19. Cf. Ch. Perrot, *op. cit.*, p. 54.

20. Cf. Isa 40:1-2; 49:10, 13; 57:18; 61:2; 66:12-13.

21. Cf. A. George, *art. cit.*, p. 36, who refers back to Luke 8:1-2; Acts 1:13-14; Luke 11:5 and 18:3; 13:19, 21; 15:4, 8.

22. Origen, *Sur Luc*; trans. M. Crouzel, F. Fournier and P. Perichon (Paris: Cerf, *Sources chrétiennes* 87, 1962) 233.

23. The expression is a favorite of C. Moeller, which he uses in many of his writings, e.g., *Mentalité moderne et Evangélisation. Dieu, Jésus Christ, Marie, l'Eglise* (Bruxelles: Editions de Lumen Vitae, 1955) 295.

BAPTISM OF THE LORD—Pages 294–312

1. In those countries where Epiphany is celebrated on Sunday (between January 2 and 8), when it falls on January 7 or 8, the feast of the Baptism of the Lord is celebrated on the following Monday, January 8 or 9 (such is the case in 1989, 1990, 1995, 1996, 2001, 2006, 2007).

2. In the Eastern Churches, Epiphany does not celebrate the adoration of the magi, but the manifestation of the Lord at his baptism. See O. Raquez, "Les saintes Théophanies dans le rite byzantin," in *Assemblées du Seigneur*, first series, n. 13 (Paris: Cerf—Publications de Saint-André, 1962) 7-18.

3. In certain areas, since the end of the eighth century, an octave of Epiphany was instituted, and on the octave day the gospel of the Baptism was read. In the eighteenth cen-

tury, January 13 became, in French liturgies, the feast of the Baptism of the Lord (see J. Lemarie, "Le Baptême du Seigneur dans le Jourdain d'après les textes scripturaires en usage dans les Eglises d'Orient et d'Occident," in *La Maison-Dieu 59* (1959) pp. 96–980. Included in the Roman calendar in 1960, its present date was determined in 1969. But then, the Lectionary offered a different reading for each year for the gospel, whereas the first two readings were the same (Isa 42:1-4, 6-7 and Acts 10:34-38). In the second edition (1981) of the *Ordo lectionum missae*, each year has its own set of readings, but the first two are still *ad libitum:* one can still read the readings of Year A each year.

4. Matt 3:13-17; Mark 1:9-11; Luke 3:21-22; John 1:29-34.

5. The *TOB* uses the variant reading "the son of God."

6. Mark and Luke are not more specific than this.

7. The Missal offers a choice between two opening prayers.

8. Isa 42:1-4, 6-7 (Year A); Isa 55:1-11 (Year B); Isa 40:1-5, 9-11 (Year C).

9. Acts 10:34-38; 1 John 5:1-9; Titus 2:11-14; 3:4-7.

10. Isa 42:1-9; 49:1-6; 50:4-9; 52:13–53:12.

11. Acts 2:14-40; 3:12-26; 4:8-12; 5:29-32.

12. To introduce both the presence and preaching of the Baptist and Jesus' coming to be baptized by John, Matthew writes: "In due course" (Matt 3:1, 13, *JB*). This stereotypical expression merely marks a transitional passage.

13. Cf. *The Jerusalem Bible*.

14. These various texts have parallels in Mark and Mark.

15. This detail found in each of the Synoptics is often overlooked: the theophany took place after the baptism. This is not an incidental detail. To represent the Spirit descending on Jesus during his baptism would suggest that at least in the case of Jesus, the gift of the Spirit was dependent upon the baptism by John. In other words, this representation excessively accentuates the significance of the baptism of Jesus as prototypical of Christian baptism. Consequently, far too many sermons rely on this interpretation, bypassing the central point: what happened for Jesus and for us is, above all, that there was a revelation, i.e., epiphany, of his status as Son of God.

16. Isa 61 has been popularized today by the well-known hymn of L. Deiss (K 35). Note, however, that in this composition, the prophecy is applied to the Christian. This is why the author noted in the index: "from Isa 61."

17. "The biblical title 'Son of God' does not necessarily express natural sonship, but can simply refer to adoptive sonship, which results from a divine choice to establish a particularly intimate relationship between God and his creature." See the lengthy note in *The Jerusalem Bible* on Matthew 4:3.

18. From the creed said at baptism and the Easter Vigil.

19. Rite of baptism, imposition of hands. See also chrismation, communion antiphon for the ritual Mass of baptism.

20. Baptism is second birth. There are numerous affirmations of this, particularly by Paul in his letters: Rom 6:1-4; 8:14, 15, 19; 9:26; Gal 3:26; 4:6; Eph 1:5; etc.

21. There are many representations of the baptism of Jesus: the frescoes in the catacombs (Callistus, Peter and Marcellus, etc.), other frescoes (above all at Ravenna), bas-reliefs on sarcophagi, sculpture in the Church of St. Basil in Bruges (between 1050 and 1187), basins of baptismal fonts at N.-D. de Furnaux, also in Belgium (these last two appear in A. Ourtens, *Belgique romane. Architecture, art monumental* (Paris: Ed. Braun, 1969). It would be impossible to catalogue the numerous and diverse modern instances of such representations.

22. *Commission Francophone Cistercienne, Tropaires des dimanches* (Dourgne: Le livre d'Heures d'Encalcat, 1980) 16 (Chant FLH 142: music by Ch. Villeneuve).

23. This text is found, almost in its entirety, in the Sunday Lectionary for Ordinary Time, Year A, but broken up: Isa 55:1-3, eighteenth Sunday; Isa 55:6-9, twenty-fifth; Isa 55:10-11,

fifteenth. Such is the way of the liturgy: it selects from a single passage of Scripture what will fit well with a given celebration.

24. The translation of *The Jerusalem Bible* is closer to the Hebrew: "My heart recoils from it, my whole being trembles at the thought."

25. The first six verses of this passage (1 John 5:1-6) are found on the Second Sunday of Easter, Year B.

26. According to John's vocabulary, the "world" often has a pejorative connotation. Used in this way, it denotes everything that is opposed to God, Christ, and even the disciples (John 1:10; 7:7; 15:18, 19; 17:14; etc.). In the Book of Revelation, "earth" has the same meaning (Rev 6:15; 13:3, 8; 14:3; 17:2, 5, 8).

27. The text of the Lectionary has retained two verses that talk about John's preaching.

28. On Sundays we read 420 of the 679 verses this Gospel contains. It is read integrally, except for what concerns the Passion (read on Palm Sunday, Year B), during the first nine weeks of Ordinary Time each year.

29. Literally: "No sooner had he come up out of the water than he saw . . . " *(JB)*.

30. Text by Nicole Berthet, in *Commission Francophone Cistercienne, Prières aux quatre temps: Des poèmes et des chants* (Paris: Cerf—Publications de Saint-André-Centurion, Vivante liturgie 101, 1986) 32–33.

31. See text, p. 75.

32. The first part—Titus 2:11-14—is also read for the Nativity of the Lord, Mass at night. The second—Titus 3:4-7—at the Mass at dawn.

33. See N. Egender, "La philantropie de Dieu chez les Pères grecs," in *Assemblées du Seigneur*, first series, n. 57 (Bruges: Publications de Saint-André, 1965) 53–66.

The Vulgate edition by St. Jerome translates *philanthropia* (philanthropy) by *humanitas* (Titus 3:4). On the meaning and significance of the Latin word, see Y. Congar, "Dum visibiliter Deum cognoscimus . . . Méditation théologique, in *La Maison-Dieu 59* (1959), pp. 132–161, especially pp. 144–159, "Dieu révélé dans son 'humanité.' "

34. In the original Greek, Titus 3:1-4 forms one extremely complex sentence that must be rendered in several clauses in any translation.

35. This passage, augmented by the two following verses, was read the Third Sunday of Advent, Year C. The two verses omitted here continue the description of judgment, evoked by the expression of baptism "in the Holy Spirit and in fire.

36. In addition to verses 17-18, the Lectionary omits verses 19-20, which evoke the end of John's ministry and his imprisonment by Herod. Luke readily follows this pattern: anticipating his chronology, he freely refers to later events (Luke 1:56, 80).

37. Daniel 2:18 (revelation of the meaning of Nebuchadnezzar's dream); 9:3-19 (revelation of the meaning of the prophecy of the seventy weeks); Luke 9:28-29 (Transfiguration); Acts 9:11 (call to Ananias to baptize Saul); 10:30 (Cornelius' vision that Peter would come and baptize him); 22:17 (Paul's vision that directed him to leave Jerusalem).

38. Luke 11:13; Acts 1:14; 3:15; 4:31.

39. Luke 5:16; 6:12; 9:18, 28-29; 11:1; 22:32, 41, 44.

40. Another variant could be "You are my beloved Son; to you have I given all my love."

41. Text from the Armenian liturgy, cited in J. Lemarie, *La Manifestation du Seigneur* (Paris: Cerf, Lex orandi 23, 1957) 366.

MYSTERIES OF EPIPHANY—Pages 313-14

1. Antiphon of the *Magnificat*.

2. This day—the day after the Baptism—begins the first part of Ordinary Time, which runs until the Tuesday before Ash Wednesday and resumes the Monday after Pentecost.

3. The antiphon seems to ignore the Nativity. But one must remember that it is of Eastern origin and that for the Eastern Churches, December 25 combines both the solemnity

of the Nativity and the adoration of the magi, while Epiphany is the celebration of the Baptism of the Lord. Christmas-adoration of the magi constitutes, consequently, one "mystery." The same thing happens somewhat in the West, even though they are divided into two feasts.

4. The gospel of the wedding at Cana is read for the Second Sunday of Ordinary Time C.

5. See P. Danet, "Noël et Pâques, mystères de paix," in *Assemblées du Seigneur*, first series, n. 10 (Bruges: Publications de Saint-André, 1963) 93–103.

6. Constitution on the Liturgy, n. 102.

7. This is expressed quite rightly, regarding the Eucharist, in the antiphon of the *Magnificat*, *O sacrum convivium* for the Office of the Holy Sacrament, attributed to St. Thomas Aquinas (1225–1274): "Banquet most holy where Christ is received as nourishment, the memorial of the passion is celebrated, our soul is filled with his grace, and the glory to come is already given."

8. Antiphon of the *Benedictus*.